ADVANCES IN STRATEGIC MANAGEMENT

Volume 16 • 1999

POPULATION-LEVEL LEARNING AND INDUSTRY CHANGE

ADVANCES IN STRATEGIC MANAGEMENT

POPULATION-LEVEL LEARNING AND INDUSTRY CHANGE

Series Editor: JOEL A.C. BAUM
Rotman School of Management
University of Toronto

Volume Editors: ANNE S. MINER
School of Business
University of Wisconsin—Madison

PHILIP ANDERSON
Amos Tuck School of Business Administration
Dartmouth College

VOLUME 16 • 1999

100 Prospect Street
Stamford, Connecticut 06901

ISBN: 0-7623-0500-2
ISSN: 0742-3322

Manufactured in the United States of America

CONTENTS

LIST OF CONTRIBUTORS

Philip Anderson	Amos Tuck School of Business Administration Dartmouth College
Linda Argote	Graduate School of Industrial Administration Carnegie Mellon University
Joel A.C. Baum	Rotman School of Management University of Toronto
Whitney B. Berta	Rotman School of Management University of Toronto
Kathleen M. Carley	Department of Social and Decision Sciences Carnegie Mellon University
Alan B. Eisner	Lubin School of Business Pace University
Ari Ginsberg	Stern School of Business New York University
Henrich R. Greve	Institute of Policy and Planning University of Tsukuba, Japan
Pamela Haunschild	Graduate School of Business Stanford University
Ingo W. Holzinger	School of Business University of Wisconsin-Madison
Ji-Yub (Jay) Kim	School of Business University of Wisconsin-Madison
Theresa K. Lant	Stern School of Business New York University
Eric R. Larsen	City University Business School London
Alessandro Lomi	School of Economics University of Bologna, Italy
James G. March	Stanford University

Stephen J. Mezias	Stern School of Business New York University
Anne S. Miner	School of Business University of Wisconsin-Madison
Corey Phelps	Stern School of Business New York University
Joseph F. Porac	Goizueta Business School Emory University
Thekla Rura-Polley	School of Management University of Technology, Sydney, Australia
James B. Wade	School of Business University of Wisconsin-Madison
Monica Yang	University of Illinois, Urbana-Champaign

ACKNOWLEDGMENTS

This volume is the child of all its authors and we appreciate their persistence. We also thank Linda Argote who, with Anne Miner, organized the Carnegie Mellon and University of Wisconsin conference on Knowledge Transfer and Levels of Learning, June 12-14, 1998, at which these papers were first presented. Pamela Haunschild not only helped shape early approaches to population level learning but played an active role in the creation of this volume. Conversations with Paul Ingram, Dan Levinthal, James G. March, James Brian Quinn, Gabriel Szulanski and Sid Winter contributed to our perspective, as did work by doctoral students Jay Kim, Ingo Holzinger and Andreas Schwab.

We thank Dean Andrew Policano at the University of Wisconsin-Madison School of Business, along with the Tuck School of Business at Dartmouth College, and Carnegie-Mellon University for their crucial support for the conference and book. We also appreciate the editorial assistance of Linda Johansen, and Charlotte Frascona, coordination help by Donna Wallace, and exceptional production support by Rona Velte.

As is his want, Joel A. C. Baum, series editor for *Advances in Strategic Management*, played a positive role at many levels of action, from collecting forms to influencing the contours of our thought, for which we thank him.

PRELUDE

The study of organizational learning has suffered from three particularly conspicuous problems. The first is the tendency to define learning both as improvement and as a particular set of processes. This makes learning a good thing by definition and begs the question of when particular learning processes do or do not lead to intelligent behavior. The second is the tendency to view the learning of particular learners, whether individuals, groups, or organizations, as occurring within an environment dominated by exogenous factors. This ignores all of the ecological interactions that occur as learning in one part of a system affects learning in other parts. The third is the tendency to underestimate the shortsightedness of learning, the fact that learning processes respond primarily to outcomes that are near to action in time and space. This myopia of learning favors immediate local efficiency over returns that are more distant in time and space, a property that is particularly troublesome when assessing learning by an individual organization from the perspective of a population of organizations.

All three of these problems run through current enthusiasms for learning as a source of competitive survival advantage. The proposition that learning improves chances for survival often seems to reduce either to the tautological proposition that improvement leads to improvement, or to the false proposition that learning processes invariably lead to improvement. The emphasis on augmenting organizational capabilities through learning often seems to ignore the competitive and cooperative consequences of interactive learning, the networks of connections that facilitate and inhibit the flow of knowledge within and among organizations, the complications of combining learning from others with learning from experience, and the difficulty of specifying a criterion for improvement without specifying the time and space perspective involved. The rush to strategies for improving a firm's learning abilities often seems to ignore the many features of learning that can lead one astray.

The present book provides a powerful set of reminders about these complications of learning, as well as others. It offers a rich elaboration of learning's complexity. For example, it illuminates three classical issues that are easily overlooked in the casual application of learning ideas to the giving of advice:

- The circumstances under which fast learning, that is the rapid response to signals of advantage, is inferior (as a long run instrument of advantage) to slow learning, for example, by developing high levels of competence at an inferior technology.
- The circumstances under which learning at the individual organizational level is deleterious to improvement at the population level, for example, by reducing diversity in a population below what is optimal for long run population advantage.
- The circumstances under which learning by one organization interferes with learning by another, for example, by making the outcomes of action difficult to interpret.

None of these issues is easily resolved. Learning clearly is not a panacea for organizational shortcomings. Strategic management is, as usual, revealed to be more complicated than is comfortable for those seeking simple advice given quickly. Nevertheless, as these chapters reveal, a complicated world is still amenable to elements of understanding.

There is, perhaps, a broader lesson to be learned from the research reported here. The giving of advice, whether to managers, children, or lost drivers, involves compromises among what is known, what can be said, and what can be heard. In any domain of interest, what is known is invariably more complex than what can be said or heard. As a result, people who give advice are continually torn between saying what is true and saying what will be heard. It is a delicate task worthy of enormous social approbation when accomplished well.

The art of giving good advice is the art of moving managers, children, and lost drivers in the right directions, taking into account the advice givers' limitations of speech and their clients' limitations of hearing. From this perspective, the real complaint about the courtiers of the emperor with new clothes is not that they failed to tell him he was naked, for he would not have heard that, but that they failed to nudge him to a course of action that would lead him to discover his nakedness.

Any system for giving good advice has to maintain a tension between telling the truth and not being heard, on the one hand, and telling what can be heard but is not true, on the other. In such a system, the role of academic researchers is not so much to give advice as it is to generate knowledge and to provide critical commentary on advice that is given. Along the way, an academic tries to counteract the natural tendency of advice givers to become more attentive to the hearing of their clients than to the knowledge underlying what they say. This book is in that tradition. It honors the noble tradition of giving advice on strategic management and organizational learning by exploring some elements of fundamental knowledge that might inform such advice.

James G. March
Stanford University

PREFACE

In 1995 Miner and Haunschild published an influential theoretical piece on population-level learning that argued for the importance of studying learning at a more macro level than is customary: at the level of the population. Miner and Haunschild focused on changes in the mix of routines that occurred at the level of the population as a key learning outcome. This outcome can arise from parallel organizational learning (i.e., how organizations learn from their own experience), recurrent interorganizational learning (i.e., how organizations learn from the experience of other organizations), and collective learning (i.e., how a collective or population of organizations learns from its experience). An example of population-level learning provided by Miner and Haunschild occurred in the U.S. semiconductor industry in the 1980s. U.S. semiconductor firms were losing market share at a rapid rate to their Japanese counterparts. U.S. firms looked to Japanese firms for models of effective management. U.S. firms collectively formed Sematech, a cooperative research organization that was modeled on industry cooperative research organizations in Japan. Thus, learning occurred at the population level: U.S. semiconductor firms, as a collectivity, created a new industry form and thereby changed the mix of routines in the population.

Miner and Haunschild's influential piece has sparked considerable research on population-level learning in a short time. The rapid rise of research on population-level learning reflects the power of the construct—at both a theoretical and a practical level.

At a theoretical level, interest in population-level learning reflects a convergence of two intellectual trends in the organizational sciences. The first is the increased interest in the concept of organizational learning. While the concept of organizational learning arguably goes back to Cyert and March's *A Behavioral Theory of the Firm* first published in 1963, interest in the concept of organizational learning exploded in the late 1980s and 1990s (Argote, 1999; Huber, 1991; Leavitt & March, 1988). A particularly positive trend in organizational learning research during this period was the increasing accumulation of empirical evidence about the phenomenon (Miner & Mezias, 1996). Although most previous work on organizational learning occurred at the organizational (or organizational subunit) unit of analysis, a new trend in the organizational learning area is examining how organizations learn from each other—how knowledge transfers across organizations. Research on population-level learning brings this interorganizational learning to the fore and also adds learning at the level of the population.

The second intellectual trend reflected in research on population-level learning is the importance of the environment in current research traditions. Although several early researchers appreciated the importance of the environment in understanding organizational behavior, organizational-environmental relations did not move to center stage in the organizational sciences until the late 1970s and 1980s (Aldrich, 1979). Theoretical perspectives such as population ecology (Hannan & Freeman, 1977), resource dependence (Pfeffer & Salancik, 1978), and institutional theory (DiMaggio & Powell, 1983; Meyer & Rowan, 1977; Scott, 1987) that were developed or elaborated during this period to explain how the environment selects or affects firms.

Current industry trends such as the increased use of joint ventures and strategic alliances, the increased rate of mergers and acquisitions the increased globalization of firms all point to the importance of population-level learning arising from repeated interorganizational learning. Realizing benefits from joint ventures or merged organizations often requires that one organization learns from another. Similarly, knowledge transfer is an especially important process in firms that are organized on a global basis to take advantages of differences in expertise, labor costs, or access to markets around the world. Thus, current business trends underscore the importance of repeated interorganizational learning, and its impact on firms, industries, regions, and other populations of organizations.

One measure of the value of a new theoretical perspective, such as population-level learning, is whether it helps us see and understand important phenomenon that existing theories do not. The papers in this volume provide convincing evidence of the value of the population learning perspective.

Linda Argote
Carnegie Mellon University

REFERENCES

Argote, L. (1999). *Organizational learning: Creating, retaining and transferring knowledge.* Norwell, MA: Kluwer.

Aldrich, H. E. (1979). *Organizations and environments.* Englewood Cliffs: Prentice-Hall.

Cyert, R. M., & March, J. G. (1963). *A behavioral theory of the firm.* Englewood Cliffs, NJ: Prentice-Hall.

DiMaggio, P. J., & Powell, W. W. (1983). The iron cage revisited: Institutional isomorphism and collective rationality in organizational fields. *American Sociological Review, 48,* 147-60.

Hannan, M. T., & Freeman, J. (1977). The population ecology of organizations. *American Journal of Sociology, 83,* 929-84.

Huber, G. P. (1991). Organizational learning: The contributing processes and the literatures. *Organization Science, 2,* 88-115.

Levitt, B., & March, J. G. (1988). Organizational learning. *Annual Review of Sociology, 14,* 319-340.

Meyer, J. W., & Rowan, B. (1977). Institutionalized organizations: Formal structure as myth and ceremony. *American Journal of Sociology, 83,* 340-63.

Miner, A. S., & Mezias, S. J. (1996). Ugly duckling no more. Pasts and futures of organizational learning research. *Organization Science, 7,* 88-99.

Pfeffer, J., & Salancik, G. R. (1978). *The external control of organizations.* New York: Harper & Row.

Scott, W. R. (1987). The adolescence of institutional theory. *Administrative Science Quarterly, 32,* 493-511.

INDUSTRY AND POPULATION-LEVEL LEARNING: ORGANIZATIONAL, INTERORGANIZATIONAL, AND COLLECTIVE LEARNING PROCESSES

Anne S. Miner and Philip Anderson

OVERVIEW AND IMPLICATIONS

One important school of strategic management theory has long adopted an implicit learning perspective in describing how strategies are formed (e.g., Burgelman, 1988; Mintzberg & McHugh, 1985; Noda & Bower, 1996; Quinn, 1980). These authors have focused on the ways organizational strategies emerge as individuals and groups come to learn about their own situation and to converge on patterns of behavior that appear to work. Mintzberg, Ahlstrand and Lampel (1998, pp. 208-9) argue that the role of leadership is not to preconceive deliberate strategies but to manage a process of strategic learning in which novel strategies can emerge, noting that strategies often first appear as patterns from the past and only later become plans for the future.

Even strategy perspectives that emphasize formal analysis, planning and formal strategic choice increasingly emphasize learning and knowledge deployment

Advances in Strategic Management, Volume 16, pages 1-30.

ISBN: 0-7623-0500-2

strategies. Early research on the resource-based view of the firm (e.g., Wernerfelt, 1984) directed attention to knowledge-based resources that are imperfectly tradable in factor markets. Those focusing on the strategic management of technology argued that firm prosperity depends on the proper assessment and deployment of knowledge assets, including both information and competencies (Teece, 1986; Winter, 1987). These concerns naturally stimulated research on how such resources are created (e.g., Leonard-Barton, 1995; Nonaka & Takeuchi, 1995), and empirical studies of knowledge transfer between firms (Darr, Argote & Epple, 1995; Hamel, 1991; Ingram, 1997; Ingram & Baum, 1997), and in broader networks (Powell, Koput, & Smith-Doerr, 1996). Indeed, the study of dynamic capabilities lies at the heart of cutting-edge strategy research today (Iansiti & Clark, 1994; Teece, Pisano & Shuen, 1997), focusing on organizational systems for creating and harvesting knowledge that is difficult to imitate and offers sustainable advantage. Links between learning and competition also inform important work on the dynamics of international competition and industry evolution as well as research on the co-evolution of technologies and industries (Kogut, 1993; Teece, 1986).

At the same time, learning research has also moved center stage in organization theory. Dissertations and major academic journals increasingly highlight organizational learning (e.g., Argote & Epple, 1990; Lant & Mezias, 1992; Levitt & March, 1988; March, 1991; Miner & Mezias, 1996; Walsh & Ungson, 1991). The growing body of related empirical research builds on two traditions. The first emphasizes learning through the selective retention of standard operating procedures or routines. In the traditional behavioral theory of the firm, search for new routines is triggered by periodic performance gaps (Cyert & March, 1963; Lant, 1992), while other models emphasize less purposeful search and varied selection processes (Burgelman, 1988; March, 1981; Miner, 1990, 1994). Consistent with very broad models of adaptive systems (Holland, 1996; Huberman, 1989) the key learning outcome is change in behaviors.

The second tradition envisions learning as a cognitive process, involving inference, computation, and understanding (Glynn, Lant & Milliken, 1994; Weick, 1979). Here, the key learning outcome is change in knowledge structures or mental models. Recent work has supplemented previous simulation (Levinthal & March, 1981; Lounamaa & March, 1987) and qualitative or conceptual studies (Cangelosi & Dill, 1965) with systematic empirical research (Argote, 1999). Contemporary research addresses learning subprocesses such as knowledge creation, memory formation and access, search, forgetting and knowledge transfer, and has provided evidence of distinct individual, group and organizational level learning processes (Argote, 1999; Epple, Argote & Devadas, 1991; Levinthal & March, 1993; March, 1999).

In this volume of *Advances in Strategic Management*, we bring together a set of papers that link strategy and learning models, and emphasize the way recurrent learning at several levels of analysis produces change in collectivities of organizations. We define *a population level learning outcome* as systematic change in the nature and mix of routines, strategies or practices enacted in a population of organizations, arising from experience (Miner & Haunschild, 1995). The population level learning framework focuses on how repeated learning processes affect the distribution of routines and competencies in an organizational population. These iterated learning *processes* include recurrent (1) independent organizational, (2) interorganizational, and (3) collective learning. The framework explores how iterated learning at several levels of analysis will generate systematic population level change. We believe many of the patterns discussed will have important implications for organizational fields, communities and regional clusters, but we emphasize industry transformation and use the terms *population* and *industry* interchangeably.

Although each paper contributes to its own distinct nexus of theory and practice, taken as a whole they illuminate three central issues in strategic management:

1. **Industry structure and learning:** *Does recurrent learning at different levels of action tend to produce convergence of practices and organizational forms in industries and organizational populations? Or will it produce emergent substructures—which may later influence further organizational action?* These questions address a central puzzle of strategic learning: how can organizations differentiate themselves and develop distinctive capabilities at the same time they learn from others? They illuminate how nonlinear industry transformation processes affect important strategic choice considerations for individual organizations.
2. **Industry evolution and learning:** *What factors moderate how recurrent organizational, interorganizational and collective learning influence population/industry transformation?* If recurrent learning at varied levels of analysis can produce different population level transformation patterns, what are some common moderators of these outcomes? These concerns address factors that strategists would need to consider in attempting to anticipate how their own and others' repeated learning processes may produce unanticipated population/industry transformation patterns over time.
3. **Industry attractiveness and robustness:** *How do different learning processes influence population/industry survival and prosperity?* Does recurrent learning at one level of analysis help learning at higher levels? Or can firm and population level learning processes conflict, creating tension between adaptive learning at different levels of analysis? These concerns focus attention on whether organizations may benefit from considering both their own and industry-level survival, and on factors making industries more or less attractive to learning organizations. They highlight crucial issues for strategists seeking to enhance the fate of industry or regional groups.

Table 1. Links Between Chapters and Issue

Chapter	*Industry Structure*	*Industry Evolution*	*Industry Attractiveness (Robustness)*
Miner & Anderson	•	•	•
Carley	•	•	
Greve		•	•
Ginsberg, Larsen & Lomi	•	•	•
Mezias, & Eisner		•	•
Wade , Porac & Yang	•	•	
Baum & Berta		•	•
Miner, Kim, Holzinger & Haunschild		•	•
Lant & Phelps	•	•	•
Rura-Polley		•	•
Anderson	•	•	

In Table 1, we indicate links between specific chapters and these issues, based on our perceptions of the papers' explicit statements as well as their implicit assumptions.

Insight into these three broad areas takes on increased urgency as organizations, industries and regions actively seek to use learning strategies and manage knowledge in pursuit of survival and prosperity. These issues also resonate with long-standing theoretical questions about organization learning more broadly and its links to strategic management. The framework also has special salience as organizational boundaries become more fluid, because it focuses on practices and guiding recipes, rather than numbers of organizations in the population.

In this chapter, we first clarify the population learning framework and definitions that inform our approach, to lay the foundation for considering specific papers. Next, we highlight selected ways specific papers provide insight into the three questions above, noting implications for strategic management. To conclude, we flag selected additional themes raised by the papers, areas we see as ripe for further research, and key contributions of the population-level learning framework to strategic management and organization theory.

LEARNING OUTCOMES, PROCESSES, AND LEVELS

In this section, we introduce our approach to learning outcomes, processes and levels, to clarify the overall population-level learning framework. We then build on these ideas in the following section to argue that strategy development and deployment unfold in the context of population-level learning. After summarizing several illustrative links between the three key strategic issues listed above and population-level learning concepts, we consider each issue's links to the specific chapters in more detail.

Learning as process and outcome. One reason "learning" papers usually start by defining the concept is that many plausible learning types and levels have been subsumed under this construct in varied literatures. Despite—or perhaps because of—the burgeoning interest in learning, the term itself has become contentious. Are cognition and understanding essential for learning? Does knowledge creation represent learning? At what level(s) of analysis does learning take place? Early writers were frequently charged with committing the ecological fallacy, inappropriately transporting concepts from one level of analysis to another and engaging in reification of groups and organizations. Do organizations learn, or do only individuals learn? Do organizations have memories?

We begin with a basic, but inclusive definition of *the process of learning: An agent learns when experience systematically alters its behavior and/or its knowledge* (Argote, 1999; Miner & Mezias, 1996). This definition characterizes both simple trial and error repetition of apparently fruitful actions and complex intellectual discovery as forms of learning. Consistent with this definition, we see *a change in the distribution of routines, practices or behaviors in the learning system as an important learning outcome.* This might, but does not necessarily, include cognitive routines such as scripts, mental models or theories. Like March and his colleagues, we define the learning outcome as a change in organizational routines or practices, not in terms of outcomes such as greater productivity (Levitt & March, 1988).

The link between a context and behavioral routines evoked in that context may or may not, then, be mediated by knowledge. For example, an adaptive system that adjusts future behavior through a simple feedback loop can be seen as "learning," although no intellectual activity is taking place. On the other hand, sometimes learning involves creating or updating a mental map, theories about cause and effect, or changing taken-for-granted assumptions (see Walsh, 1995, for a review of managerial cognition and collective memory). In this case, experience alters behavior by re-shaping the connections in a knowledge structure, which can then lead to change in the distribution of behavioral routines, practices or strategies. This process involves interaction with the world—or experience—with action informing understanding and understanding potentially informing action (Daft & Huber, 1987; Glynn, Lant & Milliken, 1994).

Levels of learning. Viewing a learning outcome as change in the distribution of routines and practices in a system sheds a different light on concerns about levels of analysis in learning. Rather than asking whether only individuals, or also collections of individuals can learn, we point out that the distribution of routines, or patterned behavior can shift at many levels of analysis. Clearly experience can systematically alter the future behavior and/or knowledge structures of both individuals and collective actors.

In recent years scholars have increasingly emphasized that learning at a focal level of analysis is not merely the simple aggregation of learning at lower levels of analysis. Even the individual mind may be thought of as a complex ecology of interacting ideas (Bateson, 1972). Complex systems of interaction produce emergent properties that cannot necessarily be predicted by understanding the individual propensities of the systems' components (Cowan, 1994; Hutchins, 1991; Simon, 1996). Learning at one level may be unrelated to, or even inconsistent with effective learning at another level. For example, Argote (1999) shows how learning at the individual level can inhibit learning at the group level, and a simulation by Lounamaa & March (1987) suggests simultaneous rapid learning by different parts of organizations can reduce learning effectiveness. These considerations suggest that collective learning is a worthy object of study in its own right. We cannot always reduce a collectivity's learning to the sum of learning processes at the next lower level of analysis and action.

For this reason, to understand learning as a driver and instrument of strategy, we not only need to investigate lower levels of analysis, such as learning by individual strategists or top management teams (e.g., Huff, 1990; Reger, 1990). We must also examine the context provided at higher levels of analysis. Organizational learning must be placed in the context of learning processes and outcomes at the next higher level of analysis. This involves multiple organizations that interact as they learn (March, 1991). The emergent pattern of behavior which can become strategy at the organizational level both influences and is influenced by the distribution of routines, strategies and practices in the population to which it belongs. Expanding the definition of Baum (1996, p. 77) we define an organizational population as *a set of organizations that share at least one major semi-stable trait, activity or resource utilization pattern.* An industry, for example, would represent an organizational population; a regional collection of organizations might also represent a local organizational population.

Population-level learning as outcome. Miner and Haunschild (1995, p. 115) originated the term *population-level learning* to denote the outcome of *"systematic change in the nature and mix of routines in a population of organizations as a result of experience."* Miner and Haunschild used the term "routine" to refer to a broader class of activities than narrow, repetitive sets of micro-actions in organizations. Their use of the term included systematic bundles of activity such as practices, programs, search rules, strategies, and other patterned behaviors or cognitive activities (Miner & Haunschild, 1995).

These routines can be enacted at many levels of analysis; they might include organizational roles, group practices, organizational strategies, or patterned behaviors enacted at the level of a population itself, such as an industry-level coordination "routine" used in a research consortium or trade association (Aldrich & Sasaki, 1995; Aldrich, Zimmer, Staber, & Beggs, 1994). Because it is based on experience, this learning outcome is distinct from shifts in distribution of routines that result from differential births and deaths of organizations. That is, we do not see population level learning outcome as a compositional effect, in which some routines, practices and strategies become more frequent because the organizations which implement them become more frequent. Rather, the change in distribution is itself the product of experience of some unit or units in the population.

For example, consider the U.S. radio industry in the 1960s and 1970s (Smith, Wright & Ostroff, 1998). AM radio stations exhibited a distribution of programming formats skewed heavily toward top-40-singles music. But by the 1990s, most music formats were offered by FM radio stations, and the distribution of AM formats was skewed toward syndicated talk-radio programs. How did this shift in the distribution of routines occur? In part, the transformation was driven by differential births and deaths—founders of new AM stations tended to adopt talk formats instead of music formats, and stations featuring music formats tended to be sold to new owners who switched to talk formats. However, this transformation is also in part a story of population-level learning. Some AM radio stations learned from observing other stations that talk-radio could attract listeners and advertisers, so they changed routines. Additionally, supra-organizational institutions emerged that made it easy for stations to institute talk-radio formats (in this case, widespread syndication and the emergence of recognized talk-radio personalities with nation-wide visibility) (Smith, Wright & Ostroff, 1998).

A population-level learning outcome, then, represents a sociological fact that characterizes a collective entity, not its individual members. Individual organizations or groups of organizations enact routines; populations exhibit a distribution of routines. To say that a population-level learning outcome has occurred is to say that the distribution of routines (practices and strategies) in a population has shifted over time, as a result of experience somewhere within the population. This experience may be direct or vicarious, as when the population observes the outcome of another population's actions.

We emphasize three learning processes that can produce this population level outcome, each at a different conceptual level of analysis. First, *parallel independent organizational learning* can produce new distributions of routines. As Carley shows (this volume), a set of organizations that are initially similar can learn independently in the same context with the same tasks, yet end up stratified in terms of practices and performance. Variety in practices occurs as the result of different organizational experiences and learning trajectories.

Second, *recurrent interorganizational learning* can produce new distributions of routines. Interorganizational learning takes place when an organization learns by observing other organizations, by exchanging knowledge with others, or by generating knowledge through joint interaction. This learning may be either vicarious (when one organization observes another) or interactive (when learning arises from active contacts between two or more organizations). Considerable research focuses on the impact of interorganizational learning on the individual learning organization. Does an organization gain from attempting to share knowledge in alliances (Aldrich & Sasaki, 1995; Mowery, Oxley & Silverman, 1996;

Powell et al., 1996)? Can a second mover learn effectively from observing a first mover (Antonelli, 1990)? Yet the research often stands silent on the way repeated instances of interorganizational learning influence the shape of an entire industry or organizational population (but cf. Suchman, 1994).

Third, whole industries and populations can observe other industries or populations, drawing on their shared experience to enact or inform population-level routines. This represents *a collective population learning process* at the population or industry level. A collective population-level learning process occurs when at least one learning step—such as knowledge discovery, retention, retrieval from memory, or contemporary experience—is collective. For example, a population may observe its own shared experience and collectively develop an interorganizational coordination device (a population-level routine). It might also develop a formal collective entity after watching another population/industry do so, build norms based on prior shared experience, or evolve shared mental models of population/industry identity, boundaries or performance standards. The United States semiconductor industry's observation of Japanese research consortia, and the consquent development of its own research consortia (such as SEMATECH; see Corey, 1997) represents a collective learning process. An emerging industry's development of a trade association group in response to the shared experience of an external threat could also represent collective learning (Bresser, 1998).

An important goal of this volume is to explore the claim that learning processes at one level may or may not mirror learning processes at another. At the same time, it is clear that the degree to which learning processes are collective represents a continuous rather than a discrete variable. For example, if an industry association (a collectivity) draws on data about the range of industry level performance (information from the memory of the whole population) to develop a new coordination routine between industry members (new population-level routine) and codified it in an industry level rule (new form of population level memory), then the entire learning process would be collective at the industry level. At the other extreme, population-level learning might involve primarily one collective learning step combined with other processes. For example, organizations might draw on but not share their separate experiences with different technological variants to decide on a shared industry standard. The original knowledge acquisition at the firm level would have been organizational, but the codification into industry-level norms would represent a collective process.

While most papers in this volume emphasize one of the three levels of learning processes, many also consider more than one process, and also address collective learning processes. Carley, for example, presents a simulation study of parallel independent organizational level learning. Baum and Berta, Greve, Ginsberg, Larsen and Lomi, and Mezias and Eisner primarily explicate interorganizational learning. Anderson, Lant and Phelps, Miner et al., and Rura-Polley emphasize collective learning issues. At the same time, the authors frequently show how learning processes occur at more than one level, and most imply that different learning processes influence population level transformation in non-obvious ways. The power of learning's impact on industries and organizational populations can be overlooked when one focuses solely on strategy as organization-level learning.

LINKS BETWEEN POPULATION LEVEL LEARNING AND STRATEGY DEVELOPMENT AND DEPLOYMENT

Why should students of strategic management care about population-level learning outcomes and the learning processes that produce them? Industry and competitive analysis (e.g., Oster, 1999; Porter, 1980) represent frameworks that scholars and managers use to understand the context of an organization's strategic position. These analyses help us assess which industries are more or less attractive environments, and how a firm's strategy positions it with respect to other enterprises. Much traditional industry analysis has drawn on fairly static concepts of industry structure. The changing nature and mix of routines, strategies and practices in a population that result from experience is the context in which the strategy-making process takes place. By considering how learning processes produce such changes, we begin to develop models of dynamic transformation of the industry and population context for firm level strategies. Theories about population-level learning help us assess why some organizational populations learn faster than others do, and how a firm is positioned with respect to other enterprises.

In the following three sections we consider specific implications of the chapters in this volume for each of the three major themes: (1) industry structure, (2) industry evolution, and (3) industry attractiveness and robustness. To highlight some common issues and implications, Table 2 summarizes several key insights developed in this volume that relate to each theme. Specific nuances of related chapters and arguments are noted in the detailed sections in Table 2.

Industry Structure and Learning

If firms repeatedly learn from their own experience and that of others, one might expect populations and industries to become homogeneous in their routines, strategies, and practices. The well-known evolutionary economics model of Nelson and Winter (1982), for example, assumes that a firm can copy any superior technology in the neighborhood of its current techniques, and can imitate the practices of higher-performing firms, subject to some error. But if firms learn repeatedly from the same reality, or from each other, how can they create and sustain competitive advantages over time in knowledge-based competition?

Several papers in this volume illuminate aspects of this central puzzle in strategic management. They explicate how repeated learning at several levels can produce inter-firm differences. Firms can become segregated into persistently different performance categories characterized by different learning paces.

Table 2. Illustrative Links: Strategic Issues and Implications of Chapters

Key Strategic Issue	*Theme*	*Key Concepts*	*Implications for Strategy*	*Relevant Chapters*
Industry structure	Repeated independent learning can lead to persistent performance differences.	Initially similar organizations can become locked into different learning mechanisms that lead to different results.	Learning per se does not produce competitive advantage. Internal learning mechanisms can reinforce or clash with one another.	Carley
Industry structure	When firms imitate the strategy of high performers in their neighborhood, patches of firms pursuing different strategies with different results can emerge.	The emergence of cooperative patches depends on the distribution of initial strategies, and the degree to which competition is localized. Recurrent interorganizational learning can produce population level contours that constrain further organizational learning.	A firm that prefers to maintain a cooperative strategy might intentionally look for contexts with combine a starting group which a high proportion of firms following a cooperative strategy, larger scope of interaction and more sensitivity to diffuse competition in the process.	Ginsberg, Lomi & Larsen
Industry structure	Learning and changing performance standards; routines may rise and fall.	Organizational learning involves adaptive search on a performance landscape. Collective learning and action may change the performance standards which later shape future learning.	Firms can affect the outcome of competition among clusters of routines by influencing how a population collectively defines and influences which dimensions of merit matter.	Anderson; Lant & Phelps

Industry evolution	Firms often imitate others outside their local neighborhoods. Such learning may depress the performance of individual units, but may be important when it is necessary to import new routines.	Learning from firms in different settings often fails, because a particular routine works only in the context of a particular environment.	Superior selection of individual interorganizational learning targets could provide firm level competitive advantage within an industry or strategic group. At the same time, inadequate permeability of neighborhood boundaries may reduce the viability of the whole industry/population.	Baum & Berta; Greve; Ginsberg, Lomi & Larsen; Wade, Porac, Wang; Lant & Phelps
Industry evolution	Firms may imitate practices based on how widespread they are, organizational traits or on the outcome of a specific practice. Such learning may produce unexpected outcomes when many firms employ the same learning mode at the same time.	No single mode produces the "best" results, but frequency- trait- and outcome-based learning may produce different learning rates.	Firms may profit from considering the broader pattern of interorganizational learning within which they function and the interorganizational learning modes of *other* organizations, to gain insight into how the collective pattern of imitation can transform the industry's practices over time.	Mezias & Eisner; Baum & Berta

(continued)

Table 2 (Continued)

Key Strategic Issue	*Theme*	*Key Concepts*	*Implications for Strategy*	*Relevant Chapters*
Industry attractiveness/ robustness	Individual organizational failures may enhance the profitability and survival chances of an industry as a whole	Failed experiments provide valuable lessons of experience for organizations that observe them	High failure rates could sometimes produce a potentially attractive industry	Miner et. al; Greve
Industry attractiveness/ robustness	Organizational learning can reduce the variance in organizations, lowering the survival chances of an industry as a whole. Exogeneous factors may enhance the presence of variance in potential practices.	Learning as reduction in variance versus learning as change in the mean. Semi-permeable boundaries permit subpopulations to escape the dangers of too little variation.	Organizations could profit from assuring semi-permeable boundaries around their subgroups, including strategic groups or others.	Lant & Phelps; Wade, Porac, & Yang; Carley; Rura-Polley
Industry attractiveness/ robustness	The speed at which an industry learns influences its overall performance.	Population performance suffers in very speedy and very slow learning populations.	When learning rates are too high, individual and collective organizations may benefit from taking steps to retard the rate of learning; more and faster learning is not always better.	Baum & Berta; Mezias & Eisner

Patches of collective strategies can emerge that are isolated from each other, and populations can break up into local learning neighborhoods. Importantly, heterogeneity does not simply arise because of barriers to efficient or effective learning; rather, it is generated by the dynamics of learning processes themselves. Furthermore, in some cases, learning produces industry level contours that shape further organizational learning and industry transformation, so that the trajectory of learning over time depends heavily on history. We highlight here four specific factors that may influence industry structure: recurrent independent learning, emergent patches of collective strategies through cycles of competition and learning, collective learning, and changing diversity in pools of routines.

Stratified industry/population through recurrent independent learning. Carley (this volume) describes results of a simulation study that models internal organizational learning with individual level learning and organizational features that shape individuals' interactions. Organizations begin with roughly similar features, and face the same tasks. Although the organizations are all learning, they do not converge to a single type of organization or set of organizational features. Repeated parallel independent organizational learning (by organizations that do not learn by observing each other) can lead to different strata, each containing a set of organizations that is locked into a particular change strategy. Although there is oscillation in specific rankings, the high-performing organizations in one period are also typically the high performers in the next.

Carley observes that even the high performers in this stratified system do not necessarily share fixed features with each other. Rather, their internal learning processes and pace of internal change tend to be similar. The important general insight is that these *quasi-stable industry patterns emerge not because some organizations are learning from their experience while others are not, but because of detailed, local features of learning processes within each organization.* These features in turn affect each organization's specific internal networks and procedures, which, in a path dependent process, produce quasi-stable industry/population distributions of routines, strategies and practices—along with persistent performance differences.

This simulation's results contradict the popular assumption that repeated independent learning by initially similar firms charged with the same task will necessarily produce convergence to a shared set of practices and routines. However, the results support predictions that firm level learning mechanisms tend to lock in, and this in turn produces population-level patterns that are not easily altered. Firms can't generate superior performance simply by emphasizing the importance of learning, or by imitating other population members whose results are superior. *The simulation implies that learning firms need to attend to the fine-grained details of their internal learning pace and processes if their learning is to provide competitive advantage, and that they can expect high and low performance to persist even if all firms pursue a learning strategy.*

Emergent patches of collective strategies. In Ginsberg, Larsen & Lomi's simulation (this volume) firms compete in rounds of a prisoner's dilemma within neighborhoods of interaction, then adopt the strategy of the winner of the competition in their own neighborhood. This method of determining their competitive strategy for the next round can be seen as interorganizational learning in the form of outcome imitation (Haunschild & Miner, 1997; Miner & Raghavan, 1999). The simulation explicates how repeated rounds of competition and interorganizational learning, under suitable conditions, produce patches of organizations that follow a collective cooperative strategy: the firms in each patch "lock-in" to cooperation with each other. Their model shows how local decision rules followed over time induce and sustain aggregate regularities in the industry/population as a whole. Ginsberg et al. find that the initial proportion of cooperative strategists in the population influences whether patches of interfirm cooperation form. Increased scope of interaction produces larger islands of cooperation. They interpret this range of interaction in terms of the cognitive limitations of participating organizations, but the range of interaction could also be determined by such factors as shared sense of identity among organizations or simple geographic proximity (Anderson, this volume; Lant & Phelps, this volume).

Like Carley's simulation, this one shows how learning at a lower level of analysis can produce regularities at the industry level that then shape future interactions among organizations. In these models, collective learning emerges from interaction. Lower level learning produces stable contours at the industry level that constrain the ongoing strategies and behavior of firms in the future, as well as the learning strategies open to these firms. Again, these models imply that firms pursuing a learning strategy may need to consider whether the collective impact of firm learning may be creating broader industry/population patterns that will constrain the focal firm in the future. For example, in Ginsberg, Larsen & Lomi's set-up, *a firm that prefers to maintain a cooperative strategy might look for contexts that combine a high proportion of other firms following a cooperative strategy, a larger scope of interaction and more sensitivity to diffuse competition.*

Collective learning and industry heterogeneity. Anderson (this volume) tracks changes in the distribution of two competing production routines in the cement industry. He describes how the U.S. cement industry moved from a period in which dry mixing dominated, through a period in which wet mixing of raw materials was most common, and then returned to a preponderance of dry mixing. Early in the period studied, the U.S. cement industry developed a shared emphasis on quality as the key competitive dimension. Customers had no reliable technical way to assess cement quality directly, so they used social cues, reputation or high price as indicators of quality.

After World War I, a new wave of foreign competition led to a shared belief that thorough mixing of ingredients produced better cement that achieved load-bearing strength more quickly. Although this view was not grounded in direct scientific evidence, it became a shared, taken-for-granted belief—derived through interorganizational learning—that helped generate a shift to the use of water to gain more thorough mixing at the cost of fuel efficiency and throughput. Industry-sponsored research eventually generated ways to test quality (e.g., durability) of cement directly, which in turn permitted technical standard levels to be adopted by the industry. It also vastly improved dust control, thereby eliminating a key advantage of the wet-mixing process. Eventually, through further innovation, dry mixing re-emerged as the dominant routine in the industry.

In this case both simple imitative learning and a change in knowledge structures occurred. Indeed, collectively sponsored research led to more accurate shared theories about what produced more durable and reliable cement. More interestingly, the original shared performance standards shaped collective and firm level learning. But the results of this learning then transformed the industry's performance standard, which provided a new learning landscape for both firms and collective learning. Which routine prevails as the distribution of routines shifts as a result of experience—and which firms win and lose as their routines fall into and out of favor—is a function of collective action, not economic superiority alone. *Firms can affect the outcome of competition among clusters of routines by influencing the way a population collectively defines which dimensions of merit matter, what standards collective bodies set, and what research trajectories such bodies pursue.*

In another approach emphasizing collective learning, Lant and Phelps (this volume) argue that crucial learning occurs in the interactions among the organizations (rather than only within firms). They build on emerging sociocognitive theories of strategic groups and on situated learning theory to consider the process of collective learning, drawing upon observations of the emerging media industry of Silicon Alley in New York City. Lant and Phelps go beyond the idea of shared mental models by conceptualizing population-level learning as occurring within the ongoing interaction of the firms over time. *Lant and Phelps' approach implies that the development of cognitive groups does not always result in the strategic myopia described in Scottish knitwear makers (Porac, Thomas & Baden-Fuller, 1989). They suggest that variations in perceived boundaries and strength of identity can generate heterogeneity within cognitive strategic groups.*

Changing pools of diversity of routines. Rura-Polley (this volume) tackles potential origins of population heterogeneity of practices by studying directly the nature and degree of variation in proposed childcare practices in two distinct organizational subpopulations: Catholic childcare institutions in Germany and those in the United States over a 75-year period. She argues that the two differing national contexts produced very different patterns of variation among proposed practices, even though the overarching institution—the Catholic Church—maintained its underlying values and policies related to children's institutions. Rura-Polley's qualitative analyses indicate that variation in these candidate routines and strategies—at least in the German case—reflects broader social trends. The degree and nature of variation in candidate practices was clearly different in the two countries. Temporal patterns were not the same, and the two countries differed in which topic areas showed most variation. Rura-Polley's work implies that the candidate pool of routines/strategies available varies between subpopulations. The data provide important evidence that the number and nature of publicly available "recipes" for action (Spencer, 1989) can vary between regions and times, even within a single fairly hierarchical organization. *This suggests industry structure may arise in part from the degree of available diversity of practices and strategists might consider the nature and pool of available practices in choosing industries to enter.*

Taken together, these papers demonstrate ways in which all three levels of learning can—separately and in combination—produce population/industry heterogeneity, which in some cases may be sustained through lock-in processes. One of the most important features of this insight, we think, is the notion that *while individual firms learn, they may be creating unintended contours within their own industries that constrain their own fate later on.* Insight into the dynamics of such processes provides a potential strategic factor for organizations whose fate will depend on the survival and prosperity of their industries as a whole.

Industry Evolution and Learning: What Moderates the Impact of Recurrent Organizational, Interorganizational and Collective Learning?

Population-level learning occurs when the distribution of routines—broadly defined—in an industry changes as a result of experience. Industry evolution occurs when the distribution of organizations themselves, or organizational *forms* in an industry, changes over time. For example, when a change in the proportion of generalists versus specialists, M-form versus U-form enterprises, or independent firms versus joint ventures persists over time, the industry has evolved, with important strategic consequences. Since an organization's routines help govern its form and indeed some forms can be seen as complex bundles of routines, it is clear that these two dynamic processes are interrelated. Traditional industry-level competitive analysis ascribes industry transformation to exogenous factors, such as technological or regulatory change, and to the winnowing effects of competition. The articles in this volume suggest that *who organizations learn from* and *why they adopt routines* from each other is an endogenous factor that also contributes to the transformation of a population over time.

The chapters highlight three features of learning processes that may shape industry evolution: learning from near versus learning from distal neighbors, within-group versus across group learning, and modes of organizational learning.

Learning from near vs. learning from distal neighbors. Several papers explicate important ways in which distance between organizations—whether in terms of space or other dimensions—moderates the impact of learning processes on industry evolution.

For example, Greve studies organizations with multiple branches. The evolution of the radio broadcasting industry in recent years has been marked by a rise in the number of stations belonging to multi-station, multi-geography companies (Smith, Wright & Ostroff, 1998). Is this because branch systems facilitate the transfer of routines from one region to another? In his empirical study of format changes in radio stations in varied regions, Greve finds that greater experience of a branch system's units *outside* a given geographic market causes lower performance of each branch in a focal market. He also finds that the more experience a branch system has outside a given local market, the greater the variation in performance in that market. The results imply routines or format strategies transferred from distant neighborhoods actually harm rather then help the imitating stations. Greve argues that the difference in competitors between different regions creates this effect. These findings imply that if firms repeatedly imitate practices from distant neighborhoods, interorganizational imitation may decrease the immediate performance of imitators. However, Greve points out bringing in routines from distant organizational neighborhoods could help the local neighborhood as a whole, if other organizations learn from the failed routines that local branches borrowed from their sister stations.

Distal learning also occurs among organizations that do not share common ownership. Baum and Berta (this volume) study a group of firms competing in a behavioral simulation. They find that organizations learn from other organizations when their members interact with each other as individuals more frequently, and when the imitating organizations have similar market shares. Interestingly, they find that firms do not tend to imitate the most successful competitors in their local populations. Rather, they look further afield, imitating the most successful firms in other populations. In addition, Ginsberg, Larsen, and Lomi's study suggests that the further away from their neighborhoods firms search for successful organizations to imitate, the less fragmented an industry becomes.

These studies imply the boundaries of neighborhoods of interaction will powerfully influence industry evolution, and that choice of neighborhoods of interaction as well as imitation may represent an important strategic choice for individual organizations.

Within-group versus across-group learning: Neighborhood boundaries and their permeability. The distance between two organizations that may learn from one other is not simply a continuous measure in social or physical space. Industries can fragment into subgroups; firms that belong to different subgroups must cross boundaries to learn from one another, even if they are close demographically or geographically. A change in the distribution of firms across such subgroups constitutes industry evolution, if group membership is relatively distinct and persistent. How are such changes influenced by learning processes?

Wade and Porac's chapter in this volume builds a model suggesting that the movement of personnel among firms in an industry is an important conduit for interorganizational learning which influences subsequent industry structures.

Industry evolution in turn creates opportunities that encourage or discourage certain types of managerial migration among firms. In this way, interorganizational learning (through the movement of people between organizations) and industry evolution are linked in a mutually causal loop.

Early in an industry's history, these authors suggest, key managers from different firms tend to migrate from the same industries, bringing with them a common set of routines. For example, German experts greatly influenced the early practice of both the American beer brewing industry and the American cement manufacturing industry. Consequently, routines tend to be fairly homogenous across firms, and collective structures that promote collective population-level learning emerge fairly easily.

As an industry evolves, Wade and Porac suggest, it tends to split into two subsectors, a core and a periphery, differentiated by status, size, and/or performance. Organizations belonging to the core tend to monitor and learn from each other. Population-level learning takes place as routines diffuse through movement of managers from core to peripheral organizations, and through experimentation among peripheral firms, leading to the emergence of novel routines. When an industry is jolted by a shock, personnel flows tend to reverse: core firms begin to recruit from the periphery in order to import novel routines.

In considering implications of their observations, Wade and Porac argue that the degree of permeability of an industry's core may have important implications for the industry's long term adaptation. If core and periphery boundaries are nearly impermeable, the core may fail to learn new routines, strategies and practices, and over time fade. In contrast, if the core/periphery boundary is permeable, personnel movement from the periphery may introduce routines and practices that permit the to core to adapt through the adoption of these new practices. Lant and Phelps make a similar argument, pointing out that permeable boundaries between cognitive strategic groups may permit new routines and strategies to move into established groups, providing variance permits adaptive learning that can enhance long term survival of the strategic group.

These theories imply that industry evolution will be influenced by the permeability of boundaries around subpopulations, and that important strategic action can include choices about the strength and type of boundaries maintained.

Taken together, these moderating effects of neighborhoods on the population impact of interorganizational imitation have important strategic implications. Greve's work implies that learning from organizations too distant from oneself often reduces performance, yet imitating nearby competitors can produce escalation in which all firms "improve" in absolute terms but not in relative position (the so-called Red Queen effect in evolutionary theory) (Kauffman, 1993; March, 1991; Van Valen, 1973). This underscores the significance of carefully selecting interorganizational learning targets. These localized neighborhood effects on repeated interorganizational learning also suggest that strategists may benefit from considering the general pattern of interorganizational knowledge flow in their own industry or strategic group. *Superior selection of individual interorganizational learning targets could provide firm level competitive advantage within an industry or strategic group. At the same time, inadequate permeability of neighborhood boundaries may reduce the viability of the whole industry/population.*

Modes of interorganizational learning. Imitating other organizations constitutes one form of interorganizational learning: imitating another organization means using that organization's experience as a basis for one's own actions. The process may or may not involve forming inferences or causal theories about the imitated practice. On what basis do organizations choose which routines to imitate? Three different modes of interorganizational learning are addressed by various papers in this volume: (1) *frequency-based* learning (when organizations adopt the practice of a large number of other organizations), (2) *trait-based* learning (when organizations adopt the practice favored by organizations with a distinct trait such as size or prestige), and (3) *outcome-based* learning (when organizations observe the apparent results of a practice and adopt it or not based on those results) (Haunschild & Miner, 1997; Miner & Raghavan, 1999).

Baum and Berta's behavioral simulation presents further evidence for the use of more than one mode of interorganizational learning and imitation: their groups appear to choose learning targets on the basis of both traits and outcomes. Mezias and Eisner theorize that each learning/imitation mode produces a different pattern of industry transformation, due to differences in their relative speed and cost. They contend that outcome-based learning leads to the most rapid evolution when ambiguity is low, because successful new organization forms diffuse rapidly, and firms quickly exit highly competitive niches. However, they believe the costs of searching for a new form and adopting a new form are highest when firms employ outcome-based learning. Combining intuitions about costs and speed, Mezias and Eisner predict that both frequency-based and trait-based learning will lead to long periods of stability in the distribution of organizational forms, punctuated by short periods of rapid, large-scale change. In contrast, outcome-based learning will result in smaller, more frequent changes in an industry's mix of organizational forms.

One implication of the work on modes of imitation is that firms may profit from considering the broader pattern of interorganizational learning within which they function. They can try to anticipate where their industry/population may be moving, given that recurrent interorganizational imitation can produce unexpected effects. *Firms may need to pay attention to the interorganizational learning modes of other organizations—not to understand what specific knowledge a competitor may be gaining, but to gain some insight into how the collective pattern of imitation might transform the industry's practices over time.*

Population and Industry Attractiveness/Robustness: Learning's Impact on Population Survival and Prosperity

We assume if that individual organizations are all learning in sensible ways, the aggregate result will be adaptive for the industry as a whole and all its members. Yet the research in this volume belies this assumption, and explicates how different learning processes may interact to promote or detract from industry survival and prosperity. The chapters in this volume imply that two powerful factors shape the way learning influences survival and prosperity of the whole industry: the degree and nature of tensions between organizational and population-level learning, and temporal learning patterns.

Tensions between organizational and population-level learning outcomes. Several papers imply that lower-level learning may not only have unintended impact on population/industry transformation, but may in some cases conflict with fruitful population-level learning outcomes. These studies raise important questions about the impact of learning processes on organizational and population-level performance, including both survival and prosperity.

Miner, Kim, Holzinger and Haunschild draw on historical reports of organizational populations and industry transformations to examine ways failure and near-failure by individual organizations may spur different degrees of collective learning processes. The authors describe learning processes in which failing organizations stimulate other organizations to avoid specific routines/strategies/practices, to search for and imitate nonfailing organizations or to reinforce their own current practices. They also describe learning processes in which the population/industry develops new collective routines such as research consortia or federated political groups.

Miner and colleagues argue these processes produce shifts in the distribution of routines/strategies in a population in several nonobvious ways. For example, they observe how dominant firms may imitate challengers in the periphery of an industry and lose ground, even while legitimating the routines they imitate. This chapter does not imply that all learning from the failure of others is valuable. However it suggests that the failure or near failure of some organizations in many cases does spurs fruitful learning by other organizations and by the population as a whole. In fact, the authors argue the population may learn more from failures or near failures than from apparent successes, because of their greater visibility and potential for developing more accurate causal models.

Similarly, Greve shows in his radio study how organizations that imitate practices from distant regions reduce the level and increase the variance in their own performance. He suggests this helps the industry by introducing new routines/strategies and allowing others to observe their impact. He argues such firms engage—in effect—in altruistic learning: their experience detracts from their own performance but may enhance that of the industry/population to which they belong.

Three other papers point to the complementary situation in which fruitful firm-level learning detracts from learning at the population/industry level. Lant and Phelps, Wade and Porac, and Carley all describe organizational learning processes that reduce variance within firms. They point out that this useful firm-level learning may restrict population learning and adaptation by reducing the variation in routines/strategies available in the future. These situations can be seen as a complement to the failure argument, which hinges on the idea that contrasts between failure, near-failure and success provide the variance in both behavior and outcome that represents the most valuable learning context.

At the heart of all these studies lies the notion that individual organizations face trade-offs between potentially valuable organizational and population-level learning processes. This dilemma is familiar to firms in the area of knowledge deployment in research consortia, where firms try to balance supporting collective discovery of knowledge useful to the entire industry with safeguarding their own knowledge and avoiding free-riding by others (Mowery, Oxley & Silverman, 1996). The papers in this volume suggest that the dilemma may apply more broadly than in the obvious context of research and development. Efficient solutions to this puzzle are not apparent. It is hard to devise appropriate systems of side payments that reward failing firms for enhancing the knowledge of others or deviant, low-performing firms for preserving variance potentially useful to the whole population. *This issue suggests that collective consortia and industry associations could fruitfully facilitate diversity in the populations/industries they represent, rather than relentlessly promoting "best practices" in all members.*

Population/Industry performance impact of temporal learning patterns. March (Lounamaa & March, 1987; March, 1991) has illustrated several potential dangers of overly-rapid learning in simulations of organizations learning from their own experience, especially in the presence of noise and multiple learning entities. The papers here underscore potential tradeoffs between fast and slow experiential learning at the population level.

Baum and Berta's paper explores the vital question of how speed of population-level learning affects industry performance and survival. Speed is an important issue in all forms of learning (Argote, 1999). Baum and Berta provide the first systematic empirical evidence supporting the prediction that populations face windows of opportunity in which learning is most fruitful (Miner & Haunschild, 1995). Baum and Berta find that their behaviorally simulated population's speed of overall learning (using numbers of learning events in specific time periods) affected the population average performance as predicted. Population performance suffered in very speedy and very slow learning populations. The authors argue that some populations learn too slowly to harvest learning while others learn too rapidly to discover effective routines.

Mezias and Eisner's discussion of varied modes of interorganizational learning also raises questions of the impact of speed in population level transformation. Mezias and Eisner argue outcome-based imitation will result in the most rapid diffusion of a new high performance organizational form, and produce frequent change in the mix of forms, but the magnitude of such changes will be more modest than for frequency or trait-based imitation. Since these dynamics may themselves affect population survival in the face of competing populations, imitation mode may affect population survival or prosperity indirectly through its impact on the pace of population-level learning.

These and other papers taken together underscore how behavioral versus cognitive learning may moderate the impact of both speed and variance (including contrasts between failure and success) in the impact of different learning levels on population level performance. *If other organizations can easily generate valid insights and strategies by observing failing organizations, (including those that fail from overly rapid organizational learning); the industry may thrive even in the presence of high failure rates or overly-rapid learning by individual organizations. To the degree such inferential learning is difficult, dangers of overly rapid organizational learning increase.*

THE FUTURE OF POPULATION-LEVEL LEARNING RESEARCH

The population-level learning framework represents work in progress. Although learning models are attractive because they embrace dynamic processes and fit contemporary emphasis on the role of knowledge, their very richness and complexity can be a disadvantage in focusing further research. By raising common themes in different contexts, the studies in this volume point to key issues for further investigation. These include the roles and impact of neighborhoods of interaction, interorganizational imitation modes, population contours (such as performance standards or identity) and interactive learning.

Systematic empirical research on the way *neighborhoods of interaction* moderate learning's impact on population heterogeneity, survival and prosperity shows promise. It may make sense to contrast learning models here with related work examining regional populations and traditional agglomeration processes (Cooke & Morgan, 1998; Krugman, 1995; Suchman, 1995).

Similarly, empirical research on the impact of different *interorganizational imitation modes* will be important. Formal models of interorganizational imitation imply that interorganizational learning processes can produce heterogeneity (Miner & Raghavan, 1999). Because most prior empirical research has emphasized only one learning mode, we have little systematic evidence about the impact of combined frequency, trait and outcome imitation processes and their implications for strategic management.

One important notion presented in this volume is that certain *population level contours,* such as shared performance standards or identities, can arise from learning processes. These contours then also shape future behavior, including future learning at lower levels. This insight implies that collective outcomes may limit future strategic choice for learning organizations in unexpected ways. Systematic empirical research on such contours may reveal that they are more than simple moderators influencing the impact of repeated organizational or interorganizational learning. Research on the competitive structures in which learning outcomes are judged may also have important strategic implications (March, 1991). For example, performance could be judged by organizations' peak performances, or by their average performances. Each would represent a different way of keeping score of organizational success. The score-keeping system provides the incentive structure within which organizations compete and learn. Different structures would make high-risk learning strategies valuable in some cases, and low-risk learning strategies best in others.

Interactive and *situated learning*, as well as the notion of networks as the memory banks for populations also deserve continued attention (Powell, Koput, & Smith-Doerr, 1997; Powell, 1998; Suchman, 1995). In fact, the broad definition of learning used in the population-level learning framework mandates careful empirical work to tease out what specific learning processes apply under what conditions This emphasis is consistent with growing empirical work on specific learning processes (Argote, 1999). The idea that networks represent a form of memory—a learning element—for example, represents a crucial focus for continued empirical work. It also makes sense to examine related analytic work done by evolutionary economists and historians who have considered learning models in some detail (England, 1994).

Other significant issues for continuing work were not highlighted in this volume. These areas already support vigorous research that will play a vital role in illuminating population-level learning. They include the impact of levels of prior collective experience, differences in organization-level learning competencies, nuances of local learning contexts, and cross-industry and cross-region learning. For example, related prior research indicates that the *level of collective experience* can affect organizational survival chances, which in turn influence population/industry survival and prosperity (Baum & Ingram, 1998; Ingram & Baum, 1997). Research on ship-building and hotels suggested individual organizations may not be able to continue learning from others after their founding (Argote, Beckman, & Epple, 1990; Baum & Ingram, 1998). However, the potential impact of what can be learned after start-up may be weak because of the large capital investments needed in these industries. Future work should examine conditions under which ongoing population experience may or may not enhance the survival and growth of firms.

Additionally, clearly, some organizations are better at learning than are others (Carley, this volume; Leonard-Barton, 1995; Nonaka & Takeuchi, 1995). Improving an organization's ability to learn, from its own experience and that of others has been a principal focus of the burgeoning literature on organizational learning and knowledge management (e.g., Argote & Epple, 1990; Grant, 1996). Further work exploring *firm level differences in learning capabilities* represents an obvious focus for future research, going beyond the notion of absorptive capacity to a more comprehensive vision of strategic choices in targets, modes and capabilities for interorganizational learning.

The population-level learning framework suggests that in addition to studying the internal mechanisms through which firms generate or absorb routines, we should understand *the local context within which they learn.* For example, Wade and Porac describe how transferring knowledge from managers who bring core-firm experience to a firm operating in the periphery can be helpful or not, depending on how industry evolution alters the opportunity structure, opening or blocking career paths within core enterprises. Similarly, Carpenter and Westpal (1999) show how the influence of board interlocks on firm strategic decision making depends on the external, social-structural context in which the directors were embedded. More precise understanding of these areas would have value not only for firm level strategists, but also for collectivities of firms and groups such as policymakers charged with the well-being of organizational populations or industries.

International and historical research by Kogut (1993) and others (Nelson, 1993; Suchman, 1995) points to a final area we think vital for continued research: *the dynamics of whole populations, regions and industries learning from each other.* In many cases, such learning may involve the transfer of population-level routines including not only technological standards, for example, but also routines or strategies for coordinating members of a population. Additionally, while we emphasize industries as important populations, populations defined by geography and culture represent an important frontier. Waller, Gibson and Carpenter (1999), for example, argue that cultural differences are likely to influence the type, amount and pace of knowledge transfer at both firm and population levels. Insight into these processes can inform strategists concerned with the survival or growth of their own industries or regions, and appear increasingly relevant in contemporary economic settings.

THEORETICAL VALUE

We believe that a focus on the way recurrent learning influences industry and population transformation makes a distinct contribution to scholarship in both strategic management and organization theory.

For strategic management theory, this work—as we note in several places above—supplements the existing focus on interactions between learning and competition from the firm's point of view. It highlights the potential value of firms trying to understand the nonlinear dynamics of the way their own learning may alter the context in which they act and continue to learn. It is consistent with efforts to think more carefully about how regions, nations or industries can promote their own survival and prosperity in the face of knowledge creation and learning by competing regions, nations and industries (Kogut, 1993; Porter, 1990; Teece, 1986).

Research on population-level learning also continues to develop themes raised by the resource-based view of the firm, through emphasizing the importance of understanding mixes of resources in the form of routines, strategies and practices at a higher level of analysis. The framework also opens the door to conceptions of industry development that do not take the firm itself as the most crucial unit of analysis. To the degree that it emphasizes organizations, population-level learning focuses attention on learning differences among firms rather than structural regularities. This slight adjustment of focus may offer insights we could not easily achieve when we assume the nature and distribution of firms represent the most crucial unit for thinking about industry prosperity. This emphasis may also be timely. Attention to changes in the mix of routines enacted in a population directs attention to changes in what is actually getting done rather than to changes in organizational size or boundaries. To the degree that organizations are increasingly transient or maintain very cloudy borders, this focus is increasingly relevant.

In organization theory, the population-level learning framework offers a natural extension of learning theories, which have moved from individuals, to groups, to whole organizations but stopped short of any higher level. By examining the impact of learning on higher-level collectivity the population level learning framework responds to Stern and Barley's call to address organization theory's "neglected mandate": the impact of organizations on the broad social systems in which they are embedded (Stern & Barley, 1996).

While overlapping in some areas, our framework differs in emphasis from several related perspectives, however. Research on the diffusion of innovations, for example, tends to study the fate of individual innovations over time rather than the overall mix of practices. It could not easily account for Anderson's case of a single routine dominating, receding, and returning to prominence in a population, nor can it easily consider how routines interact with each other.

The population learning framework also provides a different account of many processes than does traditional neoinstitutional theory. The population-level learning perspective predicts the presence of other organizations early in an emerging industry may enhance survival of new firms and industry growth because real discovery of useful knowledge occurs and advances through interorganizational learning. This provides an alternative explanation for why increased density enhances survival—an explanation not based on social legitimacy (Aldrich, 1999; Delacroix & Rao, 1994; Miner & Haunschild, 1995).

This framework also implies that organizations may converge on some traits while diverging on others, even without the influence of social legitimacy questions, due to variation in learning modes targets and neighborhoods (Suchman, 1994). The framework also differs from organizational ecology approaches to industry transformation by shifting the focus of attention away from distribution of organizational forms and toward changes in distributions of routines, strategies and practices in a population (McElvey & Aldrich, 1983).

Learning processes that involve pure behavioral trial and error learning can often be conceptualized as evolutionary processes at a lower level of analysis. Some conceptualizations of nested evolutionary systems, for example (e.g., Baum & Singh, 1994), can be seen as learning at a higher level of analysis, but the population learning terminology may not be needed for additional insight. To the degree that transformations involve aspiration levels, intentional experimentation, knowledge structures and cognition, learning models contain elements not easily incorporated in traditional evolutionary models of change. These models often emphasize blind variation rather than search, and do not envision a separate system of representations of the world as change occurs. Cultural evolutionary theorists (Boyd & Richerson, 1985) offer approaches closer to our framework, but have tended to emphasize individual-level processes. Our perspective predicts that organizations and industries may achieve useful and valid mental representations of the world. Yet by assuming barriers, stages and limits to learning the framework also makes different predictions than do economic models that assume efficient knowledge spillover.

CONCLUSION

Vital strategy research has long focused on how firms can balance knowledge creation and deployment with efforts to find sustainable competitive advantage (Boisot, Griffiths, & Moles, 1997; Dickson, 1992; Teece, 1986; Teece, Pisano, & Shuen, 1997). Organizations seek to gain knowledge efficiently and quickly from others, yet also to harvest the value of their own knowledge and competencies without appropriation by others. Difficulties in accomplishing this, combined with increasing rates of change in contexts of competition and technology have persuaded some that learning itself represents a crucial organizational competency (e.g., Lei, Hitt, & Bettis, 1996; Teece, Pisano, & Shuen, 1997). At the same time, international competition and the pace of technological change have brought to light ways in which entire populations or industries compete with each other over time (Kogut, 1993; Porter, 1990).

The papers in this volume explore how parallel independent organizational learning, recurrent interorganizational learning and collective population learning processes can change the nature and mix of routines, strategies and practices in a population of organizations (or industry). The population-level learning perspective supplements existing work with two distinct emphases. First, it directs attention to the impact of recurrent learning at different levels on population-level transformation, rather than only on the firms directly involved in the learning. Second, it emphasizes change in the mixes of routines/ practices in the population, rather than change in the mix of organizations themselves. This focuses attention on what the organizations in a population are actually doing rather than on how many organizations the population contains, a focus that will be more relevant if boundaries become more plastic. These emphases lead to models that underscore multiple interactions between competition and learning, and suggest important issues pertinent to strategic managers and policymakers. We invite the reader to consider the work here, and to join the conversation represented by this rich set of papers.

REFERENCES

Aldrich, H.E. (1999). *Organizations evolving*. London: Sage Publications.

Aldrich, H.E., Zimmer, C. R., Staber, U. H., Beggs, J. J. (1994). Minimalism, mutualism, and maturity: The evolution of the American trade association population in the twentieth century. In J. Baum & J. Singh (Eds.), *Evolutionary dynamics of organizations* (pp. 223-39). New York: Oxford University Press.

Aldrich, H. E., & Sasaki, T. (1995). R&D consortia in the United States and Japan. *Research Policy, 24*, 301-316.

Antonelli, C. (1990). Profitability and imitation in the diffusion of process innovations. *Rivista Internazionale di Scienze Economiche e Commerciali, 37*, 109-126

Argote, L. (1999). *Organizational learning: Creating, retaining & transferring knowledge*. Boston: Kluwer.

Argote, L., Beckman, S. L., & Epple, D. (1990). The persistence and transfer of learning in industrial settings. *Management Science, 36,* 140-154.

Argote, L., & Epple, D. (1990). Learning curves in manufacturing. *Science, 247*, 920-924.

Bateson, G. (1972). *Steps to an ecology of mind: Collected essays in anthropology, psychiatry, evolution, and epistemology*. San Francisco: Chandler Publishing Company.

Baum, J. (1996). Organizational ecology. In S. R. Clegg, C. Hardy, & W. R. Nord (Eds.), *Handbook of organization studies* (pp. 77-114). London: Sage.

Baum, J., & Ingram, P. (1998). Survival-enhancing learning in the Manhattan hotel industry, 1898-1980. *Management Science, 44*, 996-1016.

Baum, J. A., & Singh, J. V. (1994). *Evolutionary dynamics*. Oxford: Oxford University Press.

Boisot, M., Griffiths, D., & Moles, V. (1997). The dilemma of competence: Differentiation versus integration in the pursuit of learning. In R. Sanchez & A. Heene (Eds.), *Strategic learning and knowledge management* (pp. 65-82). Chichester: John Wiley & Sons.

Boyd, R., & Richerson, P. J. (1985). *Culture and the evlutionary process*. Chicago, IL: University of Chicago Press.

Bresser, K. F. (1988). Matching collective and competitive strategies. *Strategic Management Journal, 9,* 375-385.

Burgelman, R. A. (1988). Strategy making as a social learning process: the case of internal corporate venturing. *Interfaces, 18*, 74-85.

Cangelosi, V. E., & Dill, W. R. (1965). Organizational learning: Observations toward a theory. *Administrative Science Quarterly, 10*, 175-203.

Carpenter, M., & Westphal, M. J. (1999). *A network perspective on how outside directors impact strategic decision making*. Academy of Management Best Papers Proceedings.

Cooke, P., & Morgan, K. (1998). *The associational economy: Firms, regions and innovation*. Oxford, UK: Oxford University Press.

Corey, E. R. (1997). *Technology fountainheads: The management challenge of R&D consortia*. Boston: Harvard Business School Press.

Cowan, G. A. (1994). Conference opening remarks. In G. A. Cowan, D. Pines, & D. Meltzer (Eds.), *Complexity: Metaphors, models, reality* (pp. 1-4). Reading, MA: Addison-Wesley.

Cyert, R. M., & March, J. G. (1963)[1992]. *A behavioral theory of the firm*. Englewood Cliffs, NJ: Prentice-Hall.

Daft, R. L., & Huber G. P. (1987). How organizations learn: A communication framework. *Research in the sociology of organizations* (vol. *5,* 1-36). Greenwich, CT: JAI Press.

Darr, E. D., Argote, L., & Epple, D. (1995). The acquisition, transfer, and depreciation of knowledge in service organizations: Productivity in franchises. *Management Science, 41*, 1750-1762.

Delacroix, J., & Rao, H. (1994). Externalities and ecological theory: Unbundling density dependence. In J. A. C. Baum & J. V. Singh (Eds.), *Evolutionary dynamics of organizations* (pp. 255-268). New York: Oxford University Press.

Dickson, P. R. (1992). Toward a general theory of competitive rationality. *Journal of Marketing, 56,* 69-83.

Dollinger, M. J. (1990). The evolution of collective strategies in fragmented industries. *Academy of Management Review, 15,* 266-295.

England, R. W. (1994). *Evolutionary concepts in economics*. Ann Arbor: University of Michigan Press.

Epple, D., Argote, L., & Devadas, R. (1991). Organizational learning curves: A method for investigating intra-plant transfer of knowledge acquired through learning by doing. *Organization Science, 2*, 58-70.

Glynn, M. A., Lant, T. K., & Milliken, F. J. (1994). Mapping learning processes in organizations: A multi-level framework linking learning and organizing. In *Advances in Managerial Cognition and Organizational Information Processing* (pp. 43-83). Greenwich, CT: JAI Press, Inc.

Grant, R. M. (1996). Toward a knowledge-based theory of the firm. *Strategic Management Journal, 17,* 109-122

Hamel, G. (1991). Competition for competence and interpartner learning within international strategic alliances. *Strategic Management Journal 12*, 83-103.

Haunschild, P. R., & Miner, A. S. (1997). Modes of imitation: The effects of outcome salience and uncertainty. *Administrative Science Quarterly, 42*, 472-500.

Holland, J. (1996). *Hidden order: How adaptation builds complexity*. Reading, MA: Addison-Wesley.

Huberman, B. (1989). The adaptation of complex systems. In B. Goodwin & P. Saunders (Eds.), *Theoretical biology* (pp. 124-133). Edinburgh: Edinburgh University Press.

Huff, A. S. (1990). *Mapping strategic thought*. Chichester: John Wiley.

Hutchins, E. (1991). Organization work by adaptation. *Organization Science, 2,* 14-39.

Iansiti, M., & Clark, K. B. (1994). Integration and dynamic capability: Evidence from product development in automobiles and mainframe computers. *Industrial and Corporate Change, 3*, 557-605.

Ingram, P., & Baum, J. A. C. (1997). Opportunity and constraint: organizations' learning from the operating and competitive experience of industries. *Strategic Management Journal, 18*, 75-98.

Kauffman, S. A. (1993). *The origins of order: Self organization and selection in evolution*. New York: Oxford University Press.

Kogut, B. (1993). *Country competitiveness*. Oxford: Oxford University Press.

Krugman, P. (1995). *Development, geography, and economic theory*. Cambridge, MA: MIT Press.

Lant, T. K. (1992). Aspiration level adaptation: An empirical exploration. *Management Science, 38*, 623-644.

Lant, T. K., & Mezias, S. J. (1992). An organizational learning model of convergence and reorientation. *Organization Science, 3*, 47-71.

Lei, D., Hitt M., & Bettis, R. (1996). Dynamic core competences through meta-learning and strategic context. *Journal of Management, 22,* 549-569

Leonard-Barton, D. (1995). *Wellsprings of knowledge*. Boston: Harvard Business School Press. Levinthal, D. A., & March, J. G. (1993). The myopia of learning. *Strategic Management Journal, 14*, 95-112.

Levinthal, D. A., & March, J. G. (1981). A model of adaptive organizational search. *Journal of Economic Behavior and Organization 2,* 307-333.

Levinthal, D. A., & March, J. G. (1993). The myopia of learning. *Strategic Management Journal, 14:* 95-112.

Levitt, B., & March, J. G. (1988). Organizational learning. *Annual Review of Sociology, 14,* 319-340.

Lounamaa, P. H., & March, J. G. (1987). Adaptive coordination of a learning team. *Management Science, 33,* 107-123.

March, J. G. (1981). Footnotes to organizational change. *Administrative Science Quarterly, 26,* 563-577.

March, J. G. (1991). Exploration and exploitation in organizational learning. *Organization Science, 2,* 71-87.

March, J. G. (1999). *The pursuit of organizational intelligence.* Oxford: Blackwell.

McElvey, B., & Aldrich, H. E. (1983). Populations, natural selection, and applied organizational science. *Administrative Science Quarterly, 28,* 101-128.

Miner, A. S. (1990). Structural evolution through idiosyncratic jobs: The potential for unplanned learning. *Organization Science, 1,* 195-210.

Miner, A. S. (1994). Seeking adaptive advantage: Evolutionary theory and managerial action. In J. A. C. Baum & J. V. Singh (Eds.), *Evolutionary dynamics of organizations* (pp. 76-89). Oxford: Oxford University Press.

Miner, A. S., & Haunschild, P. R. (1995). Population level learning. *Research in Organizational Behavior, 17,* 115-166.

Miner, A. S., & Mezias, S. J. (1996). Ugly duckling no more: Pasts and futures of organizational learning research. *Organization Science, 7,* 88-99.

Miner, A. S., & Raghavan, S. V. (1999). The hidden engine of selection: Interorganizational imitation. In J. A. C. Baum & Bill McKelvey (Eds.), *Variations in organization science: In honor of Donald T. Campbell* (forthcoming). Thousand Oaks, CA: Sage.

Mintzberg, H., Ahlstrand, B., & Lampel, J. (1998). *Strategy safari: A guided tour through the wilds of strategic management.* New York: Free Press.

Mintzberg, H., & McHugh, A. (1985). Strategy formation in an adhocracy. *Administrative Science Quarterly, 30,* 160-197.

Mowery, D. C., Oxley, J. E., & Silverman, B. S. (1996). Strategic alliances and interfirm knowledge transfer. *Strategic Management Journal, 17,* 77-91.

Nelson, R. R. (1993). *National innovation systems.* New York:Oxford University Press.

Nelson, R. R., & Winter, S. G. (1982). *An evolutionary theory of economic change.* Cambridge, MA: Belknap Press of Harvard University Press.

Noda, T., & Bower, J. L. (1996). Strategy making as iterated processes of resource allocation. *Strategic Management Journal, 17,* 159-192.

Nonaka, I., & Takeuchi, H. (1995). *The knowledge-creating company.* New York: Oxford University Press.

Oster, S. (1999). *Modern competitive analysis* (3rd ed.). New York: Oxford University Press.

Porac, J. F., Thomas, H., & Baden-Fuller, C. (1989). Competitive groups as cognitive communities: The case of Scottish knitwear manufacturers. *Journal of Management Studies, 26,* 397-416.

Porter, M. E. (1980). *Competitive strategy: Techniques for analyzing industries and competitors.* New York: Free Press.

Porter, M. E. (1990). *The Competitive Advantage of Nations and Their Firms.* New York: Free Press.

Pouder, R., & Caron, H. S. (1996). Hot spots and blind spots: Geographical clusters of firms and innovation. *Academy of Management Review, 21,* 1192-1225.

Powell, W. W. (1998). Learning from collaboration: Knowledge and networks in the biotechnology and pharmaceutical industries. *California Management Review, 40,* 228-240.

Powell, W. W., Koput, K. W., & Smith-Doerr, L. (1996). Interorganizational collaboration and the locus of innovation: Networks of learning in biotechnology. *Administrative Science Quarterly, 41,* 116-145.

Quinn, J. B. (1980). *Strategies for change: Logical incrementalism.* Homewood, IL: Richard D. Irwin.

Reger, R. K. (1990). Managerial thought structures and competitive positioning. In A. S. Huff (Ed.), *Mapping strategic thought* (pp. 71-88). Chichester: John Wiley.

Simon, H. A. (1996). *The sciences of the artificial* (3rd ed.). Cambridge, MA: MIT Press.

Smith, F. L., Wright, J. W., & Ostroff, D. H. (1998). *Perspectives on radio and television.* Mahwah, NJ: Lawrence Erlbaum.

Spender, J. C. (1989). *Industry recipes:The nature and sources of managerial judgement.* Oxford: Blackwell.

Stern, R. N., & Barley, S. R. (1996). Organizations and social systems: Organization theory's neglected mandate. *Administrative Science Quarterly, 41,* 141-146.

Suchman, M. C. (1994). *On advice of counsel: Law firms and venture capital funds as information intermediaries in the structuration of Silicon Valley.* Unpublished doctoral dissertation, Stanford University.

Suchman, M. C. (1995). Localism and globalism in institutional analysis: The emergence of contractual norms in venture finance. In W. R. Scott and S. Christensen (Eds.), *The institutional construction of organizations* (pp. 39-63). Thousand Oaks, CA: Sage.

Teece, D. J. (1986). Profiting from technological innovation: implications for integration, collaboration, licensing and public policy. *Research Policy, 15,* 285-305.

Teece, D. J., Pisano, G., & Shuen, A. (1997). Dynamic capabilities and strategic management. *Strategic Management Journal, 18,* 509-533.

Van Valen, L. (1973). A new evolutionary law. *Evolutionary Theory, 1,* 1-30.

Waller, M., Gibson, C., & Carpenter, M. (1999). *Time's arrow: The impact of differences in the time perspective of knowledge management in a multicultural context.* Presentation, Academy of Management, Chicago, IL.

Walsh, J. P. (1995). Managerial and organizational cognition: Notes from a trip down memory lane. *Organization Science, 6,* 280-321.

Walsh, J. P., & Ungson, G. R. (1991). Organizational memory. *Academy of Management Review, 16,* 57-91.

Weick, K. E. (1979). *The social psychology of organizing* (2nd ed.). Reading, MA: Addison-Wesley.

Wernerfelt, B. (1984). A resource-based view of the firm. *Strategic Management Journal, 5,* 171-180.

Winter, S. G. (1987). Knowledge and competence as strategic assets. In D. J. Teece (Ed.), *The competitive challenge: Strategies for industrial innovation and renewal* (pp. 159-183). Cambridge, MA: Ballinger.

PART I

RECURRENT LEARNING BY ORGANIZATIONS FROM THEIR OWN EXPERIENCE

Learning Stra Plan & Implementation.
↳ It's key!
See discussion at end of paper.

LEARNING WITHIN AND AMONG ORGANIZATIONS

Kathleen M. Carley

ABSTRACT

Change is readily seen both within organizations and within populations of organizations. Such change has been characterized as organization or population-level learning or evolution. Underlying such change is change at the individual human and social network level. Herein, it is asked, how does the way in which individuals learn and the way in which networks evolve reflect itself in organizational and population-level learning? What changes should emerge at the organization and population level due to learning, information diffusion, and network change at the individual level? Herein it is argued that organization and population-level phenomena, such as performance improvements, mis-learning, and shakeouts, emerge from the on-going processes of change at the individual level. Looking at learning and information diffusion enables the organizational theorist to link micro and macro level organizational phenomena.

Few organizations can characterize themselves as unchanging. Although longevity is a sign of success, inability to, unwillingness to, or simple lack of change is

Advances in Strategic Management, Volume 16, pages 33-53.

ISBN: 0-7623-0500-2

not considered a sign of success in contemporary society. Indeed, organizations and their environments are continually in a state of flux. Change within and among organizations can have dramatic organizational consequences, although the degree of flux, and the extent to which it has major consequences on the organization's performance and the population of organizations, varies both by industry and over time. Drawing on metaphors from human psychology and biology, organizational scholars often characterize such change as organizational learning or evolution. The presence of this continual change, this learning, this evolution does not imply unpredictability. If we are to understand, and possibly even predict, the behavior of organizations and populations of organizations, then we will need to understand the mechanics which bring about the observed change. We will need to understand the mechanics by which change occurs within and among organizations.

An initial basis for such mechanics lies in the underlying cognitive and network processes. That is, whether or not learning and evolution occur at the organizational level, it is irrefutably the case that individual humans do learn, exchange information, and alter their networks (who talks to, works with, reports to, whom). What changes should emerge at the organization and population level due to learning, information diffusion, and network change at the individual level?

Looking at organizations from an individual learning and network perspective enables the micro and macro levels to be linked. This linkage comes about for several reasons. Two are particularly relevant. First, the dual focus on learning and networks leads to a set of base principles for reasoning about organizations. Second, since individual learning is a dynamic process co-occurring for all individuals in a group, group level phenomena emerge automatically.

Herein, a set of learning and network based principles are first described. These principles collectively define a cognitive-network way of thinking about organizations. Then a computational model that is consistent with these principles is briefly described. This model is used to generate a series of predictions about organization and population-level phenomena. Implications from this model are then discussed.

COGNITIVE-NETWORK PRINCIPLES

To develop our understanding of organizations and populations, we need to develop a cognitive-network mechanics. In this paper, some of the basic principles of such a theory are put forward. These principles rest on research in a number of disciplines and are related to a variety of theoretical conceptions. Collectively, however, these principles provide a basis for understanding organizational change from the ground up.

The principles to be discussed here are: primacy of learning, an ecology of learning, synthetic adaptation, an ecology of networks and constraint based action. Each will be described in turn. In describing these principles the goal is not to provide an exhaustive list of all the necessary underlying principles. For example, to understand organizations in greater detail and to relate their behavior to other types of social groups, additional principles relating to issues such the nature of action, agency and knowledge, are needed (see Carley, 1999). Herein the goal is more modest. It is simply to provide a discussion of a few core ideas that differentiate this perspective from other approaches to organizational learning and that provide guidance in thinking through how change occurs at the organization and population level.

Primacy of Learning

Individual humans learn. This learning is ubiquitous—any time any place and in many ways, individuals learn. Such learning is a concurrent activity in which all individuals take part, and does two things. First, cognitive learning alters what individuals know. As individuals learn cognitively their mental models evolve. Second, learning alters how they relate to others (humans or artificial agents or animals) and other objects (resources, tasks, technology). From a network perspective, individual cognitive learning results in the construction of nodes (ideas) and relations (connections among ideas) within and among individuals. Moreover, as individuals learn, who they share what information with changes. This can result in changes in the underlying social network (Carley 1991; Kaufer & Carley, 1993). This form of learning results in change not only in the network of ideas, but the network of interactions that connect individuals.

Ecology of Learning

Not all learning is of the same type. We can think of an ecology of learning types, some of which build on or rely on others and many of which can come into competition with each other or clash. There are knowledge networks (networks connecting agents to knowledge) within and between agents, networks formed of interactions, and networks formed by joint decisions. As agents learn these networks change. There are at least two dimensions on which types of learning can be characterized—mode and activity.

For example, some of the modes in which individuals learn are observation, direct experience, expectation, and by being told. These different types of learning, or "learning mechanisms" differ in the feedback that is available to the individual.[1] Observational learning relies on a variety of types of information as feedback, with the key being that the individual learner selects which information to attend to and so use as feedback at the time of the observation. Experiential learning has its basis in task repetition by the individual and the provision of feedback by an external source. Expectation based learning occurs when individuals plan and think ahead about the future, and then use these expectations, rather than or in addition to experience, as a basis for future reasoning. Communication based learning, learning by being told, occurs when the individual learns something simply by listening without also observing, doing or planning. Although these types of learning may rely on common cognitive processes and may be related at the cognitive level, from an organizational perspective we can think of them as being relatively distinct. The important factor from an organizational point of view is that these different types of learning can be going on simultaneously. Thus, even though all individuals within the organization may be learning at the same time, what they are learning may vary in part because they are utilizing different learning mechanisms.

By activity, I mean that learning can take place in a passive or pro-active fashion. Individuals can sit back and act as information receivers, such as when they watch television or listen to a lecture. In this case, the information they learn may or may not be new. Or they can be pro-active and go out and seek information. In this case, the intent is to seek out information that is not known; although the individual may not be successful in acquiring exclusively novel information. Learning can occur during passive exchanges, such as when individuals garner new ideas from the mass-media. Many actions and interactions are accidental. Even such non-purposive behavior can result in stability at the organization and population level. Goal directed, or purposive, behavior can be characterized in terms of optimization; i.e., in an unchanging environment stability is reached when some function is optimized. Such purposive behavior can also result in at the organization and population level.

Synthetic Adaptation

Composite agents can be formed through the synthesis of other agents. Human beings are the quintessential agent. They are intelligent, adaptive and computational. Composite agents include teams, groups, organizations, population of organizations, industries, institutions, societies, and so forth that are composed of human beings. Synthetic adaptation refers to the idea that the synthesis process which creates composite agents also endows these composite agents with knowledge based properties akin to those of the underlying agents (see Carley, 1999). Specifically, any agent composed of intelligent, adaptive, and computational agents is also an intelligent, adaptive, and computational agent. Since humans are intelligent, adaptive and computational all teams, groups, organizations, institutions, societies, and so forth that are composed of humans are also intelligent, adaptive and computational agents.

Through synthetic adaptation composite agents can form which can interact with and perform the same tasks as non-composite agents. For example, in response to natural or technological disasters, there are different composite and non-composite agents all of which act as response units—single companies, consortiums of companies, network organizations, and groups of individuals acting collectively as an institutional unit all play a similar role (Dynes & Quarantelli, 1968; Topper & Carley, 1997). Synthetic adaptation enables the composite agent to take action distinct from, and not predicated on, an aggregation of individual actions. Thus the organization, in and of itself, is an intelligent, adaptive and computational entity (Carley & Gasser, in press) whose capabilities result from the detailed, ongoing, interactions among, decisions of and behavior of the member agents. Group behavior emerges from complex interactions and concurrent activity and not through simple aggregation. This conception is consistent with the work on distributed cognition (Hutchins, 1991, 1995) and transactive memory (Moreland, in press; Moreland, Argote, & Krishnan, 1996; Wegner, 1987, 1995).

One result of synthetic adaptation is that learning can and does occur at multiple levels—for example, individual, group organization, and population or industry. It is particularly useful to distinguish between individual and structural learning (Carley & Lee, 1998; Carley & Svoboda, 1996). Individual learning occurs within the agent. As agents alter their mental models by adding or dropping either ideas and/or relations among ideas we say that individual learning has occurred. Such changes may precipitate structural learning changes in interaction among agents (Carley, 1991; Kaufer & Carley, 1993). In this way individual learning mediates structural learning. When the agents are human beings, we think of such changes as changes in the agent's mental model. When the agents are composites, such as teams, organizations, industries, and populations of organizations, we think of such individual learning in terms of the shared mental model, group knowledge, or culture. Structural learning occurs among agents and within composite agents (such as groups, organizations, or institutions). Structural learning occurs as the composite agent adds or drops member agents (individual or composite) and/or the relations among member agents. Changes in interaction that result from such structural learning can influence others' knowledge and so attitudes and beliefs (Krackhardt & Porter, 1985). Individual and structural learning can occur at the organization and population level.

Ecology of Networks

Within organization theory the term network is often used to refer to the set of social or work related connections among individuals within an organization or institutional or economic arrangements among organizations. However there are many other networks. Indeed, we can think of networks as existing within an ecology of networks. For example, the social network denoting who talks to whom is intertwined with each individual's cognitive network (the way in which each individual links ideas, i.e., the individual's mental model) and the transactive knowledge network (each individual's perception of the network linking people to their ideas). Within organizations, the authority or reporting network (who reports to whom) is connected to many other networks including the task structure (which tasks are connected to which), the task access structure (who is assigned to what task), and the capabilities networks (who has what capabilities or access to what resources).

Change in any network results in a cascade of complex repercussions for the other networks in this ecology. Consider the space defined by the interaction networks and the knowledge network. One of the most common bases for interaction is similarity. One basis for similarity is shared knowledge. Change in who knows what (the knowledge network) alters the distribution of knowledge and who is similar to whom. This results in changes in the interaction network. Thus, learning results in individuals moving about in the interaction-knowledge space. As individuals within organizations learn, the organization's knowledge also changes. Learning results in people, organizations, and populations of organizations moving through the interaction-knowledge space.

Constraint Based Action

Cognition and networks mediate agent action. Interaction is a function of external constraints (opportunity), cognitive and knowledge constraints (such as agent's perception of their relative similarity to others). The actions of all agents, synthetic or not, are constrained and enabled by the learning mechanisms they employ and the networks in which they are embedded. If we imagine a hierarchy of agents then higher-order composite agents constrain the actions of their member agents. The networks in which agents are embedded influence and constrain individual and group behavior (McPherson, 1983) and serve to constrain and facilitate change (Granovetter, 1985). Constraints reduce the set of potential actions to the set of acceptable actions. Constraints can be so severe that they define all activity; for example, certain assembly line technologies define a network ordering of tasks that severely constrains which agent does what when. This notion of constraint based action appears in the information processing (March & Simon, 1958; Galbraith, 1973), social information processing (Salancik & Pfeffer, 1978) and resource dependency perspectives (Pfeffer & Salancik, 1978). However, from an applied or modeling perspective, specifying constraints requires more than a recognition that constraints exist. To really evaluate the impact of constraints, and to make concrete predictions, the precise set of tasks, networks, institutions, resources, knowledge, agents and technology that affect the flow of information need to be specified (Carley & Prietula, 1994).

MODEL AND METHODOLOGICAL APPROACH

Computational models consistent with these principles can be, and have been, used to illustrate, explain and theorize about organizational behavior. Using such a computational model, ORGAHEAD,[2] some of the implications of this theoretical approach are described and illustrated for organizations. ORGAHEAD has been previously described in detail in the literature (Carley & Svoboda, 1996; Carley & Lee, 1998; Carley, 1998). Thus, only a cursory description is provided below, with a focus on the learning aspects.

ORGAHEAD is a model of organizational performance and dynamics. ORGAHEAD has been informed by empirical studies on human learning and adaptation within human organizations. Within ORGAHEAD both individual and structural learning are present. Organizational action proceeds at both the operational and strategic level. Operational personnel learn as they work on a series of quasi-repeated tasks, which can vary in complexity. Both experiential and communication mechanisms are employed by these agents. The position of agents in the organization (as defined by the authority network, communication network, capabilities network, and so on) constrains what information is available to whom and who communicates with whom. This in turn affects what is learned by whom. At the strategic level, the CEO (or team manager) employs both experiential and expectation mechanisms. The CEO makes a decision about the task for the organization as a whole. CEOs can alter the organizational structure and so alter access to information. All agents have mental models which contain a task model, past experiences, expectations, and a knowledge network for subordinates (which subordinates know what). The CEO's mental model includes information on organizational performance, who knows what, previous structural changes, and expectations about alternative structures. ORGAHEAD has been used to look at a variety of organizational issues including the impact of different change strategies, training scenarios, constraints on organizational re-design, in both stable and changing environments.

ORGAHEAD is a dual-level model of organizational adaptation in which the organization can change at both the strategic and the operational level. At the operational level the organization is modeled as a collection of adaptive agents, each of whom occupies a particular organizational position, can learn over time, and gain task based experience. Individual learning is operationalized using a variant of a Bush and Mosteller (1955) stochastic learning model with additional limits on attention, memory, and information processing which bounds the agent's rationality more than in the original stochastic models. At the strategic level, the organization adapts strategically in response to changes in its performance through structural learning (which results in hiring, downsizing, expansion, and re-engineering). Structural learning is operationalized as a simulated annealing process.

Why Use a Computational Model?

Recent advances in computational analysis and distributed artificial intelligence (DAI) suggest that multi-agent models can be usefully employed for theory creation in the domain of organizational dynamics. In these models, core organizational processes are abstracted so as to lay bare the relationships among the various key components of organizational design and adaptation. Despite such abstraction, complex non-linear processes are a central feature of these models. Computational analysis is one of the few techniques that enables the theorist to think through the possible ramifications of non-linear processes and to develop a series of consistent predictions. Within organization theory, computational models can be, and have been, used in a normative (and sometimes a prescriptive) fashion to generate hypotheses that can then be tested in other empirical settings. Running a virtual experiment on the model and then statistically analyzing the result generates hypotheses.

Adaptive agent models, such as genetic algorithms and neural networks, are being used to answer questions about the evolution of industries and the sets of organizations within a market (Axelrod 1987; Axelrod & Dion 1988; Crowston 1994; Holland 1975; Holland & Miller, 1991; Padgett, 1997). Experiential and symbolic learning models are being used to answer questions about turnover, organizational learning, CEO activity, agent activity (Carley, 1992; Lin & Carley, in press; Lant, 1994; Verhagan & Masuch, 1994), learning ecologies (Carley & Svoboda, 1996; Kim, 1993). Issues examined include coordination and communication (Levitt et al, 1994; Durfee & Montgomery, 1991; Ishida, Gasser & Yokoo, 1992), planning (Gasser & Majchrzak, 1994), monitoring (Elofson & Konsynski, 1993) and socially shared cognition (Hutchins, 1990, 1991).

Virtual Experiments

A virtual experiment is an experiment conducted using a computer model. They are computational analogues of human laboratory experiments. The agents are computational not human beings or animals. The term simulation has been used in many ways. For example, it has been used to refer to both the computational model and the result of running that computational model at least once. Modern computational models define a space of options that is sufficiently large that virtual experiments become a feasible technique for defining the response space. One difference here from a laboratory experiment is that many more data points can be collected. Using ORGAHEAD two different virtual experiments were done to look at the impact of individual and structural learning on change at the organization and population level.

Experiment 1 was done to explore the over time behavior for a small population of organizations for an extremely long period of time. In this case, the behavior of a set of 100 organizations varying in structure and faced with a sequence of 40,000 tasks (one per time period) was simulated. Experiment 2 was done to explore the types of organizations and change patterns that emerged over time within a large population. In this case, the behavior of a set of 1000 organizations varying in structure and faced with a sequence of 20,000 tasks (one per time period) was simulated. Analysis shows that there is no fundamental difference in the way the organizations behaved in these two experiments.

In both experiments the organizations were defined such that their initial size and authority/communication structure was selected at random from all possible organizations with between 2 and 45 personnel and 1 to 4 levels in the hierarchy. In each organization the individual agents, or people, could learn and the organization as a whole engaged in structural learning. Agents were treated as being boundedly rational in terms of how many pieces of the task they could process (at most 7), how many others they can communicate with (at most 7) in one time period, how much they can remember. The CEO could alter the organization by hiring or firing personnel, changing who reported to whom, and changing who did what. The number of such changes in one time period could vary between 1 and 15. Initially, all such changes were equally likely. All organizations faced a set of 2,000 tasks, one per time period. This enables sufficient time for noticeable patterns of organization and population-level change to emerge. The over-arching task was a classification choice task. Variables measured include final performance (percentage of final 500 tasks for which the organization made the correct decision, number of structural changes, the size, density, number of isolated personnel, number of task factors ignored, and redundancy in the organization initially and at the end.

IMPLICATIONS FOR CHANGE

Organization and population-level change emerges out of the ongoing interactions among intelligent adaptive agents. Not only is interaction the fundamental social act, it is also the basis for individual behavior within organizations and the structuring of ties among organizations (Carley, 1991; Carley & Newell, 1994). For example, the structure of the networks and the ability to learn via communication can alter the rate at which the team learns and affect the diffusion of erroneous beliefs (Prietula & Carley, 1994). Further, sets of intelligent agents are self-organizing due to capability and knowledge constraints (Epstein & Axtell, 1997; Kauffman, 1995; Padgett, 1997). This self organization leads to the structuration of the organizational field. Thus, regularities in behavior, organizational structure, networks, and culture across, among, and over time for agents and composite agents emerge as agents interact. Consequently, the specifics of who interacts with whom when determines which norms, regulations, what type of culture, what type of organizational structure, and so on emerges (White, 1992).

These ideas are supported by the results from the ORGAHEAD model. Moreover, using ORGAHEAD, we gain a more precise notion of what it means for interactions among intelligent agents to generate a structured field of organizations. Structuration leads to the following three phenomena. First, there will ultimately be a quasi-stable pattern of behaviors; for example, a ranking among firms will appear. Second, in the process of moving toward this stability, more or less similar firms will differentiate themselves thus resulting in a stratified industry.

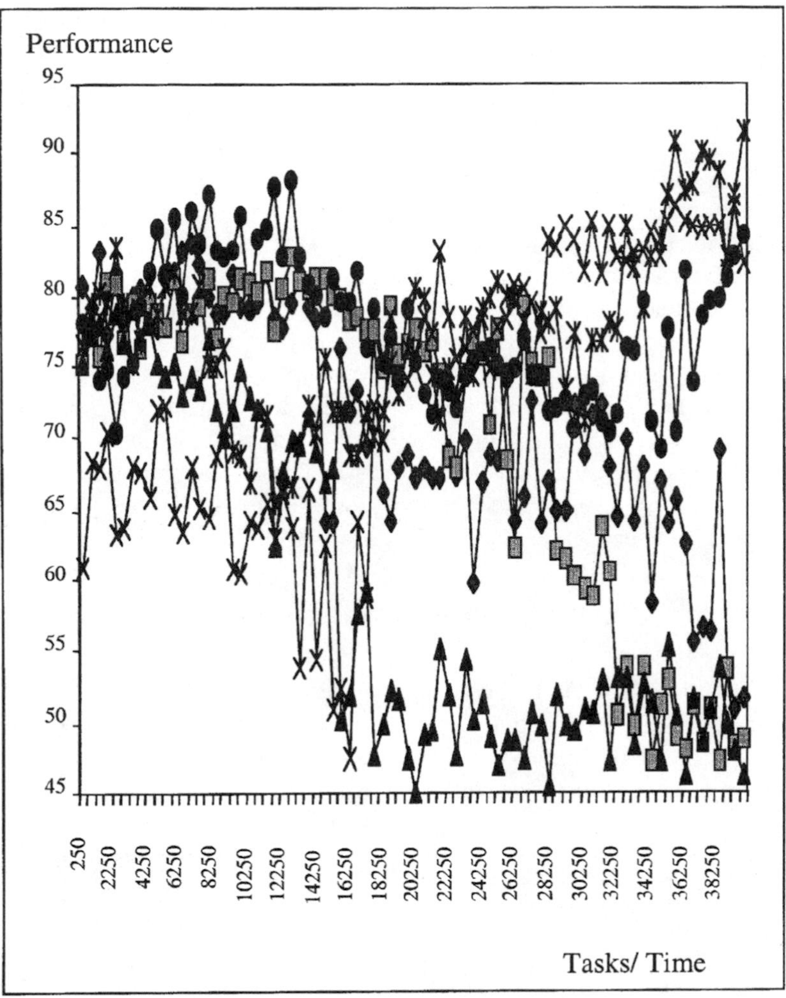

Figure 1. Over Time Changes in Performance for Lowest and Highest Performing Organizations

Third, firms will lock into strategies of change and these strategies will differ across industrial strata. However, these change strategies will not result in industrial homogeneity.

Quasi-Stability

This trend toward stability is a projected eventuality. In most cases, disruptions will occur long before stability is reached and may prevent stability from ever being achieved. The issue then is not—"what is the stable configuration?" but "what happens along the way to stability?" The results here suggest that along the way to stability, stratification and shakeouts occur. The basic cognitive-network mechanisms and the learning processes that cause short term oscillations in interaction and performance also cause organizations to enter into strategic choice sets through which they become increasingly differentiated. Many oscillations in performance and the resultant shakeouts are a result of collisions and collusions between the types of learning.

At both the organization and population level we see a general trend to stability. At the population level this trend is seen in that, in a stable environment, initially more or less equivalent firms fall into a rough rank order in performance over time. That is, clear top and bottom performers emerge. This is only a quasi-stable situation however. Due to the on-going learning the exact ranking will continue to oscillate. However, the degree of oscillation will decrease. An illustration of this appears in Figure 1.

The resultant behavior for the three organizations that ended up with the highest and lowest performance is shown in Figure 1. This figure illustrates that despite individual and structural learning, over time the variation in performance decreases for each organization even though for the population the performance bifurcates. A familiar example of such ranking shifts is the ranking of universities by national magazines. Over time, however, these organizations lock into a structure, a pattern for how to change it, and the individuals into patterned ways of responding to the environment. This trend toward quasi-stability, in a stable environment can be beneficial for those organizations that locate satisfactory structures and patterns of change. However, for those organizations that lock into poor change strategies, simply being able to learn will not alter their long-term trajectories.

In the short term, relative to the long term, there is greater oscillation in organizational behavior and firms move in their relative rankings quite dramatically. Notice in Figure 1 that all organizations are initially undifferentiated. As learning occurs both at the individual and structural level, the population of organizations stratifies. Despite appearances, the behavior of organizations and the industry is not randomly generated. Rather, this pattern of change is for each organization a reflection of the historic path it has followed in altering its structure, responding to expected changes in the environment or its own performance, and the specific nature of what the agents within the organization have learned.

Change in relative ranking across organizations is caused by different responses to the same task. These different responses are the result of the specific path of adaptation chosen by the organization; that is, history matters and there is path dependency. The specific networks within the organization, the learning

Table 1. Predicting Performance from Structural Features

Variable	*Coefficient*	*Std Coefficient*
Constant	74.89***	0.00***
Final Size	0.05	0.03
Final Number of Isolates	–0.10	–0.02
Final Amount of Ignored Information	–2.23***	–0.28***
Final Density	–14.64***	–0.09***
Final Redundancy	1.15***	0.28***

procedures within agents, the specific sequence of tasks, and who learned what information when lead organizations, even those with identical structures, to respond to the same task differently. Moreover, organizations adapt their structure given the same performance differently. There are many consequences of this differential response. For example, in some organizations the individual learning that results as the task changes clashes with the structural learning thus degrading performance; whereas in other organizations the two types of learning at that point may work synergistically to dramatically improve performance. An example of a clash is when downsizing results in laying off core talent for doing a particular task; whereas, a synergy would occur when downsizing results in laying off the key individuals who were generating erroneous decisions. Thus, the process that generates what appear to be random fluctuations, is actually non-random.

Industrial Stratification

This trend toward ultimate quasi-stability does not imply a trend toward a single outcome. In fact, in most situations there are multiple endpoints and stability means that industrial stratification has occurred. For example, the ORGAHEAD simulations (experiment 1 and 2) demonstrate that over time similar organizations will diverge into high and low performers. From a complexity standpoint we can say that there are multiple attractors to which the organizations can gravitate. Once the division has taken place most organizations will stay in their performance strata.

As performance stratification happens the internal structure of high and low performance organizations will come to be different (Carley, 1998). As noted in Table 1, based on experiment 2, in the long run the top performers will not ignore any of the information needed to do the task, will be less dense (in who talks to whom) and more redundant (in who does what) than will be low performers. They will also be slightly (though not significantly) larger.

Even though organizations begin very similarly they will tend to take different paths despite using the same learning mechanisms. Organizations will get locked into patterns of change where the internal knowledge and interaction networks that develop lock them into a particular pattern of performance. Divergence

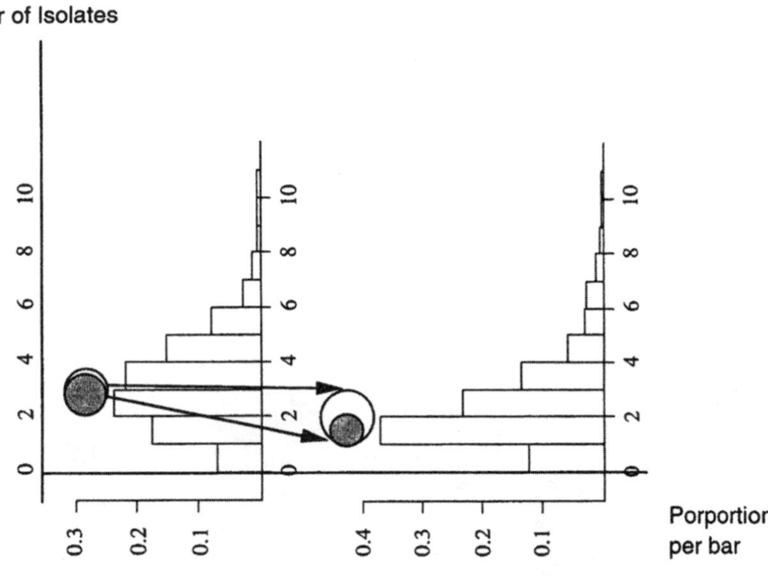

Figure 2. Change in Size of Organizations Over Time

occurs because different organizations learn different things which affects whether and when the various learning mechanisms clash or act synergistically. What this means for an organization is that learning is not guaranteed to benefit the organization. Organizational differences result from the content of what is learned, from local choices that move the organization through the interaction-knowledge space

This divergence is seen in a separation in the structure of the high and low performers (see Figure 2). In Figure 2 we see that over time, the size of the top performers increases and the size of the bottom performers decrease. In Figure 2, the mid point of the circle is the mean size of the organizations in that quartile at that time, the size of the circle is the standard deviation. The overall initial and final distribution of sizes is also shown. Over time, the population of organizations is becoming more heterogeneous in their structure.

Learning clashes result in diversity at the population level. Thus, there is not a shared experience at the population level in terms of what structure is the best. An organization that exhibits high performance has located a structure and a change strategy that is well suited for the current task environment. Poor performance organizations have not located such an ideal. However, structures and change strategies that do well in one task environment may not do well in other

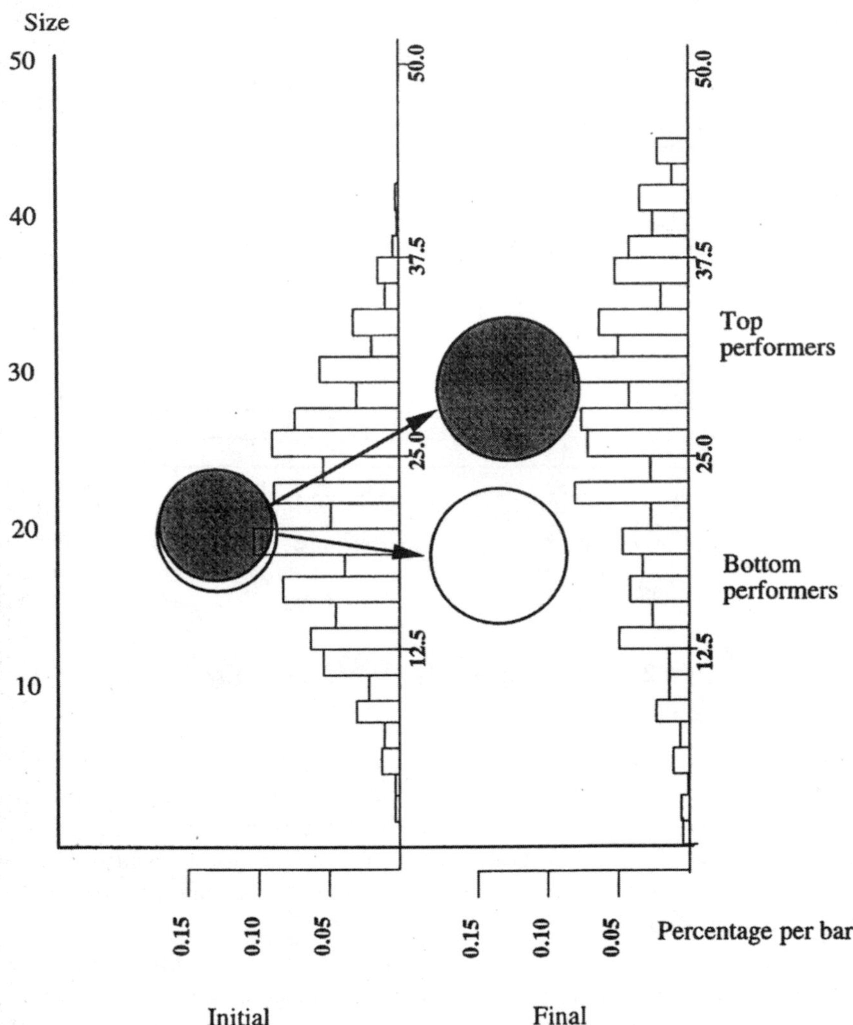

Figure 3. Change in the Number of Isolates in Organizations Over Time

environments. Thus, it may be that learning clashes, although detrimental to a particular organization, may result in sufficient population diversity that in an environmental shift there may be a pre-existing set of organizations with the appropriate structure and change strategy.

In addition to diversification, learning clashes also can result in dysfunctionality. For example, in most organizations there are a few people who are isolated. These are people who, by choice or happenstance, are loners and rarely interact with or share information with others. In some sense their knowledge and expertise is lost to the rest of the organization. Due to the potential for lost opportunities, we might think of the organization as being more dysfunctional if there are more isolates.

In experiment 2 we find that over time, for most organizations, the quest for a more high performing structure leads organizations to adopt forms in which there are fewer isolates (see Figure 3). The quest for high organizational performance results in more common individual experience. This occurs without these organizations necessarily adopting a strategy of firing these isolates. Despite this trend, low performing organizations end up having more isolates than do high performing organizations. In Figure 3, the mid point of the circle is the mean number of isolates in the organizations in that quartile at that time, the size of the circle is the standard deviation. The overall initial and final distribution of the number of isolates is also shown.

In the case of isolates, organizations are, as a population, becoming more homogeneous. The population of organizations has—in the sense of its mix of practices changing—learned, without mimicry, that isolates detract from performance. However, high performing organizations have learned the lesson better and will still have fewer isolates and exhibit less variance among themselves than will low performers. The learning clashes between individual and structural learning result in low performing organizations, despite appropriate changes, retaining their dysfunctionality and coming to appear more dysfunctional than their high performing counterparts.

Stratification Strategies and Complexity

For many tasks, and for the task used in these experiments, these attractors to which the organizations gravitate do not take the form of "the right organizational structure for this task." That is, there are structures that are known to perform optimally, and the simulated organizations do not all gravitate to these forms despite attempts to improve performance. For high performance organizations, the attractors are patterns of change. Over time, the way in which these organizations change also diverges (see Table 2). In Table 2 the percentage difference in final and initial conditions for each of the structural variables is shown.

There are two points to notice. First, top and bottom performers do not always change in the same direction. As noted earlier, learning clashes within organizations can result in diversification and stratification at the population level. Second, regardless of whether or not low and high performers change in the same direction, the variance in change is much less for the high performers than the low performers. In other words, high performing organizations may not move to the same organizational form, but they tend to change at the same rate. This is reflected in the fact that the variance in the distribution of the various structural indicators may or may not be lower for high than low performers; however, the

Table 2. Diversification in Change Strategies

Change in	Low Performers		High Performers	
	Mean	Std. dev.	Mean	Std. dev.
Size	22.54	134.08	31.35	1.48
Isolates	23.32	151.58	–17.49	86.56
Overlooked Information	45.85	137.30	–13.80	45.47
Density	–11.00	73.31	–28.92	50.74
Redundancy	–4.49	59.80	33.61	57.54

variance in the percentage change in these indicators over time is always much lower for high performers than low performers. In this sense, the experience that is shared by high performers is not experience in operating within a particular form, but experience in process and degree of change.

DISCUSSION

The argument here is quite simple: a unified theory of organizational change should be possible if it has at its basis a processual approach to learning. Principles underlying such an approach are: the primacy of learning, a learning ecology, synthetic adaptation, a network ecology, and constraint based action. Complex behavior within and among organizations result from simple learning mechanisms operating within a system of constraints and an ecology of learning mechanisms and changing networks. Importantly, these networks include both knowledge and interaction networks all of which change dynamically as agents learn.

There are many ramifications of saying that interaction and learning at the individual level result in organizational movement through the interaction-knowledge space. One implication is that structure and culture emerge at the organization and population or industry level as agents interact. This means that there is no ontological imperative that gives one agent (such as the CEO, corporate founder, or funding agency) more a priori impact on an organization's or industry's ultimate future. This is not to say that specific individuals do not play an important role, merely to say that the behavior of all individuals collectively is what is key.

Organizations that begin quite similar can end up very different. The exact same learning mechanisms result in divergence in form, strategy and performance for organizations. Learning in and of itself will result in a stratification of the organizational landscape and a potential shakeout in terms of firm survival. Firms do not fail because they are not learning, but because they are learning the wrong things, or learning the right things in the wrong order and at the wrong time. Path, or history, matters. What is interesting is despite the importance of history, and hence the exact networks within and among organizations, the organizational structures and patterns of change that emerge at the population level are not random. For individuals, experiential learning results in improved performance, which can be mitigated by changes in the structure of the organization (structural learning). For an organization, individual learning results in performance improvements, but the structure of the organization places a cap on these improvements. Structural learning can remove these caps but can result in clashes or synergies with individual or experiential learning. These clashes or synergies result at the population level in industrial stratification and the appearance of mimicry in process among high performers.

In general, this work illustrates how complex dynamics at the organization and population level result from simple, but non-linear processes, at the individual level. Consequently, thinking through the implications of adaptation processes is non-trivial even given simple starting conditions. For example, herein, all the behavior that emerged did so under the following conditions. All organizations began with different, but randomly chosen structures. All individuals learned in the same way. All organizations were faced with the same sequence of tasks and receive the same feedback. Individual, organizational, and population-level changes that emerged did so because of the specific networks, the position of individuals and organizations in the interaction-knowledge space, and their specific history of response to events. Complexity emerged simply due to learning occurring within a system of cognitive and network based constraints.

Taking a population ecology perspective, we recognize that organizations can, unlike those in the foregoing virtual experiments, cease to exist. A cause of such organizational death is low performance. In the foregoing simulations performance was measured as accuracy—the percentage of tasks in a decision window that were correctly classified by the organization. If we expect returns on accuracy, then we can think of this as a proxy for profits. Low accuracy would indicate low profits. Low profits, or lack of profits, over an extended period could lead to the demise of the organization. Such determination of the economic well being of an organization would occur at a slower rate than the task decision-making rate. That is, it is reasonable to assume that the organization does not fail after mis-classifying a single task. Rather, sustained poor performance is more likely to result in organizational demise. Based on these assumptions we can ask what would be the impact of organizational death?

If in fact, organizations only fail if their performance goes under a particular threshold for an extended period of time then what should happen, in the absence of mimicry, is that there will be an initial shakeout in most industries. This shakeout will occur as organizations get locked into change strategies that push them to the lower strata. The severity of the shakeout and when it occurs will vary by industry depending on initial conditions and the complexity of the task. A consequence of the shakeout will be increased homogeneity in the population; although this homogeneity will be far from perfect. Since learning does not stop, at any level, organizations will continue to change after the initial shakeout. However, to the extent that they have locked into high performance change strategies then fewer organizations are likely to fail at later dates than in the initial shakeout (barring major changes in technology or environment). Additionally, it is likely that it the organizations that are in the middle strata that will be most at risk. Future work using these computational models in conjunction with population-level learning models are needed to make predictions about the distribution and timing of these shakeouts.

At the population level another type of learning exists that has not been considered—mimicry. Mimicry, may alter the severity and timing of the shakeout, as well. We see among high performers behavior that looks like mimicry of process. However, there is no process in the model for individuals to transfer among organizations or to lean via communication from those in other organizations. The apparent mimicry among high performers occurs for two reasons. First, to the extent that structures have become more similar through structural learning will result in the same individual learning which means similarity in the expectation based learning among the CEOs which results in them taking similar actions. In other words, they have learned to parse incoming information on the task in the same or similar ways. Second, these organizations have locked into similar change strategies. This means that they have learned to parse information on how their own organization operates and responds to the environment in the same or similar ways.

Learning clashes for the population, result in higher diversity in form on some dimensions, and higher diversity in form for all low performers on all dimensions. In this sense, there are many ways to fail and only a few ways to succeed. But these few ways to succeed are not simple algorithms for the structure of the organization. Rather, they are a complex historical pattern of changes, networks, and cognitions all connected through simple but ubiquitous learning mechanisms.

ACKNOWLEDGMENT

This work was supported in part by the Office of Naval Research (ONR), United States Navy Grant No. N00014-97-1-0037 and by the National Science Foundation under Grant No. IRI9633 662. The views and conclusions contained in this document are those of the authors and should not be interpreted as representing the official policies, either expressed or implied, of the Office of Naval Research, the National Science Foundation, or the U.S. government.

NOTES

1. A large number of individual learning models exist (for a review see Pew & Mavavor, 1998). Some researchers argue that a single learning mechanism may be sufficient to account for all of the apparent different types of learning. Whether or not this is the case, from the vantage of organizations, learning types that take different feedback or occur at different rates have different organizational implications.

2. ORGAHEAD is written in a combination of C, PERLSCRIPT, and C++ and runs only on UNIX platforms. Interested readers should contact the author to determine the most feasible mode of access.

REFERENCES

Axelrod, R. M. (1987). The evolution of strategies in the iterated prisoner's dilemma. In L. Davis (Ed.), *Genetic algorithms and simulated annealing* (pp. 32-41). London: Pitman.

Axelrod, R., & Dion, D. (1988). The further evolution of cooperation. *Science, 242* (Dec.), 1385-1390.

Bush, R. R., & Mosteller, F. (1955). *Stochastic models for learning*. New York: Wiley.

Carley, K. M. (1991). A theory of group stability. *American Sociological Review 56*, 331-354.

Carley, K. (1992). Organizational learning and personnel turnover. *Organization Science, 3,* 20-46.

Carley, K. M. (1998). Organizational adaptation. *Annals of Operations Research, 75*, 25-47.

Carley, K. M. (1999). On the evolution of social and organizational networks. In S. Andrews & D. Knoke (Eds.), *Research in the Sociology of Organizations* (vol. 16, pp. 3-30). Stamford, CT: JAI Press Inc

Carley, K. M., & Gasser, L. (in press). Computational organization theory. In G. Weiss (Ed.), *Distributed artificial intelligence* (Chap. 7). Cambridge, MA: MIT Press.

Carley, K. M., & Lee, J-S.(1998) Dynamic organizations: Organizational adaptation in a changing environment. In J. Baum (Ed.), *Advances in strategic management: Disciplinary roots of strategic management research* (vol.15, pp. 269-297). Stamford, CT: JAI Press Inc.

Carley, K., & Newell, A. (1994). The nature of the social agent. *Journal of Mathematical Sociology, 19,* 221-262.

Carley, K., & Prietula, M. (1994). ACTS theory: Extending the model of bounded rationality. In K. Carley & M. Prietula (Eds.), *Computational organization theory*. Hillsdale, NJ: Lawrence Erlbaum Associates.

Carley, K. M., & Svoboda, D. M. (1996). Modeling organizational adaptation as a simulated annealing process. *Sociological Methods and Research, 25,* 138-168.

Crowston, K. (1994). Evolving novel organizational forms. In K. M. Carley & M. J. Prietula (Eds.), *Computational organization theory*. Hillsdale, NJ: Lawrence Erlbaum Associates.

Durfee, E. H., & Montgomery, T. A. (1991). Coordination as distributed search in a hierarchical behavior space. *IEEE Transactions on Systems, Man, and Cybernetics, 21*, 1363-1378.

Dynes, R. R., & Quarantelli, E. L. (1968). Group behavior under stress: A required convergence of organizational and collective behavior perspectives. *Sociology and Social Research 52*, 416-429.

Elofson, G. S., & Konsynski, B. R. (1993). Performing organizational learning with machine apprentices. *Decision Support Systems, 10*, 109-119.

Epstein, J., & Axtell, R. (1997). *Growing artificial societies*. Boston, MA: MIT Press.

Galbraith, J. (1973). *Designing complex organizations*. Reading, MA: Addison-Wesley.

Gasser, L., & Majchrzak, A. (1994). ACTION integrates manufacturing strategy, design, and planning. In P. Kidd & W. Karwowski (Eds.), *Ergonomics of hybrid automated systems IV*. Netherlands: IOS Press.

Granovetter, M. (1985). Economic action and social structure: The problem of embeddedness. *American Journal of Sociology, 91*, 481-510.

Holland, J. H. (1975). *Adaptation in natural and artificial systems*. Ann Arbor, MI: University of Michigan Press.

Holland, J. H., & Miller, J. (1991). Artificial adaptive agents in economic theory. *American Economic Review, Papers and Proceedings, 81*, 365-370.

Hutchins, E. (1990). The technology of team navigation. In J. Galegher, R. Kraut, & C. Egido (Eds.), *Intellectual teamwork* (pp. 191-220). Hillsdale, NJ: Lawrence Erlbaum Associates.

Hutchins, E. (1991). The social organization of distributed cognition. In L. B. Resnick, J. M. Levine and S. D. Teasley (Eds.), *Perspectives on socially shared cognition*. Washington DC: American Psychological Association.

Hutchins, E. (1995). *Cognition in the wild*. Cambridge, MA: MIT Press.

Ishida, T., Gasser, L., & Yokoo, M. (1992). Organization self-design of distributed production systems. *IEEE Transactions on Knowledge and Data Engineering, 4*, 123-134.

Kaufer, D. S., & Carley, K. M. (1993). *Communication at a distance: The effect of print on socio-cultural organization and change*. Hillsdale, NJ: Lawrence Erlbaum Associates.

Kauffman, S. A. (1995). *At home in the universe: The search for laws of self-organization and complexity*. New York, NY: Oxford University Press.

Kim, D. H. (1993). The link between individual learning and organizational learning. *Sloan Management Review,* Fall issue, 37-50.

Krackhardt, D., & Porter, L. (1985). When friends leave: A structural analysis of the relationship between turnover and stayers' attitudes. *Administrative Science Quarterly, 30*, 242-261.

Lant, T. L. (1994). Computer simulations of organizations as experimental learning systems: Implications for organization theory. In K. M. Carley & M. J. Prietula (Eds.), *Computational organization theory* (pp. 195-216). Hillsdale, NJ: Lawrence Erlbaum Associates.

Levitt, R. E., Cohen, G. P., Kunz, J. C., Nass, C. I., Christiansen, T., & Jin, Y. (1994). A theoretical evaluation of measures of organizational design: Interrelationship and performance predictability. In K. M. Carley & M. J. Prietula (Eds.), *Computational organization theory* (pp. 1-18). Hillsdale, NJ: Lawrence Erlbaum Associates.

Lin, Z., & Carley, K. (1993). Proactive or reactive: An analysis of the effect of agent style on organizational decision making performance. *International Journal of Intelligent Systems in Accounting, Finance and Management, 2*, 271-288.

March, J. G., & Simon, H. A. (1958). *Organizations*. New York: Wiley.

McPherson, J. M. (1983). An ecology of affiliation. *American Sociological Review, 48*, 519-532.

Moreland, R. L. (in press). Transactive memory in work groups and organizations. In L. Thompson, D. Messick, & J. Levine (Eds.), *Shared knowledge in organizations*. Mahwah, NJ: Lawrence Erlbaum Associates.

Moreland, R. L., Argote, L., & Krishnan, R. (1996). Socially shared cognition at work: Transactive memory and group performance. In J. L. Nye & A. M. Brower (Eds.), *What's social about social cognition? Research on socially shared cognition in small groups* (pp. 57-84). Newbury Park, CA: Sage.

Padgett, J. F. (1997). The emergence of simple ecologies of skill. In B. Arthur, S. Durlauf, & D. Lane (Eds.), *The economy as an evolving complex system II* (vol. 27, pp. 199-222). Reading MA: Addison-Wesley.

Pew, R., & Mavavor, A. (Eds.). (1998). *Modeling human and organizational behavior: Applications to military simulations.* Washington, DC: National Academy Press.

Pfeffer, J., & Salancik, G. R. (1978). *The external control of organizations: A resource dependence perspective*. New York: Harper and Row.

Prietula, M. J., & Carley, K. M. (1994). Computational organization theory: Autonomous agents and emergent behavior. *Journal of Organizational Computing, 41*, 41-83.

Salancik, G. R., & Pfeffer, J. (1978). A social information processing approach to job attitudes and task design. *Administrative Science Quarterly, 23*, 224-253.

Sanil, A., Banks, D., & Carley, K. (1995). Models for evolving fixed node networks: Model fitting and model testing. *Social Networks, 17*, 65-81.

Stryker, S. (1980). *Symbolic interactionism.* Menlo Park: Benjamin Cummings.

Topper, C., & Carley, K. M. (1997). *A structural perspective on the emergence of network organizations*. Working Paper, H. John Heinz III School of Public Policy and Management, Carnegie Mellon University, Pittsburgh, PA.

Verhagen, H., & Masuch, M. (1994). TASCCS: A synthesis of double-AISS and plural-SOAR. In K. M. Carley & M. J. Prietula (Eds.), *Computational organization theory*. Hillsdale, NJ: Lawrence Erlbaum Associates.

Wegner, D. M. (1987). Transactive memory: A contemporary analysis of the group mind. In B. Mullen & G. R. Goethals (Eds.), *Theories of group behavior* (pp. 185-208). New York: Springer-Verlag.

Wegner, D. M. (1995). A computer network model of human transactive memory. *Social Cognition, 13*, 319-339.

White, H. C. (1992). *Identity and control: A structural theory of social action*. Princeton, NJ: Princeton University Press.

PART II

RECURRENT INTERORGANIZATIONAL LEARNING

BRANCH SYSTEMS AND NONLOCAL LEARNING IN POPULATIONS

Henrich R. Greve

ABSTRACT

Interorganizational imitation transfers practices among organizations and represents an important process in population-level transformation (Miner & Haunschild, 1995). Imitation is facilitated by observation and contacts among adopters, however, suggesting that it has limited power to spread new practices across organizational populations that cover great geographical areas. This research tests whether organizations that are branch systems act as conduits of mimetic organizational learning over a distance. Building on other research on experiential learning within (Barnett, Greve, & Park, 1994) and across organizations (Baum & Ingram, 1998), this paper examines how experience affects the performance of organizations related by branch affiliation. It contrasts theory on how nonlocal learning may help or harm local branches and shows that nonlocal learning exists in the radio broadcasting industry and is harmful for the performance of branch organizations.

Advances in Strategic Management, Volume 16, pages 57-80.

ISBN: 0-7623-0500-2

INTRODUCTION

Interorganizational learning, the focus of this paper, can change the nature and mix of routines in a population of organizations, a result defined by Miner and Haunschild (1995) as one potentially important form of population-level transformation. Interorganizational learning can occur when structures, behaviors, beliefs, or even causal models are transferred among organizations in the population through deliberate imitation of a cooperating or noncooperating target organization, through less deliberate processes such as interorganizational job moves or transference of professional standards, or through knowledge creation arising from organizational interactions.

Interorganizational learning is facilitated by observation and contacts among early and later adopters of particular practices (Rogers, 1983: chap. 6, 8), however, suggesting that it has limited power to spread new routines across organizational populations that are geographically dispersed. Some see the short-distance spread of valuable routines as an important reason why industries are often highly clustered geographically (Porter, 1990, pp. 154-159). Others have suggested that while contacts are important, they can also be widespread geographically, because large corporations form networks among their dispersed branches and suppliers, and these networks transfer routines (Harrison, 1997, pp. 125-149). The literature does not give clear answers. Some have found stronger short-distance diffusion (Anderson, this volume; Burns & Wholey, 1993; Davis & Greve, 1997; Greve, 1998; Knoke, 1982), but others have not (Rao & Drazin, 1998; Soule & Zylan, 1997). The geographical reach of routine transfer may depend on the routine being learned and the organizational networks transferring it (Davis & Greve, 1997). This paper tests whether organizations that are branch systems act as conduits of long-distance mimetic learning. Building on research on experiential learning within (Barnett et al., 1994) and among organizations (Baum & Ingram, 1998; Ingram & Baum, 1997), I examine how the total operating experience of a branch organization affects the performance of its individual branches.

Studying how the experience of a branch system affects the performance of its components has several benefits. First, showing effects of nonlocal experience reaffirms that interorganizational learning processes occur, at least within these organizational systems. Such evidence helps justify a search for the more elusive interorganizational learning of routines among organizations under separate ownership and management. Second, examining the performance effects of experience rather than discrete routines allows analysis of how learning of less observable skills and routines affects organizations. It is a good response to the criticism that studies of the diffusion of distinct innovations overstate the strength of interorganizational learning because they select routines that spread, as opposed to the many that never spread beyond the original innovator. Third, organizational routines distilled from experience can become enduring and unimitable organizational capabilities, so experience effects on performance provide an indirect path to understanding competence-based competitive advantage (Barney, 1991). Fourth, branch systems are a prolific organizational form that constitutes one-third of all retail sales in the United States (Bradach, 1997), so it is reasonable to examine whether their growth is caused by competitive advantages. Effects of nonlocal experience on the performance of units of branch systems will tell how branch systems differ from unitary organizations and may help in understanding why they are ubiquitous in many industries.

The study uses data from the U.S. radio broadcasting industry. Broadcasting is a typical branch-structured industry with many markets and a blend of single-market independent organizations and multi-market branch systems. The branch systems differ in the number of branches, geographical scope, and age, giving good data for testing how branch system experience affects performance, though it should be noted that unlike some other industries in which branch systems are prevalent, such as banking, hotels, and restaurants, legal restrictions on the size of a corporation have prevented the creation of very large branch systems.

In radio broadcasting, the market is differentiated by the variation of tastes in the potential audience (Steiner, 1952), giving managers two distinct strategic tasks. First, they need to find a strategic position—a niche in the market—that appeals to many listeners. Second, they need to exploit and defend this position by delivering high-quality programming suited for their target audience (Keith, 1987). Experience can help managers find good niches and allow development and testing of routines for increasing the appeal of the programming. Neither of these tasks is trivial, and they are made extraordinarily difficult by the many competitors targeting the same audiences. Urban radio markets typically have around 30 stations, and some have many more, so each station is pitted against multiple competitors. At any given time, some competitors will be dissatisfied with their current performance and will seek to improve it, challenging others if necessary and turning radio markets into relentless battles over market share. Thus, radio markets have long been hypercompetitive (D'Aveni, 1994).

THEORY AND HYPOTHESES

An organization shows behavioral learning when experience produces change in the composition of its routines, and this change in routines has some permanence (Cyert & March, 1963; Levitt & March, 1988; Miner & Mezias, 1996). Learning does not require that this change be an improvement. Learning can make organizations worse off when they learn routines inappropriate to the situation or when they learn appropriate routines more slowly than their competitors (the "Red Queen" effect, see Barnett & Hansen, 1996). A discussion of whether the organization is likely to learn appropriate routines is necessary to form hypotheses on whether it is likely to improve through learning by experience. Here I focus on the important and difficult learning process of adapting to the demands of a differentiated market.

Learning in the Market

Markets can be seen as social constructions in which consumers and firms seek to learn each other's routines and tastes by examining each other's market behaviors. This is a mutual learning problem, which causes greater difficulty in finding optimal outcomes than one-sided learning problems, in which actors explore a passive environment (Lounamaa & March, 1987). Mutual learning in the market occurs through a cycle of firm moves and customer responses (Leifer & White, 1987; Porac & Rosa, 1996; White, 1981). Managers observe the behaviors of their firm and its competitors and use the resulting performance outcomes to infer the tastes of the consumers. This gives a menu of choices that consists of the main strategies available and variations on these main strategies, which can be used to adjust the position in the market and update the routines for dealing with the market. Customers adjust to the firms' moves as soon as they discover them, which may not be immediately; the firms respond again, and the wheel of adjustments takes another turn. In this situation, suboptimal performance is not only a possible outcome, it is a likely outcome, because incremental learning can lead to local optima, and learning by large experiments requires the persistence to collect multiple performance observations before deciding whether a given strategy is good (Lounamaa & March, 1987).

Uncertainty is great in this view of the market, and observation of the market at one time point reveals little about the available opportunities. Observing the market over time gives more data on how consumers respond, and having more branches in the market gives more opportunities to experiment by making changes. Since experience in the market corresponds to the number of branches in the market and the length of time they have been in the market, and both increase knowledge of the market, it follows that experience in the local market helps the organization perform well:

Hypothesis 1. Greater total experience of a branch system's units in a given market causes higher performance of each branch unit in the market.

Learning from Outside the Market

Organizations learn from the experience of others by observing and interpreting their experiences or simply by incorporating or avoiding routines used by others (Levitt & March, 1988). Such learning is likely to be easier within a branch system than it is among branch systems, as organizations organized in a branch systems are members of a cooperative system. These systems are likely to have organizational mechanisms in place for transferring to the rest of the system routines found useful in one branch unit (Argote, Beckman, & Epple, 1990; Bradach, 1997). Consistent with this suggestion, major strategic changes appear to spread rapidly among the members of a branch system (Greve, 1995, 1996). Experience outside the local market and (possibly) routines for transferring routines used elsewhere are likely to encourage learning of new routines in branches when the branch system has great experience outside the local market and, hence, nonlocal experience is likely to affect performance.

The question that needs to be resolved is whether the nonlocal experience is likely to help or harm each branch. The effect hinges on the appropriateness of the routines that are transferred. The view of markets as social constructions in which consumers and suppliers know little about each other leads to a remarkably pessimistic view of the transferability of knowledge across markets: since the performance of each organization, which is the datum used for learning about the market, is contingent on the customers and competitors in a given market, learning in one market may not be useful in other markets. First, customers can be different in different markets. How do East Coast and West Coast radio listeners differ from each other, and how do they differ from listeners in Peoria? The answer determines the benefit of transferring a given routine across markets. Second, since the returns to each set of routines depend on the routines of the competitors in the market, the benefit of a routine can differ in different markets even if the consumers' tastes are identical.

The uncertainty introduced by differences in markets complicates the learning problem but does not preclude organizations from benefiting from experience in different markets. If branch systems can select for transfer only routines that are beneficial in a target market, then experience outside the target market is likely to benefit their branches. The problem of selecting routines for transfer across space is similar to the problem of learning from the past: the history of a given routine often provides insufficient experience to allow sound judgment of its applicability in a different situation (March, Sproull, & Tamuz, 1991). Organizations typically compensate by seeking to enrich their experience through interpretation so that the underlying mechanism can be understood. Branch systems also employ structural solutions, such as internal consultants, who accumulate experience with transferring routines across branches, presumably including experience in judging when transfers will improve the performance (Bradach, 1997). The ability to solve the problem of judging the appropriateness of transfer can be viewed as a dynamic capability (Teece, Pisano, & Shuen, 1997), as it allows organizations to transform their experience into competitive advantage. If organizations can select routines that are beneficial for transfer, then experience outside the local market is likely to be helpful:

Hypothesis 2a. Greater experience of a branch system's units outside a given market leads to higher performance of each branch unit in the market.

If the branch system cannot effectively choose only beneficial routines for transfer, the experience outside the focal market is likely to harm the branches. The branch management has a limited capacity for attention and change, so adoption of routines from outside the local market diverts attention away from developing routines in response to the local market. While routines from outside the local market have random value relative to the local market unless the organization successfully screens for appropriate routines, routines in response to local experience are likely to have positive value, so the trade-off between nonlocal and local experience harms the branch unit. This leads to the following alternative hypothesis:

Hypothesis 2b. Greater experience of a branch system's units outside a given market leads to lower performance of each branch unit in the market.

Learning by Change of Core Features of the Organization

The above hypotheses are based on the use of experience to make incremental changes to organizational routines and assume that such changes are beneficial to the organization provided they are appropriate to the context. Organizations do not make only incremental changes, however, they also occasionally make changes that abandon past routines and adopt a new set of interconnected routines. To identify such changes, the concept of organizational core is useful. The organizational core consists of the organization's goals, forms of authority, technology, or marketing strategy (Hannan & Freeman, 1984, p. 156). Other parts of the organization are designed to conform to the core, such as when organizations buffer their technological system (Scott, 1987) or adapt their structures to their strategy (Miller, 1986).

Because of the links from the core to the periphery, changes in the organizational core require adjustments in related parts of the organizations, causing coordination uncertainty that complicates change (Barnett & Freeman, 1997). Interdependence of marketing strategy, technology, and suppliers of capital equipment and knowledge, for example, means that change in one causes changes in other parts of the organization. Core change requires not only learning of new routines in isolated places in the organization but also involves coordination problems, including intraorganizational politics and learning how to use new formal structures and informal networks in the organization (Barnett & Freeman, 1997; Hannan & Freeman, 1984). Core changes may also lead to loss of support from the organization's customers and suppliers, or the organization will itself withdraw from them and seek to establish ties with others more suited to its new strategy. By disrupting internal routines and links with the environment, change lowers the organization's performance until it has rebuilt its routines and strengthened its links with supporting actors in the environment (Amburgey, Kelly, & Barnett, 1993).

Measuring core changes is clearly a useful control when studying how experience affects performance, and it is also an opportunity to contrast the effect of core changes on organizations of different size and experience. If organizational size complicates the coordination necessary to make core organizational changes (Hannan & Freeman, 1984), then size will have a negative effect on the performance after a core change (Greve, in press; Péli, Bruggeman, Masuch, & ó Nualláin, 1994). If organizational experience causes increased intraorganizational and interorganizational commitment to one set of routines (Hannan & Freeman, 1984), then greater organizational experience has a negative effect on the performance after a core change. Incremental learning will continue after a core change, so the negative effect of the core change itself dissipates over time if the organization makes appropriate incremental changes (Barnett & Carroll, 1995). The effect of a core change in strategy on performance can then be summarized as one main-effect prediction and two interactions:

Hypothesis 3. Performance will be lower just after a change in strategy.

Hypothesis 4. For large organizations, the performance decrease just after a change in strategy will be greater than for small organizations.

Hypothesis 5. For experienced organizations, the performance decrease just after a change in strategy will be greater than for inexperienced organizations.

Learning and Variability[1]

An organization's performance is not completely determined by its strategic position and capability. Uncontrollable and unpredictable factors such as moves by competitors and changes in customer tastes cause the performance to vary from one period to the next, giving the organization an expected performance and a variance around this expectation. The preceding hypotheses assume that experience affects the expected performance, but experience may also affect the variance. Managers are averse to high variation, as they are to risk in general, and will seek to reduce it (Shapira, 1994). This can be done by finding strategic positions that are infrequently attacked or developing capabilities that make customers loyal. If experience helps in doing so, the following hypotheses will be supported:

Hypothesis 6. Greater experience of a branch system's unit in a given market causes lower variation in the performance of each branch in the market.

Hypothesis 7. Greater experience of a branch system's units outside a given market causes lower variation in the performance of each branch in the market.

Alternatively, experience may cause managers to make trade-offs between expected performance and variation in performance that are different from those made by managers of corporations with less experience. Since high performance and low variance are both desired, a manager might rationally accept lower expected performance to get lower variance of performance, so if the coefficient estimates of experience have the same sign in the analysis of the level and variance of performance, the results could be interpreted as results of different trade-offs between level and variance. Hence, the only result that would suggest that experience is harmful for the organization is if greater experience lowers the level of performance and raises the variance of performance. Same-sign coefficients for the two outcomes would suggest that experience affects managerial preferences for risk rather than organizational capabilities.

DATA AND METHODS

The study examines the effects of learning by assessing the effects of changes in format in the U.S. radio broadcasting industry. A format is a combination of program content, announcer style, timing of program and commercial material, and methods for obtaining listener feedback and quality control (Keith, 1987). Radio audiences differ in tastes for music and other programming material, and the variation in preferences lets radio stations choose their strategic position by providing music or other material that appeals to their targeted audience group. Tastes for programming material vary by age and other demographic variables, so formats generally target specific demographic groups. Stations seek to improve their market shares by changing their programming within the format or finding a new position by changing the format. Format changes are costly for the station, so they are typically done only when management is sure that the present format is undesirable. Format changes often involve staff changes, market surveys, or help from format consultants and may require marketing the station to a new set of advertisers. Format changes affect all aspects of the station's operations and are clearly core organizational changes.

The radio broadcasting industry has not experienced major deregulation like some other industries. The process of granting licenses, however, involves hearings from local interests and discretion by the Federal Communications Commission, and this did restrict and slow down entry into the industry. This process was streamlined during the first Reagan presidency, leading to easier entry and increased competition in many markets. While this is not a major deregulation, the entry of new competitors may have changed the effect of experience on performance and may have introduced new routines in the population. Because of this possibility, experience before and after 1980 is treated separately in the analysis.

To test hypotheses 1-5, the market share of radio stations was used as the dependent variable. To test hypotheses 6-7, the absolute value of the standard deviation of market shares was used as the dependent variable. The experience of the radio corporation and the format changes of its stations are the main independent variables. The control variables include sets of indicator variables for the market (city) population rank and the station's niche (format), so the effect of experience is measured holding total market size and market niche constant.

Sample and Data Sources

The study uses data from stations in 160 U. S. radio markets measured by Arbitron, which is the leading audience measurement provider in U.S. radio broadcasting. It tracks formats and format changes of stations from January 1, 1984, to December 31, 1992, and has annual performance measures for the same period. This sample was determined by the availability of performance measures comparable across markets and stations and measures of format change. Data on format changes were coded from the *M Street Journal* (1984-1993), a weekly newsletter (biweekly in the first 10 months of publishing) monitoring the radio broadcasting industry. Each change noted in the newsletter contained data on origin (previous) and destination (new) formats, station call letters, state, and market. The newsletter reports are based on information supplied from a network of industry insiders who monitor markets and alert the editor whenever they judge that a station has changed its format (Greve, 1996).

Data on the corporate structures came from *Duncan's Radio Group Directory* (1993). This directory includes all stations owned by radio branch systems active in 1992 and contains records of station sales that allowed me to trace the changes of these branch systems over time and discover additional branch systems that no longer operated in 1992. This could be done because groups usually sell their stations in batches, so sales by groups were recorded as purchases by other groups. This method is not perfect, as groups may hold stations for a short time and re-sell them, but seemed to yield good coverage of the groups in U.S. broadcasting during the study period.

Audience measurement data came from *Duncan's American Radio* (1992). This source shows Arbitron audience estimates for 160 different markets from 1975 (or the first year the market was measured, if that is later) to 1992 for most stations in the market. I did not use the data on audiences from before 1984 for this study because matching data on formats and other covariates were not available. The data source does not list public radio stations and some commercial radio stations that had very low ratings throughout this time period, nor does it list all Arbitron markets. Of the 261 markets measured by Arbitron in 1991, 10 are partially or wholly enclosed in others, so they are not meaningful separate markets. Of the remaining, the source omits most of the below-200 markets (nine remain), 37 of the 101-200 markets, and three of the top 100 markets. This amounts to unintentional sampling but does not appear to be a serious flaw as long as the results are interpreted with some attention to the overrepresentation of stations in large markets. All stations with performance data were included, and up to nine years were available for each station. The data set had 2,506 stations and 20,833 year-station observations. The models use lagged independent variables, causing the loss of the first year for each station and leaving 2,490 stations and 18,327 year-station observations.

Model

The first dependent variable is the market share of each station, which creates a special modeling problem. Market shares result from a process of mutual adjustment and adaptation among market participants, and in most markets this adjustment process is lengthy enough that market shares cannot be assumed to be in equilibrium at any one time. This leads to models that assume that the measured variable is out of equilibrium but moving toward it, and the most common of these is the partial adjustment model (Coleman, 1968; Tuma & Hannan, 1984). According to this model, the equilibrium is a target that the market is moving toward, not as an observable outcome. The model specifies the change in performance as:

$$dP_t / dt = r(P^* - P_t), \tag{1}$$

where P_t is the performance at time t, P^* is the target performance, and r is the rate of adjustment toward the target. Although the target performance level is not observable, it can be modeled as a function of observable variables. The target performance is modeled as:

$$P^* = \beta X_t + \lambda F_t + \delta C_t, \tag{2}$$

where X_t are covariates describing the organization and market context, F_t is a set of indicator variables for the format, and C_t is a set of covariates describing the effect on a recent change. Because partial adjustment models do not assume that social change occurs instantly but, instead, allow explicit estimation of the rate of change, they have been used to estimate change in variables such as organizational growth (Freeman & Hannan, 1975), strategy (Haveman, 1993), performance (Barnett et al., 1994; Haveman, 1992), sales (Boeker, 1991), and structure (Strang, 1987).

The partial adjustment model can be estimated by substituting (2) into (1) and solving the resulting differential equation to give:

$$P_{t+\Delta t} = exp(-r\Delta t)\, P_t + [1 - exp(-r\Delta t)](\beta X_t + \lambda M_t + \delta C_t). \quad (3)$$

This is a nonlinear equation, which can be estimated directly by nonlinear least squares (Strang, 1987). The nonlinear estimation routine LSQ provided by TSP was used (Hall, 1993).

The second dependent variable is the absolute deviation in market shares. A model with fixed effects for each station and no covariates was fitted to obtain the station-specific mean performance (P_i) and the standard error of this performance (ε) for each period:

$$P_{i,t} = P_i + \varepsilon_{t.} \quad (4)$$

The absolute standard error for each period, $|\varepsilon_t|$, was then taken as the dependent variable in the analysis. This variable was autocorrelated, so TSP's maximum likelihood estimator for time-series cross-sectional data with first-order autoregression was used.[2]

Measures

Market Share

Arbitron reports many market share measures showing audiences in specific demographics and time segments. This analysis used a broad measure, the 12+ Metro audience share (Monday-Sunday, 6 a.m.-midnight), which shows the average proportion of all listeners over 12 years old tuned in to the focal station during the broadcast week. This measure gives a gross market share and has the advantage of being widely recognized, since it is reported in the usual industry data books (Duncan, 1992; M Street Corp., 1992), and of being useful in analyzing the shares of stations with different formats, since it captures the total audience instead of specific segments of it.

Experience Variables

The main effect on performance of branch affiliation is measured by an indicator variable showing whether the station was owned by a *branch system*, defined as an individual or organization with three or more rated stations in at least two markets and a revenue of $3 million or more (Duncan, 1993).[3] Two variables measure the post-deregulation experience of the branch system within the focal market and outside the focal market. *Experience within* the local market is the number of years it has operated its current stations in the local market after 1980. Regulations prohibited more than two stations in each market, so the experience is either the experience of its only station in the market or of its two stations in the market. The branch organization's experience with stations in the market that were sold before the focal year are not counted because it is very difficult to ensure that all sales of stations are known (some branch systems are older than the data sources). *Experience outside* the local market is the number of years it has operated its current stations outside the local market after 1980. *Early experience* is the total (within and outside market) years of operation before 1980. The experience is divided into experience before and after 1980 because firm behaviors and the consequences of firm behaviors may change when regulations change, decoupling learning before a regulatory change and organizational performance after the regulatory change (Barnett et al., 1994). If the experience effect is unchanged, the estimates will show the same coefficients before and after the regulatory change. The early experience is thus a control variable in the analysis. These experience variables are based on the years of operation instead of the production, as in the learning curve studies (e.g., Argote et al., 1990). This simplification is possible because the rate of production is constant for radio stations—they produce a single broadcast, so their production and learning are not dependent on the size of their audience.

There may be decreasing returns to experience, and old experience may be less valuable than recent experience (Argote et al., 1990; Ingram & Baum, 1997), so I tried different specifications of experience. I compared linear (constant returns), logged (decreasing returns), and discounted (obsolescence) specifications and found the discounted specification with a discount factor of 0.9 to have the highest log likelihood. This specification is shown in the tables, but it should be noted that the logged specification and the discounted specification with factor 0.8 had log likelihoods so similar to the shown model that a Bayesian test (Raftery, 1995) could not select among them. These specifications showed the same results except that the logged specification had greater significance levels for experience outside the market.

Format Change Variables

Because format changes are core organizational changes, they may negatively affect the performance of the station. This was measured by the variable *format change*, which captures whether the station made a change of format the year before. Three variables were formed as interactions of *format change* with other covariates. These are *Change×Branch system,* which interacts format change with the indicator of branch systems, *Change×Experience*, which interacts format change with the sum of experience inside and outside the local market, and *Change×Lagged Share*, which interacts format change with the lagged share. The first two of these test hypotheses 4 and 5, and the last is a control for regression toward the market mean when making changes. Regression toward the market mean occurs when uncertainty in the evaluation of alternative strategies introduces randomness into the selection of a new strategic position (Harrison & March, 1984). Organizations that change when they have low performance can then fortuitously improve, as most alternative strategies are better than their current ones, but organizations changing when they have high performance are likely to experience reduced performance because few alternative strategies are better than the current ones (Greve, in press). In the two last interaction variables, experience and lagged share are expressed as deviates from their means so that the coefficient estimate of *format change* will reflect the effect of change for stations with average experience and performance before the change.

Control Variables

The competition in the local market was controlled for by including the number of stations in the market (*market density*) and the number of changes by other stations (*market change*). Market density counted all stations in the market, including those that did not appear in the data for performance measurements (i.e., public stations and stations without measurable influence). The number of other stations in the same market with the same format measures competition within the strategic position and is called *niche density*. These variables were constructed from M Street Corp. (1992) and the event data and updated annually. The concentration of the market was measured with the *C4 concentration index*, which sums the shares of the top four stations in the market. It is commonly used, as it gives similar results as the Herfindahl index of concentration, but can be computed even when the shares of the lowest-share firms are missing (Scherer & Ross, 1990, pp. 71-79). Indicator variables for 23 different market population ranks (1-10, 11-20, and so forth) were included to control for the fixed-effect differences among markets of different population size. Finally, to capture the effect of the current format, indicator variables for 23 different formats were included (the omitted category includes some rare formats and stations with unknown or hard-to-categorize formats). These were included both as origin formats and (except for two that were collinear) as destination formats, since the performance change of a station that changes its format depends both on the format it leaves and the format it enters. Controls for the past and current strategy are important when estimating the effect of a change in strategy, since inertia effects can only be estimated when the value of the organization's strategic position is accurately measured (Barnett & Carroll, 1995; Greve, in press).

RESULTS

Table 1 shows the means, standard deviations, and correlation matrix of the analysis data set. Related variables are placed next to each other, so the highest correlations are found near the diagonal. Three groups of variables covary: the market density and changes per year; branch system and experience within and outside the market; and format change with its interaction variables. None of the

Table 1. Descriptive Statistics

Variable	*Mean*	*Std.dev*	*(1)*	*(2)*	*(3)*	*(4)*	*(5)*	*(6)*	*(7)*	*(8)*	*(9)*	*(10)*	*(11)*	*(12)*
1 Share	5.289	4.492												
2 Market density	30.04	18.17	–.254											
3 Niche density	1.086	1.253	–.071	.195										
4 Market change	3.911	2.89	.169	.511	.133									
5 Market concentration	40.589	11.23	.328	–.534	–.118	–.250								
6 Branch system	0.315	0.465	.116	.197	.052	.108	–.153							
7 Experience within	1.676	3.428	.085	.179	.036	.104	–.118	.725						
8 Experience outside	9.738	19.19	.045	.235	.062	.143	–.177	.752	.601					
9 Early experience	8.308	27.39	.050	.206	.041	.054	–.127	.450	.404	.609				
10 Format change	0.120	0.325	–.176	.019	.013	.040	–.016	–.016	–.014	–.012	–.021			
11 Change × Lag share	–0.248	1.217	.261	–.077	–.023	–.070	.090	.015	.008	.003	.018	–.551		
12 Change × Branch	0.036	0.185	–.090	.070	.022	.054	–.061	.283	.201	.213	.102	.519	–.270	
13 Change × Experience	–0.020	0.683	.017	.075	.018	.039	–.065	.322	.205	.306	.274	–.079	.066	.765

Note: Pearson correlation coefficients are shown.

zero-order correlations are alarmingly high, but they may combine to cause inefficiency in estimation. Tests of dropping or adding one or more variables at a time showed that entering the interactions of format change with branch system and experience increased the standard errors of the estimates, so they were added one by one in this analysis. Entering the three experience variables together also increased standard errors somewhat but did not affect coefficient estimates or significance levels.

Table 2 shows the estimates of the models with the variables entered in groups. Model 1 does not measure the effect of strategy changes, so it only contains tests of hypotheses 1 and 2. Experience inside has an insignificant coefficient, showing no support for hypothesis 1, which predicted that it would increase performance. Experience outside has a negative and significant coefficient, providing support for hypothesis 2b—experience in other markets appears to be harmful in a focal market. Experience before 1980 has an insignificant coefficient. Model 2 retains the finding on hypothesis 2b, as experience outside the focal market is still significant, and also shows a negative effect of format change in support of inertia (hypothesis 3). Model 3 adds two interactions with format change: lagged share, which controls for regression to the mean, has the expected negative sign and is significant. Branch system, which tests the effect of size (hypothesis 4) has the expected negative sign and is significant. Model 4 adds the experience interaction and shows an insignificant coefficient estimate, indicating lack of support for hypothesis 5, which predicted that experienced organizations would have a greater loss of performance after the change than inexperienced organizations.

The control variables show that stations have lower performance when they have many competitors, especially if the competitors have the same format. Competition within the niche is stronger than competition across niches, as one would expect. The positive effect of being a member of a branch system is an interesting contrast to the negative effects of experience outside the focal market and suggests that there is some immediate benefit of having links to other organizations, but this benefit is not associated with learning advantages over time. This seems paradoxical, and it may be worthwhile to remember that branch systems seek to buy successful independent stations, and hence the main effect of being a member of a branch system may reflect how branch systems select members rather than how they manage them. The main effect may also reflect the greater resources of branch systems (Miner, Amburgey, & Stearns, 1990).

Models 1-4 pool independent and branch-system stations, which may obscure differences within branch systems. To ensure that the conclusions are also valid within branch systems, the models were reestimated on data including only stations that were members of branch systems. In these data, the main effect of a branch system and its interaction with format change cannot be estimated, so those variables were omitted. Model 5 in the table replicates model 2 on the within-branches data, and model 6 replicates model 4. The conclusions are unchanged in these analyses. As before, only experience outside the market has a

Table 2. Partial Adjustment Models of Audience Shares with Fixed Effects for Origin and Destination Format

	Independent and Branch Stations				*Branch Stations Only*	
Variable	*Model 1*	*Model 2*	*Model 3*	*Model 4*	*Model 5*	*Model 6*
Lagged share	0.893***	0.893***	0.893***	0.893***	0.914***	0.916***
	(0.006)	(0.006)	(0.006)	(0.006)	(0.010)	(0.010)
Market density	−0.011*	−0.010†	−0.011*	−0.011*	−0.003	−0.004
	(0.005)	(0.005)	(0.005)	(0.005)	(0.010)	(0.010)
Niche density	−0.690***	−0.652***	−0.665***	−0.666***	−0.997***	−1.026***
	(0.110)	(0.107)	(0.110)	(0.110)	(0.242)	(0.250)
C4 concentration	0.066***	0.070***	0.071***	0.071***	0.080**	.080**
	(0.011)	(0.011)	(0.011)	(0.011)	(0.027)	(0.028)
Branch system	2.190***	2.174***	2.388***	2.384***		
	(0.483)	(0.471)	(0.494)	(0.503)		
Experience within	−0.057	−0.057	−0.060	−0.060	−0.079	−0.083
	(0.052)	(0.051)	(0.052)	(0.052)	(0.067)	(0.069)
Experience	−0.021*	−0.021**	−0.021*	−0.021*	−0.019†	−0.020†
outside	(0.009)	(0.009)	(0.009)	(0.010)	(0.011)	(0.011)
Early experience	0.004	0.004	0.004	0.004	−0.003	0.004
	(0.004)	(0.004)	(0.004)	(0.004)	(0.006)	(0.005)
Format change		−1.706***	−2.215*	−2.227*	−2.762***	−4.148**
		(0.352)	(0.856)	(0.872)	(0.781)	(1.596)
Change×Lagged			−0.461†	−0.461†		−0.792†
share			(0.279)	(0.279)		(0.461)
Change×Branch			−1.475*	−1.440		
system			(0.749)	(0.974)		
Change ×				−0.001		−0.039
Experience				(0.008)		(0.098)
R-square:						
Unadjusted	0.85676	0.85693	0.85708	0.85711	0.88545	0.88561
Adjusted	0.85636	0.85653	0.85666	0.85668	0.88442	0.88456
Coefficients	52	53	55	56	52	54
Observations	18,327	18,327	18,327	18,327	5,731	5,731

Notes: †$p < 0.10$;
*$p < 0.05$;
**$p < 0.01$;
***$p < 0.001$;
two-sided *t* tests.

significant effect, and this effect is negative. Format change has a negative effect, showing inertia, and the interaction with lagged share has a negative effect, showing regression to the mean. The interaction with change and experience is not significant, so hypothesis 5 is not supported in this analysis. Thus, branches are more inert than independent stations, but greater experience in a branch system does not seem to increase the inertia of its branches.

Table 3 shows the analysis of the variation in performance. For brevity, only one model is shown for all stations and for branch stations, but the results remain

Table 3. AR(1) Models of Absolute Residuals

	All Stations		Branch Stations Only	
Variable	Model 1		Model 2	
Intercept	0.535	(0.064)	0.419	(0.124)
Lagged share	0.085^{***}	(0.003)	0.090^{***}	(0.005)
Market density	-0.008^{***}	(0.001)	-0.006^{***}	(0.001)
Niche density	0.029^{***}	(0.008)	0.024	(0.015)
C4 concentration	0.010^{***}	(0.001)	0.012^{***}	(0.002)
Branch system	0.090^{*}	(0.041)		
Experience within	-0.010^{*}	(0.005)	-0.010^{*}	(0.005)
Experience outside	0.0013	(0.001)	$0.0018^{\dagger}$	(0.001)
Early experience	-0.0017^{**}	(0.0005)	-0.0018^{**}	(0.0005)
Format change	0.177^{***}	(0.028)	0.141^{**}	(0.052)
Change×Lagged share	0.021^{**}	(0.008)	0.012	(0.015)
Autocorrelation coefficient	0.367^{***}	(0.007)	0.366^{***}	(0.013)
R-square:				
Unadjusted	0.2746		0.2871	
Adjusted	0.2742		0.2860	
Coefficients		12		11
Observations	18,327		5,784	

Notes: $^{\dagger}p < 0.10$;
$^{*}p < 0.05$;
$^{**}p < 0.01$;
$^{***}p < 0.001$;
two-sided *t* tests.

the same if the variables are entered in groups. This analysis shows a significant negative effect of experience within the market, supporting hypothesis 6: branches of corporations with greater experience in the local market have less variation in performance. Experience outside the local market has a positive sign, which is significant in the analysis of only branch stations and contrary to hypothesis 7's prediction that branches of corporations with greater experience outside the local market have less variation in performance. Experience outside the local market causes greater variation and lower level of performance, which strongly suggests that it causes routines to be inappropriately transferred across markets, lowering performance by diverting managerial attention away from local development of routines.

Some additional analyses were done to look for moderators of the experience effects. First, transfers of routines may be more difficult across great distances and across markets of different sizes, since audience tastes show regional variation, and market size determines the smallest viable niche width. To test this, a measure of regional and market size diversity was included along with its interaction with experience outside the market. No significant results were obtained for the interaction variable, but the main effect of diversity was a marginally significant positive estimate. Thus, there is no reason to view transfers across markets of different regions or sizes as particularly risky. This suggests that of the two possible differences among markets—customer tastes or strategies of competitors—it is the difference in competitors that causes difficulty for radio managers. Regional and size differences of market tastes, though present, are understood well enough to be managed. Second, corporate experience could have nonmonotonic effects if experience has a positive effect initially but gradual hardening of routines causes organizations with great experience to become inert (Ingram & Baum, 1997). This was tested by including squared terms of experience, but they were not significant. Thus, there is no evidence that experience outside the focal markets is initially beneficial.

CONCLUSION

The findings showed two main effects of branch systems on market share. First, there was a positive effect of being a member of a branch system. Second, there was a negative effect of the branch system's experience outside the local market. This negative effect shows that transfers of routines occur but that this long-distance learning is harmful for the branch's performance. The positive effect of belonging to a branch system may then reflect either the greater resources of such systems or their selection of successful independent stations as acquisition targets. Experience outside the market increased the variation of market shares, strengthening the case for its harmful effect on the station. Experience within the market and before the regulatory change showed no effects on market shares. While zero effects cannot be interpreted with confidence, these are not completely surprising findings. Experience within the market was hypothesized to be helpful, but this benefit may have been canceled by a "Red Queen," which represents a competitive stalemate (Barnett & Hansen, 1996): if all stations learn at the same rate, then the experience within the market will not give any comparative advantage and will not affect the market share. The rule limiting each corporation to two stations within each market may have limited the opportunity for large corporations to learn at a higher rate than independent stations by having multiple stations in which to experiment. Also, the high job mobility of radio personnel may enable recently founded stations to hire personnel experienced in the market, thus substituting personal for organizational experience. Both experience within the market and early experience reduced the variation of performance, suggesting that managers of stations experienced in the local market and managers of old and large corporations successfully stabilize their market shares.

The findings that change reduced performance and that branch systems experienced greater reduction in performance when changing were expected, since they had been obtained before in the same data, though in models without experience variables (Greve, in press). Experience from outside a given market has also been shown before to harm the performance of branches (Baum & Ingram, 1998), but this finding is counterintuitive and seems to need an explanation. If the experience of the corporation in other markets impedes local adaptation, the cause may be competency traps (Levitt & March, 1988, pp. 322-323). Branch organizations transfer routines from successful to less successful ones, ignoring differences in market context that might make the routines less effective in their new context. Transfer of inappropriate routines is harmful in two ways. First, these routines may themselves reduce the performance of the organization by driving out better, existing routines. Second, the process of transferring these routines occupies decision makers' attention, making exploration of new routines less likely. Routines that succeed in one market are likely to be reapplied in other, perhaps inappropriate contexts, creating a structural bias toward nonlocal transfer rather than local experimentation, just as organizational decision making is often biased toward exploiting existing routines rather than exploring new ones (Levinthal & March, 1993; March, 1991).

The inappropriate transfer of routines across contexts is seen in corporations managing businesses in multiple industries as well as in corporations managing branches in multiple markets of the same industry. It has often been attributed to poor management, but this seems to understate the frequency of its occurrence and the strength of the processes that lead to it. Managers who transfer "best practices" from successful organizational units are engaging in reinforcement learning, which is the basic psychological process of repeating behaviors that have led to good outcomes in the past (Milliken & Lant, 1991). Often, these transfers are accompanied by interpretation and explanation of why these routines are so good, but the construction of such explanations is closer to intuitive science (Nisbett & Ross, 1980) than rigorous science, causing the inferences to be more local to a given context than the decision maker realizes (Levinthal & March, 1993). The multi-market organizational structure is a powerful tool, but it shapes attention and learning processes so that managers can get caught in traps while seeking to repeat past successes. Only managers who are highly alert and selective in determining when to transfer routines will avoid the competency trap.

The findings have interesting implications for the effect of branch systems on population-level transformation. Clearly, branch systems can accelerate population-level change of routines because branches are prone to make changes even in the face of considerable uncertainty, in contrast to White's (1981) prediction that organizations will rarely reposition themselves in the market. Such changes create variation in market behaviors that others can observe, respond to, and learn from, driving forward the variation-selection-retention process of evolution (Campbell, 1965). Changes reveal information about customers, accelerating the mutual adjustment process between firms and consumers. Do they also benefit the individual firm attempting change? These results give empirical grounds for questioning whether the benefit to the market adjustment process is realized as a benefit to the individual branch making changes. Instead, they suggest that branch organizations that bring new routines into a market are engaged in unintentional altruism (March, 1981, pp. 572-573): new routines sustain the evolution of the market but are costly for the organization introducing them. The beneficiaries are the organizations that can use the information from failed introductions of new routines into the market to infer the market structure and develop more appropriate routines (Miner, Kim, Holzinger, & Haunschild, this volume). In this view, the contribution of a branch organization to a market is not its local efficiency or adaptiveness but the import of new routines that propel the evolution of the market as a whole.

For managers, these findings raise difficult questions about strategic conduct and organizational design. The negative value of routine transfer indicates that caution is needed for managers of branch systems who wish to standardize routines or transfer best practices across units. The warning is not universal, as the value of routine transfer depends on the diversity of customer demand and competitor strategies across markets. This is only a small consolation, however, since these findings suggest that managers have difficulty judging when routine transfer is appropriate and when it is not. Determining the appropriateness of a strategy of transfer and standardization requires an impartial review of the diversity of markets and the strengths of competitors specializing in one market. The insights from such a review should also be used to decide whether to design the organizational form to encourage contact among branch managers, and the informal transfers of routines resulting from such contacts, or whether isolation should be encouraged. It is difficult to imagine branch systems pursuing a complete decoupling of branch strategies, but the degree of coupling of branches is clearly a strategic variable that should be adapted to the diversity of their markets.

Similarly, policymakers with an interest in the performance of markets should note that differences across organizational forms in how experience is accumulated and acted on make it difficult to equate the short-term efficiency of a form with its long-term contribution to market performance. An organization can affect the performance of a market by its static efficiency, its behavioral learning from experience, and its contribution to the behavioral learning of other organizations. It is clear that branch systems greatly affect markets, but it is less clear how and in what direction. A branch system's duplication of routines across markets gives any adoption of a new routine greater economic impact, positive or negative, than its adoption by a unit organization. Their greater rate of accumulating experience and transferring its implications across markets makes branch systems quick learners, but as this research shows, they are not selective enough for their own good. The social prominence of branch systems makes them targets of imitation and of differentiation by competitors, so their adoption of routines often initiates responses by competitors. The last of these effects, their contribution to experiential learning by competitors, could be the most important contribution of branch systems to population-level learning and market performance. Unit organizations learn primarily based on their experience in the local market, and are slow to take advantage of routines developed elsewhere. Thus, a mix of branches and unit organizations gives a population a high learning potential, since the nonlocal bias of branches and the local bias of unit organizations can reduce market performance unless checked by market interaction with the other form.

ACKNOWLEDGMENTS

This paper was greatly improved by comments from Joel Baum, Whitney Berta, Pam Haunschild, Jay Kim, Dan Levinthal, Anne Miner, and participants of the Carnegie Mellon-Wisconsin learning conference.

NOTES

1. I am grateful to Dan Levinthal for suggesting the analysis of variation in performance.
2. This standard error is autocorrelated, unlike the standard error of the partial likelihood estimator above, because it is generated by a model with only fixed effects.
3. These branch systems do not have to be formally incorporated organizations. Some branch systems are an assembly of stations owned individually by a person or a partnership; others belong to a division of media-related businesses.

REFERENCES

Amburgey, T., Kelly, D., & Barnett, W. P. (1993). Resetting the clock: The dynamics of organizational change and failure. *Administrative Science Quarterly, 38,* 51-73.

Argote, L., Beckman, S. L., & Epple, D. (1990). The persistence and transfer of learning in industrial settings. *Management Science, 36,* 140-154.

Barnett, W. P., & Carroll, G. R. 1995. Modeling internal organizational change. In J. Hagan & K. S. Cook (Eds.), *Annual review of sociology* (vol. 21, pp. 217-236). Greenwich, CT: JAI Press.

Barnett, W. P., & Freeman, J. (1997). *Too much of a good thing? Product proliferation and organizational failure.* Research Paper No. 1425. Graduate School of Business, Stanford University.

Barnett, W. P., Greve, H. R., & Park, D. Y. (1994). An evolutionary model of organizational performance. *Strategic Management Journal, 15,* 11-28.

Barnett, W. P., & Hansen, M. T. (1996). The Red Queen in organizational evolution. *Strategic Management Journal, 17,* 139-157.

Barney, J. (1991). Firm resources and sustained competitive advantage. *Journal of Management, 17,* 99-120.

Baum, J. A. C., & Ingram, P. (1998). Survival-enhancing learning in the Manhattan hotel industry, 1898-1980. *Management Science, 44,* 996-1016.

Boeker, W. (1991). Organizational strategy: An ecological perspective. *Academy of Management Journal, 34,* 613-635.

Bradach, J. L. (1997). Using the plural form in the management of restaurant chains. *Administrative Science Quarterly, 42,* 276-303.

Burns, L. R., & Wholey, D. R. (1993). Adoption and abandonment of matrix management programs: Effects of organizational characteristics and interorganizational networks. *Academy of Management Journal, 36,* 106-138.

Campbell, D. T. (1965). Variation and selective retention in socio-cultural evolution. In H. R. Barringer, G. I. Blanksten, & R. Mack (Eds.), *Social change in developing areas* (pp. 19-49). Cambridge, MA: Schenkman.

Coleman, J. S. (1968). The mathematical study of change. In H. M. Blalock, Jr. & A. Blalock (Eds.), *Methodology in social research* (pp. 428-478). New York: McGraw-Hill.

Cyert, R. M., & March, J. G. (1963). *A behavioral theory of the firm.* Englewood Cliffs, NJ: Prentice-Hall.

D'Aveni, R. A. (1994). *Hypercompetition: Managing the dynamics of strategic maneuvering.* New York: Free Press.

Davis, G. F., & Greve, H. R. (1997). Corporate elite networks and governance changes in the 1980s. *American Journal of Sociology, 103,* 1-37.

Duncan, J. H. J. (1992). *American radio: Sixteenth anniversary issue 1976-1992. A statistical history.* Indianapolis, IN: Duncan's American Radio, Inc.

Duncan, J. H. J. (1993). *Duncan's radio group directory.* Indianapolis, IN: Duncan's American Radio, Inc.

Freeman, J., & Hannan, M. T. (1975). Growth and decline processes in organizations. *American Sociological Review, 40,* 215-228.

Greve, H. R. (1995). Jumping ship: The diffusion of strategy abandonment. *Administrative Science Quarterly, 40,* 444-473.

Greve, H. R. (1996). Patterns of competition: The diffusion of a market position in radio broadcasting. *Administrative Science Quarterly, 41,* 29-60.

Greve, H. R. (1998). Managerial cognition and the mimetic adoption of market positions: What you see is what you do. *Strategic Management Journal, 19,* 967-988.

Greve, H. R. (in press). The effect of change on performance: Inertia and regression toward the mean. *Administrative Science Quarterly, 44.*

Hall, B. H. (1993). *Time series processor version 4.2 user's guide.* Palo Alto, CA: TSP International.

Hannan, M. T., & Freeman, J. (1977). The population ecology of organizations. *American Journal of Sociology, 82,* 929-964.

Hannan, M. T., & Freeman, J. (1984). Structural inertia and organizational change. *American Sociological Review, 49,* 149-164.

Harrison, B. (1997). *Lean and mean: Why large corporations will continue to dominate the global economy.* New York: Guilford Press.

Harrison, J. R., & March, J. G. (1984). Decision making and postdecision surprises. *Administrative Science Quarterly, 29,* 26-42.

Haveman, H. A. (1992). Between a rock and a hard place: Organizational change and performance under conditions of fundamental environmental transformation. *Administrative Science Quarterly, 37,* 48-75.

Haveman, H. A. (1993). Organizational size and change: Diversification in the savings and loan industry after deregulation. *Administrative Science Quarterly, 38,* 20-50.

Ingram, P., & Baum, J. A. C. (1997). Opportunity and constraint: Organizations' learning from the operating and competitive experience of industries. *Strategic Management Journal, 18,* 75-98.

Keith, M. C. (1987). *Radio programming: Consultancy and formatics.* Boston: Focal Press.

Knoke, D. (1982). The spread of municipal reform: Temporal, spatial, and social dynamics. *American Journal of Sociology, 87,* 1314-1339.

Leifer, E. M., & White, H. C. (1987). A structural approach to markets. In M. S. Mizruchi & M. Schwartz (Eds.), *Intercorporate relations: The structural analysis of business* (pp. 85-108). Cambridge: Cambridge University Press.

Levinthal, D. A., & March, J. G. (1993). The myopia of learning. *Strategic Management Journal, 14,* 95-112.

Levitt, B., & March, J. G. (1988). Organizational learning. In W. R. Scott & J. Blake (Eds.), *Annual review of sociology* (vol. 14, pp. 319-340). Palo Alto, CA: Annual Reviews.

Lounamaa, P. H., & March, J. G. (1987). Adaptive coordination of a learning team. *Management Science, 33,* 107-123.

M Street Corp. (1992). *M Street radio directory*. New York: M Street Corp.

March, J. G. (1981). Footnotes to organizational change. *Administrative Science Quarterly, 26,* 563-577.

March, J. G. (1991). Exploration and exploitation in organizational learning. *Organization Science, 2,* 71-87.

March, J. G., Sproull, L. S., & Tamuz, M. (1991). Learning from samples of one or fewer. *Organization Science, 2,* 1-13.

Miller, D. (1986). Configuration of strategy and structure: Towards a synthesis. *Strategic Management Journal, 7,* 233-249.

Milliken, F. J., & Lant, T. K. (1991). The effect of an organization's recent performance history on strategic persistence and change: The role of managerial interpretations. In P. Shrivastava, A. Huff, & J. Dutton (Eds.), *Advances in strategic management* (vol. 7, pp. 129-156). Greenwich, CT: JAI Press.

Miner, A. S., Amburgey, T. L., & Stearns, T. M. (1990). Interorganizational linkages and population dynamics: Buffering and transformational shields. *Administrative Science Quarterly, 35,* 689-713.

Miner, A. S., & Haunschild, P. R. (1995). Population-level learning. In L. L. Cummings & B. M. Staw (Eds.), *Research in organizational behavior* (vol. 17, pp. 115-166). Greenwich, CT: JAI Press.

Miner, A. S., & Mezias, S. J. (1996). Ugly duckling no more: Pasts and futures of organizational learning research. *Organization Science, 7,* 88-99.

Nisbett, R., & Ross, L. (1980). *Human inference: Strategies and shortcomings of social judgment.* Century Psychology Series. Englewood Cliffs, NJ: Prentice-Hall.

Porac, J., & Rosa, J. (1996). Rivalry, industry models, and the cognitive embeddedness of the comparable firm. In J.A.C. Baum (Ed.), *Advances in Strategic Management* (vol. 13, pp. 363-388). Greenwich, CT: JAI Press.

Porter, M. E. (1990). *The competitive advantage of nations.* New York: Free Press.

Péli, G. O., Bruggeman, J., Masuch, M., & ó Nualláin, B. (1994). A logical approach to formalizing organizational ecology. *American Sociological Review, 59,* 571-593.

Raftery, A. E. (1995). Bayesian model selection in social research. In P. V. Marsden (Ed.), *Sociological methodology* (vol. 25, pp. 111-163). Cambridge, MA: Blackwell.

Rao, H., & Drazin, R. (1998). *Executive migration and organizational foundings: Portfolio manager movement and the creation of international stock funds by mutual fund families, 1986-1994.* Manuscript, Emory University.

Rogers, E. M. (1983). *The diffusion of innovations* (3rd ed.). New York: Free Press.

Scherer, F. M., & Ross, D. (1990). *Industrial market structure and economic performance.* Boston: Houghton Mifflin.

Scott, W. R. (1987). *Organizations: Rational, natural and open systems* (2nd ed.). Englewood Cliffs, NJ: Prentice-Hall.

Shapira, Z. (1994). *Risk taking*. New York: Russell Sage.

Soule, S. A., & Zylan, Y. (1997). Runaway train? The diffusion of state-level reform in the ADC/AFDC eligibility requirements, 1950-1967. *American Journal of Sociology, 103*, 733-762.

Steiner, P. O. (1952). Program patterns and preferences, and the workability of competition in radio broadcasting. *Quarterly Journal of Economics, 66*, 194-223.

Strang, D. (1987). The administrative transformation of American education: School district consolidation, 1938-1980. *Administrative Science Quarterly, 32*, 352-366.

Teece, D. J., Pisano, G., & Shuen, A. (1997). Dynamic capabilities and strategic management. *Strategic Management Journal, 18*, 509-533.

Tuma, N. B., & Hannan, M. T. (1984). *Social dynamics: Models and methods*. Orlando, FL: Academic Press.

White, H. C. (1981). Where do markets come from? *American Journal of Sociology, 87*, 517-547.

THE ORGANIZATIONAL ECOLOGY OF STRATEGIC INTERACTION

Ari Ginsberg, Erik R. Larsen, and Alessandro Lomi

ABSTRACT

Cooperation is both essential for evolution as well as difficult to obtain in a Darwinian world in which defectors tend to enjoy a short-term competitive advantage. The problem of how cooperation can be sustained in a population of self-interested agents is particularly salient in fragmented industries characterized by the fact that discrete organizational entities produce and reproduce industry-level structures by processing only strictly local information. To illuminate selected aspects of this apparent paradox in industry evolution we present a computational model of how individual competitive behavior evolves into aggregates with complex collective properties that determine the structural context of future individual action. According to the model, aggregate regularities (or "structures") emerge from the local interaction among agents playing a spatial version of the repeated prisoner's dilemma. At each round the local strategy that yields the maximum individual benefit will survive and replace the strategy having inferior local fitness. This can be seen as a process in which organizations imitate the what appears to be the most successful strategy used by others in their own neighborhood (outcome-based imitation). Through this mechanism, the strategy with the highest reproductive value at the strictly local level propagates to

Advances in Strategic Management, Volume 16, pages 81-112.

ISBN: 0-7623-0500-2

more distant sites by influencing the choice of units in partially overlapping neighborhoods, and generates emergent collective consequences. The model is simulated under a variety of conditions to explore the effects of the range of local interaction and of frequency-dependent selection on the emergence of population level or collective strategies.

INTRODUCTION

The micro-structure of organizational populations rarely resembles that of biological populations with homogeneous mixing, in which every member is equally likely to compete with or—in more general terms—counter any other (Kephart, 1994). Typically, organizations in industry directly affect—and are directly affected—only by the behavior of a limited number of other organizations with whom they have direct contact without necessarily being aware of the diffuse consequences of their actions (Schelling, 1972, 1978, Chap. 4). The iteration of patterns of local interaction induces the fragmentation of competitive environments which become partitioned into discrete clusters whose members build a shared understanding of competition, enforce agreed behavioral rules, learn specific roles and develop coherent identities (Odorici & Lomi, 1999; White & Eccles, 1987). Empirical evidence supporting this view of competition as a local process has been found for a wide variety of organizations including—among others—banks, breweries, hotels, automobile producers, and newspapers (Baum & Haveman, 1997; Carroll, 1985; Carroll & Swaminathan, 1992; Freeman & Lomi, 1994; Hannan & Carroll, 1992; Hannan, Carroll, Dundon, & Torres, 1995; Lomi, 1995).

A general indication emerging from this expanding body of empirical research is that organizations operating in fragmented industry settings craft their competitive strategies in response to (and anticipation of) a restricted number of rivals that depend on similar combinations or resources—or niches (Baum & Mezias, 1992; Baum & Singh, 1994). Yet, the fact that niches are partially overlapping triggers an indirect chain of connections by which local competitive strategies propagate throughout an organizational population giving rise to indirect—or diffuse—competitive pressures that cannot be linked back to the action of any specific rival (Lomi & Larsen, 1996; McPherson, 1983).

Fragmented industry settings pose a particularly critical challenge for the formation and development of collective strategies and inter-organizational co-ordination. To be sustainable, collective strategies require a balance between the need to control critical resources and the costs of interorganizational cooperation (Contractor & Lorange, 1988), but this is difficult to achieve when members of an industry face heterogeneous and, at the limit conflicting, resource constraints and dependencies. Fragmented industries are typically characterized by a large number of small and medium-sized, privately held firms that have neither the economic might to control important resources nor the slack to absorb such costs

(Dollinger, 1990). Examples of industries that have been defined as fragmented based on the observation that their top-four concentration ratio is forty percent or less (Porter, 1980) are: textile and apparel manufacturers, jewelry retailing, and house building. The atomistic and diffuse nature of competition makes information exchange and the recognition of interdependence difficult (Dollinger, 1990, p. 268). Private ownership inhibits public scrutiny, thereby hindering the development of a central authority to regulate industry members or enforce compliance with a standard set of rules and procedures.

Absent a central authority to coordinate a formal and deliberate strategy for interorganizational cooperation, how does a collective strategy develop? How can the decentralizing forces triggered by fragmented competitive environments produce and *reproduce* recognizable "structures" at more aggregate levels? In other words, how can local strategists—endowed with only limited information-processing and cognitive capacities—manage to impose and maintain order in their environments? One possible answer to these questions is that, other than the formation of trade and professional associations or other forms of centralized regulatory mechanisms, collective strategies are not a sustainable solution to the problem of social and economic order (Nielsen, 1988). A second possible answer to the problem of social and industrial order is that order is produced by the state and reproduced by the professions (Meyer & Rowan, 1977; DiMaggio & Powell, 1983), but while this particular perspective might help to understand how order is enforced it does not seem to explain how order arises in the first place. Another possible answer—one that we will seek to examine in this paper—is that population-level (collective) strategies are induced by the cumulation of a large number of dyadic (i. e., strictly local) interactions (Bresser, 1988). In turn, this implies the existence of distinct population-level learning processes that cannot be reduced to learning activities going on within individual organizations or within intermediate organizational aggregates.

In this paper we concentrate on the dynamics of strategic interaction in fragmented industries because fragmented industries provide a valuable opportunity for exploring possible links between macro views of collective strategy based on ecological and institutional theories of organizations, and more micro perspectives based on the economics and psychology of strategic choice (Oliver, 1988). If individual rivals in a fragmented industry compete locally, but organizational populations (and markets) evolve globally, questions arise about what level of analysis is the most appropriate and—more importantly—how individual learning activities might link different levels of action.

To address these and related issues, we propose an autogenetic approach to the emergence of collective strategies. As opposed to an endogenetic perspective, which emphasizes the role of intentional design choices, or an exogenetic view, which emphasizes the importance of institutional forces outside the control of any individual actor, an autogenetic perspective of strategy emphasizes the role of the self-organizing capacities of individuals interacting in a social field (Ginsberg,

Larsen, & Lomi, 1997). A key theme of autogenesis—or self-organization—is that the interactions among micro-level entities (organizations in the present case) are governed by local decision rules and behavioral routines (Drazin & Sandlands, 1992). For example, an organization might follow a rule of examining the practices of other near-by organizations, and adopting a practice that appeared to generate the best outcome for those organizations. When iterated, these rules and routines of local interaction induce and sustain aggregate regularities—or population-level strategies.

To capture the emergent character that cooperation often assumes among direct rivals (Axelrod, 1984) in this paper we rely on the decision routines of the prisoner's dilemma—a well-known two-person non-zero sum game which provides a baseline model for studying the evolution of cooperation in a variety of social, political and economic contexts (Axelrod, 1997). We do not use the decision routines implicit in the prisoner's dilemma because we are convinced that they provide a complete or universal representation of how members of an organizational population interact. Rather, we exploit the unambiguous decision rules of the prisoner's dilemma because the corresponding game has been argued to represent some key features of many social situations and its properties have been extensively explored in a variety of contexts (Axelrod, 1984, 1997; Macy, 1991; Heide & Miner, 1992).

Against this general background, in this paper we develop a set of four key research questions regarding the emergent process though which a decentralized system of dyadic interactions among individual organizations produces population-level results that are tempting to identify as the outcome of collective—or population-level—strategies. To examine these questions, we employ a simulation methodology that allows us to test a computational model of how behavior of individual organizations (or—in more general terms—"agents") with spatial extension may evolve into aggregates with complex collective properties, which in turn, determine the structural context of future action. In this model, the learning processes by which a population of organizations evolves and changes are embedded in ongoing networks of local interactions. These local interactions involve both interorganizational competition and imitation (or interorganizational learning). According to the model, the iteration of these local interactions among individual agents over time induces distinct structural configurations at the population level.

THEORETICAL BACKGROUND

One way to think about collective strategies is as emergent population-level configurations induced by repeated interaction among individual micro-level units. In this paper we emphasize two basic properties of this (competitive and cooperative) interaction out of which collective strategies emerge. First, interaction is local—that is, it occurs at the level of individual dyads and is direct only among units living in neighborhoods of a given (finite) size. Learning is an eminent example of a family of important organizational processes that are localized because—as James March put it: "[M]ost theories of learning and selection are theories of local adaptation. They assume a process in which the relevant factors are localized in time and space" (March, 1994, p. 42). Second, interaction among elementary units is governed by recursive rules and routines that—over time—become the main "source of continuity in behavioral pattern of organizations" (Nelson & Winter, 1982, p. 96). These two essential features of interaction among members of organizational populations represent the point of departure of our attempt to articulate a model to capture both the spatial as well as the temporal dimension of the evolution of population-level learning processes.

Mechanisms of Emergent Cooperation

The prospects for market-wide cooperation and the concomitant importance of cooperative strategy to firms in a fragmented industry has been a subject of controversy among researchers. Some have argued that reliance on the market mechanism appears to preclude the use of cooperative strategy by firms in a fragmented industry (e.g., Nielsen, 1988). Others have argued that these firms also have the capabilities and requirements for collective strategy options that can increase their power and performance in the organizational field (e. g., Skinner, Donnelly, & Ivancevich, 1987).

More recently, Dollinger (1990) has argued that collective strategy is less visible in fragmented industries because much of it has an emergent character. Based on Axelrod's (1984) seminal work on the evolution of cooperation, Dollinger argues that a mechanism exists within a population of firms in a fragmented setting for initiating and transforming firm-level behavior into population-level behavior without a central organizing authority.

Axelrod (1984) describes a mechanism of emergent collective strategy that is operationalized in a series of computer simulation tournaments of the prisoner's dilemma (PD) game. The Prisoner's Dilemma is a two-person non-zero sum game, frequently used in experimental and theoretical investigation of competitive and cooperative behavior in populations of self-interested individuals. The assumptions used for the PD game display a congruity to the conditions of fragmented industries, in which there are no large firms that dominate or lead (Dollinger, 1990, p. 274). Specifically, these are: (a) the absence of a mechanism available to enforce threats or commitments; (b) the uncertainty regarding the other player's move; (c) the absence of signaling or communication; (d) the inability to change the other's payoffs; and (e) the inability to eliminate the other player.

	Cooperate	Defect
Cooperate	R,R	S,T
Defect	T,S	P,P

Figure 1. The Pay-off Matrix for the Repeated Prisoner's Dilemma Game

Building on the above framework, we can model the strategic interactions of firms in a fragmented industry as a population of agents playing a spatial variation of the Repeated Prisoner's Dilemma (RPD) game, where in every round of the game each firm can choose between two possible actions D for "defect" and C for "cooperate. " Figure 1 shows the payoff matrix (M) of the RPD. The environmental assumptions are that the game will be played for an indefinite number of times (that is players cannot apply backward induction) and that the discounted value of the payoff for the next exchange is sufficiently high. The payoff matrix is specified such that $T > R > P > S$, where T is the temptation award for non-cooperation, or defection; R is the reward for local cooperative behavior, P is the punishment for defection, and S is the sucker payoff for cooperating while the other player defects. An additional constraint that is needed when the game is repeated is that $2R > T + S\ (>2P)$, which prevents players from taking turns exploiting each other and earning higher rewards. These constraints define the standard version of the repeated prisoner's dilemma according to which (cooperate, cooperate) and (defect, defect) are, respectively, the best and the worst possible outcomes in terms of the sum of payoffs (Rasmusen, 1989). As we mentioned in the introduction, in the present context we are not interested in justifying this specific choice of rules of local interaction on empirical grounds. Rather our choice of individual decision routines reflects analytical convenience and generality (Binmore, 1992).

Our attempts to impose meaningful constraints on the specific forms that interaction among individual units may take reflects our conviction that collective strategies cannot "emerge" as the result of just any kind of local interaction. In particular, collective strategies—or "order" at the population level—cannot be obtained by random interaction at the micro-level (a point that we illustrate below). For something that we might legitimately identify as a "collective strategy" to become observable, assumptions about decision routines that guide micro-behavior are necessary. Thus, in studying the effects of interorganizational activity on the evolution of collective strategies, we first examine:

Question 1: *To what extent can we think of collective strategies in a fragmented industry as the emergent product of repetitive patterns of local competitive and imitative interactions among individual organizations?*

Sensitivity to Initial Conditions

Dollinger (1990) argues that collective strategy in fragmented industries evolves through a series of stages: first comes individual (i. e., dyadic) cooperative behavior, next comes the formation of clusters of cooperation, and last comes the emergence of a collective strategy. The achievement of critical mass is the key to what Axelrod (1984) called the process of colonization, that is, the transformation of dyadic interaction to clusters, and finally to the population (Dollinger, 1990). Critical mass is the minimum level of cooperative activity needed to make the activity self-sustaining, that is the minimum size of any coalition that can gain from abstaining from the preferred choice (*T*) (Schelling, 1978).

The process of colonization itself cannot be adequately captured in a linear or cyclical model. The presence of feedback loops between the motor of change operating at the firm level and the evolutionary motor of change operating at the population level requires the use of a nonlinear dynamical systems model (Van de Ven & Poole, 1995). Such models assume that the operation of the change motors is a function of (at least partly) the same operation at an earlier time and that there are feedback loops that vary in strength and direction over time between opposing forces (Larsen & Lomi, 1999; Radzicki & Sterman, 1994).

These characteristics highlight the path dependent nature of the process of colonization. The sensitivity of this developmental process to initial conditions means that small initial differences in trajectories of cooperation and competition may grow into large differences over time, and as they move far from equilibrium, they may bifurcate into patterns resembling chaotic behavior (Wolfram, 1983; Hilborn, 1994; Ginsberg, Larsen, & Lomi, 1997). Thus, in studying the impact of colonization on the emergence of collective strategy in a fragmented industry, we examine:

Question 2: *How does the initial distribution of individual cooperative strategies influence the aggregate long term distribution of strategies in organizational populations?*

Scope of Local Interaction

Strategy researchers have tended to define the boundaries of markets and rivalry in terms of characteristics of the external environment, such as, customer choice sets (Day, Shocker, & Srivastava, 1979), cross-elasticities of demand (Friedman, 1983), and strategic groups (Porter, 1980). In contrast to these approaches, however, social construction theorists have argued that markets are inherently equivocal and that market boundaries are defined by the players themselves rather than the resource environments in which they act (see, e.g., Leifer, 1985; Porac, Thomas, Wilson, Paton, & Kanfer, 1995; White, 1992).

Within the very broad, diffuse, and ambiguous resource constraints that characterize a fragmented industry setting, competitive ties are mostly local, that is, among organizations that are proximate in a multidimensional attribute space. In fragmented industries the relevance of local ties for the determination of competitive strategies reflects the difficulty of expressing accurate similarity judgments in environments characterized by the presence of a number of heterogeneous and partially overlapping resource sub-spaces (or niches).

When there is sufficient agreement among actors about the particulars of an organization type, such boundaries may be commonly recognized. For example, Porac and colleagues (1995) found that many Scottish knitwear producers recognized the existence of a group of large industrial knitwear firms geographically concentrated in the Borders region of the country.

Geographical proximity among small firms in a fragmented industry makes it likely that they will know more about each other than about competitors outside of their neighborhood. Managers tend to give more weight to opinions expressed by individuals whom they consider more socially proximate (e.g., because they are sensitive to similar sets of issues or face similar constraints), or imitate individuals whom they consider more prominent in their social networks (Kahneman, Slovic & Tversky, 1982).

Proximity may also lead to a variety of judgmental biases whose net effect is to bound processes of competitive imitation and diffusion to local niches or "neighborhoods. " For example, research suggests that the simplification and narrowing of focus propagated by social proximity also leads to competitive blind spots, such as incorrect generalization (Nisbett & Ross, 1980) and insensitivity to challenges from unexpected directions (Porac & Thomas, 1990). Conversely, the more complex and comprehensive are managers' mental models of their competitive environments, the more likely they are to overcome the judgmental biases that pervade strategic decision making (Ginsberg, 1995).

The above discussion suggests that the broader the scope of competitors with which a firm interacts, the better should be managers' strategic information and the decisions they make regarding local interactions. However, we have little evidence of how the overall evolution of collective strategy is influenced when individual managers compare their performance with that of a larger, or smaller, set of competitors. Thus, in studying the effects of individual decision making on the emergence of collective strategy in a fragmented industry, we examine:

Question 3: *How does the scope of local interaction among firms in a fragmented industry affect the evolution of collective, population-level strategies?*

Awareness of Indirect Competition

Bounded rationality considerations suggest that at any given time individual agents are able to process only a limited amount of information, that is, can compute the strategic implications of their actions by taking into account the behavior of only a limited number of competitors with whom they directly interact. This direct competition or, more precisely, rivalry (or "conflict") occurs between pairs of actors each identifiable to the other and implies mutual awareness. This notion of competition goes back at least to Simmel (1908) who described conflict as a concrete social relation between parties who take one another into account, and orient their action to one another. Simmel's definition represents the sociological basis of the concept of competition which became dominant in the analysis of economic competition and collusion (Tirole, 1988, chapters 5 & 6).

However, conflict is responsible only for a fraction of the overall competitive pressure experienced by individual actors because competition can also be indirect, that is, can occur among many actors, with competitors largely anonymous to one another. Indirect or diffuse competition emerges from overlaps in basic resource requirements, and does not imply mutual awareness (Brittain & Wholey, 1988). In fact, as noted by Hannan and Carroll (1992, p. 127), the existence of (indirect) competition is often the consequence of the absence of interaction across some boundary. The coexistence of diffuse and direct competition—that is, of competition *and* conflict—is puzzling because while *individual organizations* craft their competitive strategies in reaction to and anticipation of the behavior of a small number of other clearly identified competitors *organizational populations* evolve according to global processes involving both direct and diffuse competition. As Hannan and Carroll (1992, pp. 127-128) put it: "The utility of a view of competition depends on the capacity to deal with the sometimes diffuse nature of competition and with the possibility that intense competition can eliminate interaction and overlap." Clearly, the existence of diffuse competition poses fundamental attribution problems related to how individual organizations understand and represent the global structure of their competitive environments. Therefore, we examine:

Question 4: *How does awareness of indirect (or diffuse) competition by members of a fragmented industry affect the evolution of population-level collective strategies?*

METHODS AND RESEARCH DESIGN

Simulating the Model

To clarify how ecological macro-dynamics interact with firm-level processes to influence the emergence of collective strategies in fragmented industries, we simulated a cellular automata-based computational model under a variety of conditions. Our reasons for relying on simulation to study the relationship between micro-behavior and macro-dynamics in the evolution of collective strategies are threefold. First, rules and routines that regulate the behavior and performance of individual organizations are essentially unobservable at the population level. Second, macro theories of organizations are often silent on the role of action at lower levels of analysis while behavioral theories of organizations are silent on the role of population evolution and transformation. Hence, very little theoretical guidance is available to discipline the search for empirical specification. Consequently it is difficult to discriminate empirically between alternative micro-evolutionary processes, and to test their macro-implications for the dynamics of organizational populations (Levinthal, 1990). Finally, simulation methods are increasingly being used to further our understanding of key issues in organizational ecology such as adaptation and selection (Levinthal, 1990) and the relationship between local interaction and population density (Lomi & Larsen, 1996).

We simulated the evolution of collective strategies by considering the agents as computational units or cells operating in discrete space (i.e., capable of processing only local information), discrete time (i.e., their state gets updated synchronously at discrete time steps), and which can take on discrete states (defined in terms of the two actions available) (Lindgren & Nordahl, 1994).

Cellular Automata Models of Self-Organizing Behavior

As observed by Stern and Barley (1996, p. 157), "Computational techniques have progressed to the point where researchers can rise above the individual firm to examine structural patterns that are often imperceptible from the vantage point of an individual or even an organization." To apply concepts from computation theory to the sociology of collective strategy we first need to find an appropriate framework for modeling the relationship between the observable qualitative behavior of a social system (in our case, a population of firms in a fragmented industry) and the operation of a computing machine.

Cellular automata (CA) are mathematical models of dynamic systems that provide such a framework. Their connection with collective social entities made up of elementary decision units performing logical operations on their inputs, and the operations of a parallel computer, is particularly transparent (Gutowitz, 1991; Hogeweg, 1988). In both cases, the solution of a global problem and the efficiency of this solution do not depend on the power and speed of a central control mechanism, but on the coordination of a large number of decentralized processors. Thus, cellular automata lend themselves particularly well to portray the macrobehavior produced by diffused positional externalities among micro-elements processing local information—a situation that may represent the single most important problem in developing a theory of emergent collective strategy. Cellular automata models have been increasingly used in a variety of research areas, including physics, chemistry, artificial life, and computer science. The application of cellular automata has found its way less frequently into economics and other social sciences (Albin, 1987; Keenan & O'Brien, 1993; Lomi & Larsen, 1996).

A two dimensional CA model of dyadic interaction can be seen as an *n* x *n* chess board where each square has some computational power to perform a local action depending on the state of the neighborhood A formal representation of such a CA is:

$$x_{i,j}^{t} = \phi\left(\sum_{h=i-k}^{h=i+k} \sum_{g=j-k}^{g=j+k} x_{h,g}^{t-1}\right) \tag{1}$$

where x is the value of cell *i, j* at time *t* and ϕ is a boolean function which specifies the rule of the automata. The parameter *k* determines the range of the rule, i. e., how many neighboring sites are taken into account in (and affected by) the evolution of the automata. In other words, the parameter *k* defines "how local is local," or the propagation feature of the automata. The value of a given site depends at most on *2k+1* sites and the region affected by a given site grows at most *k* sites in each direction every time step *t*. See Packard and Wolfram (1985) for a more detailed description of two dimensional CAs.

Building on the work of May and Nowak (1992), in our computational model of cooperative behavior, the RPD game described earlier is played by agents (who, in our case, are firms in a fragmented industry) represented as cells arranged on a two-dimensional spatial array—or lattice—of size *n* x *n*. At any given time every cell on the array can occupy only one of the two states (C or D). To incorporate the effects of diffuse competition in our study, we fix the advantage of defecting (*T*) in any one round as a function of the global number of defectors rather than as in the usual RPD game described above. As detailed in Appendix 1, in this version P = S = 0 and *T* is a variable, which is at times smaller than R because of its dynamic nature.

The strategy of a cell can be seen as emerging from the results of a series of games played with cells living in a neighborhood of radius *K*. In any one round, the payoff for each individual cell is computed as the sum of the payoffs across the games played with the neighboring cells. For example, when $K = 1$ the game will only be played with the eight cells that touch a given cell c_{ij}. When $K = 2$ the number of games each cell is playing per round is 24, and for $K = 3$ the number of games per round is increased to 48. In every round, the state of every cell in the lattice is updated in two steps: (1) computation of the maximum payoff received by any cell in the neighborhood and (2) occupation of each site by either the original "owner" or by one of its neighbors, depending on who obtains the highest score in that round.

Appendix 3 illustrates the process from the perspective of a participating organization. In a nutshell, the organization (1) plays one round of the game with its neighbors, (2) identifies the winning strategy within its local neighborhood, and (3) switches strategy to the winning strategy if and only if the winning strategy is different from the focal organizations' original strategy. These steps are repeated over in successive rounds of play.

In this sense, the propagation of strategy across the system is strictly related to its adaptive value or "fitness." Appendices 1 and 2 formalize the assumptions underlying these rules. Appendix 3 provides a schematic representation of the logical structure of the model from the point of view of each individual cell on the lattice.

Analytical Issues

A problem commonly encountered in the literature of dynamic lattice models concerns the boundary conditions of the system (Wolfram, 1983). One solution is to impose periodic boundary conditions whereby the lattice is "folded" and the cells arranged on a torus. The second solution is to assign a null value to the cells nearest to the boundary. Here we follow this second method, that is, we assume that the m cells nearest to the boundary will always cooperate, that is, play C. We use m=5 and correspondingly reduce the numbers of effective cells on the lattice to $(n - 2m)^2$.

A second analytical issue in need of clarification concerns the initialization of the system, that is, the initial assignment of strategies to lattice sites. One possible analytical strategy is to start from a single "seed" typically placed in the center of the lattice. In the present context this would involve placing a single "defector" in a sea of "cooperators" and study how competitive strategies unfold over time. Starting with a single cooperator in a sea of defectors does not produce an interesting dynamics because the cooperator dies out in the second round after playing CD (winning 0) while all of its neighbors play DC (and win T). The second possibility is to assign strategies to sites according to some random mechanism. In the present context, this would involve starting with a certain percentage of "cooperators" and "defectors" as an initial state. This option is particularly useful to analyze path dependence and sensitivity to initial conditions. To explore the transformation of dyadic ties to clusters after critical mass has been achieved, we adopt the latter initialization strategy.

RESULTS

In presenting our analysis of the simulation results, we will first illustrate the broad range of qualitative behaviors that our dynamic model is capable of producing. After establishing a general connection between individual strategies and the dynamics of the system (Question 1), we then examine how initial conditions may influence this connection (Question 2). Finally, we examine how the scope of interaction (Question 3) and awareness of indirect competition (Question 4) substantially alter the spatial and temporal distribution of collective strategies.

Localized Interaction and Self-Organizing Structures

To understand the qualitative behavior of the model, we start from the basic question: Does individual strategy make a difference in terms of the overall evolution of the population? To answer this question we need to see what the evolutionary dynamics of a system look like when local interaction is random rather than rule-based. Figure 2 shows two space-time frames illustrating the evolution of cooperative strategy when local action is based on flipping a coin. The system advances one frame every period, and the second frame in Figure 2 displays the system configuration after 50 periods. As expected, a system with random interaction does not display any tendency toward self-organization over time.

In contrast, a system in which local interactions are governed by rules displays distinct patterns of self-organization regardless of the specific initial distribution of cooperators and defectors: Figures 3 and 4 show six space-time frames illustrating the evolution of cooperative strategy under different initial conditions. In

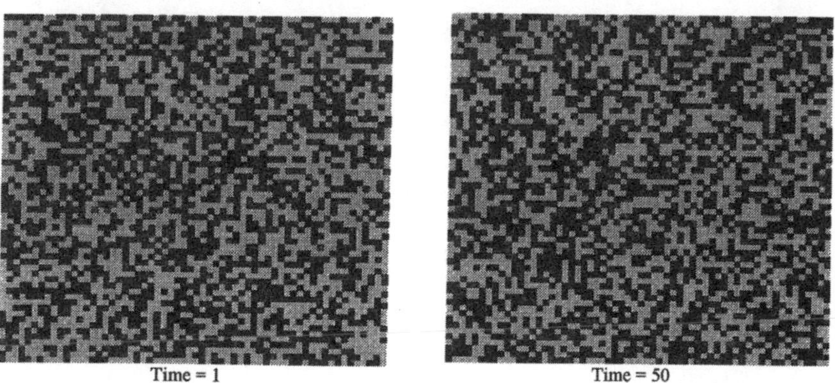

Figure 2. Spatial Evolution When Local Interaction is Random

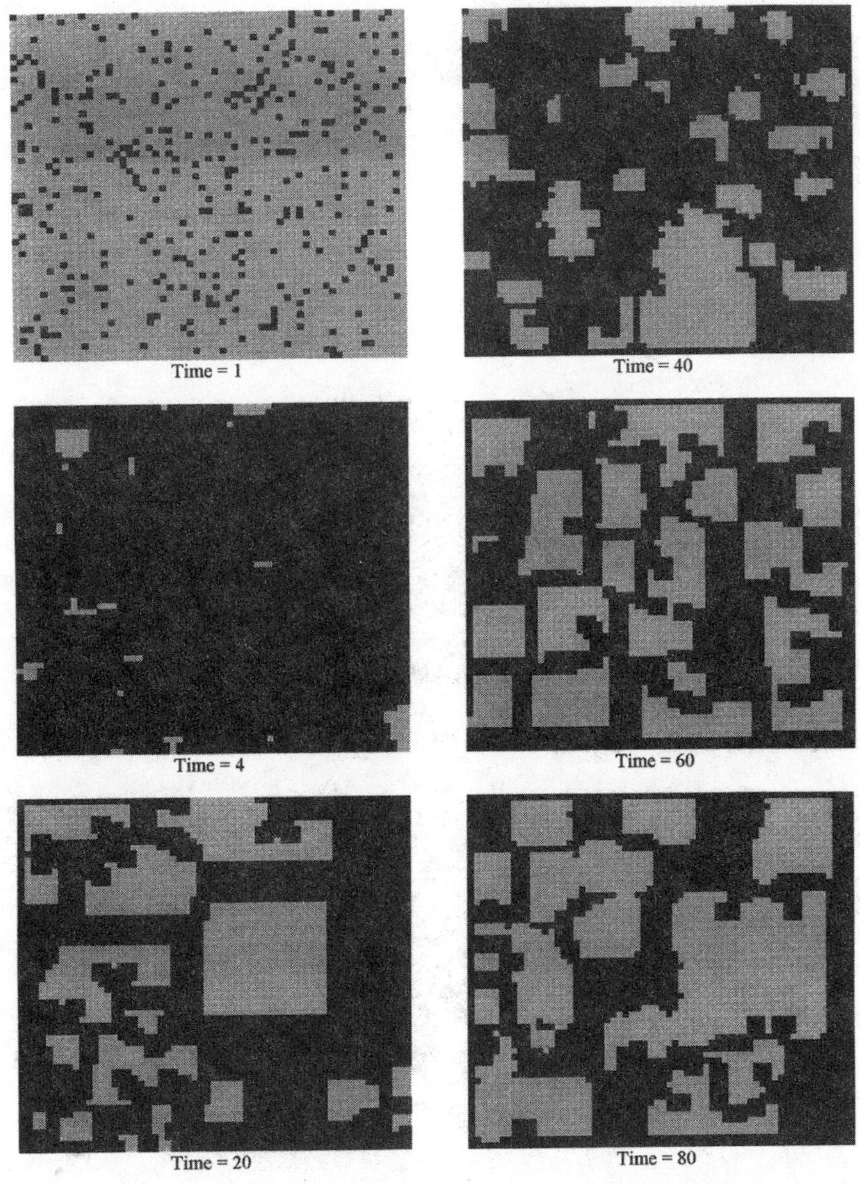

Figure 3. Spatial Evolution of the Computational Model Initialized by 90% Cooperators

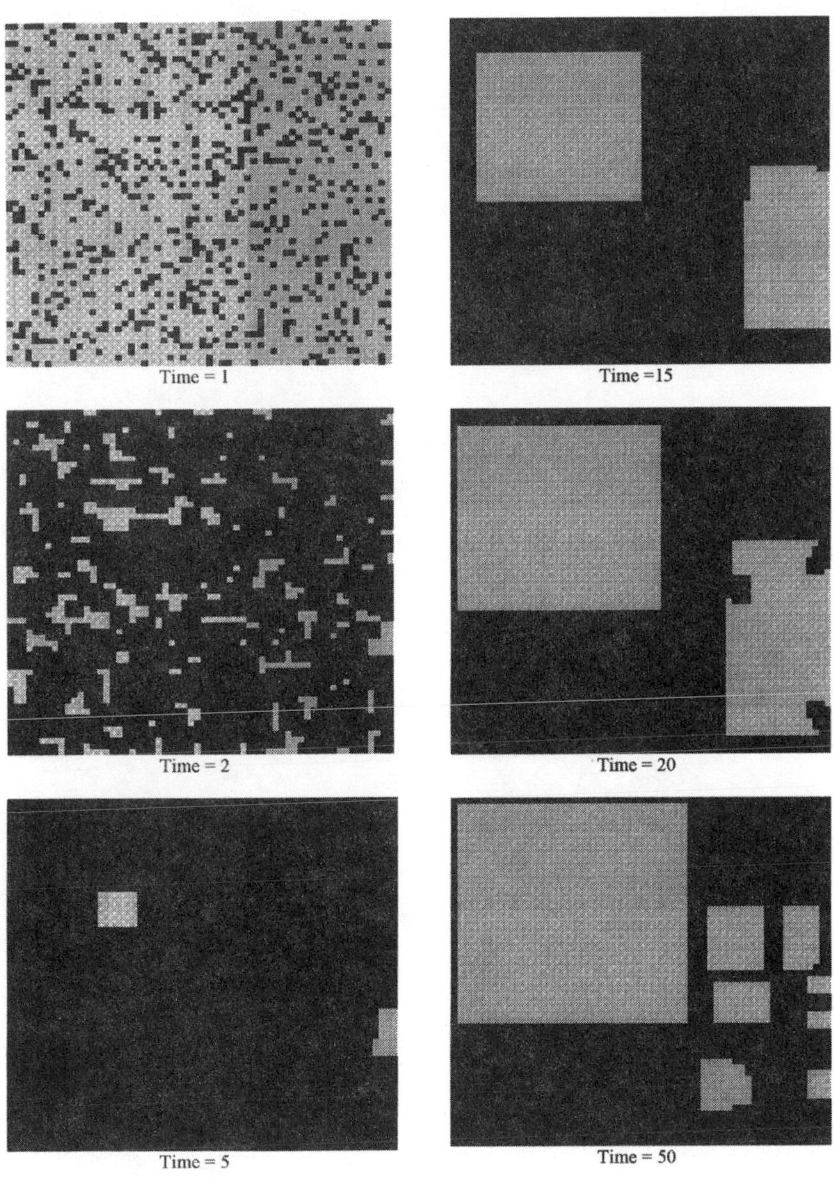

Figure 4. Spatial Evolution of the Computational Model Initialized by 80% Cooperators

both figures the D-strategists are represented as black, and C-strategists as white cells. Figure 3 shows evolutionary patterns starting from an initial condition of 90% cooperators (i.e., a unit has a 10% chance of becoming a defector and a 90% chance of becoming a cooperator) randomly spread out in the lattice; Figure 4 shows evolutionary patterns starting from an initial condition of 80% cooperators (i.e., a unit has a 20% chance of becoming a defector and an 80% chance of becoming a cooperator) randomly spread out in the lattice. In both these cases, individual agents choose and update their local strategies according to equations (2) through (7), that is, when they "play" the spatial version of the RPD specified above with their eight nearest neighbors ($K = 1$) and $\alpha = -0.001$.

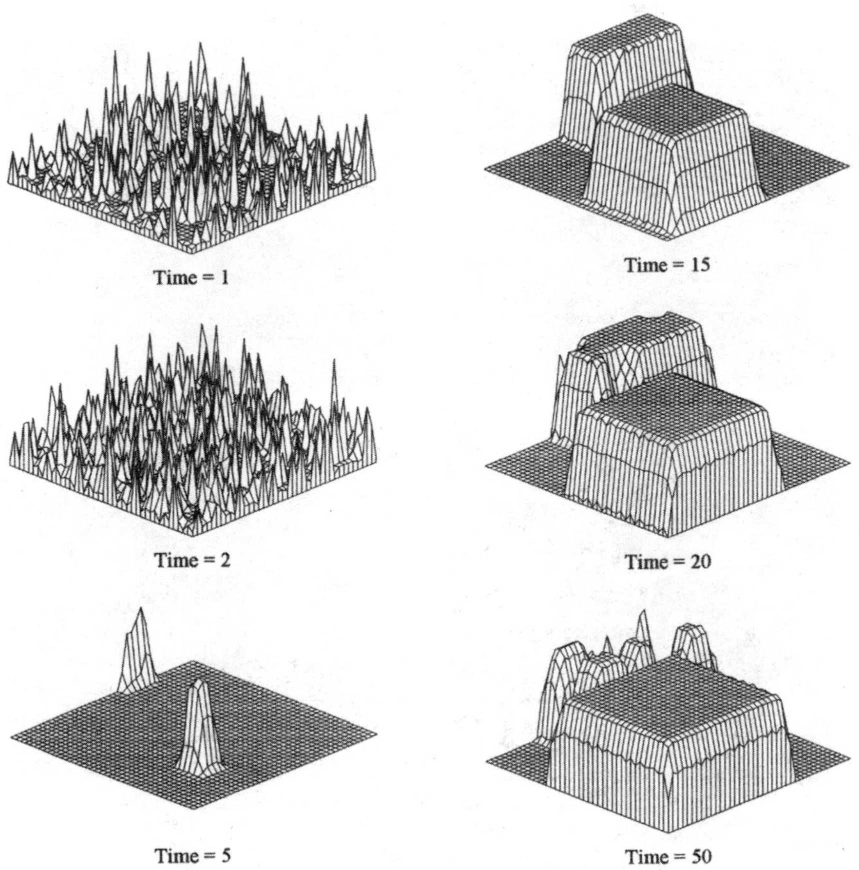

Figure 5. Three-dimensional Representation of the Spatial Distributions (Corresponding to the States in Figure 4)

The process of colonization generated by the spatial distribution of D-strategists and C-strategists can be clearly seen in Figure 5, which reports the payoffs received on the vertical axis. (Compare it with the two-dimensional version in Figure 4.) The valleys in Figure 5 represent clusters of D-strategists, corresponding to the black areas, while the peaks represent clusters of cooperators, corresponding to the white areas in Figure 4. All players located in the "valley of defectors" get the payoff (=0) corresponding to the DD combination in M (the payoff matrix). The vertical dimension in the figures (the "height" of the clusters) is defined by the payoff achieved by C-strategists, each of which gets 8, corresponding to the CC combination in M multiplied by the number of players in the neighborhood.

Sensitivity to Initial Conditions

Initial levels of cooperative activity affect the evolution of collective strategies in two ways. First, they determine whether cooperative activity dies out and second they determine whether and when cooperative activity reaches a state of equilibrium in the population. The distribution of the amount of initial cooperation may vary from one fragmented industry setting to another. Differences may

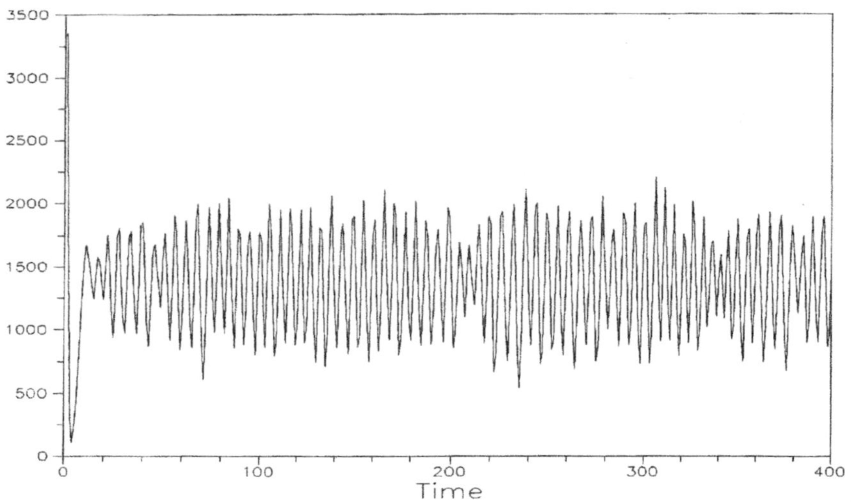

a) Number of cooperators

Figure 6. Temporal Evolution of the Model Initialized by 90% Cooperators

depend on industry tradition, the perceived advantage of C instead of D, the actual advantage of C instead of D, and the preferences of banks or venture capitalists. To determine the minimum level of initial activity needed to make cooperation self-sustaining, we simulated different initial coalition sizes. We found that any initial state in which there were fewer than 75% cooperators lead to the disappearance of cooperative activity (this result is in part due to the set-up of the parameters in the automata, i.e., α and 4 in the indirect competition).

To examine the influence of initial cooperative activity on the achievement of equilibrium, we compared evolutionary processes of 90% versus 80% cooperators in the initial condition. As shown in Figure 3, the result of the interaction processes with 90% cooperators is a series of continuously changing symmetric spatial patterns, with cooperators (C-strategists) and defectors (D-strategists) persisting indefinitely, but in fluctuating proportions. By plotting the time series of the aggregate numbers of "cooperators" (i.e., cells in state "C"), Figure 6 shows that with an initial condition of 90% cooperators the number of cooperators fluctuates in a chaotic motion that does not achieve an equilibrium condition.

In Figures 3 and 6, we see an industry which continues to evolve over time, where collective strategies never reach an equilibrium. There is a constant change of collective strategies, although we can observe some structure at each point in time, that is, a network of defector strategies with islands of cooperative strategies. Incumbents cannot afford to routinize cooperation where the environment

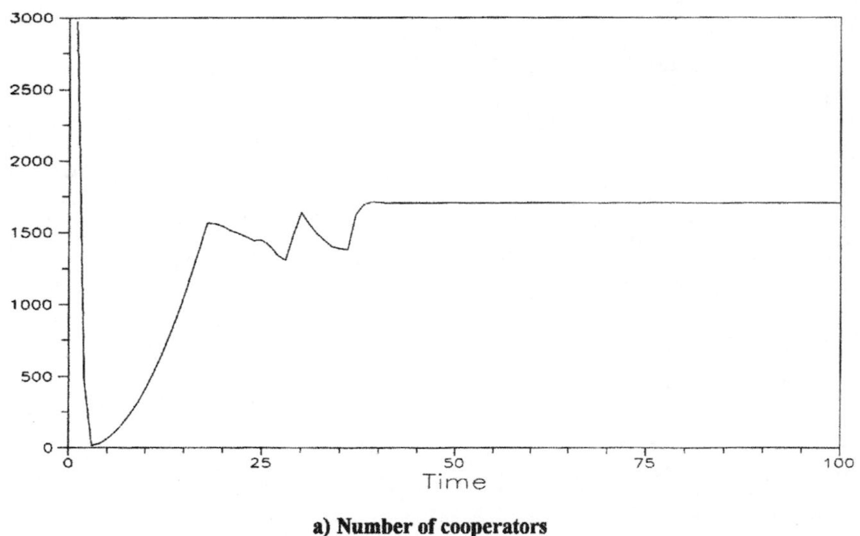

a) Number of cooperators

Figure 7. Temporal Evolution of the Model Initialized by 80% Cooperators

keeps changing fast enough to require constant reassessment of strategy and periodic change.

In the case of 80% cooperators (Figure 4), the lattice almost becomes all D, but there are just enough Cs left at time 5 to start building the C areas. Finally, at time 50, the system reaches equilibrium, that is, a state of no more changes. Figure 7 shows that with an initial condition of 80% cooperators the number of cooperators declines very rapidly during the first 3 generations, after which the effect of diffuse competition sets in and the number of C-strategists rises and fluctuates as a function of T. After 40 generations the system reaches a stable equilibrium where no further change occurs, that is, no single firm changes strategy after this point. The number of defectors stabilizes around 1600 units.

In Figures 4 and 7, we see how self-organization from a randomly distributed mix of cooperators and defectors can lead to a fragmented industry environment partitioned into well defined clusters of dominant C and dominated D strategists with no tendency toward change.

Increased Computational Capability

Having established a connection between the role of local strategies and the importance of initial conditions in shaping the collective motion of the system, we now explore the significance of the scope of local interaction and of information about the global state of the system. In other words, we increase the computational power of the firms so that they are now able to interact with a larger number of neighbors and compare their performance with that of a larger number of direct competitors. At the same time we manipulate the global sensitivity of the system to individual action to explore how this affects the adoption of locally best strategies.

In Figure 8, horizontal variation across space-time frames reflects differences in the range of local interaction (K) for a given $\alpha = -0.0015$. For example, in the first column to the left of the figure where $K = 1$, in every round every cell plays against the eight others in its neighborhood. Similarly, in the last column to the right where $K = 3$, in every round every cell plays against the 48 others in its neighborhood. Each column in Figure 8 captures a set of time variations within models for a given range of local interaction. For example, the second column contains three space-time frames of the model to illustrate the different configurations reached by the system after 20, 40, and 60 generations, respectively, as a function of K. Only K is changed experimentally while everything else—including the initial conditions—is kept constant across models.

The very different patterns emerging after the first 60 generations in the three situations indicate that the scope of direct competition significantly alters the (spatial and temporal) distribution of C- and D-strategists, and strongly affects the evolution of collective strategy. Specifically, as K increases, groups (or networks) of adjacent actors adopting the same strategy increase in size. This results in an

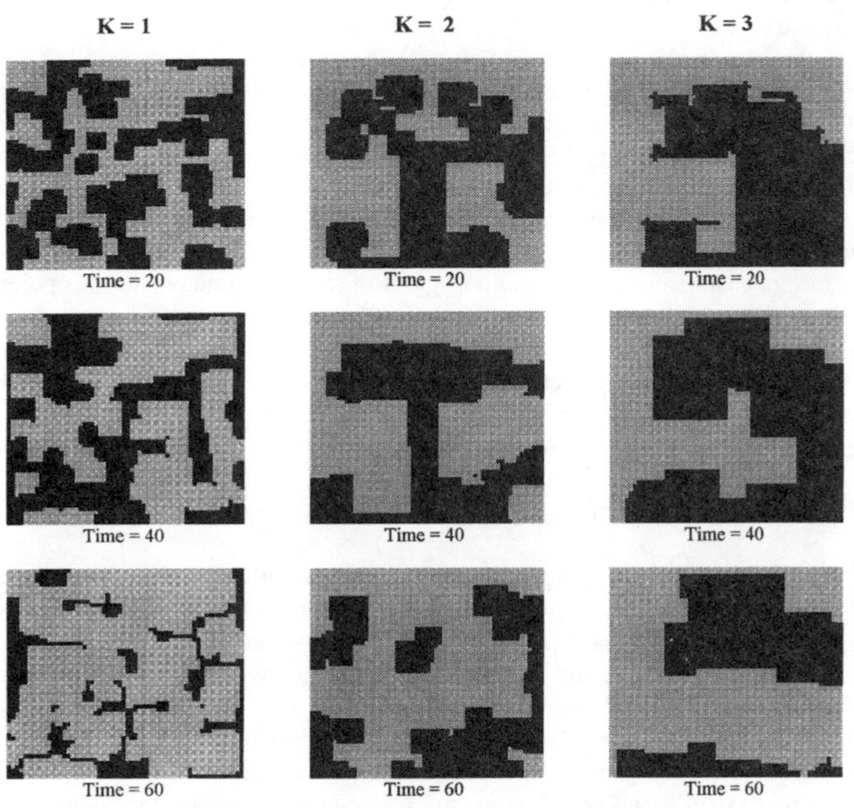

Figure 8. The Influence of Interaction Range (K) on the Evolution of the Population

overall decrease in the complexity of the patterns, that is, in a coarser spatial distribution of strategies.

As mentioned above, increases in *K* can be seen as a way of representing an expanded computational power of individual units or firms in members of a fragmented industry. For example, the capacity of a player to compare his or her performance with that of a set of competitors, and therefore to react to direct competition, increases by a factor of 3 (8 cells to 24) when *K* goes from 1 to 2. In other words, as *K* increases, the industry becomes less "computationally" fragmented. One can think about this in terms of geographical market space, where *K* = 1 means that the manager of a small business is only aware of what is going on in a very limited geographic area, say a neighborhood within a city. There is no coordination outside this very narrow area except through indirect competition, of which the manager might not even be aware. When K is increased to 2 individual agents directly affect (and are directly affected by) 24 alters, that is, agents now can compare their performance over a broader local range.

Figure 8 shows that by increasing the market space that managers keep under control, the distribution of various strategies becomes more coherent since the manager is now benchmarking against more companies in a larger area. What were earlier on local collective strategies now disappear as the industry becomes increasingly less fragmented. As K is increased further to 3, we start to observe an even more coherent set of collective strategies, where there is even less room for local alternatives. This implies that as K increases, the permanence of suboptimal local strategies decreases. At the limit where $K \rightarrow N/2$, each agent would possess the computational power to compare a unit's performance with the performance of all others. This would result in a situation where the competitive structure of the fragmented industry could be represented as a fully connected graph. Such a system will simply converge to the individually best solution in the second round without any further tendency toward change.

Awareness of Diffuse Competition

Finally, we explore the implications of the diffuse nature of competition in a fragmented industry by experimentally varying a the intensity of the relation

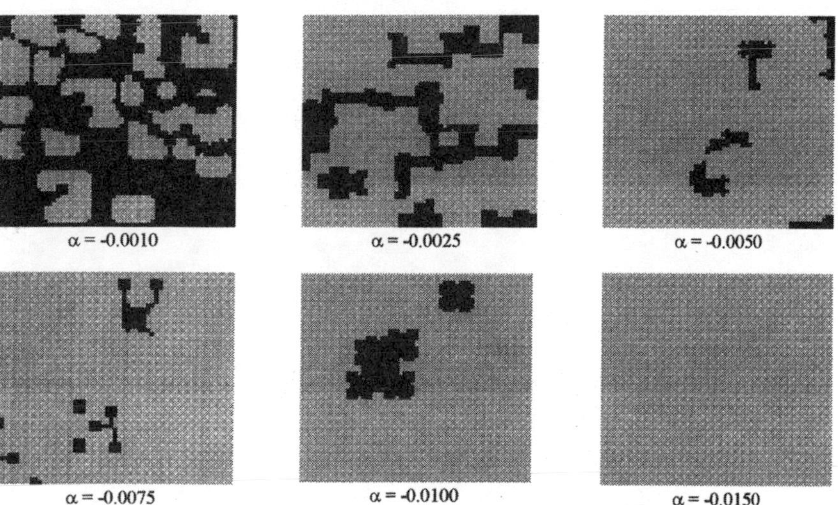

Figure 9. The Influence of Decision Heuristics (α) on the Evolution of the Population (from the model in Figure 3, K=1)

between the aggregate number of defectors and the expected payoff of defecting. We analyze what happens to the evolutionary dynamics of the system when the individual short term advantage of defecting decreases as a function of the aggregate number of existing D-strategists—in other words what happens when the incentive to form or not to form collective strategies changes. Figure 9 shows the effect of α on a system where cellular agents play the RPD with their eight nearest neighbors ($K = 1$). As α becomes more negative the effects of diffuse competition become stronger for any individual player, that is the reward for any organization to not cooperate becomes smaller as a few non cooperative organizations will erode the premium for defection over cooperation.

As α becomes more negative, D-strategists not only become fewer, but they also become much more spatially concentrated. As diffuse competition reduces the adaptive value of employing a rational competitive strategy in any one individual game, D-strategists are confined to a progressively narrower region of the system and only rarely can they propagate through space to form elaborate networks, or stable clusters. Again the limited and rapidly decreasing incentive for defecting will limit the spread of non-cooperative strategies at the population level and as a becomes more negative we observe that there in the limit ($\alpha = -0.015$) only cooperative strategies survive in the population.

Figure 10 illustrates the close connection between the number of cooperators and the strength of diffuse competition by plotting the average number of cooper-

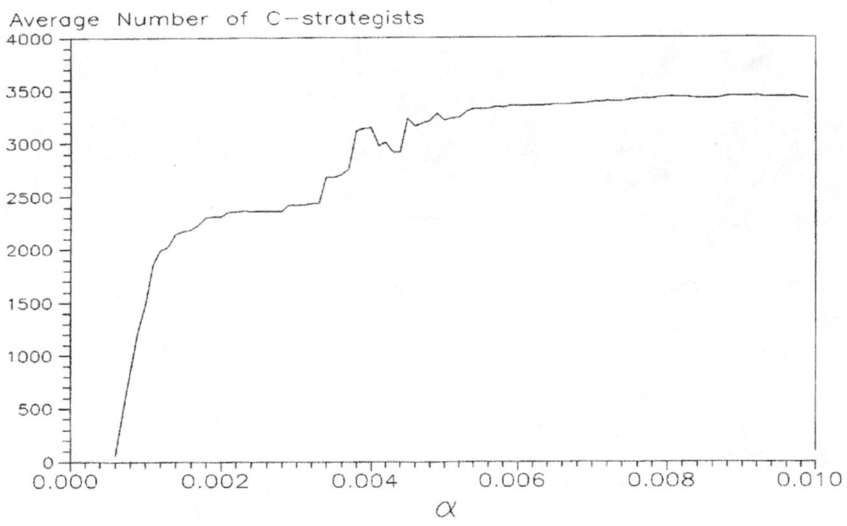

Figure 10. Awareness of Diffuse Competition and Number of Cooperators

ators from time $t = 500$ to $t = 600$ against α based on 100 simulations—where α is a parameter which captures the sensitivity of individual agents to the aggregate consequences of their actions (see appendix 2). While the advantage of cooperating increases linearly as the number of C-strategists increases, the average number of C-strategists increases exponentially with the decision heuristic a. Changing the strength of diffuse competition from $\alpha = -0.0006$ to $\alpha = -0.003$ increases the population of C-strategists from around 100 to around 2,300, corresponding to an increase of around 96 percent. Changing the strength of diffuse competition from $\alpha = -0.003$ to $\alpha = -0.01$ increases the population of C-strategies from around 2,300 to 34,000, that is, by approximately 48 percent.

DISCUSSION AND CONCLUSIONS

We began by drawing attention to the special problems that fragmented industries pose for the formation and development of collective strategies. If interorganizational activity occurs locally, but cooperative strategies evolve at the population level, questions arise about what level of analysis is the most appropriate and—more importantly—how different levels of action might be linked.

To address the weakness of the theoretical linkage between existing micro and macro perspectives on organizations, we proposed an autogenetic perspective, which emphasizes the role of the self-organizing capacities of individuals interacting in a social field. Based on the image of firms as units performing a complex collective computation by processing strictly local (and therefore incomplete) information, we used computational techniques inspired by the theory of cellular automata to develop a formal evolutionary model. Within this framework, the evolution of collective strategies in fragmented industries begins through the dyadic interaction of individual agents who operate in a spatially extended environment and play the infinitely repeated version of the Prisoner's Dilemma with their neighbors. We simulated the model under a variety of conditions to illustrate how interactions in fragmented industries between managers with limited computational and cognitive capacities induce and sustain collective strategies at the population level.

Most of the results produced by our models are consistent with conjectures about the ecological consequences of niche desegregation and institutional change which, by breaking the boundaries around technical or institutional sectors, make individual organizations more sensitive to competitive pressures coming from more remote sites (Hannan & Freeman, 1986). Similar processes of diffuse competition are triggered when markets expand to surpass local geographical boundaries (Hannan & Carroll, 1992). Take, for example, Avis Sports, a Moorehead City, North Carolina, distributor of hunting and fishing equipment, which, three years ago formed a purchasing and marketing cooperative that now has more than 500 independent sporting-goods-retailer members around the country. This process of colonization is, in large part, the result of sensitivity to widespread competition. As observed by Gary Zurn, executive vice president of Avis Sports, "If something wasn't done to help these dealers compete, our customer base was going to continue to erode" (Dale E. Buss, "The Little Guys Strike Back," *Nation's Business*, July, 1996, p. 20).

In more general terms, the findings confirm that the connection between individual behavior and its aggregate system-level consequences is not easily predictable. However, social order in general, and collective strategy in particular, cannot arise spontaneously from random interaction. Aggregate regular structures with clear boundaries at the macro level emerge from as well as shape the patterns of interaction at the micro level. What is interesting about these population-level regularities is that they surface and persist without any intentional design or "central" control, even though it is generally impossible to predict them.

Population-level structures appear to partition the population into sharply distinct classes characterized by persistent performance differences. More specifically, we found that strategies with different fitness values not only persist over time, but coexist in varying proportions and are localized in clearly bounded clusters. This result is genuinely emergent because the agents are not programmed to form stable clusters. It also substantiates theoretical arguments regarding the emergence of collective strategy (Dollinger, 1990).

The evolution of individual cooperative activity into a population-level phenomenon appears also to be highly path dependent or sensitive to initial conditions. More specifically, we found that unless the process begins with a critical mass of C-strategists, cooperation cannot become self-sustaining at the population level. Moreover, different levels of initial activity lead to very different trajectories, those that achieve equilibrium and those that resemble a chaotic decision tree.

The extent to which competition is direct significantly alters the (spatial and temporal) distribution of strategic activities, and strongly affects the emergence of collective strategy. As the range of local interaction increases, the permanence of suboptimal local strategies decreases. More specifically, as individual agents are given the computational power to compare their performance with that of a larger number of direct competitors, the distribution of strategic activities becomes less spatially fragmented, but more temporally unstable. Interestingly enough, when the range of local interaction increases the system no longer reaches a unique equilibrium configuration and, when $K = 3$, it enters a periodic collective motion where the same state will be visited every five generations, infinitely many times. This result is important because it demonstrates how the structural stability of a social system, such as is represented by the interactions of firms in a fragmented industry, depends systematically on the range and structure of social networks.

Finally, we found that as organizations in a fragmented industry become more sensitive to the collective consequences of their local strategies—that is, as they become more sensitive to the effects of diffuse competition—D-strategies are confined to a limited region around the initial defector, and do not propagate beyond the local level. This result is the consequence of the simple frequency-dependent selection mechanism that we set up according to which the payoff from defection is a monotonically decreasing function of the aggregate numbers of defectors. Clearly, questions remain open about the possible implications of nonlinearities in this simple incentive structure on how organizations in fragmented industries learn to cooperate.

Our results regarding the influence of the range of interaction K and the effects of α—the global penalty for defecting—are consistent with the argument that the formalization of an emergent collective strategy occurs if environmental elements at the population level create some "consciousness" among the firms and the gains from joining the collective exceed the costs (Dollinger, 1990). What is particularly interesting, however, is the sensitivity of the qualitative behavior of the system to relatively small changes in the scope of interaction and to the intensity of the relationship between density of D-strategists and individual reward associated with defection.

Limitations of the Modeling Framework

Despite the value of these results for understanding the emergence of collective strategy in fragmented industries, it is important to acknowledge the limitations of our modeling framework. The first basic limitation of our modeling framework is its reliance on a synchronous updating mechanism. The state of every site on the lattice is updated at the same discrete time steps. While this computational structure is generally considered a reasonable assumption in models of physical and chemical systems (Wolfram, 1986), its realism for modeling the mechanics of social and ecological processes can be questioned (Hogeweg, 1988). For example, Huberman and Glance (1993) convincingly argued that the behavior of certain systems can be extremely sensitive to the assumption of synchronous updating.

The second limitation derives from the fact that the same rule of local interaction is used to update the state of every cell in the lattice. In principle, it is possible to think of different rules competing for sites, or to design individual cells which draw rules of interaction from a distribution of possible rules. However, we are not aware of any work that has implemented such a model, possibly because the computational burden would quickly become prohibitive if the number of possible combinations was left unconstrained.

Future Directions

To simulate the behavior of our models we relied on a number of ancillary assumptions, which correspond to a set of constraints that can be relaxed in future studies. For example, we assumed that all players have equal information (or understanding) of the global consequences of individual action. This assumption is easy to relax by adding a random, time varying and/or location-specific disturbance term in the relation defining the advantage of defecting as a function of the density of D-strategists. We also assumed that each player can consistently and readily emulate the strategy which satisfies a local fitness criterion. This situation can be modified by allowing players to make mistakes, for example, by designing an updating mechanism according to which there is a small probability that players will choose a local strategy that is the opposite of what they intended. This is a generally accepted approach to the modeling of mutation in biological systems (Lindgren & Nordahl, 1994).

A third assumption is that players have no expectations about future encounters because they have no memory of past events. This assumption could easily be abandoned by following the pioneering work of Axelrod (1984) and including history as a determinant of future strategy, with memory structure operating as a sort of genetic code (Lindgren & Nordahl, 1994). Future explorations may employ models that can incorporate the less "Pavlovian" processes of expectation formation suggested by Huberman and Glance (1993) to control the behavior of individual players. While the absence of an explicit mechanism of expectation formation and memory at the individual level severely reduces the realism of our models, this element of oversimplification at the individual level did not prevent various forms of order—or "organization"—to become apparent at the population level. We believe this is in itself an important result because it indicates one way in which different structural levels can be decoupled.

Despite its limitations, we believe that the current research illustrates the great potential of using computational models and computer simulations to advance our understanding of the impact of firm-level strategies on the broad business systems in which firms are embedded. In so doing, we aspire to help strategic management shift from an entity point of view to one that makes frameworks of cooperation and coevolution central (Moore, 1996). To shed light on the connection between strategies of local interaction involving both competition and imitation and their global population consequences, we sought, in particular, to examine the evolution of collective strategies in fragmented industries. We hope that our study helps open new frontiers for analyzing industry environments as dynamically complex organizational ecosystems and for understanding the self-organizing properties of strategic interactions.

APPENDIX 1

Let f_1 be a function which relates the aggregate number of agents choosing D to the payoff of defection expected by each individual player. Thus T^t—the expected payoff associated with defection at time t—is:

$$T_t = f_1(D_{t-1}) \tag{2}$$

Let $a_{i,j}^{t-1}$ be the state of cell c_{ij} at time t-1 (i. e., D or C), $a_{i,j}^{t-1}$ the state of any other cell $c_{h,g}$ in the neighborhood σ_K directly playing with c_{ij}, T^t, R, P, S the payoffs associated with the different strategies in M, and let K be the range of the local interaction. Then the total payoff for cell ij at time t, which is repeated for all $n \times n$ cells in the lattice, can be computed as:

$$\Pi_{i,j}^{t} = \sum_{h=i-K}^{h=i+K} \sum_{g=i-K}^{g=i+K} (a_{i,j}^{t-1}, a_{h,g}^{t-1}, T^t, R, P, S) \tag{3}$$

Every round, the state of every cell in the lattice is updated in two steps. The first step involves the computation of $\pi_{i,j}^t$. This quantity can be computed as:

$$\pi_{i,j}^{t} = \text{Max}(\Pi_{h,g}^{t}\ for((((i-K) < h < (i+K)) \wedge ((i-K) < g < (i+K))) \tag{4}$$

where $\pi_{i,j}(t)$ is the maximum payoff received by any cell c_{ij} in a K-neighborhood.

In the second step, every site is either occupied by the original "owner" or by one of the neighbors, depending on who obtains the highest score in that round. Another way of saying this is that agent c_{ij} will abandon the strategy chosen in the previous round if a neighbor with a different strategy outcompeted all the others in the neighborhood, that is, managed to obtain the highest pay-off. So in every round c_{ij} updates its strategy according to the rule:

$$a_{i,j}^{t} = \begin{cases} D\ if \exists\ a_{h,g}^{t-1} \in \sigma_K = D\ |\Pi_{h,g}^{t} \rightarrow \pi_{i,j}^{t} \\ C\ if \exists\ a_{h,g}^{t-1} \in \sigma_K = C\ |\Pi_{h,g}^{t} \rightarrow \pi_{i,j}^{t} \end{cases} \tag{5}$$

This equation reflects the idea that agents evaluate their strategy relative to (or "given") their knowledge of what the other players in the K-neighborhood received at t-1.

At every generation (or round) all the cells in the system revise their strategy according to this two-step updating process and adopt the locally "best" course of action.

APPENDIX 2

We define f_1 in equation (2) as a linear function of the global number of defectors where α is the slope of the line, N is the total number of defectors, and 4 is the payoff for defecting if no cell defects (i. e., if $N = 0$). The relationship is given as:

$$T^t = \alpha N^t + 4 \tag{6}$$

where

$$N^t = \sum_{i=l+m}^{i=n-m} \sum_{j=l+m}^{j=n-m} \begin{cases} 1 \text{ if } a_{i,j}^{t-1} = D \\ 0 \text{ if } a_{i,j}^{t-1} = C \end{cases} \tag{7}$$

The slope of the line is an expression for how sensitive individual agents are to the aggregate consequence of their actions, or if $\alpha < 0$, it can be seen as a global level penalty for defecting. When $\alpha = 0$, there is no diffuse effect and the model becomes similar to May and Nowak's model (1992). A positive α is associated with increasing returns on defection, and a negative α—as we use in the baseline case where $\alpha = -0.001$—puts a penalty on individual defection, which increases with the aggregate number of other agents choosing the same uncooperative course of action.

APPENDIX 3

Decision routines for individual cells on the lattice.

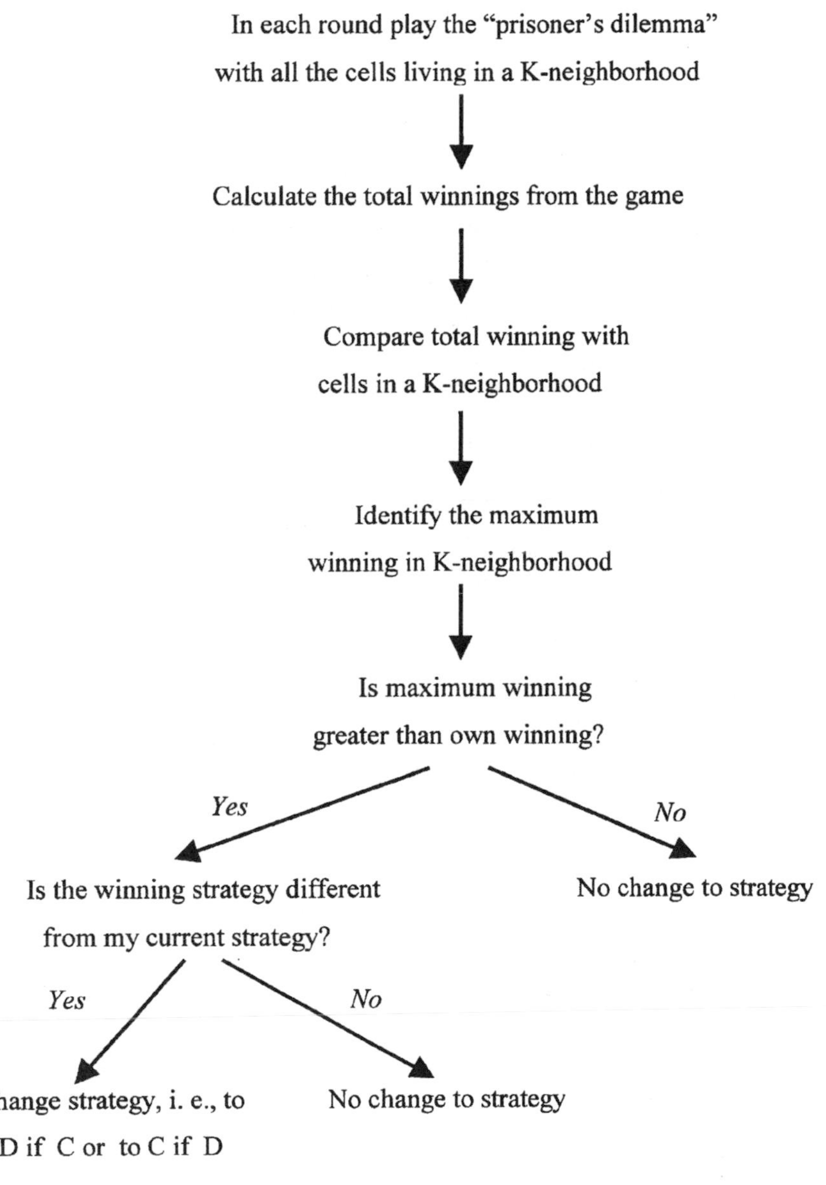

ACKNOWLEDGMENTS

A preliminary version of this work was presented at the Carnegie Mellon-University of Wisconsin Joint Conference on Organizational Learning and Knowledge Transfer that was held in Pittsburgh June 12-14, 1998. We are grateful to Anne Miner for her encouragement and careful advice.

REFERENCES

Albin, P. (1987). Microeconomic foundation of cyclic irregularities or "chaos." *Mathematical Social Research, 13*, 185-214.

Axelrod, R. (1984). *The evolution of cooperation*. New York, NY: Basic Books.

Axelrod, R. (1997). *The complexity of cooperation*. Princeton, NJ: Princeton University Press.

Baum, J. A. C., & Haveman, H. (1997). Love thy neighbor. Differentiation and agglomeration in Manhattan hotel industry:1898-1990. *Administrative Science Quarterly, 42*, 580-604.

Baum, J. A. C., & Mezias, S. J. (1992). Localized competition and organizational failure in the Manhattan hotel industry, 1989-1990. *Administrative Science Quarterly, 37*, 580-604.

Baum, J. A. C., & Singh, J. V. (1994). Organizational niches and the dynamics of organizational mortality. *American Journal of Sociology, 100*, 346-380.

Binmore, K. (1992). *Fun and games*. Lexington, MA: D. C. Heath Company.

Bresser, R. K. (1988). Matching collective and competitive strategies. *Strategic Management Journal, 9*, 375-385.

Brittain, J. W., & Wholey, D. H. (1988). Competition and coexisting in organizational communities: population dynamics in electronics components manufacturing. In G. R. Carroll (Ed.), *Ecological models of organizations* (pp. 195-222). Cambridge, MA: Ballinger.

Carroll, G. (1985). Concentration and specialization: dynamics of niche width in populations of organizations. *American Journal of Sociology, 90*, 1262-1283.

Carroll, G., & Swaminathan, A. (1992). The organizational ecology of strategic groups in the American brewing industry from 1975-1990. *Industrial and Corporate Change, 1*, 65-97.

Contractor, F., & Lorange, P. (Eds.) (1988). Cooperative strategies in international business: Joint ventures and technology partnerships between firms. NewYork: Lexington Books.

Day, G. S., Shocker, & Srivastava, R. K. (1979). Customer-oriented approaches to identifying product markets. *Journal of Marketing, 43*, 8-19.

DiMaggio, P., & Powell, W. (1983). The iron cage revisited: Institutional isomorphism and collective rationality in organizational fields. *American Sociological Review, 48*, 147-160.

Dollinger, M. J. (1990). The evolution of collective strategies in fragmented industries. *Academy of Management Review, 15*, 266-285.

Drazin, R., & Sandlands, L. (1992). Autogenesis: A perspective on the process of organizing. *Organization Science, 3*, 230-249.

Freeman, J., & Lomi, A. (1994). Resource partitioning and foundation of banking cooperatives in Italy. In J. A. C. Baum & J. V. Singh (Eds.), *Evolutionary dynamics of organizations*. New York: Oxford University Press.

Friedman, J. (1983). *Oligopoly theory*. New York: Cambridge University Press.

Ginsberg, A. (1995). Minding the competition: From mapping to mastery. *Strategic Management Journal, 15*, 153-174.

Ginsberg, A., Larsen, E., & Lomi, A. (1997). Generating strategy from individual behavior: A dynamic model of structural embeddedness. In J. A. C. Baum, & J. E. Dutton (Eds.), *Advances in strategic management* (vol. 13, pp. 121-147). Greenwich, CT: JAI Press.

Gutowitz, H. (1991). *Cellular automata: Theory and experiment*. Cambridge, MA: MIT Press.

Hannan, M. T. (1986). Ecological theory: General discussion. In S. Lindenberg, J. S. Coleman, & S. Nowak (Ed.), *Approaches to social theory*. New York: Russell Sage Foundation.

Hannan, M. T., Carroll, G., Dundon, E., & Torres, J. (1995). Organizational evolution in a multinational context: Entries of automobile manufactures in Belgium, Britain, France, Germany and Italy. *American Sociological Review 60*, 509-528.

Hannan, M. T., & Freeman, J. H. (1986). Where do organizations come from? *Sociological Forum, 1*, 50-72.

Heide, J., & Miner, A. S. (1992). The shadow of the future: The effect of anticipated interaction and frequency of contact on buyer-seller cooperation. *Academy of Management Journal 35*, 256-291.

Hilborn, R. C. (1994). *Chaos and nonlinear dynamics*. New York: Oxford University Press.

Hogeweg, H. (1988). Cellular automata as a paradigm for ecological modeling. *AppliedMathematics and Computation, 27*, 81-100.

Huberman, B., & Glance, N. (1993). *Evolutionary games and computer simulations*. Proceedings of the National Academy of Science, *90*, 7716-7718.

Kahneman, D., Slovic, P., & Tversky, A. (1982). *Judgement under uncertainty: Heuristic and biases*. Cambridge: Cambridge University Press.

Keenan, D., & O'Brien, M. (1993). Competition, collusion and chaos. *Journal of Economic Dynamics and Control, 17*, 327-353.

Kephart, J. (1994). How topology affects population dynamics. In C. Langton (Ed.), *Artificial Life III* (pp. 447-63). Reading, MA: Addison-Wesley.

Larsen, E. R., & Lomi, A. (1999). Resetting the clock: A feedback approach to the dynamics of organizational inertia, survival and change. *Journal of the Operational Research Society*, forthcoming.

Leifer, E. M. (1985). Markets as mechanisms: Using a role structure. *Social Forces*, *64*, 442-472.

Levinthal, D. (1990). Organizational adaptation: Environmental selection and random walks. In J. Singh (Ed.), *Organizational evolution* (pp. 201-233). Newbury Park, CA: Sage.

Lindgren, C., & Nordahl, M. (1994). Evolutionary dynamics of spatial games. *Physica D, 75*, 292-309.

Lomi, A. (1995). The population ecology of organizational founding: Location dependence and unobserved heterogeneity. *Administrative Science Quarterly*, *40*, 11-144.

Lomi, A., & Larsen, E. R. (1996). Interacting locally and evolving globally: A computational approach to the dynamics of organizational populations. *Academy of Management Journal, 39*(4), 1287-1321.

Macy, M. W. (1991). Learning to cooperate: Stochastic and tacit collusion in social exchange. *American Journal of Sociology, 3*, 808-843.

March, J. G. (1994). The evolution of evolution. In J. A. C. Baum, J. V. Singh (Eds.), *Evolutionary dynamics of organizations* (pp. 39-52). New York: Oxford University Press.

May, R. M., & Nowak, M. A. (1992). Evolutionary games and spatial chaos. *Nature*, *359*, 826-829.

McPherson, M. J. (1983). An ecology of affiliation. *American Sociological Review, 48*, 519-532.

Meyer, J., & Rowan, B. (1977). Institutionalized organizations: Formal structure as myth and ceremony. *American Journal of Sociology, 83*, 340-363.

Moore, J. F. (1996). *The death of competition*. New York: HarperCollins Publishers.

Nelson, & Winter, (1982). *An evolutionary theory of economic change*. Cambridge, MA: Belknap Press.

Nielsen, R. P. (1988). Cooperative strategy. *Strategic Management Journal, 9*, 475-492.

Nisbett, R., & Ross, L. (1980). *Human inference: Strategies and shortcomings of social judgement,* Englewood Cliffs, NJ: Prentice Hall.

Odorici, V., & Lomi, A. (1999). Classifying the competition: An empirical study on the cognitive social structure of strategic groups. In Z. Shapira & T. Lant (Eds.), *Managerial and organizational cognition*. NJ: Lawrence Erlbaum Associates.

Oliver, C. (1988). The collective strategy framework: An application to competing predictions of isomorphism. *Administrative Science Quarterly*, *33*, 543-561.

Packard, N., & Wolfram, S. (1985). Two-dimensional cellular automata. *Journal of Statistical Physics, 38*, 901-946.

Porac, J., & Thomas, H. (1990). Taxonomic mental models in competitor definition, *Academy of Management Review, 15*, 224-240.

Porac, J., Thomas, H., Wilson, F., Paton, D., & Kanfer, A. (1995). Rivalry and the industry model of Scottish knitwear producers. *Administrative Science Quarterly*, *40*, 203-227.

Porter, M. E. (1980). *Competitive Strategy*. NewYork: Free Press.

Radzicki, M. J., & Sterman, J. D. (1994). Evolutionary economics and system dynamics. In R. W. Englan (Ed.), E*volutionary concepts in contemporary economics*. Ann Arbor, MI: University of Michigan Press.

Rasmusen, E. (1989). *Games and information: An introduction to game theory*. New York: Blackwell.

Schelling, T. C. (1972). Dynamic models of segregation. *Journal of Mathematical Sociology*, *1*, 143-186.

Schelling, T. C. (1978). *Micromotives and macrobehavior*. New York: W. W. Norton & Company.

Simmel, G. (1908). *The sociology of Georg Simmel* (1950 trans.). New York: Free Press.

Skinner, S. J., Donnelly, J. H., & Ivancevich, J. M. (1987). Effects of transactional form on environmental linkages and power dependence relations. *Academy of Management Journal*, *30*, 577-588.

Stern, R. N., & Barley, S. R. (1996). Organizations and social systems: Organization theory's neglected mandate. *Administrative Science Quarterly*, *41*, 146-162.

Tirole, J. (1988). *The theory of industrial organization*. Cambridge, MA: MIT Press.

Van de Ven, A. H., & Poole, M. (1995). Explaining development and change in organizations. *Academy of Management Review*, *20*, 510-540.

White, H. C. (1992). *Identity and control: A structural theory of social action*. Princeton, NJ: Princeton University Press.

White, H. C., & Eccles, R. (1987). Producers' markets. In M. Milgrates & P. Newman (Eds.), *The new Palgrave dictionary of economics* (vol. 3, pp. 984-986). London: MacMillan.

Wolfram, S. (1983). Statistical mechanics of cellular automata. *Review of Modern Physics*, *55*, 471-526.

Wolfram, S. (1986). Cellular automata fluids: Basic theory. *Journal of Statistical Physics*, *45*, 601-644.

MODES OF INTERORGANIZATIONAL IMITATION AND THE TRANSFORMATION OF ORGANIZATIONAL POPULATIONS

Stephen J. Mezias and Alan B. Eisner

ABSTRACT

This paper explores the possible implications of population-level learning in the evolution of organizational populations by examining the potential influence of modes of interorganizational imitation on the persistence of organization-level change in organizational populations. We use an institutionalized ecology of learning model to develop propositions about the effect of modes of interorganizational imitation on the survival of firms that change. We focus on variables and processes that can have a significant impact on the survival of firms that change, including the diffusion of new, high-performance organizational types, the rate of exit from niches that are becoming overcrowded, the costs of search and change, and endogenous processes of environmental change. We conclude that the mode of imitation that organizations use can have important effects on the transformation of organizational populations.

Advances in Strategic Management, Volume 16, pages 113-130.

ISBN: 0-7623-0500-2

What is the role of organization-level change in the evolution of firms and populations of firms? Mezias and Lant (1994) used simulations to demonstrate that a significant proportion of firms that imitate other firms will survive under a broad set of conditions. They concluded that this called into question claims that organizational level change does not affect characteristics of the population significantly (Hannan & Freeman, 1984). Haunschild and Miner (1997, p. 497) interpreted Mezias and Lant's results to suggest that "organizational learning may be a rather complex process influenced by multiple contingencies." Although they implied that different modes of imitation may be one of the important contingencies, they did not discuss how or why this might unfold. In this paper, we argue that different imitation rules may result in different outcomes over time, with differential impacts on the transformation of populations of organizations.

In distinguishing among types of imitation, we begin with the categories developed by Haunschild and Miner (1997) in a study of the use of investment bankers as advisors on acquisitions. While the categories of imitation they studied were driven by market-based criteria, they suggested that the categories of imitation may be generalizable and gave examples of how different imitation modes might be used by a printing firm. This hypothetical firm might engage in frequency imitation of accounting practices, trait imitation of the ordering practices of a large firm, and outcome imitation of the press operation practices of the fastest firm (Haunschild & Miner, 1997, p. 496). They also speculated about the implications of their study, noting the importance of "the simultaneous existence of multiple modes of imitation whose strength varies with context. The study underscores imitation's nuanced and potentially complex role in organizational and population-level transformation." We interpret this conclusion as suggesting that it would be useful to examine the role of modes of interorganizational imitation as a form of population-level transformation and learning. We do so here by examining the potential influence of modes of interorganizational imitation on the characteristics of an organizational population.

We use and extend the model of an institutionally informed ecology of learning developed by Mezias and Lant (1994), beginning with the variables that they found to have a significant effect on the viability of imitative change. These included environmental carrying capacity, the costs of search and change for imitative firms, the probability of environmental change, and the gain, or magnitude of environmental change. We extend their model by going beyond the single form of interorganizational imitation that they considered, a trait-based algorithm of copying the largest firm, to examine the effect of three modes of interorganizational imitation: frequency-based, trait-based, and outcome-based.

AN INSTITUTIONALLY INFORMED ECOLOGY OF LEARNING

A combination of organizational ecology, institutional, and organizational learning theories can offer a balanced perspective on the role of organizational-level change in the evolution of organizational populations (Fombrun, 1988; Mezias & Lant, 1994). Combining perspectives offers a more realistic picture of the evolution of organizational populations (Mezias & Lant, 1994; Fombrun, 1988; Singh & Lumsden, 1990). Further, combinations of perspectives have offered valuable insights in previous literature (e.g., Singh, House, & Tucker, 1986; Tucker, Singh, & Meinhard, 1990).

Successful organizational adaptation is more difficult and costly under conditions of ambiguity and environmental uncertainty (March, 1981; Hannan & Freeman, 1984). Organizations may exchange institutional for technical routines in the face of such environmental uncertainty (Meyer, Scott, & Deal, 1983) because institutional mimetic routines may alleviate the possible disadvantage of organizational change. For this reason, we use a model of an institutionally informed ecology of learning. We use the term *ecology* because we are interested in modeling populations of organizations, and *learning*, since each organization is an adaptive learning system (Mezias & Lant, 1994). Further, we assume that several core dimensions characterize an organization and that organizational change represents a change in one or more of the core dimensions of an organization (Hannan & Freeman, 1984; Tushman & Romanelli, 1985).

As an ecology, the economy or environmental system sustaining a population of organizations has some carrying capacity or number of competing firms (e.g., density) that can be sustained by the environment. As the carrying capacity of the environment increases, more firms can be sustained or, in the event of no new entrants, the competition among existing firms decreases. If the population density increases more rapidly than the environmental carrying capacity, then competition becomes more intense among existing firms.

Some level of environmental ambiguity also characterizes environmental systems. Environmental ambiguity in a population may cloud the underlying relationship between individual organizational core features and organizational performance (March & Olsen, 1976). Ambiguity differentially affects organizations in a population in assessing actual performance levels (Lant & Mezias, 1990; March, 1988; Mezias & Lant, 1994). The greater the level of ambiguity, the more likely that organizations may experience errors in organizational processes such as search or change.

Environmental changes may affect populations of organizations as a result of both the frequencies at which those changes take place and the level of gain or magnitude of those changes (Mezias & Lant, 1994). Fine-grained environments entail changes of comparatively small magnitude, while coarse-grained environments entail changes of relatively large magnitude (Freeman & Hannan, 1983; Hannan & Freeman, 1977). Both the independent effects and the interaction of the frequency and the magnitude of environmental change characterize the dynamics of change in a population's environment.

We view individual firms as organizational learning systems and use an organizational learning perspective to model the changes of individual organizations within a population (Mezias & Eisner, 1997; Mezias & Glynn, 1993; Mezias & Lant, 1994). Elaborating the organizational model allows for a more complete consideration of the role of individual organizational level actions in the evolution of organizational populations.

Organizations as Adaptive Learning Systems

The organizations in this ecology carry out mimetic processes by learning from experience as "routine-based, history-dependent, and target oriented" systems (Levitt & March, 1988, p. 319). Organizations act as aspiration-level adapters, comparing current performance to an object or aspiration level. Organizations decide on the amount of scanning or search they will execute based on whether their actual performance is above or below their target level, because search is costly (Cyert & March, 1963; Nelson & Winter, 1982; Payne, Laughunn, & Crum, 1980). Organizational performance above or below the target level influences the prospect of organizational change. Changes to the core features of organizations are more likely when organizational performance is below the target level (Cyert & March, 1963; Levitt & March, 1988; March & Simon, 1958). An adaptive organizational learning model suggests a system in which an organization is more likely to change when its performance is below its target level, and the outcome of the search an organization conducts will determine the substance of the change.

While is it not impossible for an adaptive organization with a performance level above its target level to change a core feature of the organization, it is considerably less likely (Cyert & March, 1963; Levinthal & March, 1981). Organizations with performance levels above their targets may engage in opportunistic searches that sporadically result in the discovery of good occasions to contemplate organizational change (Cyert & March, 1963). For an adaptive organization with performance below the target level, the likelihood of organizational change is an increasing function of the difference between actual and target performance levels (Cyert & March, 1963; Mezias, 1988; Mezias & Lant, 1994).

Search and Change

The organizational search process is the examination of novel or alternative modes of operating an organization. Ecological and institutional perspectives reveal two possible types of search: (1) search at founding of the organization and

(2) search during the operating lifetime of the organization (Mezias & Lant, 1994). Search at the inception of an organization is assumed to have one of two possible main effects on the variety of organizational forms in a population. According to Hannan and Freeman (1987, p. 911), "Some foundings initiate an entirely new form and thus contribute qualitatively to the diversity of organizational forms in society. Most foundings replicate an existing [organizational] form and contribute quantitatively to diversity." Thus, search at founding may either create a new organizational form or replicate an existing form in a population.

The second type of organizational search is conducted after the organization is in operation. The rules of his type of stochastic search are derived from both the ecological and institutional perspectives. First, following the ecological or selection perspective, some organizations that have just undergone their initial foundings experience inertial forces that make them structurally rigid: "These organizations follow a fixed strategy and do not search or change at any time after founding" (Mezias & Lant, 1994). Second, following the institutional perspective, some organizations may follow a strategy of imitation. These organizations scan for information from their environment, acquiring "information about environments with which they then imitate competitors" (Fombrun, 1988, p. 227). Mezias and Lant (1994) suggested a model in which "there is a non-zero probability mimetic firms will change their core features so as to become more similar to [their] industry leader[s]." We extend Mezias and Lant's (1994) model to include three broad categories of mimetic behaviors that correspond with the three modes of interorganizational imitation studied by Haunschild and Miner (1997).

Neither search nor change is without costs in organizations (Hannan & Freeman, 1984). Following a learning perspective, both organizational search and organizational change become less costly over time with experience. Organizations with experience at a particular type of search process may incur lower costs associated with those activities than organizations without experience. As organizations gain more and more experience with a particular type of organizational search or change, their costs may be a stochastically decreasing function of experience.

Modes of Imitation

Copycats come in many varieties and accomplish this most "sincere form of organizational flattery" in a number of different ways. Organizational imitation is also an institutional process by which firms seek legitimization (DiMaggio & Powell, 1983). Haunschild and Miner (1997) put forth three basic modes of organizational imitation: frequency-based imitation, trait-based imitation, and outcome-base imitation. Frequency-based imitation describes organizations carrying out practices used by a large number of firms; trait-based imitation describes organizations borrowing mannerisms of organizations with particular traits, such as large size or centrality in networks; outcome-based imitation describes imitating the processes that appeared to generate specific successful outcomes in other organizations.

MODES OF IMITATION AND THE TRANSFORMATION OF POPULATONS

There are many ways that modes of imitation could affect the rates and extent of change in organizational populations (Mezias & Lant, 1994). First, modes of imitation might affect how a population approaches its carrying capacity. This involves both the rate at which new forms diffuse, so as to gain the advantages of legitimacy, and how quickly firms recognize increasing competition and leave niches that are becoming overcrowded. Second, there may be relationships between modes of imitation and the costs of search and change. Finally, different modes of interorganizational imitation are likely to affect whether the distribution of forms is likely to change over time, which is related to the endogenous component of environmental change. Especially important in this regard is whether particular modes of interorganizational imitation are likely to lead to more or less frequent change and change that is more or less extreme.

Modes of Imitation and Carrying Capacity

A major concern in the evolution of new forms of organization has been understanding the process by which new and superior forms of organization diffuse. One way of thinking about this problem from an evolutionary perspective is to consider the role of carrying capacity. The question then becomes, How quickly can the diffusion of a new and superior form of organization approach the carrying capacity of the environment? Ecological accounts of the relationship between the number of firms and the survival of firms suggest that there are systematic relationships between mortality, that is, the failure of firms to obtain resources from the environment to ensure survival, and density, or the number of firms in the population. First, at low levels of density, increases in the number of firms are beneficial to survival (Hannan & Carroll, 1992), because they enhance the ability of firms to obtain resources from the environment necessary for survival. In terms of carrying capacity, this is consistent with the claim that the carrying capacity of the environment is enhanced by increases in the numbers of a particular organizational form when numbers are low. For example, when the numbers of a new organizational form, say, a provider of Internet access services, are low, initial increases in organizations of this form increase their legitimacy (Hannan & Carroll, 1992).

Second, at higher levels of density, continuing increases in the number of organizations of a particular form are detrimental to survival. Regardless of the effect on legitimacy of a form because of a continuing increase in its numbers, higher numbers eventually lead to competition for resources. Beyond the point at which competition begins, further increases in the number of organizations of a given form increase the probability of organizational death in the population as a whole. In terms of carrying capacity, this is consistent with the claim that the carrying capacity of the environment is exhausted by the competitive effect of high levels of density. Given this framework, we can explore how different modes of interorganizational imitation might affect the carrying capacity of environments at low and high levels of density.

The question of how modes of interorganizational imitation will affect the diffusion of a new, high-performance organizational form can be answered by exploring the assumptions inherent in the framework for distinguishing among different modes. One characteristic of a form with low density is that its frequency in the population will be quite low; thus, it is hardly controversial to observe that frequency-based imitation will result in slow adoption of an emerging organizational form.

We assume that imitated traits change slowly. If so, it is unlikely that trait-based imitation will result in the rapid diffusion of a new organizational form. Thus, like frequency imitation, trait-based imitation will result in slow diffusion of a new high-performance organizational form. For either trait or frequency imitation, the enhancement of the carrying capacity resulting from increases in density at low levels is likely to be achieved very slowly. By contrast, outcome-based imitation has the potential to diffuse new, high-performance organizational forms much more quickly. To the extent that a new form achieves outcomes that are perceived as worthy of imitation, a mode of interorganizational imitation based on observed outcomes can result in rapid diffusion of an emerging organizational form:

Proposition 1. Outcome-based imitation will result in the most rapid diffusion of new high-performance organizational forms. Trait-based imitation and frequency-based imitation will result in slower diffusion.

The relationship between perceived outcomes and the worthiness of imitating the firm achieving the outcomes is important to proposition 1. By assuming that organizations operate in ecologies of learning characterized by some level of ambiguity, we have imposed the constraint that the relationship between firm characteristics and performance is characterized by some level of noise. Thus, firms with similar characteristics may achieve different levels of performance. Further, the relationship between performance achieved and the characteristics of the firm is not a one-to-one mapping (Lant & Mezias, 1992; Levinthal & March, 1981; Mezias & Glynn, 1993). As long as the signal exceeds the noise in the relationship between firm characteristics and performance, then the first proposition should hold. As the level of ambiguity increases and the quality of the signal about the worthiness of imitating the characteristics given by a firm's performance deteriorates, however, an outcome-based imitation rule is more likely to lead to errors and much less likely to converge rapidly on a single high-performance organizational form (Lant & Mezias, 1990, 1992). In this case, diffusion will be slowed and will most likely result only if a trait-based imitation rule can reveal high-performance types despite the ambiguity. For example, the continued growth of a firm or firms of the new form reveals the signal buried beneath the noise. At that point, a trait-based imitation rule based on size will result in rapid diffusion of the new form. Similarly, the expanding exchange relations of a new high-performance firm might eventually lead to its interorganizational ties becoming so dense that it is imitated because of its centrality.

Proposition 2. Under conditions of high ambiguity, trait-based imitation is more likely than outcome-based imitation or frequency-based imitation to result in the diffusion of a new high-performance organizational form.

The other part of the story of the relationship between modes of interorganizational imitation and the carrying capacity of the organizational environment concerns the ability of firms to avoid the detrimental effects of competition at high levels of density. Firms do not want to adopt forms that are so numerous that the intense competition associated with high levels of density will decrease their ability to obtain needed resources from the environment. It seems clear that at high levels of density, a frequency mode of imitation is unlikely to diffuse an organizational form. Moreover, as numerous organizations adopt a particular form, organizations may have greater difficulty distinguishing themselves in the marketplace. Similarly, since many traits, such as being the largest organization or the most central, normally change fairly slowly, a trait-based imitation rule is not likely to help organizations avoid an overcrowded niche. As with the discovery of a new organizational form, an outcome-based imitation rule is the mode of interorganizational imitation that is most likely to reveal that a niche is becoming overcrowded:

Proposition 3. Outcome-based imitation is more likely than trait-based imitation or frequency-based imitation to result in exit from competitive niches.

Once again, the level of ambiguity will affect the reliability of negative performance as a signal of the need to exit a niche because of increasing competition. At low to moderate levels of ambiguity, we expect the above proposition to hold. As the level of ambiguity increases, the quality of the performance signal deteriorates. At high levels of ambiguity, the ability of an outcome-based imitation rule to signal organizations to exit competitive niches on a timely basis is reduced (Lant & Mezias, 1990, 1992). Under these conditions, an outcome-based imitation rule is more likely to lead to errors. Exit from the niche will be slowed, and exit en masse from a competitive niche may never occur as it does under conditions of low ambiguity. By contrast, high levels of ambiguity may not have the same effect on trait-based imitation rules. For example, size can be considered the result of multiple performance observations that will be less affected by ambiguity than the single observations of an outcome-imitation rule. Similarly, being the most central firm in a population may be relatively unaffected by ambiguity, because as firms form ties with frequent exchange partners regardless of the level of variation in their performance from period to period.

Proposition 4. Under conditions of high ambiguity, trait-based imitation will be more likely than frequency-based imitation or outcome-based imitation to induce exit from competitive niches.

In summary, with respect to the rapid diffusion of a new, high-performance organizational form, frequency-based imitation should always be slow. In general, a frequency-based imitation rule will not result in rapid diffusion of any form until it becomes very frequent in the population. While the precise rate at which frequency-based imitation will take off is not necessarily clear and may vary across populations, it is clear that infrequent forms are not likely to be imitated under such a rule because there are few examples of this organizational form to imitate, so rapid diffusion would not occur. Similarly, with respect to exit from a crowded niche, frequency-based imitation will also be slow because there are too many organizations of the form that is imitated, so timely exit from an overcrowded niche does not occur. For example, the intense competition among manufacturers of personal computers based on the WINTEL operating system is likely to affect those firms that follow a frequency-based imitation rule. With low to moderate levels of ambiguity, the best mode of interorganizational imitation for both the diffusion of new high-performance organizational forms and timely exit from overcrowded niches is by outcome. With very high ambiguity, however, the high level of noise contained in performance signals can lead to many mistakes using an outcome-based mode of interorganizational imitation. At the extreme, the advantages of outcome-based imitation both in quick discovery of high-performance new organizational forms and timely exit from niches that are becoming overcrowded disappear. Diffusion will be slower but, ultimately, is more likely to occur as a result of trait imitation.

Modes of Imitation and the Costs of Search and Change

Haunschild and Miner (1997) hinted at the relationship between imitation and the costs of search and change in their concluding discussion. Comparing their findings with others' on the question of learning after founding, they observed that "factors that increase the cost of organizational change constrain vicarious learning to the time of founding" (p. 497). In other words, under conditions of costly change, the viability of organizational change driven by imitation is reduced. A parallel argument can be made about the costs of search: factors that increase the cost of search constrain the viability of organizational change driven by imitation. This is exactly what Mezias and Lant (1994) found: the survival of firms capable of trait-based imitation was reduced by increases in the costs of search and change. Here, we explore some possible mechanisms by which these liabilities of search (Mezias & Lant, 1994) and change (Hannan & Freeman, 1984) occur by developing propositions concerning modes of interorganizational imitation.

We believe that there are systematic differences in the costs of search according to the mode of interorganizational imitation being used. Typically, evolutionary and ecological models of firms have assumed that the characteristics that distinguish organizational forms are observable; for example, it is quite easy to distinguish a producer of short films from a producer of feature-length films (Mezias & Kuperman, 1998). This implies that frequency search, to discover which organizational forms are most frequent in the population, should not be too costly. In fact, the knowledge required to answer the question of whether there are more companies that produce short films or that produce feature-length films may be widely shared social knowledge. Similarly, we assume that large size and centrality in networks are observable. It may be less likely that precise knowledge of which firms are largest or most central is generally known precisely; however, we assume that the costs of the search required to obtain this information in sufficient detail to guide interorganizational imitation will be low. Once again, this implies that trait-based search, to discover large or central organizations, should not be too costly. Thus, other things being equal, we expect that the cost of search associated with frequency-based imitation will be lowest, and the costs of search associated with trait-based imitation will be relatively low as well.

With respect to outcome-based imitation, the institutionalized ecology of learning model would lead to the opposite argument. First, to discover good outcomes to imitate, the outcomes and organizational forms of a large number of firms will need to be observed. Some of this information may become known as part of the development of general social information; for example, the reputations of firms may be associated with the outcomes they have achieved (Fombrun, 1988). But it still may be costly to get a more complete reading of information on outcomes for various organizational forms. More significantly, the model of institutionalized ecologies of learning suggests that the relationship between organizational forms and performance is characterized by ambiguity. Firms may not accurately reveal, or even know, their true performance; as a result, the monitoring of performance that is the basis of outcome-based imitation will be difficult and prone to error:

Proposition 5. The cost of search associated with outcome-based imitation will be relatively high compared with that associated with frequency-based imitation and trait-based imitation.

With respect to the costs of change, our arguments concerning modes of interorganizational imitation are based on the assumption that the costs of adopting an organizational form decrease with the frequency of that form. In the extreme, an organizational form can become so widespread and well understood that, in the words of Meyer and Rowan (1977, p. 344), its building blocks "come to be littered around the social landscape." As a range of coercive, normative, and mimetic pressures to adopt an organizational form increase with its prevalence (DiMaggio & Powell, 1983), responding to these pressures by adopting the form becomes a managerial imperative. Organizations and professionals will work together to come to common solutions and adopt forms that reduce the costs of compliance with these legalistic imperatives (Edelman & Suchman, 1997). An example is the multidivisional form. University professors will do research and teaching that familiarizes their audiences with the form as it becomes more common. Executives serving on boards become increasingly likely to obtain direct experience in dealing with organizations using this form. Personnel professionals are likely to develop solutions to human resource management problems that arise under this form of organization. Legal professionals are likely to develop common solutions for conforming to legislative, executive, and judicial decrees. Other things being equal, all of these efforts will decrease the cost of changing organizations to adopt the traits of a multidivisional form. The clearest implication of this argument is that the costs of change associated with a frequency-based mode of interorganizational imitation are likely to be low. Similarly, to the extent that the form of central or large firms contributes social information that results in similar cognitive processes in a great variety of institutions at various levels of analysis in an ecology of learning, trait-based imitation will also be associated with fairly low costs of change:

Proposition 6. The costs of implementing change associated with frequency-based and trait-based modes of interorganizational imitation will be relatively low compared with those associated with outcome-based imitation.

By contrast, the assumption that there is ambiguity in the relationship between the traits of firms and their performance implies that an outcome-based mode of interorganizational imitation is unlikely to lead to widespread, long-term adoption of single organizational forms. Early on in the history of the emergence of a new form, outcome-based imitation is likely to lead to first or early movement to a new type, as we proposed in proposition 1. Later, as a form becomes more common and competition begins to reduce the performance of that form, outcome-based imitation is most likely to lead to exit from that form. In both cases, the reduction in the cost of change associated with more frequently observed organizational forms, discussed above, is not likely to have occurred. As a result, the costs of change associated with an outcome-based mode of interorganizational imitation are likely to be high. In addition, as the level of ambiguity increases, the likelihood that an outcome-based model of interorganizational imitation will lead to unnecessary and ill-advised change increases. Thus, the costs of change borne by firms following an outcome-based mode of interorganizational imitation are likely to be even greater as the level of ambiguity increases:

Proposition 7. The costs of implementing change associated with an outcome-based mode of interorganizational imitation are likely to be high and will increase with the level of ambiguity.

Modes of Imitation and Environmental Change

According to open systems theories of organizations the struggle to obtain the resources necessary for survival from the external environment is a key function of organizations (Lawrence & Lorsch, 1967; Thompson, 1967). Ecological and evolutionary theories are based on the assumption that the ability of firms of different forms to obtain resources is mediated by the external environment. This assumption is also shared by the institutionalized ecology of learning model developed by Mezias and Lant (1994), which, in the tradition of most ecological and evolutionary models, treated the external environment as largely exogenous. At the same time, there is strong empirical evidence that the ability to obtain resources is affected by density, which is determined, at least in part, by the decisions of firms to adopt different organizational forms. Thus, at least part of the relationship between firm characteristics and performance will be determined endogenously. Using a model of organizations as learning systems, Mezias and Eisner (1997) explicitly incorporated competition that increased with the number of firms of a given form. The underlying assumption is that the environmental mapping from firm characteristics to performance can be affected by the choices that firms make about forms. Thus, the ability of firms of particular forms to obtain necessary resources from the environment can be seen as having both an endogenous and exogenous component. Our discussion of the relationship between interorganizational imitation and environmental change focuses on how the decisions of individual firms to imitate might affect the ability of firms of particular forms to obtain necessary resources from the environment.

In the discussion of carrying capacity, we have already developed some ideas about the relationship between modes of interorganizational imitation and the discoveries of new high-performance organizational forms and emerging competition. Here, we discuss how the collection of the decisions to change organizational form that results from different modes of interorganizational imitation may affect the frequency and magnitude of endogenous environmental change. The logic generalizes the arguments developed in the context of identifying both new high-performance organizational forms and intensifying competition.

As we have argued, organizations using the frequency-based mode of imitation are slow to discover new organizational forms because there are few of this form to be imitated. Generally, given inertia in organizational type, frequency-based imitation will be unlikely to lead to change in the distribution of forms in the environment. Thus, frequency-based imitation is likely to lead to long periods with little or no change in the distribution of organizational forms in the environment. Change will only occur when there is a large shift in the distribution of organizational forms, which the assumption of inertia implies will be a relatively rare event. But frequency-based imitation driven by population change is also likely to be a threshold event, with episodes of change being rapid and widespread when they do occur. For example, Chandler (1977) can be interpreted as suggesting that the long dominance of the hierarchical form for large firms ended with a relatively rapid shift to the multidivisional form. Similarly, as long as the traits being imitated, such as the largest firm or the most central firm, change fairly slowly, we expect the same result. Trait-based imitation will result in long periods of stability punctuated by short periods of rapid shifts in the distribution of organizational forms in the population:

Proposition 8. Both frequency and trait-based imitation will result in long periods of stability in the distribution of organizational forms, punctuated by short periods of rapid and large-scale change in the distribution of organizational forms.

In contrast, the outcome-based mode of interorganizational imitation, as we have argued, is more likely to lead to the diffusion of new high-performance organizational forms. It is also more likely to lead to the discovery of intensifying competition and the need to exit from a niche that is becoming more crowded. Further, as the level of ambiguity increases, the probability that a firm following an outcome-based mode of imitation will perceive the opportunity to move to a higher-performance organizational form will increase. Thus, we would expect change in the mix of organizational forms in the population to be more frequent under an outcome-based mode of interorganizational imitation. At the same time, because the propensity to herd into crowded niches is tempered by an outcome-based imitation rule, we would not expect the extreme changes under an outcome-based rule that we would observe under a frequency-based or trait-based imitation mode. As firms crowd to adopt an organizational form that has achieved good outcomes, subsequent outcomes for this form will be diminished by competition. As a result, firms following an outcome-based rule in subsequent periods will be less likely to adopt a form of organization that will move them into a crowded niche.

Proposition 9. Outcome-based imitation will result in more frequent change in the mix of organizational forms in the population, but the magnitude of these changes will tend to be more modest than those that occur under frequency-based or trait-based modes of interorganizational imitation.

DISCUSSION AND IMPLICATIONS

We began with an interest in how population-level learning might affect the evolution of organizational populations. To gain closure on this broad question, we turned our attention to modes of interorganizational imitation as mechanisms of population-level learning. Further, by linking our framework with Mezias and Lant's (1994) institutionalized ecology of learning model, we also cast this study in terms of the rapprochement of institutional and selection perspectives (Singh & Lumsden, 1990). From this perspective, the important work to be done involves deepening our understanding of the implications for the evolution of organizations and populations of organizations of the interactions of various imitation strategies and selection pressures. We believe that our propositions offer some preliminary insights into this question. Haunschild and Miner (1997, p. 497), in their empirical study of the roles of imitation, concluded that they had found evidence for "the simultaneous existence of multiple modes of imitation whose strength varies with context. The study underscores imitation's nuanced and potentially complex role in organizational and population-level transformation."

We concur and believe that our study highlights the complex role of a mix of modes of interorganizational imitation in population-level transformation. The propositions put forth in this chapter specifically address several mechanisms by which modes of imitation can affect populations of organizations. These are summarized in Table 1. The mechanisms we discussed were derived from Mezias and Lant's (1994) results, which suggested that the carrying capacity, the costs of search and change, and environmental change are all important variables in understanding the viability of imitative search and change. A brief review of the effects of modes of interorganizational imitation on these variables, as suggested by the propositions, begins to illustrate how complex the effects of imitation might be.

We began with Mezias and Lant's (1994) finding that higher levels of carrying capacity enhanced the survival of imitating firms. Then we interpreted the existing evidence to suggest that the carrying capacity of the environment is enhanced by additional adoptions of a form when its density is low. Based on this, we suggested that the ability of a given imitation mode to lead to additional adoptions of a form when its density is low could affect the survival of imitative firms. It was our claim that outcome-based imitation would be the most likely mode of imitation to lead to increases in density at low levels; thus, outcome-based imitation would enhance the survival of imitative firms. Further, existing evidence can be interpreted to suggest that as density increases, the carrying capacity of the environment is approached, and competition becomes more intense. Mezias and Lant's (1994) results suggest that this will reduce the viability of imitative firms. Once again, we argued that an outcome-based mode of imitation would be most likely to lead organizations to notice the reduced performance resulting from this emerging competition. This mode would be the most likely to lead an

Table 1. Summary of the Effects of Modes of Imitation on Populations of Organizations

	Frequency-based Imitation	*Trait-based Imitation*	*Outcome-based Imitation*
Carrying Capacity	Slower diffusion of new organizational forms	Slower diffusion of new organizational forms	Faster diffusion of new organizational forms
Cost of search	Lower cost	Lower cost	Higher cost
Cost of change	Lower cost	Lower cost	Higher cost
Effects of the probability of environmental change	Lower probability of change	Lower probability of change	Higher probability of change
Effects of the magnitude of environmental change	Larger magnitude of change	Larger magnitude of change	Smaller magnitude of change

organization to discover an alternate form and lead it to exit from a crowded niche. Both frequency-based and trait-based imitation would be much less likely to lead to migration to a new form at low levels of density or to exit from a crowded niche as density increases.

These predictions change at high levels of ambiguity. Our claim was that the ability of the outcome-based mode of imitation to reveal high-performing forms, including new ones, is reduced by ambiguity. As a result, the survival advantage of the outcome-based mode in leading to quick increases in density at low levels and quick recognition and exit from a niche as density and competition increase is reduced. The signal of the viability of a form that is embedded in traits like large size or centrality will be more reliable than the signal conveyed by outcomes.

We next turned our attention to the costs of search and change, which Mezias and Lant (1994) found reduced the viability of imitation. With respect to the cost of search, we argued that the information required for frequency-based or trait-based imitation was likely to result in lower search costs than that required for outcome-based imitation. This cost disadvantage for outcome-based imitation is likely to worsen as the level of ambiguity increases. With respect to the cost of change, we argued that the more common an organizational form, the lower would be the costs to a firm that changed to that form. It follows directly from this that the frequency-based mode would have the lowest costs of change. Similarly, since trait-based imitation is likely to lead to convergence on a form of organization with a particular trait, say, the largest or most central organization, it is likely to lead to convergence on a form. As the frequency of this form increases, the cost to firms of changing to that form decreases. Thus, a trait-based imitation mode would also have relatively low costs of change. By contrast, an outcome-based mode of imitation would be less likely to lead to convergence on single forms. Further, as the level of ambiguity increases, the number of mistakes that firms pursuing an outcome-based mode of imitation would make would also increase.

Thus, we argued that an outcome-based mode of imitation would reduce the viability of imitation by resulting in higher costs of search and change.

With respect to both the frequency and magnitude of environmental change, Mezias and Lant's (1994) results are somewhat more complex. The viability of imitation is enhanced by very frequent change and, to a lesser extent, by very infrequent change. In addition, the viability of imitation is enhanced by a very high magnitude of change and, to a lesser extent, by a very low magnitude of change. In our propositions we argued that all three modes of interorganizational imitation could enhance the viability of imitation by affecting endogenous environmental change, but the mechanisms by which they might do this differ. We argued that both frequency-based and trait-based modes of imitation would lead to infrequent change but a high magnitude of change. In contrast, an outcome-based mode of imitation would lead to more frequent but lower-magnitude environmental change.

We conclude that the mode of imitation that organizations use can have important effects on the shape of an organizational population. Whether organizations use frequency-based, trait-based, or outcome-based imitation can have far-reaching effects. The mode of interorganizational imitation used can affect the diffusion of organizational forms, entry into and exit from competitive niches, the cost of organizational search and change, and the stability of the distribution of organizational forms. Haunschild and Miner (1997, p. 497) interpreted their results to suggest that "organizational learning may be a rather complex process influenced by multiple contingencies." We echo their statement in our most confident conclusion: students of organizations need to understand the powerful interplay between competitive forces and the mode and level of imitation in populations of organizations. Further research that explores the effects on organizational populations of various modes of interorganizational imitation should be one route for developing the understanding of these complex organization and population-level dynamics among both researchers and practitioners.

ACKNOWLEDGMENTS

The authors would like to thank Theresa Lant and participants at a seminar at the Wharton School, University of Pennsylvania, for comments and encouragement. In the grand tradition of such acknowledgements, we hold ourselves responsible for all remaining errors, ramblings, and confusion.

REFERENCES

Carroll, G. R., & Hannan, M. T. (1989). Density delay in the evolution of organizational populations: A model and five empirical tests. *Administrative Science Quarterly, 34*, 411-430.

Chandler, A. D. (1977). *The visible hand: The managerial revolution in American business*. Cambridge, MA: Belknap Press.

Cyert, R. M., & March, J. G. (1963). *A behavioral theory of the firm*. Englewood Cliffs, NJ: Prentice-Hall.

DiMaggio, P. W., & Powell, W. W. (1983). The iron cage revisited: Institutional isomorphism and collective rationality in organizational fields. *American Sociological Review 48*, 147-160.

Edelman, L. B., & Suchman, M. C. (1997). The legal environments of organizations. *Annual Review of Sociology, 23*, 479-515.

Fombrun, C. (1988). Crafting an institutionally informed ecology of organizations. In G. Carroll (Ed.), *Ecological models of organizations*. Cambridge, MA: Ballinger.

Freeman, J., & Hannan, M. (1983). Niche width and the dynamics of organizational populations. *American Journal of Sociology, 88,* 1116-45.

Hannan, M. T., & Carroll, G. (1989). *Dynamics of organizational populations: Density, legitimization, and competition*. New York: Oxford University Press.

Hannan, M. T., & Freeman, J. (1977). The population ecology of organizations. *American Journal of Sociology, 82*, 929-964.

Hannan, M. T., & Freeman, J. (1984). Structural inertia and organizational change. *American Sociological Review, 49*, 149-64.

Hannan, M. T., & Freeman, J. (1987). The ecology of organizational foundings: American labor unions, 1836-1985. *American Journal of Sociology, 92*, 910-943.

Haunschild, P., & Miner, A. (1997). Modes of interorganizational imitation: The effects of outcome salience and uncertainty. *Administrative Science Quarterly, 42*, 472-500.

Lant, T. K., & Mezias, S. J. (1990). Managing discontinuous change: A simulation study of organizational learning and entrepreneurship. *Strategic Management Journal, 11*, 147-179.

Lant, T. K. & Mezias, S. J. (1992). An organizational learning model of convergence and reorientation. *Organization Science, 3*, 47-71.

Lawrence, P. R., & Lorsch, J. W. (1967). *Organization and environment: Managing differentiation and integration*. Boston: Graduate School of Business Administration, Harvard University.

Levinthal, D. A., & March, J. G. (1981). A model of adaptive organizational search. *Journal of Economic Behavior and Organization, 2*, 307-333.

Levitt, B., & March, J. G. (1988). Organizational learning. *Annual Review of Sociology, 14,* 319-340.

March, J. G. (1981). Footnotes to organizational change. *Administrative Science Quarterly, 26*,, 563-578.

March, J. G. (1988). Variable risk preferences and adaptive aspirations. *Journal of Economic Behavior and Organization, 9*, 5-24.

March, J. G., & Olsen, J. P. (1976). *Ambiguity and choice in organizations*. Bergen, Norway: Universitetsforlaget.

March, J. G., & Simon, H. A. (1958). *Organizations*. New York: Wiley.

Meyer, J., & Rowan, B. (1977). Institutionalized organizations: Formal structures as myth and ceremony. *American Journal of Sociology, 83,* 340-63.

Meyer, J., Scott, W., & Deal, T. (1983). Institutional and technical sources of organizational structure: Explaining the structure of educational organizations. Reprinted in J. Meyer & W. Scott (Eds.), *Organizational environments: Ritual and rationality*. Beverly Hills, CA: Sage.

Mezias. S. J. (1988). Aspiration level effects: An empirical investigation. *Journal of Economic Behavior and Organization, 10,* 389-400.

Mezias, S. J., & Eisner, A. B. (1997). Competition, imitation, and innovation: An organizational learning approach. *Advances in Strategic Management, 14*, 261-294.

Mezias, S. J., & Glynn, M. A. (1993). The three faces of corporate renewal: Institution, revolution, and evolution. *Strategic Management Journal, 14*, 77-101.

Mezias, S. J., & Kuperman, J. (forthcoming). The community dynamics of entrepreneurship: The birth of the American film industry, 1895-1929. *The Journal of Business Venturing.*

Mezias, S. J. & Lant, T. K. (1994). Mimetic learning and the evolution of organizational populations. In J. Baum & J. Singh (Eds.), *Evolutionary dynamics of organizations* (pp.179-198). New York: Oxford University Press.

Nelson, R. R., & Winter, S. G. (1982). *An evolutionary theory of economic change*. Boston, MA: Belknap Press.

Payne, J. W., Laughunn, D. J., & Crum, R. (1980). Translation of gambles and aspiration level effects on risky choice behavior. *Management Science, 26,* 1039-1060.

Singh, J. V., House, R. J., & Tucker, D. J. (1986). Organizational change and organizational mortality. *Administrative Science Quarterly, 31,* 587-611.

Singh, J., & Lumsden, C. (1990). Theory and research in organizational ecology. *Annual Review of Sociology, 16,* 161-195.

Singh, J. V., Tucker, D., & House, R. (1986). Organizational legitimacy and the liability of newness. *Administrative Science Quarterly, 31,* 171-193.

Singh, J. V., Tucker, D., & Meinhard, A. (1988). *Are voluntary social service organizations structurally inert?* Paper presented at the Academy of Management, Anaheim, CA.

Thompson, J. D. (1967). *Organizations in action: Social science bases of administrative theory*. New York: McGraw-Hill.

Tucker, D., Singh, J. V., & Meinhard, A., (1990). Organizational form, population dynamics, and institutional change: The founding patterns of voluntary organizations. *Academy of Management Review, Vol #,* 151-178.

Tushman, M. L., & Romanelli, E. (1985). Organizational evolution: A metamorphosis model of convergence and reorientation. In L. L. Cummings & B. M. Staw (Eds.), *Research in organizational behavior* (vol. 7, pp. 171-222). Greenwich, CT: JAI Press.

INTERORGANIZATIONAL PERSONNEL DYNAMICS, POPULATION EVOLUTION, AND POPULATION-LEVEL LEARNING

James B. Wade, Joseph F. Porac, and Monica Yang

ABSTRACT

In this chapter, we develop a model that connects personnel flows with the diffusion of knowledge and population-level learning to illuminate industry evolution. The model takes into account (1) population dynamics, (2) the opportunity structure in an industry, including job vacancies and available venture capital, and (3) executive migration between existing firms and new firms and between the core and periphery of an industry. We use the model to outline how executive migration can influence population learning at different stages of an industry's evolution and in industries with resource partitioning or dominant designs.

Advances in Strategic Management, Volume 16, pages 131-153.

ISBN: 0-7623-0500-2

INTRODUCTION

An emerging literature suggests that one important determinant of organizational evolution is learning among members of an organizational population (Mezias & Lant, 1994; Miner & Robinson, 1994; Miner & Haunschild, 1995). Miner and Haunschild (1995) defined population-level learning as the systematic change in population-level routines that arise from the experiences and interactions of population members. Interactions between organizations are a source of variation in producing new routines, while selection processes determine which routines diffuse throughout the population and are retained (Miner & Haunschild, 1995).

Miner and Haunschild (1995) delineated two types of learning processes that can occur within a population of organizations. First, multiple organizations sometimes learn by observing the experiences of similar others and incorporating practices and procedures that are perceived as successful which Miner and Haunschild (1995) called vicarious learning. This type of interorganizational learning took place in the pharmaceutical industry, where large firms observed start-up biotech firms and copied routines that they deemed successful (Fildes, 1990). Similarly, the diffusion of Japanese management techniques to the U.S. automobile industry occurred as Detroit manufacturers observed the success of Toyota, Honda, and Nissan. These interorganizational transfers of practices are sometimes accomplished through informal channels. The Wagonwheel Bar in Silicon Valley, for example, was not only a place where employees of newly emerging semiconductor firms went for entertainment, it also provided a setting in which they could exchange business information and even hire new personnel (Braun and Macdonald, 1982). In other instances, formal relationships between firms such as consortia, joint ventures, interlocks, and trade associations lead to the diffusion of new routines. Davis (1991) showed, for example, that the "poison pill" strategy for defending against a hostile takeover diffused throughout corporate America partially through director interlocks.

This type of vicarious learning is a function of individual organizations scanning their environments, making assessments about the relative efficacy and feasibility of salient practices in other organizations, and then encoding and incorporating these practices into the fabric of their own processes and structure. But population learning can also occur at a *collective* level. Collective learning cannot be reduced to an aggregation of individual organizational learning but is an emergent outcome of the interactions among many organizations. This is what Miner and Haunschild (1995) have labeled collective population-level learning. Thus, for example, interactions between organizations in trade associations may lead to the emergence of new standards and industry wide strategies toward government regulation. Similarly, interactions between firms can shape the collective identity of a population by generating consensus about the identity of a firm's rivals. Porac and colleagues (1995) found, for instance, that managers of firms in the Scottish knitwear industry have a keen sense of who their rivals are and the important dimensions that define separate "categories" of firms.

In this chapter, we argue that personnel flows among organizations—the movement of managerial personnel *within* an organizational population—are critical to both vicarious and collective population learning. Moreover, the type of learning that occurs, we suggest, is closely linked to the stages in a population's evolution. In the early stages of an industry's development, the most pressing problem facing industry participants is achieving cognitive and sociopolitical legitimacy (Aldrich & Fiol, 1994; Delacroix & Rao, 1994). Consequently, personnel flows that aid or hinder collective learning during this period are critical to the industry's legitimation. For example, many of the founders and expert personnel in the early semiconductor industry came from Bell Labs (Braun & Macdonald, 1982). The common understandings and perspectives shared by these individuals facilitated the emergence of rules of interaction among players in the industry and increased the visibility and acceptability of the industry in the eyes of external constituents. In mature industries, however, vicarious learning is added to the mix because consensus has evolved around how an organization categorizes itself and its rivals. In these instances, personnel flows act primarily as a conduit by which routines diffuse through a population.

The purpose of our chapter is to flesh out how personnel flows within a population influence population evolution and learning. From a review of the existing literatures that have explored the causes and consequences of personnel mobility we develop an integrative model that describes the interplay among population-level events, such as the foundings and exits of firms, the employment opportunity structure in an industry, executive migration patterns, and population learning. We then apply this model to population evolution to suggest how executive migration influences population learning at different stages of an industry's life cycle.

CAUSES AND CONSEQUENCES OF PERSONNEL MOBILITY: AN INTEGRATIVE MODEL

Past Research on the Causes of Personnel Mobility in Organizational Populations

Recent research has begun to uncover the complex processes that causally link organizational foundings and deaths to the mobility of personnel within organizational populations. Carroll, Haveman, and Swaminathan (1992) estimated that organizational foundings and failures were responsible for 25% to 55% of all personnel movements in a typical industry. In support of this view, Haveman and Cohen (1994) accounted for significant job shifts among managers in the California savings and loan (S&L) industry by tracking S&L foundings and failures over time. They suggested that population dynamics influence the employment opportunity structure of an industry by creating vacancy patterns that lead to managerial entries and exits from existing organizations. Organizational failures directly increased interorganizational mobility by creating a pool of unemployed S&L managers who were free to move to other existing S&Ls. At the same time, failures indirectly influenced personnel mobility because personnel exits from the S&L industry increased as the number of job opportunities in the industry contracted. Substantial mobility effects were also found for organizational foundings and mergers. Haveman (1995), for example, showed that foundings and failures within the S&L industry had direct effects on managerial turnover and indirect effects on the average tenure distribution of S&L managers.

Labor economists have proposed that several distinct labor markets have strong effects on personnel mobility and operate simultaneously in modern industrialized societies. In particular, labor segmentation theorists suggest that work experiences and rewards differ significantly between an advantaged "core" and a disadvantaged "periphery" employment sector (Bluestone et al., 1973; Piore, 1980). Segmentation theorists argue that the core industrial sector of the economy, with its primary labor market, is composed of the large and powerful firms of monopoly capitalism. The secondary labor market of the peripheral sector, on the other hand, consists of the many smaller and more intensely competitive firms in the economy.

Impediments to movement between core and peripheral sectors result in stable patterns of labor inequality across the economy. It has generally been argued that mobility from the periphery into the core is limited. Such movement is impeded by the typically poor education of peripheral workers, unstable work histories and unacceptable work behavior learned from secondary-sector employment, racial and sexual discrimination in hiring, union membership rules, and peripheral employees' lack of access to labor market information. Moreover, because internal labor markets and systematic career paths are generally absent in peripheral firms, the upward mobility of workers in that sector is limited. In discussing the peripheral labor market, Bluestone and colleagues (1973, p. 30) concluded that "the working poor are trapped in the peripheral economy," although they acknowledged mobility from the periphery to the core may increase during periods of rapid economic growth and prosperity.

Piore (1980) has proposed that a similar process operates within concentrated industries. An industry becomes concentrated when there are economies of scale and cyclical demand. According to this argument, several large firms in the industry will become the dominant low-cost producers. These dominant firms will develop internal labor markets, career ladders, and employment practices similar to firms in core sectors. Firms in the periphery will offer less job security and inferior career opportunities (Smith, 1983). Again, mobility between the core and the periphery will be quite limited.

In contrast to Piore, Brittain and Wholey (1990) argued that the creation of a core and a periphery within an industry follows Carroll's (1985) logic that high concentration creates opportunities for firms to thrive in specialized peripheral niches. They suggested that high concentration will create opportunities in the periphery, thereby increasing mobility. They expected that mobility would also be high in industries with low concentration because of opportunities for specialist firms. Consistent with their expectations, they found that quit rates have a U-shaped relationship with concentration. Quit rates were highest in industries of high and low concentration, reflecting increased personnel mobility as a result of larger numbers of vacancies in the industry.

At the level of a focal firm, Brittain and Freeman (1986) found that changes in a firm's opportunity structure influenced entrepreneurial activity. Disruptive events such as mergers or outside chief executive officer successions increased the rate at which executives left firms in the semiconductor industry to found new organizations. Romanelli (1989) suggested that the creation of new organizational forms is driven by the opportunity structures within existing industries. She argued that when individuals are blocked from advancement in incumbent organizations and are in a position to see entrepreneurial opportunities, they will leave to found new organizational forms. All of these arguments are consistent with the view that opportunity structures have powerful effects on personnel flows.

Past Research on the Consequences of Personnel Mobility

Much organizational theory assumes that the transfer of managerial personnel across and within organizations plays an important role in affecting the mix of routines in organizational populations. Resource dependence theorists have argued that interorganizational mobility is an important organizational mechanism for coopting external constituencies who can contribute key organizational resources (Pfeffer & Salancik, 1978). In the aggregate, such mobility improves interorganizational communication and stabilizes the relationships among firms (e.g., Pfeffer & Leblebici, 1973). Organizational evolutionists (e.g., McKelvey, 1982) have suggested that the migration of managerial talent across organizations disseminates key organizational competencies in a population. This, in turn, influences the aggregate distribution of organizational characteristics in the population and thus the relative survival chances of population members. Moreover, entrepreneurs who found new organizations acquire the requisite skills and competencies from working in other organizations in the same population (Brittain & Freeman, 1986).

Researchers studying organizational innovation and knowledge creation have argued that the transfer of managerial and technical personnel across firms is an important source of knowledge diffusion and industry innovation (e.g., Leonard-Barton, 1995). Among other dynamics, the diffusion of ideas and skills creates communities of practice that cut across organizational boundaries and shape the technological trajectories driving innovative activity (e.g., Dosi & Orsenigo, 1988). It also is one mechanism for the diffusion of legitimated myths about proper organizing routines (e.g., Meyer & Rowan, 1977).

Despite the important role in organizational theory often attributed to managerial mobility across firms, there is surprisingly little published research directly linking personnel flows to population-level processes. One early paper by Baty, Evan, and Rothermel (1971) showed that the movement of faculty across universities facilitated the flow of information and new ideas. Kraatz and Moore (1998), who also studied educational organizations, showed that one driver of the diffusion of professional programs in liberal arts colleges was the mobility of college presidents. In studying industrial firms, Pfeffer and Leblebici (1973) observed that managerial mobility within 20 different industries was positively related to industry growth and productivity improvements. Boeker (1997) found that firms were more likely to enter the product markets of other firms from which their managers had recently migrated. One explanation for this finding is that management decided to enter a new market and then recruited appropriate personnel. In this case, environmental conditions that are common across firms in a population may lead managers to recruit similar personnel which, in turn, leads to systematic changes in population-level routines. All of these results are consistent with the argument that interorganizational mobility has a significant impact on the distribution of routines in individual organizations and populations.

An Integrative Model

Although the above studies on the causes and consequences of employee mobility are limited in number and scope, they are sufficient to suggest an underlying causal ordering linking industry-level dynamics with interorganizational personnel mobility. This dynamic can be depicted as shown in Figure 1. Population-level dynamics, such as organizational foundings, failures, and changes in industry concentration, influence the opportunity structure of managers within a population by expanding or contracting the resource base of member firms. Vacancies open and close according to these population-level processes. In addition to vacancies in existing organizations, resource availability affects access to new venture capital, thus controlling the opportunity for individuals to strike out on their own to build new firms in the industry. Together, these differential opportunities encourage managers, through displacement, recruitment, and entrepreneurship to leave their existing firms and migrate to others. In turn, the resultant mobility patterns affect the diffusion of knowledge in an industry and, hence, population-level learning. In the remainder of this chapter we use this causal dynamic to delineate how personnel flows influence, and are influenced by, industry emergence and maturation.

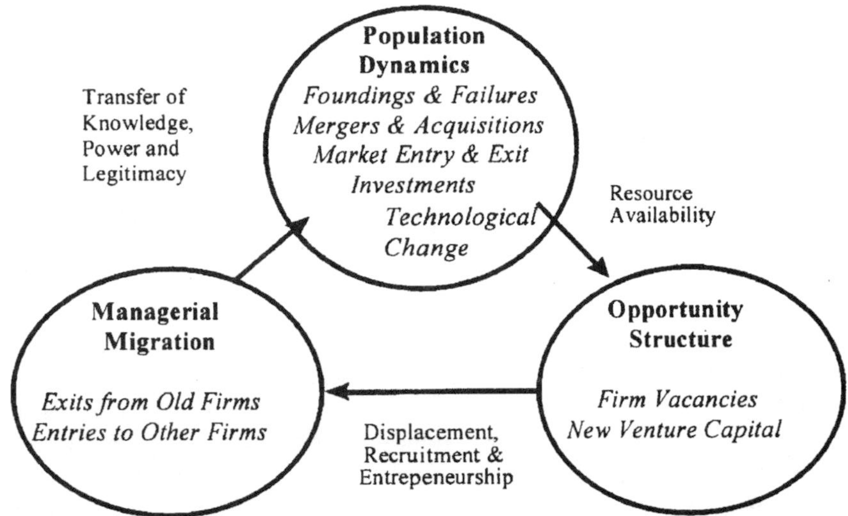

Figure 1. Effects of Personnel Flows on Population Evolution

PERSONNEL MOBILITY AND INDUSTRY EMERGENCE AND GROWTH

Scholars theorizing about industry creation assert that industry entry and exit patterns are the result of competition and industry consolidation (e.g., Delacroix, Swaminathan & Solt, 1989). Entrepreneurship is often viewed as the process of seizing opportunities through combinations of productive inputs (Dean & Meyer, 1996). The greater the changes occurring in an industry, the greater the opportunities created. The more available the market opportunities in an industry, the greater is the potential for entrepreneurial activity and new venture formations.

Romanelli (1989) argued that new organizational forms emerge in response to market changes and new social needs. She further suggested that entrepreneurs who start firms in emerging industries tend to originate from populations that already address those needs. For instance, she noted that prior research has shown that when women's medical societies were first founded, there was a high density of medical societies that, for the most part, did not allow women to be members (Marrett, 1980). Founders of these new societies generally had strong ties to the existing medical community (Marrett, 1980). Similarly, Abernathy (1978) suggested that even though railroad firms had expertise in engine technologies, bicycle manufacturers were the first to enter the automotive industry because of their expertise in providing personal transportation. In each case, changes in market needs or the emergence of new technologies provided opportunities to individuals and firms in related industries (Romanelli, 1989, 1991).

While not all entrepreneurs who enter a new industry will have experience in related industries, the degree to which a firm's executives have ties to a related industry is likely to have a strong influence on its survival chances. Carroll, Bigelow, Seidel, and Tsai (1996), for example, found that carriage and bicycle manufacturers diversifying into the automobile industry had lower failure rates than firms entering the market from other industries. They speculated that the technological spillovers from these industries led to these advantages. Auto manufacturers had higher chances of survival to the extent that a firm's executives had transferable skills and experience.

Overall, the research discussed above suggests that founders in emerging populations will tend to migrate from industries that fulfill related needs. To the extent that a founder of a focal firm migrates from such an industry, a firm's survival chances are enhanced. To the extent that founders have similar cognitive models of how to organize and have similar types of expertise, the rate at which an industry attains legitimacy and grows is likely to increase as well. Common cognitive models will increase the transfer of information across firms, facilitating population-level learning. These common cognitive models could result if a large proportion of founders tend to migrate from a common source and have similar backgrounds and expertise.

This process of migration explains an interesting empirical finding. In examining the early evolution of the United States brewing industry, Carroll and Swaminathan found that German immigration had a positive effect on the founding rate of breweries and a negative impact on mortality.[1] This effect may be related to the fact that during this period many entrepreneurs who started breweries in America had acquired brewing experience and expertise in Germany, a country well known for its high-quality beer (Baron, 1962). Because of poor economic conditions in Germany, there was a large influx of Germans into the United States during the 1840s and 1850s.

Like other immigrants, Germans experienced social discrimination and formed groups of closely knit enclave communities to steel themselves against social ostracism and isolation. These enclaves produced tight social networks that supported their entrepreneurial activity and, in turn, enhanced the brewing industry's viability. This argument is consistent with the idea that the embedded relationships that make up enclave communities encourage and support economic activity (Coleman, 1988; Granovetter, 1985; Portes & Sensenbrenner, 1993). Baron (1962) referred to this period as the German "engulfment" of the American brewing industry, and by the 1860s, German-style lager beer dominated the American marketplace.

The background of founders also seems to be tied to the emergence of collective action in a new industry. In the early stages of industry evolution, interactions between firms are often cooperative rather than competitive (Hannan & Carroll,

1992; Carroll, 1997; Swaminathan & Wade, 1999). Founders attempt to mobilize resources through collective action such as the formation of trade associations and mutual benefit societies. To the extent that founders share common cognitive models and have overlapping social and professional networks, collective action structures such as industry associations emerge more quickly. For instance, the United States Brewing Association was established in 1862 by brewers of German descent. Until 1875, the proceedings of the annual meetings were conducted exclusively in German. Similarly, Swaminathan and Wade (1999) speculated that because many entrepreneurs who started brewpubs in the 1980s were involved in home brewing clubs, common understandings were developed that facilitated future collective action. In our view, such a process would be emergent and would lead to collective population-level learning.

Thus, the degree to which early founders share common cognitive models and can mobilize collectively may have a critical impact on the viability of a new population. It is unlikely, for instance, that German immigration would have had the same effect on the development of the brewing industry had it occurred after the industry matured. Such an argument is consistent with Arthur's (1989) notion that initial conditions can have powerful effects on a system's evolution. In broad terms, the history of the American brewing industry is consistent with our general model in that a detrimental change in the opportunity structure in Germany spurred entrepreneurial activity in America, which, in turn, led to a transfer of knowledge and expertise into the American brewing industry.

Another key factor that will affect the rate of legitimation and growth of a new population is the reputational capital of the initial founders. Delacroix and Rao (1994) suggested that the legitimation process generates externalities because early founders bear more of the costs in legitimating the organizational form. If the initial founders inspire confidence in the capital market and in other potential investors, however, they will favorably alter the opportunity structure in the nascent industry. As a result, a bandwagon effect will induce other potential founders to enter the industry and thereby increase the rate at which the population grows. Burton, Sorensen, and Beckman (1998) found that the reputation and ability of Silicon Valley entrepreneurs to attract start-up capital is significantly related to the prestige and reputation of an entrepreneur's prior employing firm. Some established Silicon Valley companies are known as entrepreneurial "hotbeds" because numerous company executives have left such firms over the years and have founded successful new ventures. The benefits that accrue from having been previously employed by highly reputable firms convey significant survival advantages for newly emerging industries that are characterized by tight networks and dense local interactions in which reputational capital can be easily monitored, evaluated, and diffused. But the timing of such personnel flows is critical. Injections of personnel from external sources and from entrepreneurial hotbeds are likely to have the greatest impact in the early stages of a population's development.

PERSONNEL MOBILITY IN MATURING INDUSTRIES

Establishment of a Core and a Periphery

Over time, organizations within a population tend to develop stable recruitment patterns and career paths. DiMaggio and Powell (1983) suggested that one factor leading to the homogenization of an interorganizational field is the creation of common job titles that are well understood and which facilitate personnel flows between organizations. Stable personnel flows will lead to common belief systems and serve as conduits for reinforcing common norms within a population. Such a pattern predominates in the academic market where research-oriented schools almost exclusively recruit from each other. Moreover, these universities have the common career titles of assistant, associate, and full professor.

Often there is differentiation within an organizational field between central and peripheral organizations. In organizational fields that have a large professional workforce, and where outputs are hard to measure, status will determine which organizations are most central (DiMaggio & Powell, 1983). In other, more competitive settings, such differentiation may be a function of other salient dimensions, such as size or performance. In either case, consensus evolves around how an organization categorizes itself and its rivals (Porac, Thomas, & Baden-Fuller, 1989). While there will often be multiple categories in a field, organizations will not tend to have a detailed knowledge of all "types" because of limited attention and cognitive limitations (Porac & Rosa, 1996). At the same time, however, organizations will have a detailed knowledge of their own local "type" and of the dominant organizations in the field. Porac and colleagues (1995), for instance, found that both small and large organizations in the Scottish knitware industry perceived large organizations as their rivals.

In general, common norms and beliefs are intensely developed among the elite organizations and then diffused to the remainder of the organizational field. This type of process is consistent with what Haunschild and Miner (1997) have referred to as trait learning. This type of interorganizational learning occurs when practices adopted by firms with certain characteristics tend to diffuse through the population (Haunschild & Miner, 1997). One mechanism that can support the transference of elite values and norms from elite to peripheral organizations is personnel flows. The flow of personnel from the center to the periphery promotes the homogenization of an organizational field through incremental change as peripheral firms adopt the practices of core members of the field (DiMaggio & Powell, 1983). In turn, personnel flows among firms in the center support the development of common values and beliefs.

Such a view is only partially consistent with the literature on dual labor markets within and between industries. Labor economists would likely agree that there is mobility within each sector and that mobility from the periphery to the core is restricted because workers in the periphery generally have lower education, training, and applicable job skills (Bluestone et al., 1973). In contrast to our arguments, however, they contend that workers in the core will be unlikely to migrate to the periphery because the jobs there will generally offer less job security and opportunities for advancement (Smith, 1983). Even if firms in the periphery offer favorable employment contracts, they are unlikely to be able to match those offered to the top performers in the core firms. Because core firms have better developed career ladders and superior opportunities for advancement than peripheral firms (Smith, 1983), it is quite likely that they will be able to retain their top performers.

Managers in core firms that are blocked from advancement often, however, may find viable opportunities in peripheral firms. Lazear and Rosen (1981) suggested, for instance, that a series of rank-order tournaments determine advancement in organizations. Prizes in the form of increased compensation and promotions are awarded to winners of a tournament. These survivors compete in subsequent tournaments in which the value of the prize sharply increases at higher levels in the organization. While empirical research has generally supported tournament theory (Bull et al., 1987; Main, O'Reilly & Wade, 1993), little research has examined how individuals who are denied "prizes" remain motivated. Main and colleagues (1993) suggested that while tournaments do operate, they are more akin to a relay race in which winners are given incremental raises and promotions, but the losers still have the opportunity to compete in future tournaments and potentially leapfrog over earlier winners. It is possible, however, that the opportunity structures in peripheral firms will attract many of these individuals, particularly those who lose in multiple tournaments.

Of course, this argument suggests that workers leaving core firms either of their own volition or through layoffs will tend to be "lemons." Consistent with this view, Gibbons and Katz (1991) showed empirically that workers who were laid off had longer spells of unemployment and received lower wages in their subsequent job than those who were displaced because of a plant closing. Presumably, future employers can infer that laid-off workers are of low quality but can make no such inference about workers displaced because of plant closures. This begs the question, however, of why peripheral firms offer displaced personnel favorable employment packages and high-level positions if such personnel tend to be lemons.

The answer may lie in the signaling effect embedded in the reputation of the core firms. Because core firms serve as high-status models for peripheral players in the industry (DiMaggio & Powell, 1983), peripheral organizations are likely to believe that such recruitment would result in a transfer of prestige and legitimacy. For instance, when the first author worked at a peripheral company that was in a specialized market segment of the oil industry, it was considered a coup to attract an executive from the dominant firm in this industry segment. The general consensus in the firm was that such a person would introduce practices that would increase the firm's performance and ultimately its status. Not surprisingly, the performance of these recruits was less than stellar, particularly those who were recruited following a layoff.

Such a process also clearly occurs in the academic market. A small number of top research universities are the dominant institutions, while universities that focus more on teaching than research form the periphery. As would be expected, mobility from the periphery to the core is quite limited. Mobility from the core to the periphery is much more common and consists to a large degree of people who could not satisfy the research demands of the top universities.

If this type of adverse selection process occurs in industries, it raises the possibility that peripheral firms that recruit from the core may be actually lowering their survival chances. The poor position of the peripheral firms could be exacerbated if the low-quality managers recruited from core firms are placed in high positions because of the status accruing to them from their prior work experience. We are not claiming that such personnel flows will always be undesirable for peripheral firms because all personnel that migrate from core firms might not be "lemons." In many cases, such people may simply be a poor fit with the bureaucratic structure of the large dominant firms. As we note below, such migration can promote variation in the periphery.

While these patterns of personnel flows promote stability and homogeneity, particularly within the core firms, there is variation and experimentation at the periphery (Leblebici, Salancik, Copay, & King, 1991; Kraatz & Moore, 1998). Sources of variation include inexact copying of elite practices and experimentation which are quite likely if personnel flowing from the core to the periphery were not model members of their previous firms. Experimentation is also more common at the periphery because these firms inhabit inferior portions of the resource space (Carroll, 1985). As a result, search processes are more common, as firms experiment with new routines in the hope of improving their position (March, 1981, 1988).

Institutional change is triggered by intense competition or by environmental shocks that detrimentally affect the industry. Search processes are then triggered among the central players as they search for new routines (Leblebici et al., 1991). Because there is greater variability in routines at the periphery, those routines are likely to be a target of this search. Consistent with our general model, resource scarcity alters the opportunity structure in the industry. As a result, there should be a reversal in the flow of personnel, as executives move from the periphery to the center.

Mechanisms that promote this flow of personnel from the periphery to the core include the recruitment of personnel from the periphery and acquisitions of peripheral firms by the dominant players. In turn, these flows increase the probability of institutional change. While very few studies have explored this process, a notable exception is provided by Kraatz and Moore (1998) who found that the adoption of professional programs by liberal arts colleges (an illegitimate change) increased if a college recruited a president from a peripheral member of the field that had already adopted such a program. Similarly, they found that adoption was more likely when the college's performance was poor. In contrast, Kraatz and Moore (1998) found that the most prestigious liberal arts universities did not recruit from the periphery and rarely adopted professional programs, even when economic conditions indicated that it would be a viable alternative. Kraatz and Moore reasoned that the adoption of professional programs by these institutions would be perceived as illegitimate given their dominant position in the organizational field.

Industry Shakeout

The population dynamic that will be most apparent in the competition stage of the density dependence model is organizational failure. Some researchers have suggested that organizations may learn from observing failures in a population (Delacroix & Rao, 1994; Ingram & Baum, 1997; Kim & Miner, 1998; Miner et al., 1996). If failures are viewed as failed experiments, surviving members of a population may systematically change their routines to avoid a similar fate (Miner et al., this volume). Patterns of personnel flows can impede or facilitate a population's ability to learn from failure. Knowledge of failure is useful because it allows organizations to understand and respond to a significant threat (Sitkin, 1992).

When firms fail in a population, the direct effect is that personnel from the failed firms either leave the industry or fill vacancies in existing firms (Haveman & Cohen, 1994). In general, migrating executives bring with them the knowledge that they gained in their previous position (Baty et al., 1971; Boeker, 1997). Several factors determine the degree of impact that managers from failed firms have on population-level learning. One factor is the proportion of employees from failed firms who find other jobs in the industry relative to the number who exit. The lessons learned will be more salient to surviving firms if the personnel that experienced the failures are diffused throughout the industry.

The characteristics of the failed firms and of the firms that are the targets of employee migration will also be important. To the extent that selection processes operate systematically, and numerous firms with similar sets of routines fail, the potential for population-level learning is enhanced. For instance, if many of the failing firms have a similar set of routines that are not well suited to the environment, a large number of managers with similar knowledge and competencies will migrate throughout the remaining firms in the population. Failures might have an additional impact if a large proportion of the personnel from failed firms migrate to very visible firms. Because practices adopted by firms with salient characteristics tend to diffuse through a population (Haunschild & Miner, 1997), we anticipate that changes in routines implemented by these types of firms as a result of learning from failure will be imitated by other firms.

Overall, increased competition and the resultant failures in an industry should serve to fill any vacancies in the surviving organizations, thereby transferring knowledge that facilitates learning. This depends, of course, on the number of vacancies available. But, there are many other possible outcomes to intense competition. For example, in a highly competitive industry, executive migration may be driven by multiple processes, including foundings, failures, mergers, and recruitment. In such an environment, where executive migration is high, knowledge will be readily transferred throughout the industry. This process could generate a Red Queen effect, in that while an individual firm might increase its competitiveness, it will not retain any lasting competitive advantage because other firms have also become more competitive (Barnett and Hansen, 1996).[2] Beyond competition, however, are other industry conditions, including resource partitioning and the emergence of a dominant design, both of which can have profound effects on personnel flows and population-level learning.

RESOURCE PARTITIONING AND THE EMERGENCE OF DOMINANT DESIGNS

We suggested above that peripheral firms would initially recruit from the central firms. Moreover, we argued that in times of difficulty, this pattern would reverse as central firms recruited from the periphery. There are many cases, however, particularly in competitive markets, in which the opportunity structure will lead to a different outcome. For instance, if the opportunity structure were such that there were many profitable entrepreneurial opportunities at the periphery, dominant firms might not be able to recruit successfully from the periphery and peripheral firms may be able to attract the core firms' most valuable members. These processes should play out differently in environments with sharply different opportunity structures. Such situations arise in highly concentrated industries following the emergence of a dominant design.

Resource Partitioning in Concentrated Industries

Carroll (1985) suggested that when a market is crowded early on, participants vie for the widest possible resource base. Later, with increasing concentration and the resultant scale economies, the surviving generalists move to the center of the market. This, in turn, opens pockets of resources at the periphery where specialists can thrive. In support of his model, Carroll (1985) found that as concentration increased in a local newspaper market, the survival chances of specialist newspapers increased. Similarly, Carroll and Swaminathan (1992) found that the entry rate of specialist breweries increased with concentration. Although Brittain and Wholey (1990) did not track the destinations of employees who quit, their result showing that the quit rate is high in concentrated industries is also consistent with the idea that high concentration creates entrepreneurial opportunities.

The pockets of resources that emerge in a concentrated market change the opportunity structure in the industry. Entrepreneurial opportunities increase as investors make capital available for new start-ups. In turn, the founding of specialist organizations has direct and indirect effects on vacancy chains (Haveman & Cohen, 1994). Foundings have direct effects on vacancy chains in the population, as founders and many of their employees migrate from the large generalists in the industry to fill vacancies in the newly founded specialist organizations. Indirect effects also emerge, as vacancies created in the large generalist organizations are filled.

The characteristics of the personnel that create vacancies by leaving the generalists and the process by which these vacancies are filled have an important impact on population evolution. One perspective that sheds light on this process is Burt's social structural theory of competition. Burt (1992) proposed that structural holes, or nonredundant networks, provide information and resource advantages. For example, firms in industries in which firms' transaction networks are rich with structural holes are in a position to negotiate more favorable prices with customers and suppliers. As a result, these industries enjoy greater economic returns. Similarly, at the individual level, Burt (1992, 1997) found that managers surrounded by structural holes had greater entrepreneurial opportunities, which, in turn, led to greater power.

While Burt (1992) considered only the structural holes in personnel networks at the intrafirm level, patterns of interfirm personnel mobility also create networks in which an individual's access to structural holes can lead to a competitive advantage. Executives who move to different companies create an information network effectively linking them to their former employers. These executives bring with them the knowledge, competencies, and contacts acquired at their previous positions. Because of information advantages, executives who have networks rich in structural holes will be able to identify entrepreneurial opportunities. As a result, these individuals are most likely to leave and found or join specialist organizations under conditions of high concentration.

From the viewpoint of the large generalists, an adverse selection process constituting a brain drain is operating because generalists lose their most valuable personnel. Campbell (1994) argued that a similar process operated during the 1980s, when scientific personnel migrated in large numbers to regions in which the defense industry was concentrated. Because workers who eventually left the defense industry tended to stay in the defense industry regions, this migration had an important long-term impact on the areas from which the personnel migrated (Campbell, 1994). In concentrated environments, the opportunity structure may lead to a flow of talent away from the large generalists.

Another factor that favors specialist organizations in mature concentrated industries is that large generalists are likely to have formalized career ladders. Miner (1990) argued that formalized jobs are drivers of consistency in organizations. Thus, when individuals leave, consistency remains, as vacancies in existing job ladders are filled. In contrast, the creation of unplanned job positions (idiosyncratic jobs) will be very common in the new specialist organizations. Because idiosyncratic jobs are designed around an individual they are a source of unplanned variation that may lead to the evolution of new routines.

Ultimately, specialist populations that are successful are likely to be perceived by the dominant players as a competitive threat. According to our earlier model, this should lead the dominant players to recruit from the periphery (e.g., the specialists). Luring personnel from newly emerging specialist populations will be quite difficult, however, because of the nature of the opportunity structure. Moving from an idiosyncratic job that is customized to the individual to a bureaucratized career ladder is likely to be unattractive to employees in specialist organizations. Moreover, if venture capital is available to specialists, it will be even more difficult for generalists to recruit from the specialist populations.

Another option for the large generalists is to take over some of the small specialist producers to benefit from their expertise. Brittain and Freeman's (1986) findings from the semiconductor industry suggest, however, that this strategy may be futile, because mergers in the semiconductor industry increased the rate at which employees left to found new firms. In summary, the superior opportunity structure in the periphery that is sometimes present in concentrated environments may make it difficult for the dominant players to respond adequately to personnel drains.

Alternatively, Romanelli (1989) suggested that founders of specialist firms will primarily migrate from smaller firms or from those that have failed. Moreover, she argued that the prior experience of these entrepreneurs will be with tasks that were not central to the generalists' activities. In contrast to our arguments, she reasoned that core firms will be able to retain key individuals because they will still have good opportunities for advancement. In addition, institutionalized understandings about what are appropriate competitive practices may induce central members of a dominant firm to remain with the company.

These competing predictions can be partially reconciled. In supporting her view that individuals in important but noncentral tasks leave to found new specialist firms, Romanelli (1989) noted that Jim Treybig, who founded Tandem computers, was formerly a marketing manager at Hewlett Packard. While the position of marketing director is clearly an important task, a key factor may be that such a position is a boundary spanning activity in which one's skills are easily transferable across firms. It is precisely this type of person whose network is likely to be rich in structural holes.

Emergence of a Dominant Design

Dynamics similar to those in resource partitioning may explain the vulnerability of mature industries to the introduction of competence destroying discontinuities. Swaminathan (1995) suggested that there is a similarity between the dominant-design model and resource partitioning in that both suggest a cyclical process. High concentration results in a trend toward standardized high-volume production. Another trend towards specialization and differentiation arises simultaneously, however, as specialist firms emerge to take advantage of opportunities on the periphery.

Similarly, Tushman and Anderson (1986) proposed that the emergence of a dominant design leads to a period of incremental innovation that is abruptly followed by a technological discontinuity. In examining multiple industries, they found that competence-destroying discontinuities were introduced by new entrants. In resource partitioning, the emergence of a dominant organizational form sets the stage for a discontinuity in the market, as a new specialist population emerges (Swaminathan, 1995).

The pattern of personnel flows in technological communities with dominant designs will be similar to those in concentrated environments. After the emergence of the dominant design, career paths will tend to become standardized and increasingly bureaucratic. When a new technology emerges, however, career paths are likely to be more fluid and jobs more idiosyncratic. Again, this process makes it difficult for the dominant players to recruit personnel with the requisite knowledge from outside. In the early electronics industry, for instance, Raytheon and General Electric, two major vacuum tube producers, recruited large numbers of semiconductor experts in an attempt to compete in the emerging semiconductor industry. They had little success, however, and as one executive remarked, "For about a year, we had a going away party every Friday" (Braun & Macdonald, 1982, p. 65). Many of these semiconductor experts left because of the rigid hierarchy of the dominant firms and the bureaucratic decision-making process (Braun & Macdonald, 1982).

If increasing returns are present, the degree to which members of a dominant community are able to recruit from the periphery will be further reduced. Increasing returns associated with network externalities occur when the utility that a user derives from a good increases with the number of other adopters (Katz & Shapiro, 1985). Supporters of the design also invest in a variety of supporting and compatible products. Because of the costs, both to themselves and to customers, of switching technologies, firms sponsoring dominant designs will be unwilling to consider alternatives and may be vulnerable to new technological approaches developed by specialists (Wade, 1996). Hires of personnel not affiliated with the dominant standard may also be rare, further contributing to strategic myopia on the part of the dominant community. Thus, the opportunity structure generated by the emergence of a dominant design and its impact on the pattern of personnel flows may play a role in setting the stage for the next discontinuity.

IMPLICATIONS FOR FUTURE RESEARCH

Our discussion of the relationship between personnel flows and population evolution and population-level learning has several practical implications. From a strategic perspective, our arguments have implications for investors in emerging industries because they suggest that the backgrounds and cognitive models of entrepreneurs will play a large part in whether a new organizational form survives or fails. Moreover, by paying close attention to initial conditions in an emerging industry, investors may be able to predict early on whether investing would be advisable. Similarly, by examining the backgrounds of early entrants in an emerging industry, potential entrepreneurs may be able to better assess the risks of entering the industry. An interesting avenue for future empirical research would be to examine demographic similarities between founders and the timing of personnel flows to determine their relationship to the emergence of collective population-level learning and population growth.

One strategic implication of the movement of personnel between the core and the periphery of an industry is that firms in an industry must pay close attention to the opportunity structures that population dynamics create. For instance, if there is an environmental shock that causes the core firms in the industry to lay off workers, peripheral firms must carefully evaluate their worker's quality in light of the adverse selection processes that may be operating. In addition, high-status members of an industry should promote at least some migration from the periphery so that they can stay abreast of important changes in the environment and of innovative practices that emerge in the periphery. Future research should examine whether dominant industry members' neglect of variants available in the periphery persists even in the face of massive environmental change. If it does, such a process may ultimately lead to an industry restructuring in which dominant firms are replaced by more peripheral members of the industry.

Our discussion of networks and social capital also provides promising areas for future research. First, given Campbell's (1994) finding that executive migration had long-term effects, investigating the personnel networks within a high concentration industry and how they affect the founding and growth of specialist organizations would be a fruitful area for research. Second, future research might examine how population dynamics affect personnel flows into existing formalized jobs versus idiosyncratic jobs. Exploring shifts in social capital through personnel mobility under these conditions might be useful in predicting the relative success of new specialist populations. Finally, empirical research is needed to clarify how job experience and personnel networks interact in generating entrepreneurial activity in concentrated environments. All of these research areas have the potential to tell us more about how the movement of personnel affects interorganizational and collective population-level learning as industries evolve.

CONCLUSION

Currently, most population-level research ignores the role of personnel flows in shaping population evolution. In this chapter, we argued that attention to migration patterns is critical if we are to gain a fuller understanding of a wide range of organizational phenomena, including institutional change, resource partitioning, technology cycles, and processes of legitimation and competition. Our general model linking population dynamics and the opportunity structure of an industry with managerial migration should be a useful framework for investigating these issues.

In examining institutional change, we argued that population dynamics such as intense competition and environmental shocks affect the opportunity structure in the industry such that the probability of institutional change increases. More specifically, we suggested that in the face of economic adversity, central firms recruit from the periphery in the hope of improving their situation. Such recruitment patterns may play a role in radically transforming an industry.

Importantly, however, our discussion of resource partitioning and of the industry dynamics following the emergence of a dominant design suggests that under some circumstances patterns of personnel flows may result in the replacement of the core by the periphery. Thus, for example, if one considers the early electronics industry, dominant firms such as Raytheon were forced to the periphery by the emerging semiconductor industry. A key driver of this process was the dominant firms' inability to attract and retain key semiconductor experts. Consistent with our model, the cause of this problem was the entrepreneurial opportunities that were present in the market. Potentially, attention to population dynamics, the opportunity structure of an industry, and their impact on personnel flows can link these theories into an integrative framework and help establish the boundary conditions that determine which approach is appropriate.

Attention to this framework can also inform future work in organizational ecology. While research in this area has linked population dynamics to personnel flows and has shown that executive mobility can lead to knowledge transfer, our arguments suggest that personnel flows can ultimately affect the path of population evolution. For all of these reasons, we feel that by "bringing the people back in," future research has the potential to greatly enrich our understanding of population learning and evolution.

ACKNOWLEDGMENTS

We would like to thank Matthew Kraatz, Craig Olson, and the participants at the Carnegie Mellon and University of Wisconsin conference on knowledge transfer and levels of learning for their thoughtful comments.

NOTES

1. Personal communication with Anand Swaminathan.

2. Van Valen (1973) used the analogy of the Red Queen in linking this idea to evolution, referring to Lewis Carroll's *Through the Looking Glass*, in which Alice observes that although she is running, she is not going anywhere. The Red Queen answers that Alice must be from a slow world, because in a fast world, one must keep running simply to stay in the same place.

REFERENCES

Abernathy, W. J. (1978). *The productivity dilemma.* Baltimore, MD: Johns Hopkins University Press.

Aldrich, H.E., & Fiol, M. (1994). Fools rush in? The institutional context of industry creation. *Academy of Management Review, 19*, 645-670.

Arthur, W.B. (1989). Competing technologies, increasing returns, and lock-in by historical events. *Economic Journal, 99*, 116-131.

Barnett, W.P., & Hansen, M.T. (1996). The red queen in organizational evolution. *Strategic Management Journal, 17*, 139-157.

Baron, S. (1962). *Brewed in America.* Boston, MA: Little, Brown and Company.

Baty, G. B., Evan, W.M., & Rothermel, T.W. (1971). Personnel flows as interorganizational relations. *Administrative Science Quarterly, 16*, 430-443.

Bluestone, B., Murphy, W.M., & Stevenson, M. (1973). *Low wages and the working poor*. Ann Arbor: Institute of Labor and Industrial Relations, University of Michigan.

Boeker, W. (1997). Executive migration and strategic change: The effect of top manager movement on new product entry. *Administrative Science Quarterly, 42*, 213-236.

Braun, E., & Macdonald, S. (1982). *Revolution in miniature: The history and impact of semiconductor electronics.* Cambridge: Cambridge University Press.

Brittain, J. W., & Freeman, J. (1986). Entrepreneurship in the semiconductor industry. Paper presented at the Academy of Management Meetings, New Orleans.

Brittain, J. W., & Wholey, D. (1990). Structure as an environmental property: Industry demographics and labor market practices. In R. Breiger (Ed.), *Social mobility and social structure* (pp. 155-182). Cambridge: Cambridge University Press.

Bull, C., Schotter, A., & Weigelt K. (1987). Tournaments and piece rates: An experimental study. *Journal of Political Economy, 95*, 1-33.

Burt, R. S. (1992). *Structural holes: The social structure of competition.* Cambridge, MA: Harvard University Press.

Burt, R. S. (1997). The contingent value of social capital. *Administrative Science Quarterly, 42*, 339-465.

Burton, D., Sorensen, J., & Beckman, C. (1998). *Coming from good stock: Career histories and the formation of new ventures*. Working paper presented at the 1998 Academy of Management Meetings, San Diego, CA.

Campbell, D. T. (1994). How individual and face-to-face-group selection undermine firm selection in organizational evolution. In J. A. Baum & J. V. Singh (Eds.), *Evolutionary Dynamics of Organizations* (pp. 23-38). New York: Oxford University Press.

Carroll, G. R. (1985). Concentration and specialization: Dynamics of niche width in populations of organizations. *American Journal of Sociology, 90*, 1262-1283.

Carroll, G. R. (1997). Long term evolutionary change in organizational populations: Theory, models, and empirical findings in industrial demography. *Industrial and Corporate Change, 6*, 119-143.

Carroll, G. R., Bigelow, L. S., Seidel, M. L., & Tsai. (1996). The fates of de novo and de alio producers in the American automobile industry 1885-1981. *Strategic Management Journal, 17*,117-137.

Carroll, G. R., Haveman, H. A., & Swaminathan, A. (1992). Careers in organizations: An ecological perspective. In D. L. Featherman, R. M. Lerner, and M. Perlmatter (Eds.). *Life span development and behavior* (vol. 11). Hillsdale, NJ: Lawrence Erlbaum.

Carroll, G. R., & Swaminathan. A. (1992). The organizational ecology of strategic groups in the American brewing industry, 1975-1990. *Industrial and Corporate Change, 1*, 65-97.

Coleman, J. (1988). Social capital in the creation of human capital. *American Journal of Sociology, 94*, s95-s120.

Davis, G. F. (1991). Agents without principles: The spread of the poison pill through the intercorporate network. *Administrative Science Quarterly, 36,* 605-633.

Dean, T. J., & Meyer, G. D. (1996). Industry environments and new venture formations in U.S. manufacturing: A conceptual and empirical analysis of demand determinants. *Journal of Business Venturing, 11*, 107-132.

Delacroix, J., & Rao, H. (1994). Externalities and ecological theory: Unbundling density dependence. In J. A. C. Baum & J. V. Singh, (Eds.) *Evolutionary dynamics of organizations* (pp. 255-268). New York: Oxford University Press.

Delacroix, J., Swaminathan, A., & Solt, M. (1989). Density dependence versus population dynamics: An ecological study of failings in the California wine industry. *American Sociological Review, 54*, 245-262.

DiMaggio, P. J., & Powell, W. W. (1983). The iron cage revisited: Institutional isomorphism and collective rationality in organizational fields. *American Sociological Review, 48*, 147-160.

Dosi, G., & Orsenigo, L. (1988). Coordination and transformation: An overview of structures, behaviors and change in evolutionary environments. In G. Dosi, C. Freeman, R. Nelson, G. Silverberg, & L. Soete (Eds.), *Technical Change and Economic Theory*. Pinter Publishers.

Fildes, R. A. (1990). Strategic challenges in commercializing biotechnology. *California Management Review* (Spring), 63-72.

Gibbons, R., & Katz, L. (1991). Layoffs and lemons. *Journal of Labor Economics, 9*, 351-380.

Granovetter, M. (1985). Economic action and social structure: The problem of embeddedness. *American Journal of Sociology, 91*, 481-510.

Hannan, M. T., & Carroll, G. R. (1992). *Dynamics of organizational populations: Density, legitimation, and competition*. New York: Oxford University Press.

Haunschild, P. R. & Miner, A. S. (1997). Modes of interorganizational imitation: The effects of outcome salience and uncertainty. *Administrative Science Quarterly, 42*, 472-500.

Haveman, H. A. (1995). The demographic metabolism of organizations: Industry dynamics, turnover, and tenure distributions. *Administrative Science Quarterly, 40,* 586-618.

Haveman, H. A., & Cohen, L. E. (1994). The ecological dynamics of careers: The impact of organizational founding, dissolution, and merger on job mobility. *American Journal of Sociology, 100*, 104-152.

Ingram, P., & Baum, J. A. C. (1997). Chain affiliation and the failure of Manhattan hotels, 1898-1980. *Administrative Science Quarterly, 42*, 68-102.

Katz, M. C. & Shapiro, C. (1985). Network externalities, competition, and compatibility. *American Economic Review, 75*, 424-440.

Kraatz, M. S., & Moore, J. H. (1998). *Executive migration and institutional change.* Working paper, University of Illinois at Urbana-Champaign.

Kim, J., & Miner, A. (1998). *Crash test without dummies: Learning from failure of others.* Working paper, University of Wisconsin-Madison.

Lazear, E., & Rosen, S. (1981). Rank-order tournaments as optimum labor contract. *Journal of Political Economy, 89*, 841-864.

Leblebici , H., Salancik, G. R., Copay, A., & King, T. (1991). Institutional change and the transformation of interorganizational fields: An organizational history of the U.S. radio broadcasting industry. *Administrative Science Quarterly, 36*, 333-363.

Leonard-Barton, D. (1995). *Wellsprings of knowledge*. Boston, MA: Harvard Business School Press.

Main, B., O'Reilly, C.A., & Wade, J. (1993). Top executive pay: Tournament or teamwork? *Journal of Labor Economics, 11*, 606-628.

March, J. G. (1981). Footnotes to organizational change. *Administrative Science Quarterly, 26*, 563-577.

March, J. G. (1988). *Decisions and organizations.* Cambridge, MA: Basil Blackwell.

Marrett, C. B. (1980). Influences on the rise of new organizations: The formations of women's medical societies. *Administrative Science Quarterly, 25*, 185-199.

McKelvey, W. (1982). *Organizational systematics*. University of California Press.

Meyer, J. W., & Rowan, B. (1977). Institutional organizations: formal structure as myth and ceremony. *American Journal of Sociology, 83*, 340-363.

Mezias, S. J., & Lant, T. K. (1994). Mimetic learning and the evolution of populations. In J. A. C. Baum & J. V. Singh (Eds.), *Evolutionary Dynamics of Organizations* (pp. 179-198). New York: Oxford University Press.

Miner, A. S. (1990). Structural evolution through idiosyncratic jobs: The potential for unplanned learning. *Organization Science, 1*, 195-210.

Miner, A. S., & Robinson, D. S. (1994). Organization and population-level learning as engines for career transitions. *Journal of Organizational Behavior, 15*, 345-364.

Miner, A. S., Kim, J., Holzinger, I., & Haunschild, P.R. (1996). Fruits of failure: Organizational failure and population-level learning. *Academy of Management Best Paper Proceedings.*

Miner, A. S., & Haunschild, P. R. (1995). Population-level learning. In L. L. Cummings & B. M. Staw (Eds.), *Research in organizational behavior* (vol. 17). Greenwich, CT: JAI Press.

Pfeffer, J., & Leblebici, H. (1973). Executive recruitment and the development of inter-firm organizations. *Administrative Science Quarterly*, 449-460.

Pfeffer, J. M. & Salancik, G. R. (1978). *The external control of organizations: A resource dependence perspective*. New York: Harper and Row.

Piore, M. J. (1980). The technological foundations of dualism and discontinuity. In S. Berger & M. J. Piore (Eds.), *Dualism and discontinuity in industrial societies* (pp. 55-82). Cambridge, England: Cambridge University Press.

Porac, J. F., & Rosa, J. A. (1996). Rivalry, industry models, and the cognitive embeddedness of the comparable firm. *Advances in Strategic Management, 13*, 363-388.

Porac, J. F., Thomas, H., & Baden-Fuller, C. (1989). Competitive groups as cognitive communities: The case of Scottish knitwear manufacturers. *Journal of Management Studies, 26*, 397-416.

Porac, J. F., Thomas, H., Wilson, F., Paton, D., & Kanfer, A. (1995). Rivalry and the industry model of Scottish knitwear producers. *Administrative Science Quarterly, 40*, 203-227.

Portes, A., & Sensenbrenner, J. (1993). Embeddedness and immigration: Notes on the social determinants of economic action. *American Journal of Sociology, 98*, 1320-50.

Romanelli, E. (1989). Environments and strategies of organization start-up: Effects on early survival. *Administrative Science Quarterly, 34*, 369-387.

Romanelli, E. (1991). The evolution of new organizational forms. *Annual Review of Sociology, 17*, 74-103.

Sitkin, S. (1992). Learning through failure: The strategy of small losses. In L. L. Cummings & B. M. Staw (Eds.), *Research in organizational behavior* (vol. 14). Greenwich, CT: JAI Press.

Smith, D. (1983). Mobility in professional occupational-internal labor markets. *American Sociological Review, 48*, 289-305.

Swaminathan, A. (1995). The proliferation of specialist organizations in the American wine industry. *Administrative Science Quarterly, 40*, 653-680.

Swaminathan, A. (1998). Entry into new market segments in mature industries: Endogenous and exogenous segmentation in the U.S. brewing industry. *Strategic Management Journal, 19*, 389-404.

Swaminathan, A., & Wade, J. B. (1999). *Social movement theory and the evolution of new organizational forms* in C. B. Schoonhoven and E. Rommelli (Eds.), *The entrepreneurship dynamic in industry evolution.* Stanford University Press (forthcoming).

Tushman, M. L., & Anderson, P. (1986). Technological discontinuities and organizational environments. *Administrative Science Quarterly, 31*, 439-465.

Van Valen, L. (1973). A new evolutionary law. *Evolutionary Theory, 1*, 1-30.

SOURCES, DYNAMICS, AND SPEED: A LONGITUDINAL BEHAVIORIAL SIMULATION OF INTERORGANIZATIONAL AND POPULATION-LEVEL LEARNING

Joel A. C. Baum and Whitney B. Berta

ABSTRACT

Using a longitudinal behavioral simulation, we study the sources and dynamics of interorganizational and population-level learning and the impact of interorganizational learning speed on population-level performance. Our study reveals a range of forces that foster convergent learning among organizations: firms target others that are *high-status*, *socially proximate*, and *strategically similar* for interorganizational learning. Firms also pursue differentiation strategies, importing routines from successful organizations *outside* their local population but *within* the industry. We also show how interorganizational learning that occurs too rapidly or too slowly has a significant, negative impact on population-level performance. The paper also highlights important tensions between the implications of interorganizational learning and imitation for competitive advantage at organizational and population levels.

Advances in Strategic Management, Volume 16, pages 155-184.

ISBN: 0-7623-0500-2

Many formal organizational activities, including joint ventures and other collaborations, benchmarking, and the identification of best practices, are intended to acquire information or knowledge through learning. As researchers have considered the stability of differences in firm performance in the face of changing business environments, many have come to view the ability to learn as an important source of competitive advantage (Levinthal & March, 1993, p. 96) and perhaps one of the only sources of sustainable competitive advantage (Miner & Mezias, 1996).

Typically, learning by organizations is viewed as an organization-level phenomenon that entails "the patterned transformation of a system, arising from the selective retention of (1) behavioral routines or (2) information" (Miner & Robinson, 1994, p. 348). Work by organizational ecologists, neo-institutionalists, and network theorists, however, all demonstrates that learning may often be produced by interactions among organizations, rather than within isolated organizations. Such *interorganizational* learning may either be strictly *vicarious*, when one organization observes but does not necessarily interact with another, or *interactive,* when the learning process arises from active interactions between two or more organizations. Both processes produce organizational learning based on shared experience rather than individual organizational experience. Learning may thus commonly unfold in organizational populations and communities as well as individual organizations. In some cases, the entire learning process may involve higher-level routines, as when a whole population of organizations experiments with collective coordination routines over time.

An important *population-level learning* outcome occurs when interactions between organizations in a population produce "a systematic change in the nature and mix of routines in an organizational population arising from [shared] experience" (Miner & Haunschild, 1995, p. 115). The distinction between individual organization-level and population-level learning reveals important tensions between organization-level and population-level outcomes.

While examples of population-level learning—both effective and ineffective—are quite common (Miner & Haunschild, 1995), our understanding of such phenomena is limited by limited prior theory and empirical research. A range of processes have been identified through which interorganizational and population-level learning may occur: variation explored by new organizations that influences the larger population (Baum & Ingram, 1998), introduction of new routines to the population at large (Lant & Mezias, 1990), bursts of technological innovation that inspire variations in routines, harvesting by large firms of new routines developed by smaller firms (Tushman & Anderson, 1986), and the formation of research consortia to perform deliberate experiments, for example, with new organizational forms (Aldrich & Sasaki, 1994).

Outlining a framework within which population-level learning concepts can be integrated and investigated, Miner and Haunschild (1995) called for work that establishes more completely the features of imitators, population-learning models, and the key aspects of organizations that provoke others to imitate or cooperate with them. Miner and Mezias (1996) suggested some additional key questions that need to be addressed including who or what is doing the learning? what are the key learning processes? and when is learning valuable? We investigate several of these facets of interorganizational and population-level learning in a longitudinal behavioral simulation. The simulation permits us to study the entire interorganizational learning histories of industries and to test a range of ideas on population-level learning. We distinguish three types of interorganizational learning by organizations: *cooperative* learning through direct interaction among organizations, *mimetic* learning through selective copying of other organizations, and *inferential* learning from the perceived experiences of other organizations. Bringing together ideas from various research streams, we develop and test hypotheses examining the *sources* and *dynamics* of interorganizational learning and the effects of the *speed* of such learning for population-level performance.

ORGANIZATION-LEVEL LEARNING

Individual organizations face the question of how to divide attention and resources to *explore* new knowledge and *exploit* existing knowledge. *Exploitation* refers to learning gained through refinement and selection of existing routines. *Exploration* refers to learning gained through processes of search, concerted variation, planned experimentation, and play. March (1991) advocated that organizations endeavor to strike a balance between exploitation and exploration. Too much emphasis on exploitation can lead to the adoption of suboptimal routines, while too much emphasis on exploration can lead to incurring the high costs of experimentation without realizing its benefits. In practice, achieving this balance is challenged by a number of factors both internal and external to the organization. The sure short-run rewards of exploitation distract organizations from exploration, where returns are far less certain. Even if the expected value of exploration is greater than that of exploitation, loss aversion might still lead to a preference for exploitation (Kahneman & Tversky, 1979). The short-run rewards of exploiting organizational routines learned in the past thus typically quickly drive out exploration of novel, potentially superior, behaviors. Consequently, early experiences may prove especially fateful as organizations commit to routines shaped more by early, sometimes arbitrary, conditions, experiences and actions than by information gained from later learning situations (Hedberg, Nystrom, & Starbuck, 1976; Levitt & March, 1988; Stinchcombe, 1965). Experiential organizational learning processes are thus strongly *history-dependent*.

Each time an organization engages in a particular activity, its members increase their competency at that activity, although at a decreasing rate (Argote, Beckman, & Epple, 1990; Argote & Epple, 1990; Epple, Argote, & Devadas, 1991; Yelle, 1979). Given initial success at applying a routine, organizations are likely to gain more experience with it and continue applying it because they know increasingly well how to apply it, and because it is less risky to apply an existing, proven routine than alternatives with which organizations have limited experience. Managers' attributions of success to their own abilities and to the policies and practices (correct or not) they previously adopted, limits the likelihood that they will initiate experimentation. This is especially true if there are few negative results, a situation that increases the likelihood that any false or superstitious beliefs that managers hold will be reinforced (Levinthal & March, 1993; Miller, 1990, 1993, 1999). "Beautifully tuned with its environment, [the organization] can beat anything in sight. And these successes are impossible to forget; they tempt and tantalize managers to go just a little bit further" (Miller, 1993, p.134). "Successful organizations, like temples, are places of worship—worship of heroes, ideologies, and recipes. The potential for superstition, idolatry, intolerance, and extremism is…ever present" (Miller, 1999, p. 94).

Together, these forces and processes create *organizational momentum*, the tendency to maintain the direction and emphasis of prior actions in current behavior (Amburgey & Miner, 1992; Miller & Friesen, 1980). Once a pattern or direction of organizational action is initiated, the pattern or direction itself may become routinized and subject to strong inertial pressures. As a result, the actions of organizations *today* are strongly channeled by enduring routines resulting from experiences and actions of *long ago*. Substantial research evidence indicates that past experience strongly influences the direction and emphasis of current strategic behavior, including changes in strategic orientation (Amburgey, Kelly, & Barnett, 1993; Baum & Singh, 1996; Delacroix & Swaminathan, 1991; Kelly & Amburgey, 1991), merger and acquisition activity (Amburgey & Miner, 1992; Ginsberg & Baum, 1994), and investments in foreign environments (Chang, 1995; Hennart & Park, 1993; Kogut & Chang, 1994; Mitchell, Shaver, & Yeung, 1994; Wilson, 1990). These studies consistently show that the more experienced an organization's members become with a particular strategic activity or direction, the more likely they are to repeat or reinforce it in the future.

Attention and effort applied to exploratory search and learning by organizations is therefore often highly discontinuous. After an initial, brief episode of exploration, production pressures, force of habit, myopia, and external demands for consistency in quality and accountability of actions all conspire to impair the organization's capacity for exploratory learning by purging variation—which might provide possible alternatives—from organizational routines (Levinthal & March, 1993). Knowledge quickly congeals, embedding unresolved or unnoticed problems (Hannan & Freeman, 1984; March, 1991; Tyre & Orlikowski, 1994). Subsequent exploratory learning is erratic and is triggered by the occurrence of poor performance and disruptive events, often entailing more "retrofitting" of existing routines than learning of new ones (Milliken & Lant, 1991; Starbuck, 1983; Tyre & Orlikowski, 1994).

In the face of ambiguity and uncertainty, however, an emphasis on exploitation can prevent organizations from adjusting their routines too quickly and detrimentally to idiosyncratic events and from engaging in costly explorations into highly uncertain domains (Levinthal, 1991). Moreover, in the face of production pressures and the need for reliability and consistency of action, exploitive learning may significantly enhance performance by reducing variability in the quality or efficiency of task performance (Hannan & Freeman, 1984). Exploitation also creates competitive advantages of experience that make imitation difficult (Barney, 1991; Peteraf, 1993). The ability of firms to acquire, develop and exploit capabilities and routines often depends on their location in space and time (e.g., Arthur, 1989). Once time and history pass, firms that do not have time and history-dependent capabilities face a significant disadvantage in developing them. When this occurs, an experienced firm may gain an advantage that cannot easily be competed away. Firms that possess and exploit experience-based capabilities may therefore enjoy a sustained competitive advantage (Barney, 1991).

Despite the potential benefits they provide organizations, gains from exploitation will be short-lived and may become harmful if the criteria for organizational success and survival change *after* the organization has learned. Then, an organization's past investments in routines can be rendered obsolete, and the lack of exploration that results from a focus on those routines can inhibit adaptation and hasten failure (Baum & Ingram, 1998; Ingram & Baum, 1997). Even doing extremely well what it learned in the past, the organization may perform poorly and even fail; it may suffer the so-called *competency trap* (Levitt & March, 1988). The notion of a competency trap suggests that organizations may reduce their exploratory activity prematurely and, even in a changing environment, not renew exploratory search and learning activities despite the fact that new opportunities and threats are present. In this way, organizations' experience contributes to the inertia that binds them to routines of the past. Exploitive learning can lead organizations to employ routines of the past well beyond their point of usefulness, which may ultimately result in organizational failure (Baum, Korn, & Kotha, 1995; Miller, 1990; Starbuck, 1983).

Even in stable environments the effects of extreme competence may be detrimental to an organization's survival. Herriot, Levinthal, and March (1985) presented the unsurprising finding that specialization in an inferior routine leads to lower long-term performance relative to that which might have been realized had a firm opted to specialize in a superior alternative. What is interesting about their model is the impact that initial conditions have on the likelihood of adopting a given routine. Early and extensive allocations in a routine—whether in the absence of other alternatives or as a consequence of internal championing or other circumstances—may serve to reinforce the adoption of an inferior routine. Under these conditions, competency traps may be avoided by asynchronous adjustments of allocations and organizational goals that effectively slow down the rate of learning or the rate at which competence is gained. By extending the time over which learning takes place, asynchronous adjustment effectively increases the probability that superior solutions will be discovered, or noticed, and given a fair trial.

Consistent with the *resource-based view* of the firm, which emphasizes the "stickiness" of strategic resources intertwined *within* the firm (Barney, 1991; Peteraf, 1993) and accumulated as an experiential result of path-dependent actions over time (Dierickx & Cool, 1989; Collis, 1991), the expectation from organizational learning theory is that the path dependency and sensitivity to initial conditions produced by experiential learning will impose constraints that limit the scope of the firm. While the resource-based view counsels the pursuit of *sustainable competitive advantage* (Barney, 1991), however, organizational learning theory clearly cautions that experience-based competitive advantages are likely to prove only temporary at best (Baum & Ingram, 1998; Ingram & Baum, 1997; Levinthal & March, 1993).

INTERORGANIZATIONAL AND POPULATION-LEVEL LEARNING

While March (1976), Miner (1994), and others have suggested that variation can be promoted in organizations through institutionalized experimentation and direct and indirect incentives to individuals to reward playfulness, over time the self-reinforcing bias toward exploitation of current routines leads inevitably toward myopia. Put succinctly, "the effectiveness of learning in the short run and in the near neighborhood of current experience interferes with learning in the long run and at a distance" (Levinthal & March, 1993, p. 97). But organizations' own experience is not the only opportunity for learning. Organizations may also learn vicariously or more directly from the experience of others in their population. Organizational learning theorists have long contended that, like individuals, organizations can learn vicariously, imitating or avoiding specific actions or practices based on their perceived impact (e.g., Cyert & March, 1963). In strategic management, for example, such imitation is the basis for the so-called "second-mover advantage" (Lieberman & Montgomery, 1988). Such vicarious learning can lead to changes in routines at the population level.

An important population-level learning outcome occurs when there is a change in the nature and mix of routines enacted in a population that results from interactions among organizations (Miner & Haunshild, 1995). Thus, interorganizational and population-level learning involve either the outcome of interactions within a population or routines that occur at the population level itself (Miner & Haunschild, 1995). Interactions arise through two key mechanisms: experimentation and interorganizational imitation. Collective *experimentation* occurs through vehicles of deliberate variation like the formation of research consortia and other cooperatives. *Interorganizational learning* refers to mimetic learning, through selective copying, and vicarious inferential learning based on *other organizations'* or *populations' experience*. Our study focuses on the latter process, and in particular, the sources, dynamics and population-level consequences of interorganizational imitation.

Population-level experience has some unique advantages over an organization's own experience. Of particular significance, as Miner and Haunschild (1995) observed, populations can be expected to engage in exploration even while the organizations comprising them engage in exploitation. Any one organization is limited in how much it can explore. The limit is not just the capacity for gaining experience on its own, but also how much variation any one organization, and its stakeholders can or will tolerate (Hannan & Freeman, 1984)—there are only so many different products and prices any one organization can experiment with. Unlike organizations, populations are nonhierarchical, noncohesive, face limited demands for integration, and therefore can be more varied in their experience than individual organizations. Compared with individual organizations, populations can explore a great deal of variation without violating internal or external standards for consistency and reliability (Baum & Ingram, 1998; Ingram & Baum, 1997).

The general lack of cohesion, the diversity of organizational goals, and the absence of any systematic harvesting or censoring of newly created routines all contribute to the proliferation of new ideas and routines, rather than encouraging incremental learning. As a result, learning at the population level may be *more exploratory than learning by individual organizations* (Miner & Haunschild, 1995). Consequently, their population's experience may often be a source of fresh experience for organizations that have fallen into competency traps. In pointing to the value of instances in which variation is sought through incorporating external competencies via *grafting* or *importing* from outside the organization to generate new goals or to produce new routines, Miner and Robinson (1994) reinforced this point. With such an approach, organizations mired in their own past can potentially learn the many strategies, management routines, and technologies employed by other successful organizations in their industry. Consequently, *the best strategy for any individual organization may often be to emphasize the exploitation of the successful explorations of others* (Levinthal & March, 1993).

Such a strategy seems at odds with resource-based theory, which suggests that if a particular capability or routine is common among competing firms, then it is *unlikely* to be a source of advantage for any one of them; common capabilities are sources of competitive *parity* not competitive *advantage* (Barney, 1991; Peteraf, 1993). In dynamic competitive environments, however, the stickiness and uncertain value of firms' capabilities means that firms will often look to others' successes to gauge the value of their own capabilities. The identification of "best practices" and the practice of "benchmarking" both typify this reality. Moreover, imitation may also provide a source of *variation* in organizational routines to the extent that routines are miscopied or recombined from multiple others (Miner & Raghavan, 1999).

These benefits at the organization level notwithstanding, excessive exploration at the population level can be devastating. A population whose members engage in experimentation but fail to arrive at a standard through population-level learning will be out-competed by a population that converges, permitting standardization and coordination (Miner & Haunschild, 1995) and development of a reputation, for example, by creating consumer awareness, familiarizing government authorities with the form, and providing financial institutions opportunity to assess its credit worthiness (Delacroix & Rao, 1994).[1] Conversely, population-level learning that is too rapid may be equally devastating. If a population arrives at a standard before its members have had the chance to discover effective routines, the standard itself will be suboptimal. Settling too early on a suboptimal standard can be disastrous for a population: lacking variation, its members may not be able respond effectively to a competing population that learns a better version of the routine (Miner & Haunschild, 1995).

Not all population-level learning is exploratory. Routines derived from the past population experience often assume the status of rules, procedures, and standard practices that organizations adopt reflexively in their current operations (Levinthal & March, 1993). Relatedly, White (1981, p. 518) attributed the similarities he observed between member firms within a given industry market to organizations' "tendencies to evolve roles from observations of each others' behaviors." Markets are self-reproducing, socially constructed entities. Instead of basing their actions upon the anticipated reactions of buyers to generated product choices, "producers watch producers, they are an interrelated set and in the pure case are a clique of mutually aware firms" (White, 1981, p. 540). This, White claimed, explains why there are a few homogeneous firms in some markets.

Further, circumstances may limit the extent of exploration in populations. Arthur (1989), for example, showed that the more rapid the process of convergence to a standard, the less likely it is that other historical small events will occur that might alter the course of history by introducing alternative routines. Speed of convergence is, in part, a function of the rate at which the payoff presented to each new potential adopter accumulates. Early adoption equates to the early accumulation of experience and learning and the early realization of returns through gains in competence. Thus small historical events, like early entry into the market, determine the dominant technology. In this way, an inferior technology or routine can readily be adopted and enjoy dominance despite the later appearance of superior technologies that are never exploited to their full potential. Further, even *expectations* about which technology will become the standard exacerbate and accelerate lock-in tendencies. Arthur's results suggest that, under conditions of increasing returns, the number of prior adopters can drive the lock-in of a technology.

Learning Sources

Under conditions of uncertainty, firms' strategists use social comparison to select and evaluate their own actions (DiMaggio & Powell, 1983). Faced with insufficient information to learn from their own experience, strategists turn to the actions of their competitors for clues about how to interpret their situation. Firms using this mode of behavior to cope with uncertainty seek to learn from the experiences of others by imitating their visible actions (Levitt & March, 1988; Levinthal & March, 1993). Since the overt actions of a firm are often accompanied by subtle subroutines and tacit knowledge, however, the true value of particular practices used by others is not always easy to gauge. Instead, the frequency with which routines are observed in use, or their prevalence in the population, is used as a proxy for value (Abrahamson & Rosenkopf, 1993; DiMaggio & Powell, 1983). More frequent use provides the information that others find a practice or action valuable, which, in turn, increases its likelihood of adoption (Haunschild & Miner, 1997). As uncertainty increases, so does the difficulty associated with estimating value; so, relying on frequency as a proxy for value is particularly prevalent when environmental uncertainty is high.

The population-level learning framework predicts the pursuit of deliberate variation through the adoption of routines at the population level; routines are adopted from among those generated through the experiences of others. Firms do not imitate routines arbitrarily, however, they are selective in their imitation of the actions or practices of other firms (DiMaggio & Powell, 1983; Haunschild & Miner, 1997). They discriminate among organizational others in the population and adopt the practices and actions of those who achieve desirable outcomes. Not all other firms, then, will be the targets of interorganizational imitation. We investigate status, social proximity, similarity, and differentiation as factors that invite targeting for interorganizational learning.

Status

As firms' strategists look for role models, high-status firms, which are typically large and successful, are particularly likely candidates. Haveman (1993) found, for example, that whether a savings and loan (S&L) entered a new market was positively related to the prevalence of large, successful S&Ls in that market. Korn and Baum (1999) showed that commuter airlines imitated the market choices of their high-performing competitors. Burns and Wholey (1993) found that hospitals adopted matrix management practices when other highly visible, prestigious hospitals had previously adopted them. Relatedly, Lant and Baum (1995) found that Manhattan hotel managers were more likely to attend to the strategic actions of larger, more luxurious hotels, and Haunschild and Miner (1997) found that when large, profitable firms had recently used an investment banker, acquiring firms were more likely to choose to use it. Certain traits, such as a firm's size, prestige, or success therefore affect the likelihood that its actions and practices will be imitated. Such high-status firms are likely targets of imitation because their success signals that they have done something right to gain access to resources and to satisfy constituents. Imitation of firms with superior access to resources may also satisfy firms' quest for legitimacy (DiMaggio & Powell, 1983). Consequently, we expect that *successful* firms will be imitated more frequently as other firms attempt to share in their success or enhance their own legitimacy:

(H1): Firms target successful organizations as sources for interorganizational learning.

Social Proximity

Researchers have found that interorganizational influence in an organizational population tends to be based on social networks. Davis (1991) studied the factors that contributed to the diffusion of poison pills—mechanisms instituted by firms' boards that discourage hostile takeovers—among the Fortune 500 industrials with the greatest sales in 1985. He found that those firms with board interlocks, a measure of the social proximity of firms whose directors sit on multiple boards, adopted poison pills at significantly higher rates than did firms without board interlocks. Haunschild (1993) found that managers in four diverse industries engaged in the same types of acquisitions as those initiated by firms with which they were tied through director interlocks. Similarly, Palmer, Jennings, and Zhou (1993) showed that M-form structures are more likely to be copied from socially proximate organizations.

(H2): Firms target socially proximate organizations for interorganizational learning.

Similarity

Similar organizations tend to monitor and copy each other (Lant & Baum, 1995). Burt (1987) showed that similarity could produce even more imitation than social proximity. Porac and colleagues (1995), who examined firms operating in the Scottish knitwear industry, found that focal firms made regular efforts to apprise themselves of the actions of others whom they believed to be similar in terms of the market segment pursued. Similar firms, then, tend to monitor and copy one another. There is a range of ways in which firms can be similar. Haveman (1993) found that large firms in the savings and loan industry imitated the market entry decisions of other large member firms, although small firms in the same industry did not adopt the routines of other small rival firms. The firms active in the Scottish knitwear industry based their perceptions of similarity largely on the extent to which products (and thus target markets) were similar (Porac et al., 1995).

(H3): Firms target similar organizations as sources for interorganizational learning.

Differentiation

Although interorganizational imitation makes it possible for an organization to realize the benefit from routines proven successful by other organizations without taking on risks of investing in exploration and innovation, imitation that enhances organizational similarity also intensifies the potential for interorganizational competition (Baum & Mezias, 1992). Organizations may, therefore, observe the actions of others in efforts to *differentiate* themselves (e.g., Porter, 1980; White, 1981). Just as with imitation, a differentiation strategy requires that firms observe the routines employed by their competitors, but the objectives of such scrutiny are very different. When pursuing a differentiation strategy, organizations choose routines that contribute to consumers' perceptions of product uniqueness. This strategy is consistent with resource-based theory, which counsels organizations to perform activities and routines differently to create a *unique* position that deters imitation so as to create competitive advantage (Barney, 1991; Peteraf, 1993). So while imitation leads to enhanced competition among competitors, routines that further differentiate organizations moderate competition and may create a basis for firm-level competitive advantage. In seeking routines that contribute to differentiation, organizations may look inward for unique innovations or they may observe and attempt to import the routines of others outside of their local population (i.e., beyond their direct competitors) or industry. Importing routines from successful organizations outside the organization's local population but within the industry may afford the dual benefit of mitigating the risks associated with relying on imitation as a learning heuristic while capitalizing on the successful explorations of highly relevant others (Levinthal & March, 1993).

(H4): Firms target successful *noncompeting* organizations in for interorganizational learning.

Learning Dynamics

Momentum

In addition to contextual factors, research by Amburgey and Miner (1992) and others (Amburgey et al., 1993; Ginsberg & Baum, 1994) suggests that an organization's patterns of learning may become routinized. Learning furnishes an organization with the opportunity to routinize learning. Each time an organization engages in a particular type of learning it increases its competency at that type. The more experienced an organization becomes with a particular type of learning, the more likely it is to engage in that type again in the future. This creates repetitive momentum, observed as a tendency to maintain the original direction and emphases in a firm's current behavior. Consequently, an understanding of interorganizational learning requires consideration of an organization's history of learning.

(H5): The greater the past use of interorganizational learning by an organization, the more likely the organization will be to engage in interorganizational learning in the future.

Timing

Starbuck (1983) observed that the attention and effort organizations applied to learning is highly discontinuous. After a brief, initial interval within which organizations might learn, routines soon congeal and become habituated in response to production pressures (March, 1991). This occurs because investment in exploration is perceived as affording uncertain, longer-term returns when juxtaposed with the more immediate and perceivably sure returns of exploitation. Levinthal and March (1993) discussed two mechanisms of learning, *simplification* and *specialization*, that dominate learning in organizations and may aggravate the propensity to underinvest, and ultimately cease investment, in exploration.

Simplification refers to the propensity of firms to discourage the complexity of simultaneous organizational learning experiences by enacting less confusing environments. *Specialization* of learning competence occurs when one work unit undertakes learning and adaptation and alleviates the need for other units to learn and adjust. Both mechanisms rely on experiential learning gained either by trial-and-error experimentation (learning by doing) or organizational search, in which routines are drawn from a pool of known alternatives and adopted when they are perceived as leading to success. Interorganizational learning represents one such mechanism by which organizations can gain access to apparently reliable alternative solutions. Once internalized, practices become routinized and institutionalized, and organizations are less likely to imitate other organizations' related practices. Therefore the tendency to engage in interorganizational learning will diminish over time; organizational resources initially employed in the acquisition of information and routines from organizational others will be redirected inward to the exploitation of the acquired routines (Tyre & Orlikowski, 1994).

(H6): The rate of interorganizational learning by organizations is initially high and diminishes over time.

Although Levinthal and March (1993) suggested that both mechanisms facilitate average performance improvements, over the long term their effects are debilitating in that organizations lose the ability to engage in exploratory learning. As a consequence, *competency traps* occur, in which experience is accumulated with a routine that changing demands render suboptimal (Levitt & March, 1988). The embedding of suboptimal routines may perpetuate unresolved problems. Subsequent learning is episodic: because their initial routines are frequently suboptimal, organizations are spurred by disruptive events (e.g., performance failures) to rethink their early choices (Starbuck, 1983; Tyre & Orlikowski, 1994). Past research has attributed these temporal patterns to organizations learning from their own experience, but interorganizational learning may be similarly episodic. DiMaggio and Powell (1983) asserted that conditions of uncertainty lead organizations to seek models and ideas from other organizations. Performance failures represent one source of uncertainty and stimulate organizations to initiate problemistic search (Cyert & March, 1963), which may involve the scrutiny of other organizations with the intent to imitate their responses to change.

(H7): The rate of interorganizational learning by organizations is stimulated by poor performance.

Learning Speed and Population-Level Performance

Diffusion is a means of retaining routines at the population level that occurs when organizations adopt the effective routines of successful organizations in the population. For organizations whose routines become the target of widespread imitation, diffusion can have negative consequences: imitation erodes sustainable competitive advantages based on unique activities and routines (Barney, 1991; Peteraf, 1993). Such diffusion also raises the potential for interorganizational competition (Baum &Mezias, 1992; White, 1981). Population-level diffusion that is *too rapid* may also be harmful at the population level: routines may diffuse widely throughout the population before truly effective ones have been discovered. Conversely, a lack of connectedness at the population level, which limits diffusion and results in a proliferation of new ideas, none of which gains widespread acceptance, may be equally harmful for the population. In the absence of systematic diffusion, effective routines of population members are not harvested in any systematic way. As a result, the population may learn *too slowly* and risks being out-competed by faster-learning rival populations (Miner & Haunschild, 1995). In either case, the implication is the same: the population's members will tend to exploit suboptimal routines and may not be able to respond effectively to a competing population that learns a better version of the core organizational routine.

(H8): Population performance is enhanced when interorganizational learning is neither too fast nor too slow.

RESEARCH DESIGN AND DATA

The data for this study were obtained from a computer-based behavioral simulation conducted in two sections of an undergraduate management-skills course. *Mercado* (Uretsky et al., 1989) is an experience-based computer simulation in which different student groups each operate a medium-sized functionally organized company. The simulation provides students with an opportunity to experience the long-term implications of effective or ineffective management skills in a complex, dynamic, competitive setting. Students in two class sections were randomly assigned to one of six competing four-member firms in one of three local populations of the same industry. The simulation lasted five weeks, during which time each firm participated in four week-long decision periods. At the end of each period, firms submitted the strategic and operating decisions required by the simulation, which were used as input to generate firm-level, local population, and industry-specific performance and market results. These results were then distributed to participants within 24 hours.

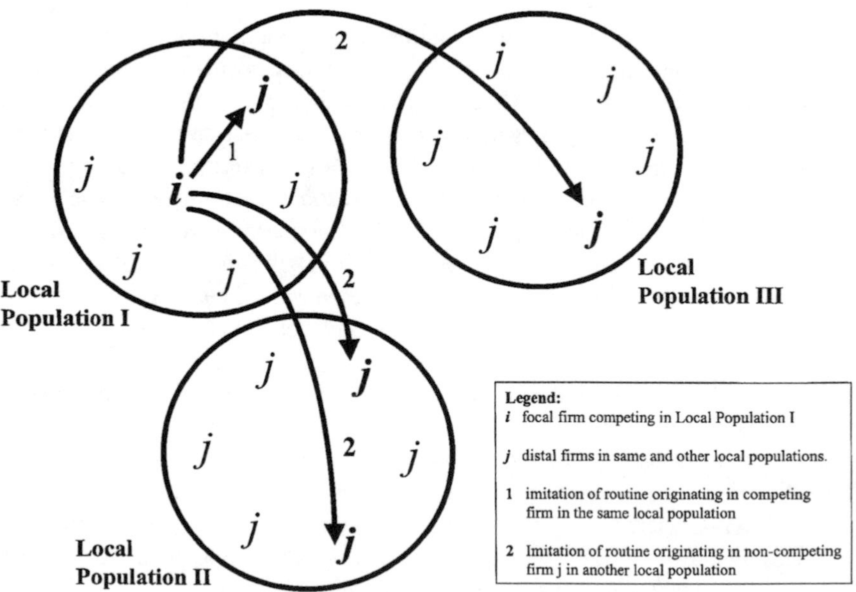

Figure 1. Potential Sources of Interorganizational Imitation in the Simulation

Dependent Variables and Analysis

Interorganizational Learning

A learning history was compiled for each firm *i* based on self-reports derived from a standard survey instrument, which was administered to the members of each firm at the end of each learning period.[2] Participants were asked to identify all interorganizational learning events that occurred during that decision period, to classify learning events by type (cooperative, mimetic, inferential), and to identify the learning sources (other firm or other firm's member). The dependent variable was defined as the number of interorganizational learning events experienced by a focal firm *i* with each other firm *j* in the same class section (but not necessarily the same local population) in each learning period. Each firm had the opportunity to learn from firms within its own local population or firms in either of the two other noncompeting local populations in their industry. Figure 1 illustrates the possible sources of interorganizational learning in the simulation.

The sample contained 2,248 firm *ij* pair/periods during which 62 interorganizational learning events (28 cooperative, 16 mimetic, 24 inferential) occurred. Since the total number of population-level learning events was so small, we aggregated the three types of learning and analyzed them together.

Because our dependent variable for hypotheses 1-6 is a count measure, we estimated the number of interorganizational learning events expected to occur within a learning period. A Poisson process provides a natural baseline model for count data that is appropriate for rare events (Coleman, 1981). The Poisson model can be modified to model diffusion by including the number of prior events as a covariate (Rasler, 1996). The basic Poisson model is:

$$Pr(Y_t = y) = e^{\lambda(x}{}_t^{)}[\lambda(xt)^y/y!],$$

where both the expected number of events in a unit interval, $Pr(Y_t{=}y)$, and the variance of the number of events in each interval equal the rate, $\lambda(x_t)$. The basic Poisson model assumes that there is no heterogeneity in the sample, but count data of rare events, the variance may often exceed the mean. Overdispersion causes standard errors of parameters to be underestimated and the statistical significance of coefficients to be overstated. We used the negative binomial regression model to correct for overdispersion. A common formulation is:

$$\lambda_t = exp(\pi' \, xt)\varepsilon t,$$

where the error term, ε_t, follows a gamma distribution. The presence of ε_t produces overdispersion. The specification of overdispersion we use takes the form:

$$Var(Y_t) = E(Y_t)[1{+}\alpha E(Y_t)].$$

We estimated this model using *LIMDEP 6.0* (Greene, 1992). In a preliminary analysis, negative binomial models failed to improve the fit significantly over Poisson models, indicating that overdispersion was not a problem. Thus, we report estimates from Poisson regression models.

Population Performance

Population performance was measured as the average profit of the firms in an industry (six competing firms) in each learning period ($x10^{-6}$ for rescaling). The sample contained 18 industry/period observations. We estimated the relationship between population performance and the independent variables as follows:

$$Population\ Performance_{it} = \beta_1\ Population\ Performance_{it\text{-}1} + \beta' X_{it\text{-}1} + \varepsilon_i$$

where $Population\ Performance_{it}$ and $Population\ Performance_{it\text{-}1}$ are the average profit of firms in industry i in the current and prior periods, respectively. We included the lagged dependent variable to account for the possibility that our performance model suffers from specification bias due to unobserved heterogeneity (Jacobson, 1990). $X_{it\text{-}1}$ are the independent and control variables.

Rather than estimating the population performance model separately for each industry i, we pooled the data and estimated a single model. This can lead to two estimation problems: autocorrelation and heteroskedasticity (Tuma & Hannan, 1984). Given these potential estimation problems, we employed a generalized least squares (GLS) model. Following Greene (1990, pp. 472-475), we transformed the data to correct for bias due to serial correlation across time (i.e., autocorrelation) and across cross-sectional units (i.e., heteroskedasticity) and then estimated GLS models using *LIMDEP 6.0* (Greene, 1992).

Independent Variables

Social Proximity (H1)

We computed the average number of self-reported (1) school-related and (2) personal interactions per week between members of the focal firm i and members of each other firm j at the start of the simulation to measure participants' proximity.

Status (H2)

The success of each other firm j was measured as its simulated profit in the prior period ($x10^{-6}$ for rescaling).

Similarity (H3)

The similarity of focal firm *i* and each other firm *j* was measured as market domain similarity defined as the absolute value of the sum of the differences in market share over three simulated product markets at the start of each period.

Differentiation (H4)

The success of each other firm *j*, measured as its simulated profit in the prior period (x10^{-6} for rescaling), was interacted with a dummy variable coded one if firm *j* was a direct competitor in the same local population and zero if *j* belonged to a different noncompeting local population.

Momentum (H5)

Following Amburgey and colleagues (1993), momentum was defined as the cumulative number of interorganizational events reported by the members of focal firm *i* prior to the start of the current period.

Time Period (H6)

Elapsed time was measured with a clock variable that counted the number of past learning periods.

Performance (H7)

The performance of the focal firm *i* was measured as its simulated profit in the last period (x10^{-6} for rescaling).

Learning Speed (H8)

We used two variables to examine learning speed effect. The first was defined as the aggregate number of interorganizational events experienced by all the firms in a local population during the last learning period. The second was defined as the cumulative number of population-level learning events reported by firms in the focal population in all prior periods. Together these variables capture and empirically separate *current* and *historical* speeds (i.e., learning per unit time) of population-level learning. To test hypothesis 8, as we describe in more detail below, we estimated both these variables as well as an interaction of the current learning speed variable with a quadratic specification of the time period variable.

RESULTS

Table 1 presents the estimates from our Poisson regression analysis of the sources and timing of interorganizational learning between firms *i* and *j*. In addition to the theoretical variables, the equation in Table 1 includes several control variables to rule out plausible alternative explanations for our findings. We include the number of school and personal interaction frequencies among the members of each firm *i* to control for the possibility that high within-firm social proximity might lower the propensity of firms to engage in population-level learning. We also include the main effect for the dummy variable differentiating firm *js* according to whether or not they are members of the same (coded 1) or different (coded 0) local population. This controls for the possibility that the greater salience of direct competitors makes them more likely to be targets of population-level learning and avoids specification bias in the estimate for the interaction term testing H4 (Cohen & Cohen, 1983).

Learning Sources

The significant positive coefficient for Profit Firm *j* supports H1, which predicted that successful, high-performing organizations will be primary targets for interorganizational learning. In addition to this main effect of high performance, we were interested in whether firms were trying to learn from high-performing competitors in their own local population or from high-performing, but non-competing, firms in other local populations (H4). If firms try to learn from their

Table 1. Poisson Regression Model of Interorganizational Learning

Profit firm *j* × 10^{-6} (H1)	.219*	(.066)
Profit firm *j* × 10^{-6} x Firm *j* Own Local Population (H4)	–.205*	(.094)
School-Related Interaction Frequency *ij* (H2)	2.712*	(1.495)
Personal Interaction Frequency *ij* (H2)	1.788*	(.923)
Market Domain Similarity *ij* (H3)	.021*	(.008)
Cumulative Past Interorganizational Learning Events by Firm *i* (H5)	.533*	(.090)
Time Period (H6)	–.574	(.371)
Profit firm *i* × 10^{-6} (H7)	.018	(.066)
School Interaction Frequency *ii*	–1.216	(1.536)
Personal Interaction Frequency *ii*	–.175	(1.154)
Firm *j* in Own Local Population	2.518*	(.888)
School-Related Interaction Frequency *ij* × Time Period	–1.592*	(.642)
Constant	–6.899*	(.903)
Likelihood Ratio	200.36	
Df	13	

Notes: * $p < .05$; standard errors in parentheses. The sample includes 2,248 firm *ij* pair/periods and 62 population-level learning events.

high-performing direct competitors, they run the risk of becoming more like them and competing more directly with them. Alternatively, if firms attempt to learn from successful firms in other local populations of the same industry, they may learn how to differentiate themselves effectively from direct competitors, but they run some risk that the routines they adopt will not be effective in their own local population. Thus, the decision of which high-performing firms to learn from is a substantive one with implications not only for individual firms, but also for the population, because of its impact on organizational diversity and intensity of competition.

The significant negative coefficient for the Profit Firm *j* x Firm *j* Own Local Population interaction indicates that high-performance makes firms likely targets as sources for interorganizational learning when the firms are in noncompeting local populations, supporting H4. Indeed, the approximately equal sizes of the coefficients for the main effect for Profit Firm *j* and its interaction with the local population dummy variable indicate that performance only influences the likelihood that firm *j* will be targeted when it is in another industry. Thus, the firms in our simulation appear to be using interorganizational learning, in part, as a basis for finding new ways to compete with leaders in their own local population. This result reinforces Greve's (1996) study of adoption of market position by organizations in the radio broadcasting industry, in which format innovations occurring *outside* of a focal organization's local market were imitated. Greve suggested that access to information about innovations in nonlocal markets is facilitated both through direct corporate contacts and the industry press. Our distribution of firm, local population, and industrywide simulation reports results may provide a similar means of information dissemination.

Another factor underlying the interaction effect may be the reluctance of firms to engage in cooperative learning (i.e., solution generation through concerted, direct interaction), which accounted for 45% of all the interorganizational learning events reported, with their direct competitors in the same local population. Nevertheless, it is evident from the significant positive coefficient for the main effect of Firm *j* in Own Local Population that much learning is taking place within the local population. Perhaps within-local-population learning is more vicarious (i.e., mimetic and inferential, in that it occurs largely through arm's-length observation instead of direct interaction) than cooperative. Alternatively, cooperative learning may be strategically undertaken with direct competitors to jointly challenge local population leaders.

Coefficients for both personal and school-related interactions between firms *i* and *j* are significant and positive. Since larger values for these variables indicate greater social proximity between two firms, in support of H2, these positive coefficients indicate that the firm *j* whose members are socially proximate to those of the focal firm *i* are more likely to be targets of interorganizational learning than the firm *j* whose members are more socially distant from firm *i*. The larger coefficient for School-Related Interaction Frequency *ij* relative to Personal Interaction

Frequency *ij* indicates that school-related proximity influences the source of interorganizational learning more strongly (comparison-of-means $t = 4.13, p < 0.001$).

We also expected that the importance of school-related interaction patterns reported at the beginning of the simulation would diminish over time. We believed our placement of students into firms—new school work groups—would substantially alter the original school-related interaction network. Reliance on prior school-related interactions would be less relevant during the simulation and might even prove detrimental if they cannibalized interactions taking place among students placed in new firms. Estimates indicate that firms do become less likely to seek routines from ties in the old school-related network. The significant negative coefficient for the interaction term, School-Related Interaction Frequency *ij* x Time Period, supports our speculation. Personal interaction networks were not disturbed in this way—including a Personal Interaction Frequency *ij* x Time Period interaction in the model did not improve the fit of the model significantly. Thus, over time, the initially stronger influence of proximity in the school-related interaction network on learning-target selection diminished, while the effect of proximity in the personal interaction network remained steady.

Similarity *ij* indicates that strategically similar firm *j*s are significantly more likely to become targets for sources of interorganizational learning by firm *i*. We found no evidence that this effect of market domain similarity depended on whether firm *j* was in the same or another industry. Thus, in contrast to high-performing firms, similar firms are targeted as sources for interorganizational learning regardless of whether they are competitors. Further, the firms in our simulation appear to be targeting organizational others with the objective of imitating routines and enhancing strategic homogeneity rather than pursuing differentiation strategies.

Learning Dynamics

The significant positive coefficient for Cumulative Population-Level Learning Events by Firm *i* supports H5. As we predicted, this coefficient indicates that each time firm *i* reported experiencing an interorganizational learning event, it significantly increased its likelihood of engaging in interorganizational learning in the future, and the effect is cumulative. With each subsequent learning event, the force of momentum on the rate of learning increases. Thus, in the context of our simulation, firms that engaged in interorganizational learning tended to routinize this activity and develop a strong learning momentum.

H6 and H7 were not supported. Neither the passage of time (i.e., Time Period) nor a decline in a firm's own profit (i.e., Profit Firm *i*) contributes significantly to explaining the incidence of population-level learning. These results may be due to the short interval over which the simulation was conducted—the time period was too short for firms' routines to congeal and become habituated and thus too short for us to observe episodic learning triggered by performance failures.

Table 2. GLS Regression Model of Population Profit Performance

Profit Local Population *i* (*t*-1) × 10^{-6}	.313*	(.125)
Cumulative # of Interorganizational Learning Events in Local Population *i* (*t*-1)	–.617*	(.161)
# of Interorganizational Events in Local Population i (t-1)	14.22*	(3.103)
Time Period	20.77*	(9.675)
(Time Period)^2	–2.702*	(1.532)
# Interorganizational Learning Events in Local Population *i* (*t*-1) × Time Period	8.826*	(2.134)
# Interorganizational Learning Events in Local Population *i* (*t*-1) × (Time Period)^2	–1.361*	(.352)
Constant	–26.27*	(13.600)
F-ratio	4.536	
Adjusted R^2	.592	
Df	8	

Notes: *$p < .05$; standard errors in parentheses. Estimates are corrected for first-order autocorrelation and heteroskedasticity. The sample included 18 firm-period observations.

Learning Speed and Population Performance

Table 2 presents the results of our GLS analysis of the relationship between learning speed and population performance. As described earlier, in addition to the theoretical variables, the model includes the total profit of firms in the focal local population (i.e., Profit Local Population *i*) in the prior period to account for specification bias due to unobserved heterogeneity.

We use two variables and two interaction terms to test H8. The two variables are (1) the Cumulative Number of Interorganizational Learning Events reported by firms in the focal local population *i* in all prior periods, and (2) the Number of Interorganizational Learning Events reported by firms in the focal local population *i* in the last period. The two interaction terms are (1) Number of Population-Level Learning Events in Local Population *i* x Time Period and (2) Number of Population-Level Learning Events in Local Population *i* x Time Period Squared. Together, these four variables capture the effects of the historical and current interorganizational learning speeds (i.e., learning event per unit time) on population performance and permit the effect of current learning speed on population performance to vary nonmonotonically over time. Main effects for Time Period and Time Period Squared are also included in the model to avoid specification bias in the estimates for the interaction effects (Cohen & Cohen, 1983).

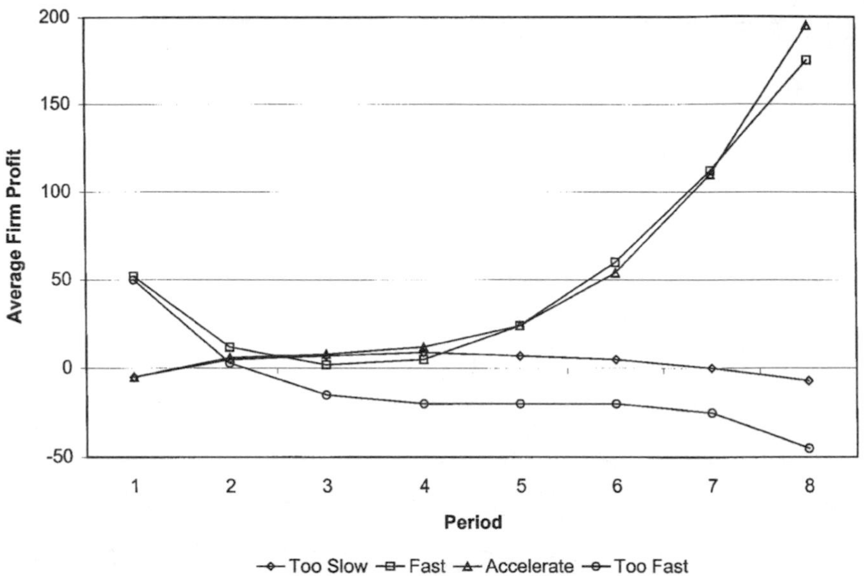

Figure 2. Learning Speed and Population Performance

Support for H8, which predicts that population performance is enhanced when population-level learning is neither too fast nor too slow, depends on the system of coefficients for these variables and interactions—several possible combinations of coefficients can support the hypothesis. Figure 2 presents the complex relationship between the speed with which interorganizational learning takes place and population performance over time based on the equation in Table 2. The figure presents estimated population performance trajectories for four hypothetical population-level learning scenarios. In the first scenario, too slow, the members of the population record one population-level learning event in each time period. In the second, fast, the members of the population record eight population-level learning events in each time period. In the third scenario, acceleration, the members of the population start slow but engage in population-level learning at an increasing rate, recording one population-level learning event in the first time period, two in the second, three in the third, and so on. And, in the final scenario, too fast, the members of the population engage in a high rate of population-level learning initially, recording eight population-level learning events in the first time period but then decrease by one event in each successive time period.[3]

In the too-slow scenario, population performance is initially low, increases modestly by the fourth period, but declines thereafter. By contrast, in the first scenario, population performance is initially high, declines until the third period, but subsequently increases rapidly. In the acceleration scenario, population performance is initially low, increases slowly until the fourth period, and then increases rapidly. Lastly, in the too-fast scenario, population performance, although initially high, declines substantially over time. As the figure shows, the effects of relatively small differences in population-level learning patterns have substantial consequences for population performance.[4]

The simulated trajectories in Figure 2 provide strong support for H8. The performance trajectories for the too-slow and too-fast scenarios clearly result in the poorest population performance. We attribute the poor performance in the slow scenario to the failure of firms in the population to harvest their population's overall prior learning systematically. And we attribute the even poorer performance in the too-fast scenario to adherence to ineffective routines learned from the population before effective routines had been discovered. By comparison, the middle-ground scenarios, fast and acceleration, were more effective. We attribute the increasing performance of fast and accelerate over time to the increasing sophistication and effectiveness of interorganizational learning skills (gained from experience), the increasing effectiveness of routines available to the learned in the population, and the ongoing exchange of ineffective routines for more effective, contemporary routines learned from others in the population.

Thus, supporting H8, performance generally suffers in populations that learn either too slowly to harvest their learning in a systematic way or too rapidly to discover effective routines. One feature of our results that is not consistent with our predictions, however, is our finding that population performance is initially high in the fast and too-fast scenarios. We speculate that the superior performance in the first period in these two scenarios resulted from the high uncertainty that prevailed during the initial period of the simulation. As DiMaggio and Powell (1983) pointed out, under conditions of high uncertainty, learning from other organizations may help reduce uncertainty and raise performance. Then the observed pattern of early superior performance followed by a succession of periods in which performance deteriorates in the too-fast scenario may reflect competency traps that arise relating to the indiscriminant learning of routines early on that ultimately prove harmful to the organization.

CONCLUSION

Our study of sources, dynamics, and speed of interorganizational and population-level learning advances knowledge about population-level learning in three essential ways. First, by tracking the prevalence and temporal patterning of all interorganizational imitation events in a simulated industry from its inception, we provide a first comprehensive look at the overall interorganizational learning configuration of an industry. Second, by simultaneously comparing diverse influences shaping the sources of interorganizational learning by organizations that have been examined separately in past studies (or not at all), we provide insight into the relative importance of a range of forces that foster convergent learning among organizations. And, third, by estimating the effects of rates of learning on population-level performance, we show how interorganizational learning can affect the fate of entire organizational populations. Exploring the impact of different rates of interorganizational learning on population-level performance represents a crucial addition to research on both learning and population-level transformation.

Our findings provide evidence that patterns of interorganizational learning are shaped, as we predicted, by the status, social proximity, and similarity of organizations to each other, as well as momentum in the learning process itself. They also indicate that populations that converge on a standard either too quickly or too slowly may find themselves at a serious competitive disadvantage. Weighing the benefits and risks associated with two broad learning strategies—exploiting the explorations of others (interorganizational learning) or exploring on one's own (organizational learning)—warrants consideration, since aggressive pursuit of either strategy exclusive of the other can affect the performance and longevity of the member organization and its population.

Our analysis also reveals apparent contradictions between the implications of interorganizational imitation for competitive advantage at the organizational and population levels. The resource-based view of the firm in strategic management advises firms' strategists to seek sustainable advantages that cannot easily be competed away by choosing to perform activities and routines *differently* to create (and then exploit) unique, path-dependent positions that defy imitation. Organizational learning theorists, in contrast, repeatedly caution that any such competitive advantage is likely to prove only temporary (Miller, 1990, 1993). Instead, they stress the advantages of population experience over an organization's own experience and contend that the best strategy for individual organizations may often be to emphasize the exploitation of the successful explorations of others (Levinthal & March, 1993). Notwithstanding these potential benefits of shared experience at the organization level, a population whose members fail to arrive at a standard—through interorganizational imitation and learning—may be out-competed by a population that converges, permitting standardization and coordination and the development of a reputation. Thus, while impediments to interorganizational imitation are crucial to gaining sustainable competitive advantage for each organization, facilitating such imitation is essential to the fate of the organization's population.

The practical implication of our findings is that organizational strategists should attend to facilitating interorganizational learning *before* impediments to it are raised at the organization level. This is because the performance and reputation of an organizational form determine, in large part, the benefits of being associated with the form. Of course, a necessary condition for building a reputation is the existence of a common set of core organizational routines that enables recognition of the form in the first place and identification of its members (Delacroix & Rao, 1994; Miner & Haunschild, 1995). Consequently, firm-level competitive advantages based on the creation of unique, inimitable positions depend on the existence of a successful organizational form in the first place. That the overwhelming majority of entrepreneurs start "reproducer" organizations (Aldrich & Kenworthy, 1999) in established industries that are only minimally different from existing organizations in the population, rather than innovative new firms that could potentially open up new niches or even entirely *new* populations, reinforces this speculation. Thus, while interorganizational imitation is vital to the emergence of organizational populations and their success *vis-à-vis* competing populations (Miner & Haunschild, 1995), creation of unique, inimitable positions is central to the emergence of performance variability among organizations *within* established populations (Barney, 1991).

Directions for future research also follow from this study. Although our simulation is a useful first step in developing our understanding of interorganizational and population-level learning, our results may be peculiar to the simulation environment we created. Consequently, future replications examining our hypotheses in other empirical settings are needed. Such replications would help establish the generalizability and broader significance of interorganizational learning for understanding organizational and population transformation. For example, it would be interesting to know whether the low rate of interorganizational learning in our simulated organizational community (62 events in 2,248 observations) is comparable to rates in other settings.

We did not examine different types of interorganizational learning in this study. Although we distinguished three different types of interorganizational learning—cooperative, mimetic, and inferential—the small number of learning events observed in the simulation precluded us from examining each learning type separately. Consequently, future research is needed to examine these learning types separately. Such research could investigate our conjecture that learning among competitors is more vicarious than cooperative. Nor did we examine learning content in this study. Our hypotheses address who is learning from whom as well as the dynamics of learning but are insensitive to the specific content of population-level learning. Interorganizational learning is a potential source of managerial competencies, operational and technical routines, and competitive strategies. More fine-grained research is needed about the content of learning to examine whether it moderates population-level learning processes. Past research demonstrating that the likelihood of adopting a particular routine depends on the proportion and status of other organizations that have adopted that routine (e.g., Burns & Wholey, 1993; Fligstein, 1985, 1991; Korn & Baum, 1999; Haunschild & Miner, 1997) reinforces the need for an emphasis on the content of learning.

In more general terms, our research contributes to the emerging evolutionary perspective on organizations. A theory of organizational evolution minimally requires an understanding of ecological processes of interaction, on the one hand, and historical processes of information conservation and transfer, on the other (Baum & Singh, 1994). With few exceptions, however, past studies of organizational evolution focus on ecological rather than historical processes (Baum, 1996). Moreover, while organizational evolution is typically conceptualized as hierarchical in form (Baum & Singh, 1994), studies of organizational evolution typically focus on a single level of analysis. Here, we emphasized the potential contribution of cooperative, mimetic, and inferential learning processes to our understanding of the conservation and transmission of organizational routines, to the emergence, stability, success, and transformation of organizational populations through time, and to the development and erosion of firm-level competitive advantages. Support for our hypotheses provides insight into forces that lead organizational populations to congeal (or not) at a rate that leads them to succeed (or not), as well as highlighting some of the divergent implications of interorganizational learning at organizational and population levels of analysis.

ACKNOWLEDGMENTS

Earlier versions of this paper were presented at the Administrative Sciences Association of Canada (Montreal, PQ, June 1996), Academy of Management (Cincinnati OH, August 1996) meetings in 1996, and the Carnegie Mellon-Wisconsin Knowledge Transfer and Levels of Learning Conference (Pittsburgh, PA, June 1998). Comments from Anne Miner, Henrich Greve, Thekla Rura-Polley, and conference participants helped us improve the paper.

NOTES

1. We refer here to the standardization of routines and invoke the definition articulated by Levitt and March (1988, p. 517), who referred to routines as "the forms, rules, procedures, conventions, strategies, and technologies around which organizations are constructed and through which they operate."
2. Copies of the survey instrument are available from the authors.
3. Because the maximum number of population-level learning events in a given decision period was eight, we developed estimates for Figure 1 using a maximum of eight population-level learning events.
4. Although these patterns in population performance are evident by the end of Period 4, we estimated values for additional Periods 6-8 to examine whether the patterns apparent at the end of the simulation (Period 5) persisted, were magnified, or diminished over time.

REFERENCES

Abrahamson, E., & Rosenkopf, L. (1993). Institutional and competitive bandwagons: Using mathematical modeling as a tool to explore innovation diffusion. *Academy of Management Review*, *18*, 487-517.

Aldrich H. E., & Kenworthy, A. L. (1999). The accidental entrepreneur: Campbellian antinomies and organizational foundings. In J. A. C. Baum & B. McKelvey (Eds.), *Variations in organization science: In honor of Donald T. Campbell.* (pp. 17-34). Thousand Oaks, CA: Sage.

Aldrich, H. E., & Sasaki, T. (1994). R&D consortia in the United States and Japan. *Research Policy*, *24*, 301-316.

Amburgey, T. L., Kelly, D., & Barnett, W. P. (1993). Resetting the clock: The dynamics of organizational change and failure. *Administrative Science Quarterly*, *38*, 51-73.

Amburgey, T. L., & Miner, A. S. (1992). Strategic momentum: The effects of repetitive, positional, and contextual momentum on merger activity. *Strategic Management Journal*, *13*, 335-348.

Argote, L., Beckman, S. L., & Epple, D. (1990). The persistence and transfer of learning in industrial settings. *Management Science*, *36*, 140-154.

Argote, L., & Epple, D. (1990). Learning curves in manufacturing. *Science*, *247*, 920-924.

Arthur, W. B. (1989). Competing technologies, increasing returns, and lock-in by historical events. *The Economic Journal*, *99* (March), 116-131.

Barney, J. B. (1991). Firm resources and sustained competitive advantage. *Journal of Management*, *17*, 99-120.

Baum, J. A. C. (1996). Organizational ecology. In S. Clegg, C. Hardy, & W. Nord (Eds.), *Handbook of organization studies* (pp. 77-114). London: Sage.

Baum, J. A. C., & Ingram, P. (1998). Survival enhancing learning in the Manhattan hotel industry, 1898-1990. *Management Science*, *44*, 996-1016.

Baum, J. A. C., Korn, H. J., & Kotha, S. (1995). Dominant designs and population dynamics in telecommunications services: Founding and failure of facsimile service organizations, 1969-1992. *Social Science Research*, *24*, 97-135.

Baum, J. A. C., & Mezias, S. J. (1992). Localized competition and organizational mortality in the Manhattan hotel industry, 1898-1990. *Administrative Science Quarterly*, *37*, 580-604.

Baum, J. A. C., & Singh, J. V. (1994). Organizational hierarchies and evolutionary processes: Some reflections on a theory of organizational evolution. In J. A. C. Baum & J. V. Singh (Eds.), *Evolutionary dynamics of organizations* (pp. 3-20). New York: Oxford University Press.

Baum, J. A. C., & Singh, J. V. (1996). Dynamics of organizational responses to competition. *Social Forces, 74,* 1261-1297.

Burns L., & Wholey, D. R. (1993). Adoption and abandonment of matrix management programs: Effects of organizational characteristics and interorganizational networks. *Academy of Management Journal*, *38*, 106-138.

Burt, R. S. (1987). Social contagion and structural equivalence: Cohesion versus structural equivalence. *American Journal of Sociology*, *92*, 1287-1335.

Chang, S. J. (1995). International expansion strategy of Japanese firms: Capability building through sequential entry. *Academy of Management Journal*, *38*, 383-407.

Cohen J., & Cohen, P. (1983). *Applied multiple regression/correlation analysis for the behavioral sciences*. (2nd ed.). Hillsdale, NJ: Lawrence Erlbaum Associates.

Coleman, J. S. (1981). *Longitudinal data analysis*. New York: Basic Books.

Collis, D. J. (1991). A resource-based analysis of global competition: The case of the bearings industry. *Strategic Management Journal*, *12*, 49-68.

Cyert, R. M., & March, J. G. (1963). *A behavioral theory of the firm*. Englewood Cliffs, NJ: Prentice-Hall.

Davis, G. F. (1991). Agents without principles? The spread of the poison pill through the intercorporate network. *Administrative Science Quarterly*, *36*, 583-613.

Delacroix, J., & Rao, H. (1994). Externalities and ecological theory: Unbundling density dependence. In J. A. C. Baum & J. V. Singh (Eds.), *Evolutionary dynamics of organizations* (pp. 255-268). New York: Oxford University Press.

Delacroix, J., & Swaminathan, A. (1991). Cosmetic, speculative, and adaptive change in the wine industry: A longitudinal study. *Administrative Science Quarterly*, *36*, 631-661.

Dierickx, I., & Cool, K. (1989). Assert stock accumulation and sustainability of competitive advantage. *Management Science*, *35*, 1504-1513.

DiMaggio, P. J., & Powell, W. W. (1983). The iron cage revisited: Institutional isomorphism and collective rationality in organizational fields. *American Sociological Review*, *48*, 147-160.

Epple, D., Argote, L., & Devadas, R. (1991). Organizational learning curves: A method for investigating intra-plant transfer of knowledge acquired through learning by doing. *Organization Science*, *2*, 58-70.

Fligstein, N. (1985). The spread of the multidivisional form among large firms, 1919-1979. *American Sociological Review*, *50*, 37-391.

Fligstein, N. (1991). The structural transformation of American industry: An institutional account of the causes of diversification in the largest firms: 1919-1979. In W. W. Powell & P. J. DiMaggio (Eds.), *The new institutionalism in organizational analysis* (pp. 311-336). Chicago: University of Chicago Press.

Ginsberg, A., & Baum, J. A. C. (1994). Evolutionary processes and patterns of core business change. In J. A. C. Baum & J. V. Singh (Eds.), *Evolutionary dynamics of organizations* (pp. 127-151). New York: Oxford University Press.

Greene, B. (1990). *Econometric analysis*. New York: MacMillan.

Greene, B. (1992). *LIMDEP*, version 6. New York: Econometric Studies, Inc.

Greve, H. R. (1996). Patterns of competition: The diffusion of a market position in radio broadcasting. *Administrative Science Quarterly*, *41*, 29-60.

Hannan, M. T., & Freeman, J. (1984). Structural inertia and organizational change. *American Sociological Review*, *49*, 149-164.

Haunschild, P. R. (1993). Interorganizational imitation: The impact of interlocks on corporate acquisition activity. *Administrative Science Quarterly*, *38*, 64-592.

Haunschild, P. R., & Miner, A. S. (1997). Modes of interorganizational imitation: The effects of outcome salience and uncertainty. *Administrative Science Quarterly, 42,* 472-500.

Haveman, H. A. (1993). Follow the leader: Mimetic isomorphism and entry into new markets. *Administrative Science Quarterly*, *38*, 593-627.

Hedberg, B., Nystrom, P. C. & Starbuck, W. H. (1976). Camping on seesaws: Prescriptions for a self-designing organization. *Administrative Science Quarterly*, *21*, 41-65.

Hennart, J. F., & Park, Y. (1993). Location, governance, and strategic determinants of Japanese manufacturing investment in the United States. *Strategic Management Journal*, *14*, 69-82.

Herriott, S. R., Levinthal, D. & March, J. G. (1985). Learning from experience in organizations. *AEA Papers and Proceedings*, May, *75*(2), 298-302.

Ingram, P., & Baum, J. A. C. (1997). Opportunity and constraint: Organizational learning from operating and competitive experience. *Strategic Management Journal*, *18* (Summer Special Issue), 75-98.

Jacobson, R. (1990). Unobservable effects and business performance. *Marketing Science*, *9*, 74-85.

Kahneman, D., & Tversky, A. (1979). Prospect theory: An analysis of decision under risk. *Econometrica*, *47,* 263-291.

Kelly, D., & Amburgey, T. L. (1991). Organizational inertia and momentum: A dynamic model of strategic change. *Academy of Management Journal*, *34*, 591-612.

Kogut, B., & Chang, S. J. (1994). Technological capabilities and Japanese foreign direct investment in the United States. *Review of Economics and Statistics*, *73*, 401-413.

Korn, H. J. & Baum, J. A. C. (1999). Chance, imitative and strategic antecedents to multimarket contact. *Academy of Management Journal*, *42*, 171-193.

Lant, T. K., & Baum, J. A. C. (1995). Cognitive sources of socially constructed competitive groups: Examples from the Manhattan hotel industry. In W. R. Scott & S. Christensen (Eds.), *The Institutional Construction of Organizations* (pp. 15-38). Thousand Oaks, CA: Sage.

Lant, T. K. & Mezias, S. J. (1990). Managing discontinuous change: A simulation study of organizational learning and entrepreneurship, *Strategic Management Journal*, *11*, 147-179.

Levinthal, D. A. (1991). Organizational adaptation and environmental selection—Interrelated processes of change. *Organization Science*, *2*, 140-145.

Levinthal, D. A., & March, J. G. (1993). The myopia of learning. *Strategic Management Journal*, *14*, 94-112.

Levitt, B. & March, J. G. (1988). Organizational learning. *Annual Review of Sociology*, *14*, 319-340.

Lieberman, M. B., & Montgomery, D. B. (1988). First-mover advantages. *Strategic Management Journal*, *9*, 41-58.

March, J. G. (1976). The technology of foolishness. In J. G. March & J. P. Olsen (Eds.),*Ambiguity and Choice in Organizations* (pp. 69-81). Norway: Harald Lyche & Co.

March, J. G. (1991). Exploration and exploitation in organizational learning, *Organization Science*, *2*, 71-87.

Miller, D. (1990). *The Icarus paradox*. New York: HarperCollins.

Miller, D. (1993). The architecture of simplicity. *Academy of Management Review*, *18*, 116-138.

Miller, D. (1999). Selection processes inside organizations: The self-reinforcing consequences of success. In J. A. C. Baum & B. McKelvey (Eds.), *Variations in organization science: In honor of Donald T. Campbell* (pp. 93-109). Thousand Oaks, CA: Sage. In press.

Miller, D., & Friesen, P. H. (1980). Momentum and revolution in organizational adaption. *Academy of Management Journal*, *25*, 591-614.

Milliken, F. J., & Lant, T. K. (1991). The effects of an organization's recent performance history on strategic persistence and change: The role of managerial interpretations. In P. Shrivastava., A. Huff, and J. Dutton (Eds.), *Advances in Strategic Management*, *7*, 129-156.

Miner, A. S. (1994). Seeking adaptive advantage: Evolutionary theory and managerial action. In J. A. C. Baum & J. V. Singh (Eds.), *Evolutionary dynamics of organizations* (pp. 76-89). New York: Oxford University Press.

Miner, A. S., & Haunschild, P. R. (1995). Population-level learning. In B. Staw & L. Cummings (Eds.), *Research in organizational behavior* (vol. *17*, pp. 115-166). Greenwich, CT: JAI Press.

Miner, A. S., & Mezias, S. J. (1996). Ugly duckling no more: Pasts and futures of organizational learning research. *Organization Science*, *7*, 88-99.

Miner, A. S., & Raghavan, S. V. (1999). The hidden engine of selection: Interorganizational imitation. In J. A. C. Baum & B. McKelvey (Eds.), *Variations in organization science: In honor of Donald T. Campbell* (pp. 35-62). Thousand Oaks, CA: Sage. In press.

Miner, A. S., & Robinson, D. F. (1994). Organizational and population-level learning as engines for career transitions. *Journal of Organizational Behavior*, *15*, 345-364.

Mitchell, W., Shaver, J. M. & Yeung, B. (1994). Foreign entrant survival and foreign market share: Canadian companies' experience in the United States medical sector markets. *Strategic Management Journal*, *15*, 555-567.

Palmer, D. A., Jennings, P. D. & Zhou, X. (1993). Late adoption of the multidivisional form by large U.S. corporations: Institutional, political, and economic accounts. *Administrative Science Quarterly*, *38*, 100-131.

Peteraf, M. A. (1993). The cornerstones of competitive advantage: A resource-based view. *Strategic Management Journal*, *14*, 179-192.

Porac, J. F., Thomas, H., Wilson, F., Paton, D., & Kanfer, A. (1995). Rivalry and the industry model of Scottish knitwear producers. *Administrative Science Quarterly*, *40*, 203-227.

Porter, M. E. (1980). *Competitive strategy*. New York: Free Press.

Rasler, K. (1996). Concessions, repression, and political protest in the Iranian Revolution. *American Sociological Review*, *61*, 132-252.

Starbuck, W. H. (1983). Organizations as action generators. *American Sociological Review*, *48*, 91-102.

Stinchcombe, A. L. (1965). Social structure and organizations. In J. G. March (Ed.), *Handbook of Organizations* (pp. 153-193). Chicago, IL: Rand McNally.

Tushman, M. L., & Anderson, P. (1986). Technological discontinuities and organizational environments. *Administrative Science Quarterly*, *31*, 439-465.

Tuma, N. B., & Hannan, M. T. (1984). *Social dynamics: Models and methods*. New York: Academic Press.

Tyre M. J., & Orlikowski, W. J. (1994). Windows of opportunity: Temporal patterns of technological adaptation in organizations. *Organization Science*, *5*, 98-118.

Uretsky, M., Gultekin, M., Miguel, M., Mullen, T. P., & Stumpf, S. A. (1989). *Mercado Foods Company*. New York: Business Simulations Inc. and the MSP Institute.

White, H. C. (1981). Where do markets come from? *American Journal of Sociology*, *87*, 517-545.

Wilson, B. D. (1990). The propensity of multinationals to expand through acquisitions. *Journal of International Business Studies*, *11*, 59-65.

Yelle, L. E. (1979). The learning curve: Historical review and comprehensive survey. *Decision Sciences*, *10*, 302-328.

PART III

COLLECTIVE POPULATION LEARNING

FRUITS OF FAILURE:
ORGANIZATIONAL FAILURE AND POPULATION-LEVEL LEARNING

Anne S. Miner, Ji-Yub (Jay) Kim, Ingo W. Holzinger, and Pamela Haunschild

ABSTRACT

In this qualitative and inductive study, we examine population-level learning by addressing the effects of failure events on the nature and mix of routines in a population. We reviewed approximately 50 failures and near-failures in 33 industry histories to assess how they affected other organizations in the industry and practices in the industry as a whole. Findings suggest that these events affect practices enacted by other organizations, or population-level patterns of routines in three broad ways: (1) through direct consequences of failure, (2) through reactions to failure by other organizations, and (3) through consequences of reactions to failure. Our analysis suggests that failure events can be a powerful engine of population-level learning. The processes and outcomes of population-level learning are complex and can lead to results that were not intended and might harm the population. Finally, we argue that managers can benefit from using the processes involved in population-level learning from failure.

Advances in Strategic Management, Volume 16, pages 187-220.

ISBN: 0-7623-0500-2

Historically, both organization and strategy theories appear to have a "success bias." Much of the empirical literature in both areas has a distinct survivor bias because most research concerns traits and processes of only surviving organizations. Theories emphasizing interorganizational learning tend to focus on the replication of routines and designs of apparently successful organizations (Burns & Wholey, 1993; Conell & Cohn, 1995), and diffusion studies suffer from an almost exclusive focus on practices that have successfully diffused (Rogers, 1995; Strang & Soule, 1998). Not surprisingly, organizational learning theory, which has gained substantial popularity in the domain of strategic management, chiefly addresses how managers can help their firms succeed and grow by learning the strategies and routines of presumably successful firms. Studies on bankruptcy and disasters, of course, represent important exceptions to this general trend (Perrow, 1984; Sutton & Callahan, 1987), and ecological studies on strategic management investigated models of organizational failure (Barnett & Hansen, 1996; Ingram, 1996). Failure, in these contexts, however, almost always represents the dependent variable. Causal models focus on what predicts it, or how to avoid it.

In this chapter, we ask a different question: What effects do the failure or near-failure of one or more organizations have on the larger groups of which they are a member? In asking this, we supplement these traditional approaches by considering organizational failure as an *independent* variable. So far a relatively small number of studies has attempted to study failure as an independent variable. Applying a learning framework, Sitkin (1992) studied the impact of failure within the firm and its use as a potential strategic asset. Ingram and Baum (1997) investigated how competitive experience or the history of failures in the U.S. hotel industry affects the survival chances of the remaining firms within this industry. Studies on rate dependence provide some evidence that the prior failure rate has a curvilinear effect on the survival prospects of other firms within the industry (Delacroix & Carroll, 1983; Delacroix, Swaminathan, & Solt, 1989).

In this chapter, we apply a population-level learning framework to explore ways in which the immanent or actual failure of an organization, routine, or set of routines affects population-level transformation. We define a population-level learning outcome as systematic change in the nature and mix of routines, strategies or practices enacted in a population of organizations, arising from experience (Miner & Haunschild, 1995). In this study, "routine" is used to refer to a broad class of activities and includes processes for producing goods and services, administrative procedures such as hiring or choosing suppliers, policies concerning research and development or financing, and strategies about product diversification and market selection (Cyert & March, 1963; March & Simon, 1958; Nelson & Winter, 1982).

In pursuing our research agenda, we followed an inductive process. We first selected industry histories that describe failures and near-failures of organizations and/or organizational routines, and then examined the apparent effects of these failure and near-failure incidents. The cases we studied pointed to two broad forms of failure-driven population-level learning. Each of these forms can produce changes in the nature and mix of routines enacted in a population of organizations. In *recurring interorganizational learning,* there is collective learning in the sense that many organizations react to the same external failures, so that shared vicarious experience informs change. The learning can be seen as collective because it arises from shared rather than independent organizational experience. It may also involve shared interpretations of the failure experience of others. For example, if a highly visible firm fails and many other firms not only observe the failure, but also develop a shared interpretation of that failure, the learning can be seen as collective. While this form of population-level learning may involve vicarious learning by individual organizations, the less each vicarious learning incident is independent, the more the process can be seen as one of collective population-level learning. The population-level outcomes can be seen as the sum of individual organizations' action in some cases, but the outcomes are not the simple sum of independent individual experience and actions.

In fully *collective population-level learning processes,* the learning activities involve at least one distinctly collective action, institution, and/or routine. For example, if a new industry association or coordination routine arises within a population of organizations, this would represent a fully collective learning process, as would a population of organizations in one country imitating the population-level practices in another. The cases suggest that ongoing interactions between many different organizations can create industry-wide effects that have meaning only at a population-level and may not even be known to some of the organizational participants.

METHOD

To explore the issues of failure's potential impact on change in the nature and mix of routines in populations of organizations, we reviewed industry histories, structuration studies, cases, and general histories of technological evolution including 10 volumes (40 issues) of *Business History Review* (1987-1996).

Our research process was inductive. Following standard methods for this research mode (Eisenhardt, 1989; Ragin, 1987; Strauss & Corbin, 1998), we did not formulate formal hypotheses prior to our research. Instead, we focused on building theory from what we observed in the cases reviewed. To achieve our inductive agenda, we first objectively coded each case and analyzed our coding afterward through iterations of independent review and discussion of incidents. We asked two research questions as we reviewed the data. First, did failure or near-failure events of one or more firms affect the industry or population to which they belong, and if so, how? Second, what processes produced such effects? Specially, how did learning processes influence the nature and mix of routines in the population as a whole? Third, what are the (strategic) implications of these processes and learning from failure?

Choice of Cases

We read and coded cases from multiple sources using two criteria to decide whether a case was appropriate for the study or not. First, at least one failure or near-failure had to be recorded in the case. Failure consisted of organizational death; near-failure consisted of reportedly very poor financial performance or an acquisition by another firm that was discussed as a "rescue" of a nearly bankrupt company. We included both failure and near-failure because we wanted to see whether both generate reactions and population-level consequences. Second, we eliminated cases in which the authors' objective was to include an analysis or interpretation of responses to the failures they recorded. The latter is important because we wanted to minimize the chance of including cases that had already been interpreted in ways that would bias our results.

Some sources contained more easily analyzable and more reliable descriptions of failures and their consequences than others. In particular, articles published in the *Business History Review* proved to be especially thorough and rich, and most depict entire histories or at least long time periods of existence of industries, organizations, or technologies. Hence, we selected many articles published in the *Business History Review*. We searched the articles for descriptions of failures or near-failures and then included those that satisfied the criteria described above. Table 1 outlines the 33 cases that informed our analysis.

Analysis

In reviewing each historical description, we first recorded every actual or immanent failure by an organization or an industry, its date, and a brief description of the failure. We then searched for any reactions to or consequences of the failure. Reactions and consequences were only recorded if they were vicarious in the sense that they affected other organizations or an entire population. We wanted to exclude any reaction that represented a firm learning from its own experience alone. Hence, if a company reacted to its own failure and that reaction did not have any apparent effect on other firms, the case was not included in our analysis. For accuracy and reliability, each case was reviewed by at least two researchers. When inconsistencies occurred between the individual reviews, the investigators met to discuss the inconsistencies and reach consensus. In most cases, the researchers were consistent in their recording of failures and reactions or consequences. In the few cases in which inconsistencies occurred, They were able to reach agreement during their discussions. In all, we considered 52 incidents in the 33 cases and noted about 75 distinct effects (the same incident sometimes had more than one effect).

After the incidents were recorded, we independently reviewed the cases for evidence of their apparent impact and met in multiple, iterative brainstorming sessions to find patterns within the reactions to and consequences of the failures

Table 1. Industry Histories and Cases Reviewed in the Study

Organization or Population	*Author (Year)*
Microelectronics and Computer Corporation (MCC)	Aldrich & Sasaki (1994); Murphy (1982)
American chicken-breeding industry	Burgos (1992)
intel (DRAM)	Burgelman (1994)
U.S. nuclear energy sector	Campbell (1994)
Rigid disk drive industry	Christensen (1993)
U.S. railway locomotive industry	Churella (1995)
American Telegraphone Company and the magnetic recording industry	Clark & Nielsen (1995)
VHS vs. Beta	Cusumano, Mylonadis, & Rosenbloom (1992)
DC (Direct current) system	David (1991)
U.S. electronics industry	Evan & Olk (1990)
U.S. tire industry	French (1986)
Ruhr region of Germany	Grabher (1990)
U.S. television manufacturing industry	Hamel & Prahalad (1988)
German and U.S. machine tool industry	Herrigel (1994)
European aerospace industry	Hochmuth (1986)
Italian chemical fiber industry	Kenis (1992)
U.S. railroad industry	Kennedy (1991)
Braniff International Corporation	Kharbanda & Stallworthy (1985)
Penn Central Transportation	Kharbanda & Stallworthy (1985)
European steel industry	Kogut (1986)
Refrigerator car and the American dressed-beef industry	Kujovich (1970)
U.S. microcomputer industry	Langlois (1992)
U.S. radio broadcasting industry	Leblebici et al. (1991)
Swiss watch industry	Porter & Hoff (1980)
Du Pont	Stabile (1987)
U.S. integrated steel mills	Scherrer (1991)
New businesses in Silicon Valley	Suchman (1994)
Venture capital firms and law firms in Silicon Valley	Suchman (1994)
Eastman Kodak and professional photography business	Utterback (1995)
Pony Express	Volti (1992)
People Express	Whitestone (1983)
Information-processing technology and tabulating machine industry	Yates (1993)
Betamax VCR	Yoffie, Aoki, & Debari (1987)

recorded. We first developed agreements on the existence of distinct incidents, then considered apparent effects of each incident through several review sessions, and finally generated higher-order groupings to all the incident-level effects. We found that a categorization scheme with three broad groupings captured meaningful variation among the cases. In addition, the apparent effects of the incidents suggested two population-level learning processes that differ in the degree to which they are collective.

FRUITS OF FAILURE: VARIED EFFECTS OF FAILURE

In reviewing the effects of failure described in the cases, we observed three broad groupings: (1) direct effects of failure, (2) reactions to failure, and (3) consequences of reactions to failure. The first category consists of consequences that affect the population directly or materially, through the simple elimination of practices carried out by the failed firms. These direct effects of failure have long been noted by students of organizations and economics and will not represent a major focus of our analysis. The second category represents the reactions of multiple individual organizations based on shared vicarious experiences, norms, or meanings as well as the reactions of entire populations. The last category entails the consequences of reactions to failure and their impact on population-level transformation.

Each category includes several subcategories that were grouped by the specific effects of failure. Based on the level of reaction or consequence, we also categorized each subcategory into two groups: (1) interorganizational and (2) collective. Table 2 summarizes our findings. In the following sections, we describe these processes and show how the studies reviewed suggest their existence.

DIRECT EFFECTS OF FAILURE

The direct effects of failure are those that affect the mix of routines in the population with no intermediate processes. We observed several cases in which organizations did not seem to change their routines intentionally as a result of the failures of other organizations, but the failures of one organization produced direct changes in the mix of routines in the population. This category includes removal of routines and industry consolidation.

Table 2. Effects of Failure

Category	*Interorganizational Level*	*Collective Level*
Direct effects of failure		**Removal of routines** Pony Express Betamax format video recorder Dry gelatin plate film firms U.S. customized machine tool firms **Industry consolidation (mergers and acquisitions)** U.S. machine tool industry Penn & New York Central railroads U.S. steel industry U.S. chicken breeding industry
Reactions to failure	**Imitation** U.S. & German machine tool industries U.S. steel industry **Inferential learning** U.S. airline industry U.S. radio industry U.S. TV industry U.S. steel industry U.S. nuclear energy industry U.S. tire industry Silicon Valley law and venture capital firms **Reinforcing existing routines** (**active inertia**) Dry gelatin plate films firms U.S. Live stock industry U.S. locomotive industry	**Compensating action** German machine tool industry European steel industry U.S. railroad industry U.S. nuclear energy industry U.S. steel industry U.S. chicken-breeding industry U.S. nuclear energy industry U.S. airline industry U.S. electronics industry **Creation of new entity** U.S. tire industry U.S. electronics industry European steel industry U.S. nuclear energy industry **Alerting effect** U.S. nuclear energy industry
Consequences of reactions to failure		**Second-hand legitimacy** U.S. radio networks U.S. steel industry **Boomerang effect** Microcomputer industry (IBM) U.S. steel industry **Poisoned well** DC system in U.S. Telegraphone in Denmark U.S. steel industry

Removal of Routines

In some of our cases, the failures of individual organizations and/or their organizational routines changed the nature and mix of routines in the population by simply removing routines from practice because the failed organization was gone. In some cases, this appeared to be related to shifts to apparently more "efficient" routines, but in others, one could not draw such a strong conclusion. For example, Volti (1992) showed how organizational death changes the nature and the mix of routines in a population of organizations. He described how, with the rise of the railroad, the Pony Express died, and the practices and organizational routines associated with the Pony Express no longer thrived in the population of organizations carrying mail and passengers.

Another example of the removal of routines is provided in Bugos' (1992) description of how, through the extinction of smaller, secondary businesses, practices associated with small hatcheries disappeared from the chicken-breeding industry, and routines became more homogenized within the industry. Initially the industry included autonomous breeders, small hatcheries, housers and distributors. In the 1950s "integrator" firms emerged that hatched, fed, vaccinated, slaughtered, and marketed their chickens. Exchange routines associated with transactions among small hatcheries and distributors disappeared. As the small firms died out, the integrator firms began to sell cut-up broilers under their own brand names to gain customer loyalty. By 1988 only 20% of all broilers were sold whole, in contrast to the 80% sold whole in the 1960s, usually with no brand label. The failure of small breeders even increased the genetic uniformity in the U.S. chicken breeding industry. Before the 1960s hatcheries bought from multiple small breeders. Later, large integrators bought from only a handful of breeders, making chickens more genetically uniform.

Industry Consolidation (Merger & Acquisition)

Failure of a set of organizations in an industry frequently produces industry consolidation. This could occur as a direct result of failure of members of an industry or as a result of subsequent mergers and acquisitions. Bugos' (1992) case provides an example of industry consolidation as a direct result of organizational failures. The number of American chicken hatcheries dropped from 11,400 in 1934 to 1,200 in 1971; many small hatcheries failed because it was difficult to place the "right" number of chicks in the reproductive pipeline. At the same time, the average size of the hatcheries rose from 46,000 to 2.5 million chicks per year (Bugos, 1992). This pattern of industry concentration among hatcheries contributed to the further demise of small hatcheries and created barriers against new hatcheries by making genetic uniformity and quality assurance more important.

An example of industry consolidation by subsequent mergers and acquisitions can be found in the history of the U.S. steel industry (Scherrer, 1991). Until the late 1960s, the U.S. steel industry was dominated by a handful of large integrated steel mills, but the emergence of new competition from both foreign steel producers and minimills severely threatened the survival of the integrated mills. After experiencing a series of failures due to their inability to compete with more efficient minimills and low-cost foreign producers, those integrated mills that survived began to consolidate their capacity through mergers and acquisitions to achieve higher efficiency.

Looking at the impact of direct removal of routines and industry consolidation, we see they may or may not produce change in the nature and mix of routines in the entire population. The direct removal of routines through organizational failure did indeed change the nature and mix of routines in some industries but this effect was compositional. It did not involve intermediary processes such as local organizations learning from observing others, or collective interpretation of the organizational failures. It did not involve an organization or larger collectivity changing behavior in response to experience. Industry consolidation in and of itself may or may not involve changes in the nature and mix of routines in a population. The same practices could continue in a smaller number of larger firms. In some instances, industry consolidation did appear to involve a change in the nature and mix of routines enacted in the population. In the chicken-breeding industry the death of smaller hatcheries also meant the loss of some of their practices. However, no intermediary learning processes were involved. Thus we turn our attention to other forms of population transformation.

REACTIONS TO FAILURE OF ORGANIZATIONS/ROUTINES

In many of the incidents we assessed, the failure of a focal organization and/or its routines appeared to stimulate reactions by other organizations. We also found evidence of collective reactions to failure.

Interorganizational Reactions

We noted that organizations often react to failure they observed by taking a certain course of actions. In many cases, *shared experiences, learning triggers, norms, or meaning played an important part in the learning process.* Two things make this analysis distinct from intraorganizational learning studies. First, although reactions occurred at the organizational level, those reactions were driven by shared vicarious experiences, norms, and meanings rather than an individual organization's unique experience. Second, in many cases the population change arose from the repeated nature of the interorganizational learning. The organizational level reactions included imitation, inferential learning, and reinforcement of existing routines triggered by the failure of others.

Failure-Triggered Imitation

One organizational level reaction we detected was the recurrent imitation of other, apparently successful routines triggered by the failure of an organization within the focal population. In his analysis of the U.S. and German machine tools industries, Herrigel (1994) described how American and German firms, pressured by severe market share losses and failures within their industries, finally shifted their focus from more traditional machines to computer numerical control (CNC) machines, thereby copying practices that Japanese producers had already applied for years. Although the American and German manufacturers had technical and managerial capabilities similar to their Japanese competitors for some time, it took failures within their populations to stimulate imitation of practices that had made the Japanese dominant in the marketplace.

The U.S. steel industry also reacted to immanent failure of some organizations by imitating competitive practices (Scherrer, 1991). After many American integrated steel manufacturers had sustained immense losses due to decreased demand for their products and increased competition by foreign firms and minimills, they decided to imitate what they perceived as the practices that provided their competitors with a competitive edge. Scherrer (1991, p. 196) noted, "since the Japanese mills represented the most efficient practice in sheet production, and since the latest minimills epitomized the best practice in production of small bars and rods, Big Steel had to follow the Japanese and the minimill examples, respectively." The American integrated steel mills never succeeded in their quest to imitate those practices effectively and recapture lost market share. Nevertheless, Scherrer's account of the U.S. steel industry provides an unambiguous example of interorganizational imitation triggered by observed failure.

Failure-Driven Inferential Learning

We also found cases in which firms clearly attempted to draw inferences from the failures they observed to avoid failing themselves. Thus, rather than imitating the routines of others perceived as more successful, these firms either avoided the failing routines of others or developed entirely new routines presumed to be better than those that had failed. For example, the failure of many new airlines that were incorporated after the deregulation of the U.S. airline industry in 1978 provided an opportunity for inferential learning by the population of the U.S. airline industry. Braniff International Corporation (BIC) and People Express (PE) were among the companies that took off right after the airline deregulation to capture the newly created market opportunities. BIC and PE were incorporated in 1978 and in 1980, respectively, and their capacities and market shares expanded at an unprecedented rate. Their fundamental marketing strategy was to create and maintain passenger volume by offering extremely low fares. But, while their cut-rate strategy allowed them to increase their market share rapidly, it did not provide them with sufficient financial return to cover the costs incurred from rapid expansion. Despite their initial success, BIC filed for bankruptcy in 1982, and PE shortly followed BIC's fate (Kharbanda & Stallworthy, 1985; Whitestone, 1983). Their failure suggested that a cut-rate, cut-throat route strategy might not be a viable strategic choice (Kharbanda & Stallworthy, 1985). Other airline companies that observed their failure slowed down price-cutting competition and began implementing other strategies, such as rigorous frequent flyer programs and improved customer services (Kharbanda & Stallworthy, 1985).

U.S. tire manufacturers also used failure to draw inferences about the appropriateness of certain practices (French, 1986). After the bankruptcy of several firms, including the reputable Carolina Rubber Company in the early 1930s, the remaining firms started to develop new practices to enhance their prospects of survival. Among these new practices were the introduction of second, third, and fourth-line tires to achieve better market segmentation, and the reduction of the number of dealers to become more cost-efficient. These practices were not copied from other organizations but were developed to avoid the fate of the failed companies.

Suchman (1994) presented a case of failure driven inferential learning that has particular potential for examining population-level learning processes. He described the role of venture capital firms in Silicon Valley, where venture capitalists inevitably observe failures of start-up firms (at a minimum in their own portfolio of investments). In Silicon Valley, venture capitalists had substantial interaction with each other and developed working norms not only about the structure of their investments but about the role of the venture capitalist. In particular, they tended to go beyond passive investment and play an active role in policy and strategic management choices of the firms in which they invested. This practice means that whatever lessons they drew from their own prior failures, or acquired from contacts with other venture capitalists, would powerfully affect activities in new businesses in which they invested.

Silicon Valley law firms also had a substantial influence on fundamental management choices that was well beyond passive legal advice, so that we would expect the lessons they drew from prior failures of organizations to be reflected in activities of many Silicon Valley firms (Suchman, 1994). In general, consulting firms and venture capitalists may be more likely than other organizations to see multiple failures and to have access to detailed organizational information from which one could draw inferences about the causes of failure. According to Suchman (1994), Silicon Valley venture capitalists and law firms are important transmitters of lessons learned from failure.

Inferential learning does not always benefit organizations that engage in such learning. Organizations can draw incorrect inferences from failure they have observed, and construct an illusionary causal relationship about the failure. This superstitious inferential learning can negatively affect the survival prospect of the organizations and the population they belong to (Levitt & March, 1988; Huber, 1991). A good example of such superstitious learning can be found in the history of the U.S. television industry. In the 1970s, the U.S. television manufacturing industry was seriously threatened by cost-efficient Japanese television manufacturers. Several U.S. television manufacturers failed to compete successfully with the Japanese television manufacturers and were consequently acquired by the large Japanese firms. U.S. television manufacturers, including RCA and Zenith, responded to this threat chiefly by taking cost-cutting measures, because they believed that the Japanese firms' primary competitive advantage was their manufacturing efficiency (Hamel & Prahalad, 1988).

The U.S. firms were not generally aware of the Japanese firms' ability to cross-subsidize market share battles. Hamel and Prahalad (1988, p. 20) noted that "by the time the U.S. firms closed the cost gap, Japanese competitors had established pre-emptive distribution and brand positions in most of the world's critical national markets." The Japanese firms had broadened their profit sanctuaries by rigorously expanding their international distribution systems and consolidating their brand names, while the U.S. firms' sales were limited to the U.S. market. Therefore, when a price war occurred, the Japanese firms could subsidize their losses in the U.S. market with the profits from their well-protected domestic market and third-country markets, while their U.S. counterparts had few options. Hamel and Prahalad (1988) argued that this superstitious population-wide reaction to potential failure by the U.S. television manufacturers eventually resulted in the virtual extinction of the U.S. television industry.

Failure-Driven Reinforcement of Existing Routines (Active Inertia)

Failure-driven imitation and inferential learning focus on change as a reaction to the failure of other organizations. However, firms did not always react to the failure they observed by changing their routines. Consistent with the ideas of competency traps (Levitt & March, 1988) and threat rigidity (Ocasio, 1995; Staw, Sandelands, & Dutton, 1981), we found that some organizations reacted to the failures of others by reinforcing their existing routines, even though those practices appear to have been closely related to the failures they observed. Thus, failure of some organizations in a population could result in a reinforcement of existing routines of organizations that observed the failure, a reaction we call "active inertia."

For example, when the diesel locomotive was introduced in the U.S. in the early 1930s, the American Locomotive Company (ALCo) was a major force in the industry (Churella, 1995). Although ALCo enjoyed sound financial status, good relations with its customers, and decades of experience in steam locomotive production, it lost market share after the introduction of the diesel locomotive. ALCo's market share dropped from about 70 percent in 1935 to 11 percent in 1957. Moreover, in 1957 ALCo observed the bankruptcies of two steam locomotive producers, Baldwin Locomotive Works and Lima Locomotive Works, which were similar to ALCo in their structures and routines. Nevertheless, ALCo continued to focus on its steam locomotive capabilities by committing more resources instead of switching to the diesel technology that apparently had come to dominate the market. In particular, ALCo developed internal promotion patterns through which only engineers with steam technology background could rise to the top and defended its strategy to concentrate on the steam engine vehemently in public. By 1969, ALCo had been completely driven out of the locomotive industry (Churella, 1995).

A second example is provided by Utterback's description of the developments at Eastman Kodak and in the American photography industry. During the 1930s, sales of roll film made of celluloid began to explode with the introduction of the Kodak system. This posed a significant threat to the survival of producers of the dry gelatin plate film that had been used by photographers before the introduction of the celluloid film. Producers reacted to this threat by improving the existing technology of dry plate photography. As a result, a number of improvements poured into the market (Utterback, 1995), but those improvements were not good enough to save them. They all eventually failed. Although some of the dry gelatin plate film producers had capabilities to develop the celluloid film, they chose to defend their old technology even in the face of technological discontinuity (Anderson and Tushman, 1990).

Collective Reactions

In analyzing the cases, we also found evidence that failure often induced a collective reaction by members of a population rather than, or in addition to interorganizational level reactions. Collective level reactions included compensating action, the creation of a new entity, and an alerting effect.

Compensating Action

Collective efforts to head off further failure in an industry represented an important reaction to immanent or actual failures of individual organizations. Compensating action took various forms and was driven by various entities. Government activity may be the most important and most prevalent form of what we call compensating action and it was typically spurred by members of an industry. For example, in 1977 the Italian government developed a concern with possible impending failure in the chemical fiber industry (Kenis, 1992). After five years of planning efforts to restructure the industry, involving some collective action by firms themselves, massive changes were finally made in the 1980s. These changes involved shifts in financial practices, legal standing, governance structures, employment practices, and organizational structures.

The European Coal and Steel Community (ECSC), a commission established in 1952 to coordinate the European coal and steel industry, responded similarly to the crisis of the European steel industry, which experienced a collapse of demand in 1975 due to the poor state of the European economies and the long-term trend toward the use of nonferrous materials. The sharp decline in steel demand coupled with the increasing global competition posed a serious threat to the survival of the industry (Kogut, 1986). To bring an end to the crisis, the ECSC developed a series of measures to balance the supply and demand of steel, including setting production targets, fixing minimum prices, regulating import competition, and decreasing production capacity.

In the U.S. electronics industry, firms concerned about immanent and actual failures in the industry in the 1980s pressured the government to change the antitrust laws in the 1980s. The subsequent changes in antitrust law permitted the creation of many cooperative research consortia in the industry, representing a shift in the nature and mix of cooperative routines at work in this population of organizations (Evan & Olk, 1990).

The German government reacted to a bitter crisis in the machine tool industry with several measures that were designed to improve the competitiveness of German manufacturers in world markets. Federal and state governments offered free consulting services to small and medium-sized firms in the industry to help them develop and market competitive technologies. Additionally, the federal government cooperated with industry associations to develop a special subsidy program to support research and development efforts associated with the CNC technology (Herrigel, 1994).

In some cases, governments dominated the compensatory reaction, especially when failure was difficult for the industry to control by itself. For example, in the 1960s, the survival of railroads in the northeastern region of the United States, the most densely populated part of the country, was substantially threatened partly because they were saddled with obligations to carry unprofitable passenger traffic. The railroads' attempts to cope with this problem proved to be a failure, as evidenced by the bankruptcies of the Pennsylvania and New York railroads in the late 1960s (Kennedy, 1991). To reduce the burden of carrying unprofitable passenger traffic on the U.S. railroads, the U.S. Congress created the national passenger railroad corporation, today called Amtrak, in 1970.

Industry-level cooperation efforts represented another form of collective response to failure. An example of this can be found in the U.S. nuclear energy sector. The accident at Three Mile Island in 1979 severely jeopardized the legitimacy and survival of the U.S. nuclear energy industry. Having realized that another accident would bury commercial nuclear power in the United States, the firms in the industry cooperated by mobilizing through associations and promotional networks to regain public confidence and improve technology. Later, several firms formed joint ventures to purchase nuclear power plants together to spread the risk and use their resources more efficiently (Campbell, 1994).

In several cases, the compensating action involved collective action within the population of organizations in combination with action taken by a government, a higher level collective actor.

Creation of New Entity

Some industries we studied reacted to a failure of subsets of organizations by creating a new entity in an effort to prevent further failures. Creating a new collective entity may yield new routines in the population and, consequently, produce population-level learning. For example, the existence of the U.S. electronics industry was severely threatened by the increasing market domination of Japanese firms throughout the 1980s. The U.S. electronics industry responded to what it perceived as immanent failure by creating the Microelectronics and Computer Technology Corporation (MCC), a major research consortium (Aldrich & Sasaki, 1994; Murphy, 1982). This, in turn, represented a new "collective routine" for the population (Miner & Haunschild, 1995) and added to the representation of collaborative routines in the population as a whole.

In other examples, German steel firms created new entities in the form of sales associations to control their prices when they were threatened by hyper-price competition (Kogut, 1986). Similarly, firms in the U.S. nuclear energy sector responded to the Three Mile Island accident by instituting an association to promote safety and R&D (Campbell, 1994), a new collective entity that added collective routines to the industry.

Alerting Effect

A less traditional impact of organizational failure is its alerting effect for other members of an industry or organizational community. Observers of organizations have long noted that failure is difficult to interpret within organizations (Sitkin, 1992). Internal actors may conclude that their own failure is a signal to work harder on a particular objective or business, rather than a sign that they are in the wrong business (Levinthal & March, 1993). Our review of industry histories seems to indicate, however, that failures or dramatic downturns of other, major firms sometimes stimulated firms to conclude that there may be fundamental problems in their industry, or at least in the implementation or execution of their own businesses, and to respond to this by developing new shared routines. In a study of industrial decline and reorganization in the Ruhr region of Germany, for example, Grabher (1990) noted that decreased demand in itself had little impact. He suggested that only after plant closures and the movement of the headquarters of the oldest firm of the coal, iron, and steel complex to another region did firms undertake a reassessment of their situation and begin to create new core business areas as well as some collaborative efforts.

Failures, in contrast to other problems or downturns, may have had a special impact because they were more salient to observers (Haunschild & Miner, 1997). An important feature of this "wake-up call" effect, however, is that it does not necessarily contain information about what firms should do differently in the future. Failure may therefore not lead to any action by the observer but rather to a firm's "non-action." The observing firms may be alerted only to avoid the actions of the failed firm. Moreover, that the alerting effect *can* occur does not, of course, mean that it always does occur. In the Swiss watch industry, for example, observers noted that for many years failures did not, in fact, appear to produce an alerting effect (Porter & Hoff, 1980).

Consequences of Reactions to Failure

In many cases we reviewed, the actions taken by individual organizations, groups of organizations, or higher-level entities worked together to create consequences that affected the entire population, frequently in unanticipated ways and sometimes without full awareness of the actors. An interesting aspect of this phenomenon is that action taken intentionally at the organizational level frequently produced unintentional population-level consequences. In all, we found three different classes of consequences of reactions to failure, which we term "second-hand legitimacy," a "boomerang effect," and a "poisoned well effect."

Second Hand Legitimacy

Leblebici, Salancik, Copay, and King (1991) described several phases of industry evolution in the U.S. radio broadcasting community. In the phase from 1950 to 1965, radio networks were concerned about potential failure because of the threat posed by the rise of television. The national networks reportedly tried to extend their businesses, experimenting with such areas as simulcasting audio portions of TV shows, stereo AM and FM broadcasts, and new forms of pay radio, none of which rescued their existing business or evolved into a new business area.

During the same period, independent, local radio stations introduced many innovative and successful practices that cut their operating costs drastically and helped them to win back advertisers who had defected to TV. The national networks then changed their radio businesses by imitating apparently successful features of local radio broadcasting, such as adding more focused programming, using pre-recorded music (rather than live), and having "special format" shows aimed at specialized audiences. These did not work to revive the national networks' programming business, evidently in part because such programming depended on local knowledge, which national networks did not have (Leblebici et al., 1991). However, the adoption of these activities in response to the threat of failure legitimized such practices and made them part of the mainstream norms of the radio broadcasting industry. We call this effect second-hand legitimization.

In essence, the networks' response to the threat of failure ultimately strengthened the standing of local radio broadcasters and the influence of their practices. From the population-level learning perspective, the radio networks' responses to potential failure eventually eroded their own strengths but produced population-level learning of new programming practices such as special formats and pre-recorded music. Leblebici and colleagues (1991) described other, similar transitions in which efforts failed to revive flagging businesses but set in motion new practices that came to permeate the industry and in some cases provide new businesses for others.

In a study of the U.S. steel industry, Scherrer (1991) provided another example of second-hand legitimacy. The U.S. steel industry had been governed by the oligopolistic structure for generations. A few, vertically integrated companies controlled most of the American steel production and dominated the market. In the 1970s, the nine largest integrated steel mills supplied about 75% of the domestic steel consumption. This oligopolistic structure, coupled with the collusive behavior of the large steel producers, enabled the integrated steel mills to effectively control the price structure and protected them from demand fluctuations. In the late 1960s, however, the emergence of new competition began to threaten the oligopolistic power of the integrated steel mills. Foreign steel producers, which benefited from low labor costs, low capital costs, and a drastic decline in ocean freight rates, rapidly expanded their market share in the United States. In addition, the widespread use of nonferrous materials such as plastics and aluminum significantly decreased the steel demand (Scherrer, 1991). At the same period, the minimills emerged, using advanced technologies such as the electric furnace and continuous casting, which provided substantial capital and labor savings (Scherrer, 1991), and began to erode the market share of the integrated mills. The use of more efficient technology, in combination with the advantage of specialization and a high-capacity utilization rate, allowed the minimills to achieve much higher productivity than the integrated mills. The higher productivity helped many minimills to remain profitable even when the steel demand was low.

In the 1970s, after experiencing severe financial and market share loss, the integrated mills attempted to improve their manufacturing efficiencies by imitating practices of the minimills. They modernized their existing facilities, and some integrated mills bought or built their own minimills. But little worked. Because most integrated minimills operated substantially below capacity, the addition of new minimills meant further deterioration of their already low utilization rates (Scherrer, 1991). The integrated mills' attempts to adopt the minimills' practices, however, led to the convergence of the integrated mills' practices with those of the minimills. While the integrated mills decreased their degree of vertical integration by importing an increasing amount of semi-finished steel, the minimills strengthened their control over their raw material. While the integrated mills narrowed down their product variety, the minimills expanded their product variety. In summary, the integrated mills' attempts to improve their productivity by imitating minimills strengthened the legitimacy of practices initially used by the minimills. From the population-level perspective, the integrated mills' attempts to address impending failure did not provide the solutions to their problems, but produced population-level learning of new practices in the U.S. steel industry.

Boomerang Effect

When IBM first entered the personal computer (PC) market in 1981, it chose not to design its own proprietary system but to adopt an open modular system, which allowed competitors to produce compatible machines. This open system strategy gave IBM a majority stake in the PC standard, but made it vulnerable to the competition from clone manufacturers. By 1988, IBM's worldwide market share of IBM-compatible PCs decreased to only 24.5% (Langlois, 1992). Clone makers also began beating IBM in introducing new technologies.

IBM's response to its impending failure in the PC market was to begin making the PC proprietary again. In 1987, when IBM announced its PS/2 line of PCs, it attempted to replace the existing 16-bit industry bus standard, called the Industry Standard Architecture (ISA), with a new 32-bit proprietary bus, called the Micro Channel Architecture (MCA). IBM's attempt to use a proprietary bus architecture was not only an attempt to replace an old dominant design but also to prevent clone makers from taking advantage of the new architecture (Langlois, 1992).

In response to IBM's strategic move, the major clone makers banded together and began to develop a competing 32-bit bus architecture, called the Extended Industry Standard Architecture (EISA). As a result, IBM lost further market share, although it sold PCs using the MCA almost exclusively. This story embraces a complex, interlevel learning process: IBM's failure to capitalize its open modular PC architecture, producing organization-level learning (the introduction of the proprietary MCA), which triggered collective knowledge creation by the clone makers (the development of the EISA). This process made IBM's strategy obsolete. We call this the boomerang effect.

Scherrer (1991) provided another example of the boomerang effect in his study of the U.S. steel mills. The strong challenge of low-cost foreign steel producers posed a significant threat to the survival of the U.S. integrated mills, which responded by persuading the government to impose import quotas that would restrict the amount of steel imported. The foreign producers reacted with a shift to higher-priced products and with a substantial increase in prices for wire rods, which had been their major export. On one hand, these foreign steel producers' reactions exacerbated the U.S. integrated mills' declining market position because the foreign producers began to erode the higher-priced product market that had been occupied by the integrated mills. On the other hand, the U.S. minimills became the principal beneficiaries of these reactions because they were able to capture the wire-rod market share that was dropped by the foreign producers (Scherrer, 1991). Thus, the collective population-level reaction of the US integrated mills (the push for protectionism) to their failure triggered a reaction that worsened the situation for one segment of the U.S. steel-producing population but benefited the other segment.

Poisoned-Well

In some of the industry accounts analyzed here, failure of one organization or routine was interpreted by other organizations as a signal that a whole type of organization or strategy was doomed. Failures and efforts to overcome them apparently produced a collective recipe or belief that certain strategies could not succeed. After that, the routine or practice no longer appeared in the population. For example, after several failing attempts to improve manufacturing efficiency, several of the U.S. integrated mills began to examine the possibility of constructing or acquiring a minimill (Scherrer, 1991). Armco built one minimill and bought another, but they both failed. Other integrated mills that attempted to enter the minimill sector followed a similar fate. These events seemed to trigger an industry-wide norm or assumption that it is inherently impossible for an integrated mill to move into the minimill sector. None of the major U.S. integrated mills operates a minimill now (Scherrer, 1991). These failures signaled that operating minimills was not a feasible strategy for the integrated mill population, and the strategy died out in the population without further attempts.

Another interesting example of this effect can be found in David's (1991) description of the so-called battle of standards over the direct current (DC) and the alternating current (AC) in the electrical supply industry. During 1887-1892, the DC system, supported by Edison, and the AC system, represented by the Westinghouse and Thompson-Houston companies, were competing for the electricity supply market. Edison vigorously opposed the introduction of the AC system, arguing it was dangerous and inefficient, but his DC system, in which he had invested his intellectual and financial assets, eventually lost out. After Edison had withdrawn from the electrical supply business, no solely DC-oriented manufacturing entity existed in the United States, although several European countries successfully developed DC-based electrical systems later. Leaving aside the issue of the relative economic and technological superiority of the two competing systems, the salient failure of Edison and his company signaled that the United States was not a fertile place for DC-based systems to thrive and further development in the area ceased.

In another example, the Danish telephone technician Valemar Poulsen invented the world's first magnetic recorder, the telegraphone. Despite the high commercial potential of the telegraphone, he failed to commercialize his invention. Poulsen and his Danish associates first tried to commercialize the telegraphone in Denmark by establishing a Danish development network and joint ventures, but with little success. Poulsen eventually closed his Danish operation and turned his attention to other countries, such as Germany and the United States. There were no further attempts to commercialize the telegraphone or other magnetic recording devices in Denmark (Clark & Nielsen, 1995).

The population-level outcomes driven by poisoned-well signals may have several significant strategic implications. The poisoned-well signal could produce harmful population-level learning, because a population might abandon routines and strategies prematurely without careful examination. For example, industry experts blamed the rigid, oligopolistic structure of the steel industry for its inability to succeed in the minimill sector, but Scherrer (1991) argued that, with a proper strategy, the U.S. integrated mills could have successfully entered the minimill sector.

DISCUSSION

Potential of Failure-Driven Learning

The above evidence suggests the power of failure in driving interorganizational and collective learning processes and illustrates a variety of ways in which the learning process may have collective elements. The evidence is qualitative and at this point does not allow statements on how frequently these events occur nor what their net impact may be. Work in progress, however, suggests that further review may refine our understanding of these processes as well as reveal other failure effects (Kim, 1999). The current work, combined with existing theory on population-level change, suggests potentially complex relationships between failure effects and population-level learning. Figure 1 diagrams the key relationships between failure and reactions to failure and population-level consequences of these reactions. This figure represents a summary of the analyses provided by our coding of the 33 failure cases.

According to the framework outlined in Figure 1, the failure of organizations leads to reactions by organizations and/or populations, which in turn produce population-level consequences. We envision that the failure of organizations will, in some cases, be independent of the failure of routines, as routines may fail without their associated organizations failing—as when Sony's Betamax format failed, but Sony did not (Cusumano, Mylonadis & Rosenbloom, 1992)—or organizations may fail although the routines they followed are still used by others in the population. In some cases organizational failure may lead to the elimination of a routine from the population, as when the cut-rate strategy of People Express was not used by other airlines. What is important here is that both failure of organizations and failure of routines create responses by other organizations. The reaction to failing organizations may be to try to figure out which routine caused the failure and use that knowledge (which may, of course, be false) to avoid that routine or develop a new alternate routine.

The reactions to failure of an organization and/or a routine vary in the ways and degree to which the learning processes are collective (Figure 1). At the primarily interorganizational level, we found four general categories of reactions. These categories include, first, reactions that result in imitation of apparently more successful organizations, as in the case of integrated steel mills attempting to imitate

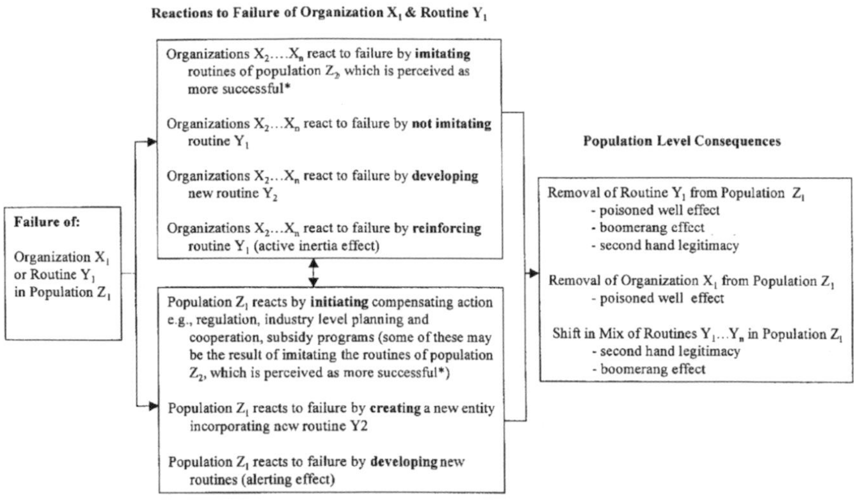

Figure 1. Failure, Reactions to Failure, and Population Level Consequences

the minimills. Another reaction is avoiding the failed routine or organization, as when airlines did not imitate People Express's cut-rate pricing strategy. A third reaction is to develop a new routine, as when surviving tire manufacturers reduced the number of dealers after several tire manufacturers went bankrupt. Finally, a fourth reaction is to reinforce a failing routine, as when American Locomotive committed more resources to steam technology after seeing other steam locomotive producers go bankrupt, as a way of attempting to stave off failure.

Also shown in Figure 1 are the various reactions to failures by populations or other collectivities of organizations. These processes mirror the processes undertaken by organizations to some extent but are distinct in that there is a population-level response in addition to or instead of the cumulative organization-level responses. For example, the U.S. electronics industry responded to the threat of industry failure by creating the MCC, an industry-level research consortium. This was a population-level response of imitating routines (industry consortium) perceived to be successful in a different national setting (Japan). This is a population-level, not an organization-level response although individual organizations were active in promoting the population-level response through lobbying and other actions. Another category of population-level responses is the creation of a new (population-level) entity, as in the case of German firms creating sales associations to control prices when threatened with failure. Finally, a third category of population-level response is through an alerting effect, resulting in the development of new routines, as when the failure at Three Mile Island stimulated the reassessment of all nuclear technologies and an effort to minimize future failures. In many cases these reactions represent a deliberate. "collective strategy" involving planned cooperation (Bresser, 1988; Dollinger, 1990).

Although our cases did not highlight population-level processes of reacting to failure by reinforcing an existing routine or avoiding a routine, these processes may still occur in some situations. The Swiss government, for example, helped the Swiss watch industry commit resources to retaining existing firms and technologies, thus reinforcing existing routines surrounding older watch technologies even after new ones were invented (Porter & Hoff, 1980).

The result of these organizational and populational responses on the population as a whole can take several forms, including the removal of a given routine from the population, removal of an organization from the population, and a shift in mix of routines with no change in the composition of organizations. These three population-level consequences are not always independent, as when the removal of an organization with a unique routine removes the routine from the population or when the removal of a routine shifts the mix of routines in the population. For example, we discussed the second-hand legitimization of the routines of local broadcasters into the mainstream of the U.S. radio broadcasting industry. The process of second-hand legitimization began with a threat of failure, which shifted the mix of routines in the radio broadcasting population (as the routines of the local broadcasters were adopted), ended with the eventual removal of some of the large network stations' older routines from the population. Finally, it is clear that responses to failure can have either positive or negative population-level consequences which have implications for the impact of population-level learning.

Positive Potential of Failure-Driven Learning

Traditionally, success has been perceived as a key generator of learning. Within organizations, success may increase slack that facilitates unintentional innovation (Levinthal & March, 1993) and can be a source of self-confidence that encourages managers to take risks (Levitt & March, 1988). March (1981) argued that organizational change can be stimulated by success. Success often decreases the intensity of search and experimentation, however (Levinthal & March, 1993). If a population observes a successful development by a firm that belongs to the population, other organizations in that population may follow the successful routine without rigorous search for new, perhaps better routines. This poses several dangers to the population. First, the lack of search and experimentation could lead the population to adopt a suboptimal technology as a standard (Cowan, 1990). Second, individual firms may fall into competency traps (Levitt & March, 1988), in which firms exploit successful procedures further, increasing the opportunity cost of exploration (Levitt & March, 1988; March, 1991).

In contrast, failure can increase the level of search and experimentation. Failure is more salient than success in many cases. Failure that serves as a signal for the danger of inertia may provide a relatively efficient device for population-level change. Like the canary in the mine, failures, which may provoke appropriate searches for causal factors leading to the failures; then benefit the population as a whole. This relatively high visibility of failure can promote organizational learning (Haunschild and Miner, 1997), with the result that firms note the failure and are encouraged to allocate more resources to exploring new business opportunities. This has population-level advantages in that it increases the number of variations in the population, facilitating innovation and reducing the possibility of being trapped in a suboptimal routine or strategy. At the organizational level, failure decreases slack (Levinthal and March, 1993). At the population-level, however, failure could sometimes increase slack because resources released by failed firms will become available to the rest of firms in the population. Thus, failures may generate experimentation within the population. The variation caused by such experimentation may increase the likelihood of discovering new successful routines (Miner and Haunschild, 1995).

Simple copying rules, such as copying successful firms, could provide faster population-level responses to changed circumstances but could also lead to only partial or inadequate changes in population practices (Miner & Raghavan, forthcoming). Two of the reactions to failure that we noted, organizations imitating the routines of another organization perceived as more successful and populations imitating the routines of another population perceived as more successful, often involve making inferences about "success." Valid inferences from the failure of a few organizations could generate understanding of causal processes that could, in principle, guide future action with more subtlety than simple copying rules (Sitkin, 1992). That this is difficult to do is revealed by the inconclusive systematic research on organizational performance outcomes. Yet, undoubtedly, making appropriate inferences from organizational failures can be done. The question is how often or in which circumstances can "appropriate" inferences occur and what are the possible problems in making such inferences?

Problems of Failure-Driven Learning

While organizational failure and/or failure of routines offer the potential for population-level learning that may benefit collectivities of organizations, it may not be always beneficial. Collective learning from failure is difficult for several reasons. First, organizations routinely mask failure to some degree, either for simple material reasons such as reducing unnecessary legal exposure, or for social reasons, such as face-saving and coalition building (Feldman & March, 1981; Pfeffer, 1981). Even more importantly, it is difficult to make good inferences from organizational failures, even if one knows the true degree of failure and the actual actions that preceded it (Sitkin, 1992). The ambiguity of organizational systems makes it difficult to link actions and outcomes (March & Olson, 1976). Gaining information on failures in many other organizations generally imposes unrealistic information gathering and processing demands, especially given the difficulty organizations have in learning from even their own experiences.

Even when interorganizational/collective learning from failure does occur, it may be the result of incorrect inferences and assumptions and thus may actually harm populations. This occurs fairly commonly in early technology trajectories. Failure of the first firms to commercialize a new invention may lead others to conclude that a particular technology cannot be developed successfully when, in fact, it can be.

For example, the possibility of raising voltage and thereby lowering the cost of DC electrical systems was explored in the late 1880s in the United States. But "because of a combination of problems associated with the battery technology available at the time, the dangers of operating a high-potential system having dynamos wired in series, and the usual run of financial difficulties, this particular project never took off, and the concept was not pursued further in the United States" (David, 1991, p. 565). The British, however, did not "learn" from this failure not to pursue this line of technological development and successfully developed it. The potential for incorrect interorganizational learning means that population-level learning processes induced by failure may lead to systematically harmful outcomes, as described above, in this poisoned-well effect, in which a promising routine is not developed in and/or removed from a population.

In other cases, organizations may be removed from a population as a result of incorrect inferences drawn from failures. For example, there are probably cases in which venture capitalists mistakenly use the failure of one type of start-up as a signal that they should not continue funding another, thus removing an organizational form from a population. Incorrect learning could also result in harmful population outcomes in periods of institutional experimentation, or in systemic technologies that require the development of standards. Indeed, these processes could lead to "runaway" outcomes in which the failure of some practices alerts a population to danger, and widespread copying of ill-advised shifts to new routines or practices ensue that harm the population as a whole (Boyd & Richerson, 1985). Our earlier case of the extinction of the U.S. television manufacturing industry illustrates this point (Hamel & Prahalad, 1988).

Even when population-level learning involves the diffusion of new routines that could be valuable for individual firms, the collective outcome can be harmful. U.S. paper manufacturers, for example, appeared to "learn" the crucial role of economies of scale, with widespread adoption of massive production equipment. The efficiency of these machines then led to an oversupply of paper, however, resulting in a dramatic decrease in profitability for the papermaking community (Taylor, 1995). In other cases, the development of new efficient technologies that are adopted on a widespread basis might benefit the entire population in terms of efficiency. Whether learning is beneficial or harmful for the population depends on many factors, including the presence of a competing population, technology factors, and product characteristics.

When collections of organizations react to failures in their midst, they frequently search for solutions that can rescue them from similar failures. The urgent need for immediate solutions can lead them to adopt myopic collective solutions at the cost of better ones. For example, in the 1970s, as we described above, the European steel industry confronted a crisis due to the sharp decline in demand and increasing competition. The European Coal and Steel Community (ECSC) developed sets of both short-term and long-term measures to head off further crisis. The short-term measures included setting production targets, fixing minimum prices, and regulating import competition, and the long-term measures included reducing the capacity of the European steel producers. This is a form of compensating action at the population-level. The short-term measures turned out to be successful, temporarily stabilizing the European steel industry, but they made the long-term measures, which could have provided the European steel industry with a permanent solution, largely ineffective (Kogut, 1986).

Overall, then, population-level learning that arises from the observation of and reaction to the failure of organizations and routines by no means assures population-level adaptation or prosperity and could, in fact, lead to population-level decline under some circumstances.

Contributions to Understanding Population-Level Learning

This work advances work on knowledge transfer and population-level learning in several ways. First, research on population-level learning is still emerging in terms of key constructs and claims. This paper represents work in progress on developing meaningful and generative definitions and partial models of population-level learning outcomes and related processes. We began with the broad definition of population-level learning by Miner and Haunschild (1995) as experience driven systematic change in the nature and mix of routines. Examining many incidents of failure and near-failure suggested two different broad forms of population-level learning, which vary in the degree to which they may be seen as collective. While consistent with the early distinction made by Miner and Haunschild concerning engines of population-level learning, these two broad forms seems to make the construct of population-level learning less ambiguous.

Specifically, the data suggested a focus on two population-level learning processes. In primarily *interorganizational learning,* failure induced multiple organizations within a population to change their routines, often as a result of shared experiences, norms, or meanings. The more shared experiences, norms, or meanings characterize the process, the more the learning process is collective. In *collective learning,* more learning elements involve collective action, or purely interactive processes. Here, organizations not only share the collective cognitions, they also act collectively, sometimes creating new population-level routines and assumptions. Further research and theoretical development will be necessary to clarify how different aspects of learning may vary across levels, including knowledge generation, acquisition, transfer, and exploitation.

We did not discuss the subprocesses involved in the various organizational reactions to failure listed in Figure 1, another important domain for further work. One such important subprocess is the movement of personnel from firm to firm, especially personnel from failing or failed organizations (Haveman & Cohen, 1994; Wade & Porac, this volume). Such movement is likely to have important effects on whether a firm reacts to failure by developing a new routine or not imitating an existing routine. Executives tend to bring routines from their previous employers to new employers (Rao & Drazin, 1998), thus affecting the distribution of routines in organizations. When executives move from failed firms to other firms, especially those outside their industry, such movement is likely to result in reactions to failure and thus population-level consequences. It would be interesting to study, for example, how personnel movement from failing U.S. television manufacturers to other firms affected the distribution of routines in the industries represented by those other firms. In addition, to the degree that we claim population-level learning processes often involve inference or shared cognition, further work can fruitfully address the interpretive aspects of population-level learning, along with issues of collective memory (Walsh, 1995).

Our research also indicates the complexity of population-level learning. Population-level learning is a multilevel phenomenon, and its processes and outcomes are difficult to predict. In this paper, we show that intentional reactions to the failure of others can have unintended outcomes for the whole population. The history of the U.S. radio broadcasting industry (Leblebici et al., 1991) and Scherrer's (1991) account of the U.S. steel industry demonstrate that the population-level consequences of organizational actions are often unpredictable to participants and perhaps more broadly. It is this complexity, however, that makes population-level learning such a fruitful and intriguing area of study.

If the effects we describe here prove pervasive or powerful, this work also has potential implications for exploring industry dynamics. At its broadest level, our work argues that patterns of prior organizational failures will substantially influence the survival and prosperity of remaining organizations. If the observation of others occurs within neighborhoods of interaction (see Ginsberg, Larsen & Lomi, Baum & Berta, Lant & Phelps, this volume), this will significantly influence collective dynamics, including both industry evolution and regional economic growth and decline. In addition, it would imply that failure events are not independent, which might in turn have implications for studies of age dependence. These potential implications and extensions of our exploratory work deserve attention.

This study focuses on failure as an engine for changes in the nature and mix of routines in a population. We do not claim that failure is the only or even the most important stimulus for learning, of course. Our research shows, however, that failure can trigger important changes within a population of organizations. There is very little research on the effects of failure as an independent variable (Sitkin, 1992). Although we have argued that this process may or may not produce adaptive or useful knowledge, we believe it represents an important form of knowledge creation and transfer. Focus on this topic raises longstanding issues concerning the adaptation of systems with multiple levels of actors and feedback (Kauffman, 1993; Levinthal & March, 1993; March, 1991). We invite others to consider the potentially complex effects of failure at this and other levels of analysis.

Finally, we note a key area related to theoretical clarification of the effects of failure. We include both failures and near-failures in our analyses in this chapter. Our work suggests that near-failures cause reactions by other firms (and thus, population-level consequences) but brings up the issue of how much failure is needed to produce these effects. How poorly does a firm or set of firms have to do to produce reactions by others? And do the reactions differ by whether a failure or near-failure is involved? Is one more salient than the other? Do firms "learn" better from failure or near-failure? A related issue is that of failure of firms versus the failure of routines. Do reactions differ in consequence of whether it was a firm that failed, a routine that failed without the firm failing, or a group of firms (or entire industry) threatened by failure? Investigating these issues may illuminate important factors in population transformation.

STRATEGIC IMPLICATIONS

The evidence presented in this chapter suggests that failures or near-failures of individual organizations, practices, or routines can have significant effects on the structure of the population to which they belong. Failure, therefore, plays a critical role in the evolution of populations or industries. Evolutionary perspectives have recently found their way into strategy research, as evidenced by the *Strategic Management Journal*'s Special Issue in 1996 "*Evolutionary Perspectives on Strategy*," and emphasize the dynamic interactions between organizations, populations of organizations, and their environments (Barnett & Burgelman, 1996; Schendel, 1996). Our analyses reinforce this notion by demonstrating the close interconnections between organizational failure on the one hand and population level transformation on the other. Failure provides individual firms as well as the collective with an opportunity to learn and actively enact their environments.

Because failure is such a significant factor for change on the level of the population, it is important that managers and other decision makers pay close attention to it. For reasons we discussed above, learning from failure may not be easy. Furthermore, one of the most consistent findings of attribution research is that observers tend to attribute failure of others to personal or organizational characteristics of the person or organization experiencing failure (Nisbett & Ross, 1980). Hence, the ability to learn from the failures of others may be inhibited by neglecting the implications for one's own organization or the collectivity.

Nonetheless, our examination of organizational failures, reactions to those failures, and the consequences of those reactions clearly demonstrates that firms may benefit from paying attention to the analysis of failure of others (Ocasio, 1997). Once attention is allocated to the identification and analysis of failure, the visibility of failures should allow firms to identify them quickly so that more energy can be allotted to the task of drawing correct inferences from the failures of others.

Intuition and common wisdom imply that the sources of failure should be avoided. Our analyses, however, suggest that managers should not simply avoid routines, technologies, or strategies connected with failed firms. As the cases in our poisoned well category indicate, such beliefs may be incorrect and leave feasible and even more profitable options neglected. Thus, making correct inferences from failure is an important task for organizational decision makers.

Failures frequently induce a shock to the industry and the individual organizations within it. Taken-for-granted rules and procedures might be questioned and collective beliefs might be challenged. While such a situation creates uncertainty for the organizations involved, it also provides an opportunity to actively shape the transformation of the industry. The cases of the U.S. radio industry (Leblebici at al., 1991), the U.S. steel industry (Scherrer, 1991), and the U.S. airline industry (Kharbanda & Stallworthy, 1985; Whitestone, 1983) demonstrate how organizations within an industry that experienced a crisis changed some institutionalized practices dramatically and, therefore, changed the fate of their industries. However, not all of those changes turned out to be successful and some organizations failed despite their active involvement in the change process.

Although we do not claim that cooperative efforts are generally superior in dealing with crisis situations, in many cases collective actions effectively stimulated survival-enhancing learning after failure for organizations and populations or industries. In our data, collective strategies appeared to be particularly effective when the entire population was threatened or affected by failure. Through collective strategies, organizations may be able to collectively enact their environments and buffer their industries from further shocks (Astley & Fombrun, 1983). While cooperative strategies, such as alliances and networks, may buffer the shock of environmental change for the firms involved (Contractor & Lorange, 1988; Miner, Amburgey, & Stearns, 1990), truly collective strategies, such as the creation of research consortia or industry associations, and lobbying efforts, may be capable of absorbing the shock for the entire industry.

Strategy revolves around the search for competitive advantage. For individual firms to achieve competitive advantage or abnormal returns, they need to differ from their competitors. Hence, variation in the population is necessary to allow for competitive advantage. Imitation of apparently successful firms, such as benchmarking the best practices in an industry, does not generally produce variation, although it may if the imitation is not perfect, is sequenced, or combines different modes of imitation (Miner & Raghavan, forthcoming). Learning from failure, however, makes use of variation within the population and thus provides an opportunity for competitive advantages for individual firms that execute it with varied levels of competence. This strategic tool goes beyond absorptive capacity (Cohen & Levinthal, 1989) to include the capability to observe and make useful inferences from the natural variation in outcomes for others (Haunschild & Beckman, 1998). Failure can spur fruitful learning by organizations and the population as a whole. In fact, the population may learn more from failure experiences than from apparent successes because of their greater visibility and the potential to develop more accurate and more sophisticated causal models.

In short, our work underscores that organizations can deliberately use failure-driven processes as a strategic tool. At the firm level, firms can look for and exploit practices incorrectly blamed for prior failure (which others will avoid through the poisoned-well effect). They can draw inferences by comparing failed with successful practices/organizations. They can stay alert to the likelihood that other firms disguise failures and avoid imitating popular practices that are not in fact producing good outcomes. They can also pool information with other allied firms to get more complete data on failed practices or firms (Haunschild & Beckman, 1998). These steps are especially promising because they encourage inferential learning and the creation of new practices or strategies. If currently successful, firms can learn to avoid reacting to failure of others in ways that actually increase their own chances of failure by drawing incorrect inferences from the failures they observed. If currently marginal, they can learn to stimulate dysfunctional reactions by more established firms to observed failures.

Collections of firms can use failure as a device to detect collective threats and as a source of collective learning (Bresser, 1988; Dollinger, 1990). Our study implies that the prosperity of an industry/population depends on a healthy balance between the dissemination of useful practices and experimentation with other practices, even though they sometimes generate failure. This means that industry association leaders face a trade-off between assisting all members to adopt perceived best practices, and encouraging variation of practices, which may generate some firm failures. Leaders may want to focus not only on how to encourage diffusion of good practices, but also on how to harvest the value of failures. Policymakers may want to consider the same balance. If the main value of firm-level failures is the removal of inefficient practices, as assumed in some economic theory, there is little role for policymakers than to make sure competition is fair. However, if firm failures play a crucial role as experiments, but such learning is difficult, policymakers may need to take action to enhance effective learning from failures of others.

CONCLUSION

Two major theories that speak to population-level change imply that the failure of organizations may be good for the collectivities to which they belong. Traditional economic theory sees failure as a way of eradicating inefficient businesses, which yields a better mix of routines in the population after the failures. Similarly, population ecology has argued that populations of organizations may move to closer alignment with environmental constraints through failures of firms (Hannan & Freeman, 1977, 1989). Competition produces failure, which leaves more valuable routines at work in the population. In these frameworks, the impact of the failure of organizations on industry evolution comes primarily from the direct subtraction of the inappropriate and inefficient activities conducted in particular organizations.

In this chapter, we have suggested additional effects of failure of individual organizations. Failures, although harmful on one level of analysis (individual organization), may be beneficial on another (population). This distinction between the prosperity of individual organizations and the systems they belong to has been noted before. Levinthal and March (1993, p. 103), for example, claimed that in nested learning systems it is "relatively unusual for a strategy that maximizes the prospects for survival of the components of a system to be the same as a strategy that maximizes the prospects for the survival of the system as a whole."

Our review indicates that population-level transformation from failure can have many forms. We differentiated among (1) direct effects of failure, (2) intentional reactions to failures of others, and (3) unintended outcomes of reactions to failures of others. We further differentiated these types by whether they occur primarily through recurrent interorganizational learning processes or as collective population-level learning processes. Interorganizational learning processes occur when multiple organizations within a population react to the failure of one or more other organizations. This type of learning has collective elements when it arises from shared rather than independent organizational experience or involves shared interpretation. Collective learning, then, involves more elements that are collective in nature, such as the creation of new entities that affect the entire population (e.g., industry associations) or the development of new coordination routines (e.g., collective standard setting).

This chapter highlighted the difference between learning from success and learning from failure and the additional benefits of learning from failure. Success of an organization in a population encourages other members in the population to copy the routines of the successful organization, often increasing homogeneity in the population. If a population consists of homogenous organizations, the survival of the population can be seriously threatened by hostile environmental changes because all the organizations in the population will be adversely affected by the changes. In contrast, failure of an organization can promote a search for alternative routines, increasing heterogeneity in the population. At the population-level, the increased heterogeneity can enhance the survival prospects of the population because not all the members in the population will be adversely affected by hostile environmental changes, and valuable new practices may be created.

By identifying some of the potentially beneficial effects of organizational failure for the population the organization belongs to, this chapter draws attention to the study of failure not only as an undesirable outcome of organizational action but also as an engine for learning. The evidence suggests that the effects of failure are a potentially fruitful area for the development of more formal propositions and further study in the field of strategic management.

REFERENCES

Anderson, P., & Tushman, M. (1990). Technological discontinuities and dominant designs: A cyclical model of technological change, *Administrative Science Quarterly*, *35*, 640-633.

Aldrich, H. E., & Sasaki, T. (1994). R&D consortia in the United States and Japan. *Research Policy*.

Astley, W. G., & Fombrun, C. J. (1983). Collective strategy: Social ecology of organizational environments. *Academy of Management Review*, *8*, 576-587.

Barnett, W. P., & Burgelman, R. A. (1996). Evolutionary perspectives on strategy. *Strategic Management Journal*, *17*, 5-19.

Barnett, W. P., & Hansen, M. T. (1996). The Red Queen in organizational evolution. *Strategic Management Journal*, *17*, 149-158.

Boyd, R., & Richerson, P. J. (1985). *Culture and the evolutionary process*. Chicago: University of Chicago Press.

Bresser, R. K. (1988). Matching collective and competitive strategies. *Strategic Management Journal*, *9*, 375-385.

Bugos, G. E. (1992). Intellectual property protection in the American chicken-breeding industry. *Business History Review*, *66*, 127-168.

Burgelman, R. A. (1994). Fading memories: A process theory of strategic business exit in dynamic environments. *Administrative Science Quarterly*, *39*, 24-56.

Burns, L., & Wholey, D. R. (1993). Adoption and abandonment of matrix management programs: Effects of organizational characteristics and interorganizational networks. *Academy of Management Journal*, *38*, 106-138.

Campbell, J. L. (1994). Contradictions of governance in the nuclear energy sector. In J. R. Hollingsworth, P. C. Schmitter, & W. Streek (Eds.), *Governing capitalist economies: Performance and control of economic sectors* (pp. 108-137). New York: Oxford University Press.

Christensen, C. M. (1993). The rigid disk drive industry: A history of commercial and technological turbulence. *Business History Review*, *67*, 531-588.

Churella, A. (1995). Corporate culture and marketing in the American railway locomotive industry: American locomotive and electro-motive despond to dieselization. *Business History Review*, *69*, 191-229.

Clark, M., & Nielsen, H. (1995). Crossed wires and missing connections: Vlademar Poulsen, The American Telegraphone Company, and the failure to commercialize magnetic recording. *Business History Review*, *69*, 1-41.

Cohen, W. M., & Levinthal, D. A. (1989). Absorptive capacity: A new perspective on learning and innovation. *Administrative Science Quarterly*, *35*, 128-152.

Conell, C., & Cohn, S. (1995). Learning from other people's action: Environmental variation and diffusion in French coal mining strikes, 1890-1935. *American Journal of Sociology*, *101*, 366-403.

Contractor, F. J., & Lorange, P. (1988). Why should firms cooperate? In F. J. Contractor & P. Lorange (Eds.), *Cooperative strategies in international business* (pp. 3-28). Lexington, MA: Lexington Books.

Cowan, R. (1990). Nuclear power reactors: A study in technological lock-in. *Journal of Economic History*, *45*, 541-567.

Cusumano, M. A., Mylonadis, Y., & Rosenbloom, R. S. (1992). Strategic maneuvering and mass-market dynamics: The triumph of VHS over Beta. *Business History Review*, *66*, 51-94.

Cyert, R. M., & March, J. G. (1963). *A behavioral theory of the firm.* Englewood Cliffs, NJ: Prentice-Hall.

David, P. A. (1991). The hero and the herd in technological history: Reflections on Thomas Edison and the battle of the systems. In P. Higonnet, D. S. Landes, & H. Rosovsky (Eds.), *Favorites of fortune* (pp. 72-119). Cambridge, MA: Harvard University Press.

Delacroix, J., & Carroll, G. R. (1983). Organizational foundings: An ecological study of the newspaper industries of Argentina and Ireland. *Administrative Science Quarterly*, *28*, 274-291.

Delacroix, J., Swaminathan, A. & Solt, M. E. (1989). Density dependence versus population dynamics: An ecological study of failings in the California wine industry. *American Sociological Review*, *54*, 245-263.

Dollinger, M. J. (1990). The evolution of collective strategies in fragmented industries. *Academy of Management Review, 15,* 266-285.

Eisenhardt, K. (1989). Building theories from case study research. *Academy of Management Review*, *14*, 532-551.

Evan, W. M., & Olk, P. (1990). R&D consortia: A new U.S. organizational form. *Sloan Management Review, 31* (Spring), 37-45.

Feldman, M. S., & March, J. G. (1981). Information as signal and symbol. *Administrative Science Quarterly, 26*, 171-186.

French, M. (1986). Structural change and competition in the United States tire industry, 1920-1937. *Business History Review*, *60*, 28-54.

Grabher, G. (1990). On the weakness of strong ties: The ambivalent role of inter-firm relations in the decline and reorganization of the Ruhr. Paper presented for the conference on "Industrial Districts and Inter-Firm Cooperation: Lessons and Policies to Implant" at the Universite du Quebec a Trois-Rivieres.

Hamel, G., & Prahalad, C. K. (1988). Creating global strategic capability. In N. Hood & J.-E. Vahlne (Eds.), *Strategies in global competition* (pp. 4-39). London: Croom Helm.

Hannan, M. T., & Freeman, J. (1977). The population ecology of organizations. *American Journal of Sociology, 82*, 929-964.

Hannan, M.T., & Freeman, J. (1989). *Organizational ecology*. Cambridge, MA: Harvard University Press.

Haunschild, P. R., & Beckman, C. M. (1998). *Learning through network: Effect of partner experience on acquisition premia.* Working paper.

Haunschild, P. R., & Miner, A. S. (1997). Modes of imitation: The effects of outcome salience and uncertainty. *Administrative Science Quarterly*, *42*, 472-500.

Haveman, H., & Cohen, L. (1994). The ecological dynamics of careers: The impact of organizational founding, dissolution, and merger on job mobility. *American Journal of Sociology, 100*, 104-152.

Herrigel, G. (1994). Industry as a form of order: A comparison of the historical development of the machine tool industries in the United States and Germany. In J. R. Hollingsworth, P. C. Schmitter, & W. Streek (Eds.), *Governing capitalist economies: Performance and control of economic sectors* (pp. 97-128). New York: Oxford University Press.

Hochmuth, M. S. (1986). The European aerospace industry. In K. Macharzina & W. H. Staehle (Eds.), *European approaches to international management* (pp. 205-225). New York: Walter de Gruyter.

Huber, G. P. (1991). Organizational learning: The contributing processes and the literatures. *Organization Science*, *2*, 88-115.

Ingram, P. (1996). Organizational form as a solution to the problem of credible commitment: The evolution of naming strategies among U.S. hotel chains, 1896-1980. *Strategic Management Journal, 17,* 85-98.

Ingram, P., & Baum, J. A. C. (1997). Opportunity and constraint: Organizations' learning from the operating and competitive experience of industries. *Strategic Management Journal, 18*, 75-98.

Kauffman, S. (1993). *The origins of order*. New York: Oxford University Press.

Kenis, P. (1992). *The social construction of an industry: A world of chemical fibers*. Boulder, CO: Westview Press.

Kennedy, R. D. (1991). The statist evolution of rail governance in the United States, 1930-1986. In J. L. Campbell, J. R. Hollingsworth, & L. N. Lindberg (Eds.), *Governance of the American economy* (pp. 138-181). Cambridge: Cambridge University Press.

Kharbanda, O. P., & Stallworthy, R. A. (1985). *Corporate failure: Prediction, panacea and prevention*. London: McGraw-Hill.

Kim, J. (1999). *Crash test without dummies: Interorganizational learning from failure experience in the U.S. commercial banking industry*. Doctoral dissertation, University of Wisconsin.

Kogut, B. (1986). Steel and the European communities. In K. Macharzina & W. H. Staehle (Eds.), *European approaches to international management* (pp. 185-203). New York: Walter de Gruyter.

Kujovich, M. Y. (1970). The refrigerator car and the growth of the American dressed beef industry. *Business History Review, 4*, 460-482.

Langlois, R. N. (1992). External economies and economic progress: The case of the microcomputer industry. *Business History Review, 66*, 1-50.

Leblebici, H., Salancik, G.R., Copay, A., & King T. (1991). Institutional change and the transformation of interorganizational fields: An organizational history of the U.S. radio broadcasting industry. *Administrative Science Quarterly, 36*, 333-363.

Levinthal, D. A., & March, J. G. (1993). The myopia of learning. *Strategic Management Journal, 14*, 95-112.

Levitt, B., & March, J. G. (1988). Organizational learning. *Annual Review of Sociology, 14*, 319-340.

March, J. G. (1981). Footnotes to organizational change. *Administrative Science Quarterly, 26*, 563-577.

March, J. G. (1991). Exploration and exploitation in organizational learning. *Organization Science, 2*, 71-87.

March, J. G., & Olson, J. (1976). *Ambiguity and choice in organizations*. Bergen, Norway: Universitetsforlaget.

March, J. G., & Simon, H. (1958). *Organizations*. New York: Wiley.

Miner, A. S., Amburgey, T. L., & Stearns, T. M. (1990). Interorganizational linkages and population dynamics: Buffering and transformational shields. *Administrative Science Quarterly, 35*, 689-713.

Miner, A. S., & Haunschild, P. R. (1995). Population level learning. In L.L. Cummings & B.M. Staw (Eds.) *Research in organizational behavior* (vol. 17, pp. 115-166). Greenwich, CT: JAI Press.

Miner, A. S., & Raghavan, S. V. (Forthcoming). Interorganizational imitation: The hidden engine of selection. In J. A. C. Baum & B. McKelvey (Eds.), *Variations in organization science: In honor of Donald T. Campbell*. Thousand Oaks, CA: Sage Publications.

Murphy, W. (1982). *The microelectronics and computer technology corporation*. Cambridge, MA: Harvard Business School Press.

Nelson, R. R., & Winter, S. G. (1982). *An evolutionary theory of economic change*. Cambridge, MA: Harvard University Press.

Nisbett, R. E., & Ross, L. (1980). *Human inference: Strategies and shortcomings in social judgment*. Englewood Cliffs, NJ: Prentice-Hall.

Ocasio, W. (1995). The enactment of economic adversity: A reconciliation of theories of failure-induced change and threat-rigidity. In *Research in organizational behavior* (vol. 17, pp. 287-331). Greenwich, CT: JAI Press.

Ocasio, W. (1997). Towards an attention-based view of the firm. *Strategic Management Journal, 18*, 187-206.

Perrow, C. (1984). *Normal accidents.* New York: Basic Books.

Pfeffer, J. (1981). Management as symbolic action: The creation and maintenance of organizational paradigms. In L. L. Cummings & B. M. Staw (Eds.), *Research in organizational behavior* (vol. 3, pp. 1-52). Greenwich, CT: JAI Press.

Porter, M. E., & Hoff, E. J. (1980). *Hattori-Seiko and the world watch industry in 1980.* Cambridge, MA: Harvard Business School Press.

Ragin, C. (1987). *The comparative method: Moving beyond qualitative and quantitative strategies.* Berkeley: University of California Press.

Rao, H., & Drazin, R. (1998). *Executive migration and organizational foundings: Portfolio manager movement and the creation of international stock funds by mutual fund families; 1986-1994.* Manuscript, Emory University.

Rogers, E. M. (1995). *Diffusion of innovations.* New York: Free Press.

Schendel, D. (1996). Editor's introduction to the 1996 summer special issue: Evolutionary perspectives on strategy. *Strategic Management Journal, 17*, 1-4.

Scherrer, C. (1991). Governance of the steel industry: What caused the disintegration of the oligopoly? In J. L. Campbell, J. R. Hollingsworth, & L. N. Lindberg (Eds.), *Governance of the American economy* (pp. 182-208). Cambridge: Cambridge University Press.

Sitkin, S. (1992). Learning through failure: The strategy of small losses. In L. L. Cummings & B. M. Staw (Eds.), *Research in organizational behavior* (vol. 14, pp. 231-266). Greenwich, CT: JAI Press.

Stabile, D. R. (1987). The Du Pont experiments in scientific management: Efficiency and safety, 1911 to 1919. *Business History Review, 61*, 365-386.

Staw, B. M., Sandelands, L. E., & Dutton, J. E. (1981). Threat-rigidity effects in organizational behavior: A multilevel analysis. *Administrative Science Quarterly, 26*, 501-524.

Strang, D., & Soule, S. (1998). Diffusion in social movements: From hybrid corn to poison pills. *Annual Review of Sociology, 24*, 265-290.

Strauss, A. L., & Corbin, J. M. (1998). *Basics of qualitative research: Techniques and procedures for developing grounded theory.* Thousand Oaks, CA: Sage.

Suchman, M. C. (1994). *On advice of counsel: Law firms and venture capital funds as information intermediaries in the structuration of Silicon Valley.* Doctoral dissertation, Stanford University.

Sutton, R. I., & Callahan, A. L. (1987). The stigma of bankruptcy: Spoiled organizational image and its management. *Academy of Management, 30*, 405-436.

Taylor, A. (1995). Why an industry that was up a tree is on a big roll. *Fortune* (April 7), 134-142.

Utterback, J. (1995). Developing technologies: The Eastman Kodak story. *The McKinsey Quarterly, 1*, 131-143.

Volti, R. (1992). *Society and technological change.* New York: St. Martin's Press.

Walsh, J. P. (1995). Managerial and organizational cognition: Notes from a trip down memory lane. *Organization Science, 6*, 280-321.

Whitestone, D. (1983). *People Express.* Boston: Harvard Business School Press.

Yates, J. (1993). Co-evolution of information-processing technology and use: Interaction between the life insurance and tabulating industry. *Business History Review, 67*, 1-51.

Yoffie, D. B., Aoki, M., & Debari, M. (1987). *The world VCR industry.* Cambridge, MA: Harvard Business School Press.

STRATEGIC GROUPS:
A SITUATED LEARNING PERSPECTIVE

Theresa K. Lant and Corey Phelps

ABSTRACT

This chapter examines learning in and among strategic groups, using a situated learning perspective in which knowledge and its meaning are negotiated and constructed by actors who interact in a community with which they identify. We explore the implications of a situated-learning perspective for individual firms, strategic groups, and populations, to develop several propositions that emphasize the trade-off between heterogeneity and homogeneity of cognition and behaviors in strategic groups. These propositions suggest that the distribution of practices in strategic groups and populations are a function of the stage of development of these collectives, the strength of the boundaries that surround strategic groups, and the configuration and actions of firms and strategic groups within a population. We conclude with a discussion of our view of strategic groups as dynamic systems and how endogenous factors in these systems influence the distribution of practices in these groups over time.

Advances in Strategic Management, Volume 16, pages 221-247.

ISBN: 0-7623-0500-2

Population-level learning is concerned with learning by collectives of organizations (Miner & Haunschild, 1995). An important collective that has received significant attention in the field of strategic management is the strategic group. Strategic groups are collectives, or substructures, within populations.

Historically, strategic groups could be characterized as populations since both are collectives of organizations that share at least one major, semi-stable trait, activity or resource utilization pattern. Howerver, treating strategic groups and populations as one in the same ignores both an important conceptual difference and potential empirical implications. Conceptually, strategic groups differ from populations in that the former include organizations who recognize each other as rivals, whereas such a cognitive component is not a necessary condition for the existence of populations. Empirically, ignoring the distinction between substructures within a population (i.e., strategic groups) and the population as a whole may blind researchers to certain sources of population-level cognitive and behavioral variety. That is, we argue that learning in, by and between strategic groups within a population has implications for population-level learning outcomes. This distinction between populations and strategic groups echoes those made early on in the development of the strategic group concept in the IO economics literature. Just as those economists who failed to identify and account for the existence of industry substructures found it difficult to explain intra-industry performance heterogeneity, organizational scholars who ignore the existence of population substructures may overlook important sources of population-level outcomes. Research has focused on economic theory to explain the emergence and relevance of these substructures within populations (Bogner, Mahoney, & Thomas, 1998), but recent research has focused on the sociocognitive basis of strategic groups (e.g., Fombrun & Zajac, 1987; Lant & Baum, 1995; Peteraf & Shanley, 1997; Porac, Thomas, & Baden-Fuller, 1989; Reger & Huff, 1993). The emerging sociocognitive theory of strategic groups emphasizes the role of managers' cognitive categorizations, enactment, and identity development. This approach is beginning to provide us with a more complete picture of how strategic groups emerge, change, and influence firm-level behavior and outcomes. In this chapter we distinguish between economic strategic groups and cognitive strategic groups and focus on the latter. We consider a cognitive strategic group to be a group of firms within a population whose members acknowledge each other as rivals and who identify with the group as a meaningful entity.

The emerging sociocognitive theory has not provided us with a complete view of strategic groups, however, because it has not considered sufficiently the extent to which processes such as enactment and identification among firms are embedded in a specific social context and evolve through interactions among actors. First, existing theory employs an individual cognitivist view of learning and action that does not take into account the extent to which learning is embedded in a social milieu. Second, it treats learning as a vicarious rather than an interactive process. Third, it treats organizations as self-contained "topographic" entities that are best modeled by considering the cognition and actions of top management teams.

In this chapter we build on the emerging sociocognitive theory of strategic groups by incorporating a situated learning perspective. We begin with the premise that sets of firms that categorize each other as competitors tend to develop similar and predictable patterns of behavior (Lant & Baum, 1995; Porac et al., 1989). Interactive learning among firms in a strategic group that results in institutionalized patterns of behavior should be viewed as situated in the particular context within which it occurs (Brown & Duguid, 1991; Lave, 1993; Lave & Wenger, 1991). The foci of learning in this perspective are not the individual firms, but, rather, the direct and indirect interactions among firms (Glynn, Lant, & Milliken, 1994).

We explore the implications of taking a situated learning view of strategic groups for population-level learning. First, the structured and predictable patterns of behavior that evolve among members of a strategic group can constrain experimentation by members. Firms participate in collective enactment; they take actions that influence their context, and their interpretations of their context influence their actions (Weick, 1979). As firms behave in accordance with their beliefs about their context and their role within that context, they contribute to the structuration of their environment (DiMaggio, 1991). Structuration yields common interpretations and predictable patterns of action (Glynn et al., 1994). Although these predictable patterns reduce uncertainty and create stability, they can inhibit firms from learning novel behavior. Second, the reduction of variance in behavior at the individual firm level may also have long-term liabilities for the collective as a whole. The lack of variability in behavior among the firms may reduce their flexibility of response under conditions of systemic change. Third, to the extent that a strategic group allows legitimate peripheral participation by actors outside the group (Lave & Wenger, 1991), situated learning processes may actually help preserve behavioral variation within strategic groups.

The U.S. auto industry in the 1970s is a classic example of a strategic group that had evolved well-defined competitive roles and predictable patterns of behavior. These firms failed to recognize that the underlying dynamics of their industry were changing, as the industry shifted to a global competitive arena. They also lacked the capability to respond effectively to this shift, and the survival of individual firms was threatened. Eventually, different practices did emerge in this industry as a result of interaction with overseas competitors. Arrangements such as joint ventures now facilitate legitimate peripheral participation of foreign competitors with U.S. automakers. This ongoing interaction among different strategic groups fosters continued experimentation and integration of alternative practices. This example demonstrates that although strategic groups tend to reduce variance in behavior among their members, they can also be the means through which new practices are shared.

The emerging sociocognitive theory of strategic groups and situated learning theory can add to our understanding of such complexities in strategic groups.

THE EMERGING SOCIOCOGNITIVE THEORY OF STRATEGIC GROUPS

The strategic groups perspective suggests that firms within an industry may not all be competitors. This insight, as well as the term "strategic group," was developed by Hunt (1972), who observed persistent intraindustry variation in the competitive behavior and performance of firms in the home appliance industry in the 1960s. His findings provided the initial empirical support and motivation for the theoretical development of the strategic group construct by Caves and Porter (1977, 1978) and Porter (1979). Reflecting its roots in industrial organization economics, the early and dominant approach to strategic group research focused on economic explanations for the existence and influence of strategic groups (Bogner, Mahoney, & Thomas, 1998).

According to the traditional, economic-based research on strategic groups, a cluster of firms competing in the same industry that pursue similar strategies, exhibit similar structures, or that have made similar combinations of scope and resource commitments constitute a strategic group (Cool & Schendel, 1987; Dess & Davis, 1984; McGee & Thomas, 1986). The degree to which these common strategies, structures, and investments are costly to imitate or substitute for represents the strength of the group's mobility barriers. Early theorists of strategic groups argued that intraindustry heterogeneity of firm strategy and performance is due to the existence of such mobility barriers. Strong mobility barriers deter the movement of a firm from one strategic position to another and the expansion of firms in one group to a position held by another group (McGee & Thomas, 1986; Porter, 1980). Consequently, firms in strategic groups protected by strong mobility barriers will persistently outperform firms in groups with weaker mobility barriers (Porter, 1980). As a direct result of these arguments, empirical investigations of strategic groups have employed a nearly uniform method of identifying strategic groups, using some form of cluster or factor analysis based on variables identified by the researcher (Barney & Hoskisson, 1990).

In recent years, however, this approach has met with significant criticism on two fronts. First, reviewers of the literature have argued that there is insufficient theoretical development of and justification for the strategic group construct (Barney & Hoskisson, 1990). Others have gone so far as to question the ontological status of strategic groups and consider them to be researcher-imposed analytical devices and statistical artifacts, rather than having any real significance for managers and firm behavior (Hatten & Hatten, 1987).

In response to these criticisms and a recognition that the dominant economic approach to strategic group research is severely limited in its ability to explain a number of dynamic issues, such as how and why such competitive structures emerge and change, on what basis specific strategies are chosen, and how strategic groups influence individual firm behavior and performance (Bogner et al.,

1998), a growing number of researchers have begun to investigate competitive structures from a cognitive perspective (e.g., Lant & Baum, 1995; Peteraf & Shanley, 1997; Porac et al., 1989; Reger & Huff, 1993). Fombrun and Zajac (1987) argued that attempting to describe the stratification of firms within an industry by using only structural factors fails to recognize the critical role of managerial perceptions, and thus managers' posture toward the environment, in determining groupings of firms that emerge.

Early work in this area was primarily exploratory and focused on demonstrating the utility of employing various techniques for mapping managerial cognitions. More recently, several scholars have advanced theoretical arguments rooted in social and managerial cognition that attempt to explain the origin, emergence, growth, and decline of strategic groups and their influence on members' behavior. Taken together, these works offer an emerging sociocognitive or "social constructionist" theory of strategic groups (Hodgkinson, 1997; Peteraf & Shanley, 1997).

Developments in the Emerging Sociocognitive Theory of Strategic Groups

Porac and colleagues (1989, p. 414) referred to the cognitive analog of a strategic group as a "primary competitive group" and defined it as "a collection of firms who define each other as rivals." More recently, Peteraf and Shanley (1997) have redefined the strategic group concept as based entirely on managerial cognition. They defined a strategic group to be "a meaningful substructure of firms within an industry—one that is acknowledged by industry participants and has significance for them" (Peteraf & Shanley, 1997, p. 166). Both of these definitions emphasize the cognitive basis of clusters of competitors. To avoid confusion about the use of the term "strategic group," however, we refer to those groups of firms discussed in the emerging sociocognitive theory of strategic groups as *cognitive strategic groups*. We use the term *economic strategic groups* to refer to those groups of firms examined using the older, economic-based research tradition. Other researchers (Bogner & Thomas, 1993; Bogner et al., 1998; Nath & Gruca, 1997; Peteraf & Shanley, 1997; Thomas & Carroll, 1994) have drawn a similar distinction between these two types of strategic groups.

Although the definition of the strategic group concept in this emerging sociocognitive theory is fundamentally based on managerial cognition, it is not necessarily inconsistent with the earlier economic-based theory of strategic groups, and recently scholars have sought to integrate and reconcile these approaches. Bogner and Thomas (1993) suggested that both types of groups influence a firm's resource allocation decision at any point in time. They argued that the economic group serves as the "raw material" for managerial perception (the cognitive strategic group), because the economic group reflects objective reality that is then interpreted by managers, while the cognitive group influences

Managerial perception and cognitive categorization

Perception

- Top managers form strategies based upon perceptions of environmental threats and opportunities.
- Strategic groups form when firms employ similar strategies based upon similar managerial perceptions of the environment (Fombrun & Zajac, 1987).

Categorization

- Top managers develop cognitive categories by assessing the similarities and differences of competitors.
- Managers sort competitors into groups based upon these categories in an effort to cognitively simplify their complex environments.
- Competitive group structures exist in the cognitive models used by managers to make sense of their environments

(Lant & Baum, 1995; Porac et al., 1987; Porac et al., 1989; Porac & Thomas, 1990; Reger & Huff, 1993)

Competitive enactment

Managers' cognitive categorizations may not only reflect the attributes of firms within competitive groups, but their actions based on these beliefs may actually create these groups.

- Managers *enact* a structure of competitive groups: they may both *respond to* and *create* their competitive environment.
- Through frequent social exchanges, top managers of different firms develop very similar cognitive models of their competitive environments.
- Shared mental models result in a shared understanding among group members of how to compete and are a potential source of the strategic isomorphism that is often observed among strategic groups.

(Lant & Baum, 1995; Porac et al., 1987; Porac et al., 1989; Porac & Thomas, 1990; Reger & Huff, 1993)

Identity

Shared mental models may not be sufficient to orient observations and behaviors of cognitive group members in a similar way.

- Through processes of social learning and social identification some cognitive groups develop a group-level identity regarding the central, enduring and distinctive characteristics of the group.
- Groups who develop a strong identity will possess members who align their activities (strategies) with those of the other group members.

(Peteraf & Shanley, 1997)

Figure 1. Major Developments in the Emerging Sociocognitive Theory of Strategic Groups

resource allocation decisions (since such decisions are based on managerial cognitions), and those decisions, in turn, affect the economic grouping. Thus, cognitive strategic groups and economic strategic groups interact in a reciprocal way (Bogner et al., 1998). Over time, cognitive groups and economic-based strategic groups may converge (Bogner et al., 1998; Nath & Gruca, 1997), although this convergence may be moderated by geography (Porac et al., 1989), industry age (Nath & Gruca, 1997; Thomas & Carroll, 1994), and environmental turbulence (Reger & Palmer, 1996). Such convergence points to the importance of understanding the sociocognitive underpinnings of the emerging theory of strategic groups.

The literature on the sociocognitive basis of strategic groups emphasizes three key elements (see figure 1). First, managers use cognitive categorization processes to simplify the monitoring of their environments, which leads them to limit their attention to groups of firms deemed similar to their own. Second, managers not only perceive groups of rivals, they enact such groups by behaving in accordance with their cognitions. Over time, these cognitions become shared by managers within the group, resulting in relatively homogenous interpretations and actions by member firms. Finally, top managers of the enacted group will identify with the group. The construction of a strong group identity will result in meaningful cognitive strategic groups that influence members' behavior. We explore each of these elements of the sociocognitive theory of strategic groups in turn.

Managerial Perception and Cognitive Categorization

According to the emerging sociocognitive theory of strategic groups, cognitive groups arise as a result of the cognitive categorization processes that managers use when making sense of their complex competitive environment (Lant & Baum, 1995; Peteraf & Shanley, 1997; Porac & Thomas, 1990; Reger & Huff, 1993).

Cognitive categorization is a heuristic that people use to simplify complex information-processing and storage tasks (Lant & Baum, 1995; Porac & Thomas, 1990; Reger & Huff, 1993). Top managers develop cognitive categories by assessing the similarities and differences of competitors along certain salient dimensions (Lant & Baum, 1995; Porac & Thomas, 1990; Reger & Huff, 1993). Managers then sort these firms cognitively into groups based on their similarity on the salient dimensions in order to simplify their complex and uncertain environments (Porac & Thomas, 1990; Reger & Huff, 1993). Rivals deemed most similar by managers of a focal firm constitute a cognitive group. Competitive group structures based on this perspective exist in the cognitive models used by managers to make sense of their environments (Lant & Baum, 1995; Porac & Thomas, 1990; Reger & Huff, 1993). These mental models define expected relationships and behaviors (Bogner et al., 1998; Lyles & Schwenk, 1992). Growing empirical evidence supports the proposition that strategic groups are readily perceived by managers.[1] Porac et al. (1989) suggested that managers in the Scottish knitwear industry constructed taxonomic mental models of the salient dimensions of competition in the industry and grouped firms based on similarities along these dimensions. Other researchers have also provided evidence that managers categorize rivals into clusters (Daniels, de Chernatoy, & Johnson, 1995; Lant & Baum, 1995; Reger & Huff, 1993). Thus, the initial empirical evidence suggests that "strategic groups are more than analytical conveniences used by researchers; they are part of the way that strategists organize and make sense of their competitive environment" (Reger & Huff, 1993, p. 115).

Competitive Enactment

While the empirical evidence suggests that managers construct mental models of competitive structures through a process of cognitive categorization, these models may merely reflect objective organizational attributes that distinguish between firms in different groups (Lant & Baum, 1995). Simple categorization processes are insufficient to explain the emergence of meaningful cognitive strategic groups—those that influence firm behavior and outcomes. From this perspective strategic groups may represent the simple aggregation of individual cognitive structures rather than a true group-level cognition (Peteraf & Shanley, 1997). Managers' cognitive categorizations may do more than reflect the attributes of firms within competitive groups, however; their actions based on these beliefs may actually create these groups (Lant & Baum, 1995; Porac et al., 1989). That is, managers may essentially *enact* a structure of competitive groups (Lant & Baum, 1995; Porac et al., 1989); they may both respond to and create their competitive environment (Weick, 1979). Porac and his associates referred to this social construction process as "competitive enactment" (Porac et al., 1989; Porac & Thomas, 1990).

Competitive enactment results in collective-level cognitive routines that in turn influence individual firm behavior (Porac et al., 1989; Porac & Thomas, 1990). Because of managers' cognitive categorization processes, certain groups of competitors in an industry will tend to view each other as the relevant players in each other's environment and, in so doing, actually create competitive groups. Firms within competitive groups may eventually enact similar *realities* through direct and indirect interaction, such as trade association membership, industry newsletters, trade conferences, informal interaction, and monitoring day-to-day activities (Porac & Thomas, 1990; Reger & Huff, 1993). As a result of these frequent social exchanges, top managers develop very similar cognitive models of their competitive environments. These shared mental models result in a shared understanding among group members of how to compete. "These shared beliefs establish the identity of individual firms and help to create a stable transactional network in which the actions of rivals are at least somewhat predictable" (Porac et al., 1989, p. 400).

When these socially constructed and shared cognitive models remain stable for a sufficient time period, yielding a shared set of beliefs about group behavior, a cognitive community is formed (Porac et al., 1989; Porac & Thomas, 1990; Thomas & Carroll, 1994). Such stable, shared beliefs are a potential source of the strategic isomorphism that is often observed among groups of firms within industries (Abrahamson & Fombrun, 1994; Powell & DiMaggio, 1991).

Similarities in behavior and beliefs among competing firms have been found in several studies (e.g., Lant & Baum, 1995; Porac, et al. 1989), providing empirical support for the competitive enactment proposition. For instance, Lant and Baum (1995) found that hotel managers in Manhattan defined a small set of rivals relative to the total number of potential competitors in the city. The managers' identification of other hotels as rivals revealed distinct clusters of firms. Firms within clusters were significantly more similar in form, practice, strategy, and belief than firms in different clusters. While these categorizations reflect managers' perceptions of actual similarities in firm characteristics such as size and strategy, the homogeneity of the cognitions of managers within groups suggests that "cognitive communities that evolve within industries tend toward isomorphism both in their practices and their beliefs" (Lant & Baum, 1995, p. 22).

Identity

Recently, Peteraf and Shanley (1997) have added to the emerging sociocognitive theory of strategic groups by arguing for the importance of identity. They maintained that the managerial categorization processes that result in similar mental models are a necessary but not sufficient condition for concluding that a true group-level cognition is operating—one that orients observations and behaviors of cognitive group members in a similar way. Building on earlier work on competitive enactment, they suggested that strategic groups develop an identity, and it is the strength of this identity, in conjunction with the shared mental models held by group members, that influences individual group members' behavior. To this end, they introduced the concept of *strategic group identity*, defined as "a set of mutual understandings, among members of a cognitive intraindustry group, regarding the central, enduring, and distinctive characteristics of the group" (Peteraf & Shanley, 1997, p. 166).

In their model, cognitive strategic groups emerge initially as a result of social learning by top managers of firms in an industry and later solidify into a true cognitive strategic group as a result of a process of social identification. These processes are embedded in a larger historical, institutional, and economic context.

Because firms face complex, uncertain, and dynamic industry environments they do not have all the relevant knowledge to cope with, managers look to competitors as strategic reference points (Fiegenbaum, Hart, & Schendel, 1996), to observe their behavior and learn from them. This process of vicarious, observational learning is consistent with the relational modeling of referent others proposed by social learning theory (Bandura, 1986). Such social learning gives direction to the categorization processes that managers use to order their environment cognitively and thus initially focuses the attention of managers on a limited group of firms within the industry (Peteraf & Shanley, 1997). As a firm gains experience through social learning of which competitors are reliable and predictable interaction partners, it may concentrate its mutualistic activities among this group of firms. Over time, this group may become a stable cognitive entity if the interactions among the group prove mutually beneficial (Peteraf & Shanley, 1997).

Social learning processes provide the foundation for a strategic group identity. Social identification processes may also operate and increase the extent to which members identify with the group. Because these processes operate over a continuous range, some groups will have stronger identities than others (Peteraf & Shanley, 1997). Only those groups that have strong identities are meaningful cognitive strategic groups, since only a strong identity can affect individual group-member behavior (Peteraf & Shanley, 1997). A group with a weak identity does not exert any influence over member behavior and is therefore not a meaningful group; rather, "it is nothing more than an aggregation of individual actors" (Peteraf & Shanley, 1997, p. 174).

The emerging sociocognitive theory of strategic groups emphasizes the fundamental role of managerial cognition and learning in explaining the emergence of cognitive strategic groups and their influence on member firms. It stresses the importance of managerial cognitive categorization, the establishment of shared cognitive models via a process of competitive enactment, and the creation of a strategic group identity resulting from processes of social learning and social identification by top managers.

In doing so, however it employs a few implicit assumptions. First, it utilizes an individual cognitivist metaphor in that knowledge is considered to be localized in individual minds or other anthropomorphized entities such as organizations (Araujo, 1998; Palinscar, 1998). Similarly, organizations are portrayed as relatively self-contained, bounded entities that learn through key individuals, such as top managers. These two points reflect the topographic view of organizations implicit in much of the organizational studies literature (Tsoukas, 1992). Finally, as exemplified by Peteraf and Shanley's (1997) paper, the nature of learning is assumed to be vicarious, in which referent others are modeled or imitated. Taken together, however, these assumptions represent an *undersituated* perspective of the learning in and by collectives.

In contrast, we assume that learning, cognition, and knowledge are inherently situated in a broader social context consisting of actors, artifacts, language, time and space. According to a situated learning perspective, knowledge and its meaning are negotiated and constructed by actors who interact within a community with which they identify and who share the practices of the community (Wenger, 1998). By applying a situated learning perspective to strategic groups and populations, we build on the sociocognitive strategic groups literature and develop a series of propositions that contribute both to the emerging sociocognitive theory of strategic groups and to population-level learning theory.

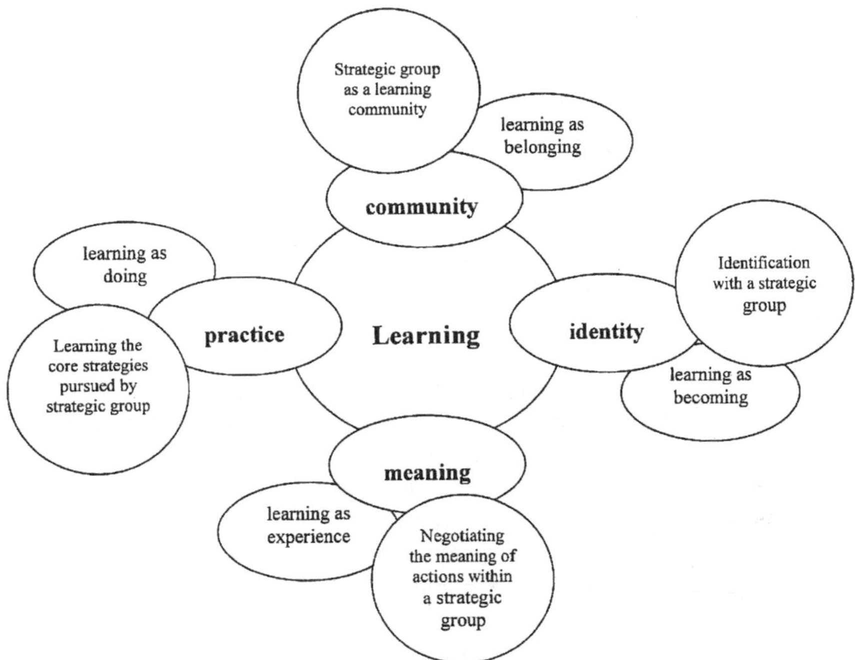

Source: Adapted from E. Wenger (1998), *Communities of Practice: Learning, Meaning and Identity,* Figure 1, p. 5, reprinted with permission from Cambridge University Press.

Figure 2. Components of Situated Learning Theory: Application to Cognitive Strategic Groups

A SITUATED LEARNING PERSPECTIVE ON STRATEGIC GROUPS

Wenger's (1998) model of social learning can be used as a lens for viewing the emergence of strategic groups as self-organizing social systems. Wenger (1998) views learning as fundamentally a social process. Social learning, is, by its nature, situated. Situated learning encompasses meaning (learning as experience), practice (learning as doing), community (learning as becoming), and identity (learning as belonging). Such a view affords a much richer sense of the learning processes that occur within and among organizations than a focus on vicarious learning by top managers. In Wenger's model, learning is not about transferring bits of information between isolated actors but is embedded in a social context. It is about creating and negotiating interpretations and identifying with a community of actors.

We can think of a cognitive strategic group as a community of practice. Porac and his associates (Porac, 1994; Porac et al., 1989) referred to such a cluster as a cognitive community. Members of a cognitive community interact frequently through various means and develop a shared language and interpretation schemes, a common understanding of how to compete, and hold each other accountable for their actions (Porac, 1994; Porac et al., 1989). Similarly, situated learning theory stresses the "mutual engagement" of members of a community of practice, the development of a "shared repertoire" among members, and the belief in "a joint enterprise" in which members develop a common goal of maintaining and preserving the community and holding each other accountable for its preservation (Wenger, 1998, p. 71). In this respect, to be a member of a community of practice is to learn how to belong to it appropriately.

In addition to community, there are three other elements of situated learning: practice, identity, and meaning. First and foremost, Wenger (1998) argued that it is the practices of the community that define it and provide it with coherence. To be a member of a community of practice is to learn how to perform competently the practices of the community. The practices that define a cognitive strategic group as a community are those strategies and tactics that most group members identify as the central and defining elements of the group (Peteraf & Shanley, 1997). Consequently, for a community of practice to exist, its members must identify with the practices of the community and feel a sense of belonging to the community. To develop an identity as a member of a community of practice is to learn how to become a practitioner in that community; actors define themselves by the ways they experience themselves through participation in the community. Peteraf and Shanley (1997) have developed the concept of strategic group identity and argued for its importance in influencing member behavior. We stipulate that the development of such an identity is integral to the learning process in collectives such as strategic groups.

Finally, the notion of meaning is inseparable from the other aspects of situated learning. "Participation [in a community of practice] goes beyond direct engagement in specific activities with specific people. It places the negotiation of meaning in the context of our forms of membership in various communities. It is a constituent of our identities" (Wenger, 1998, p. 57). The meaning that members ascribe to the experiences of the community is negotiated by them. Identity informs this negotiation process and is in turn potentially altered by it. The dense interactions among community members and the shared commitment to the preservation of the community allow for and encourage the negotiation of meaning by community members. Hence, learning is a highly interactive, situated construction process.

While a strategic group may be a community of practice, these groups themselves are also made up of other communities. Organizations comprise numerous communities of practice, and these communities transcend formal or canonical organizational boundaries (Brown & Duguid, 1991). These more numerous, deeper communities may serve as the sources of cognitive and behavioral variety for the strategic group, or the group may drive out such variety. As Wenger (1998, p. 85) stated, "the local coherence of a community of practice can be both a strength and a weakness. The indigenous production of practice makes communities of practice the locus of creative achievements and the locus of inbred failures."

The situated learning perspective emphasizes the embeddedness of social learning. Social learning includes not only processes of social comparison and imitation by managers, as described by Peteraf and Shanley (1997). It also encompasses the multifaceted learning processes of overlapping communities of actors that populate organizational fields.

According to the theory of situated action, cognitive activities should be understood primarily as interactions among actors and between actors and physical systems (Greeno & Moore, 1993). This view is in contrast to the more widely held view of cognition and knowledge as residing in the minds of individuals, where it guides perception and interpretation and from which it can be shared with or transferred to others. On the face of it, it is difficult for us to consider how cognition could reside anywhere else but in the mind. The theory of situated action, however, turns this fundamental assumption on its head (Lant, 1999).

A situated view of learning requires a different conceptualization of the locus of learning (Glynn et al., 1994). Learning neither resides in the minds of individuals nor is entirely socially constructed. Situated learning evolves within an interactive context and is embedded in the context and process of organizing. The boundaries between individuals, organizations, and their environments become less important than the interactions among them. Thus, situated learning "is best modeled in terms of the organizational connections that constitute a learning network rather than as information transfer from one individual mind to another" (Glynn et al., 1994, p. 56). Learning does not reside in individual learning entities or nodes, but in the connections between nodes (Glynn et al., 1994, p. 57; Weick & Roberts, 1994).

This view is not inconsistent with the emerging sociocognitive theory of strategic groups, but because it extends our understanding of the nature of learning, we may see relationships that we would not otherwise have seen. First, it goes beyond the emphasis on individualist cognition and the topographic view of organizations inherent in the existing literature. Second, it describes processes that transcend single levels of analysis. Third, it is dynamic, showing how the past influences the present and future. Fourth, by focusing on actors, structures, and practices as key elements in a dynamic system, we can envision how stable patterns emerge as well as how novel recombinations of these elements lead to systemic change.

Review of Situated Learning Theory

The roots of the situated action perspective can be seen in the work of cultural-historical psychologists (e.g., Leont'ev, 1932; Luria, 1928; Vygotsky, 1929). The essentials of the argument are that human thought, cognition, and knowledge are situated within a cultural system, including artifacts and practices, which is itself made up of prior thoughts and knowledge. Knowledge is embedded in these systems, which reach out across time and space, and our own thoughts are enabled and constrained by this embedded knowledge (Lant, 1999). Much knowledge is "taken for granted" in the form of artifacts, institutionalized practices, and technologies in use (Berger & Luckmann, 1967). This embedded knowledge mediates subsequent actions; actors take action in a context filled with these action mediators (Pea, 1993). Thus, our own knowledge cannot be separated from the contextual knowledge that frames it. As Pea (1993, p. 48) put it, "these ubiquitous mediating structures that both organize and constrain activity include not only designed objects...but people in social relations, as well as features and landmarks in the physical environment."

John Dewey's (1938, p. 39) words echo the same idea: "Experience does not go on simply inside a person.... We live from birth to death in a world of persons and things which is in large measure what it is because of what has been done and transmitted from previous human activities." Situated action perspectives can be found in the fields of neuropsychology (Edelman, 1987), philosophy (Wittgenstein, 1953), social anthropology (Lave, 1988), situated cognition (Suchman, 1987), and distributed cognition (Salomon, 1993).

One implication of situated action theory is that cognition and knowledge, by their very nature, are distributed and thus transcend the individual level of analysis. Clancey (1993, p. 109) suggested a dialectic process: "In a group we are mutually constraining each others' perception and sequencing, so our capabilities to interact are both developed within, and manifestations of, social, multi-agent interactions....the patterns themselves, the system of multiple situated agents constitutes a higher-order, self-organizing system."

Similarly, Cole and Engestrom (1993) argued that human behavior should be studied with "activity systems," made up of individuals, natural objects, mediating artifacts, rules, division of labor, and community, as the basic units of analysis. They view human cognition as "distributed across the loci, or nodes of an activity system...historically conditioned systems of relations among individuals and their proximal, culturally organized environments" (1993, p. 9). Accepting the system as a level of analysis provides a perspective that encompasses multilevel phenomena.

Self-organizing systems are evident in the development and perpetuation of a community. Lave (1993) argued that learning to become a community member does not entail simply the individual adoption of socially shared cognition but, rather, involves a process of situated learning in which the individual develops an identity as a member of a community. Brown and Duguid (1991, p. 48) stressed the notion of collaboration, in which individual learning is inseparable from collective learning: "Learners do not receive or even construct abstract, *objective*, individual knowledge; rather, they learn to function in a community—be it a community of nuclear physicists, cabinet makers, high school classmates, street-corner society, or ... service technicians." Wenger's (1998) description of learning communities embodies this type of self-organizing system.

Implications of Situated Learning in Strategic Groups for Firms and Populations

A situated learning perspective gives us additional insights into questions about both strategic groups and population-level learning. This view allows us to see how situated learning processes among firms will have multilevel system interaction effects (Glynn et al., 1994) because it involves trade-offs over time between variance and consistency of cognition and behavior among actors in activity systems. This is a familiar dilemma that has been pondered in the organizational learning literature in terms of the relative benefits of stability versus change (Lant & Mezias, 1992); exploitation versus exploration (March, 1991); homogeneity versus diversity (Bantel & Jackson, 1989; Milliken & Lant, 1991); turnover versus tenure (Argote, Beckman, & Epple, 1990; Carley, 1992); control versus loose coupling (Mezias & Glynn, 1993); and fast learning versus slow learning (Lant & Mezias, 1992; Levinthal & March, 1981; March, 1991).

We believe, however, that situated learning processes within and among firms in strategic groups as a source of *both* variation and consistency at the firm and population levels. We explore how factors endogenous to the system of organizations create observable distributions of beliefs and behaviors within the system, illustrating our predictions with observations from the emerging new media industry in New York City, called the Silicon Alley.

Endogenous Influences on Distributions of Practices in Populations

Stage of Community Development

The outcomes of a situated learning process within strategic groups over time may have long-term implications for the firms within these groups and for the population as a whole. As new strategic groups emerge, the level of behavioral variety, and thus innovation and sources of adaptations, will be high. As the group evolves, behavioral variety is likely to decline. The structuration of strategic groups leads to stable membership and predictable patterns of action over time: "Structuration occurs as interpretations become shared among organizations in the field; these shared interpretations yield predictable patterns of action; and these actions form the relevant context which the organizations in the field have created" (Glynn et al., 1994, p. 67.)

The development of identity in a strategic group plays a role in this structuration process. Identity evolves through a mutual interpretation process among members, and meaning and structure are attributed to patterns of behavior over time. The identity that describes the boundaries of a group influences the interpretations of member firms and tends to constrain the range of strategic actions taken (Dutton & Dukerich, 1991). Both interpretations and actions will tend toward congruence with this identity. Such a process is evident from our observations of the new media industry in New York City. This emerging industry has many examples of actors from different organizations interacting and sharing their interpretations of their evolving world. These interactions often occur during events that explicitly encourage the development of community. One example is Cybersuds™, a monthly event sponsored by the New York New Media Association (NYNMA): "Cybersuds™ is a chance to meet people from the regional new media community in a casual atmosphere— exchange ideas, business opportunities and gossip" (NYNMA announcement, January 1999). The importance of such informal gatherings to the creation of the New York new media industry can be seen in a monthly feature of the *Silicon Alley Reporter* (the regional new media magazine) called "Digital Dim Sum." This feature displays photographs of groups of new media entrepreneurs at parties, on local Web TV talk shows, at conferences, or just out on the town together. The social interactions illustrated here are examples of the processes that characterize Wenger's learning communities: learning as belonging, becoming, doing, and experience. The Silicon Alley community develops during these events, individuals identify with this emerging community, they engage in the practice of new media participants, and they negotiate the meaning of their experiences.

At the time this chapter was being written, it was still early in the evolution of the Silicon Alley community. Strategic groups were not yet well defined. Over time, we would expect that the interactions within this learning community would result in increased stability and predictability in the behaviors of the organizations in this community. As patterns of behavior are repeated, more is revealed about the strategy and competitive positioning of firms. The behaviors of member firms are likely to be consistent with the past pattern of behavior and consistent with the identity of the group of firms that is evolving. In the short term, this decreased uncertainty can benefit individual firms by making strategic decision making more straightforward and efficient.

Even though the Silicon Alley community has existed for only four years, there are some signs of a trend toward reducing variance in the culture, attitudes, and practices of community members. This can be seen in the following description of typical Cybersuds™ events:

> The mix included two partners from the Bryan Cave law firm, who were canvassing the crowd for potential clients; an associate from Coopers & Lybrand accounting firm working the door; and a woman sporting a bare midriff with a name tag that simply read "Shasha."...Some of the more over-the-top events, which have included body-piercing and go-go dancers, have raised eyebrows in the investment community and made others uncomfortable....Such is the diversity of the New York new media community—and the fragmentation that often keeps it from being taken seriously (Stites, 1998, p. C-3).

Cybersuds™ has now evolved from a beer bash where "finding a potential strategic partner and a date for the weekend were one and the same" (Stites, 1998, p. C-3) to a formal trade show frequented by established corporations as well as new media start-ups. "The evolution of Cybersuds™ from industry frat party to trade show offered evidence of how quickly New York's new media industry had emerged and matured" (Stites, 1998, p. C-3).

Proposition 1. In early stages of community evolution, firms and strategic groups will exhibit a higher variance in structures, strategies, and beliefs than in later stages of evolution.

The stage of development of learning communities (i.e., cognitive strategic groups) has implications for the distribution of practices in the population. As the community evolves and begins to share similar interpretations of its environment, members' mutual interpretations reinforce these views, and they become locked into predictable roles and patterns of behavior. This can create a situation in which it is difficult for firms to learn and exhibit novel behaviors. An example of this outcome can be found in Porac and colleagues' (1989) study of the Scottish knitwear industry. Although this industry had become global, with products from many different countries competing for customers in the same retail outlets, the Scottish firms defined only each other as relevant competitors. Their knowledge of the world evolved through interactions over time among each other; their actions became very stable and predictable. They identified themselves as Scottish knitwear makers and acted accordingly. The actions of firms outside their group were seen as irrelevant. As learning theorists have suggested, a lack of sufficient equivocal experience tends to impede learning (Levitt & March, 1988; Milliken & Lant, 1991).

Over time, the lack of new ideas emerging from the firms in a cognitive strategic group creates stagnation within the collective. Novel behaviors by individuals firms would be the alternatives that the community has to choose from when the environment changes. A lack of novel alternatives can deprive the population of the ability to respond to environmental discontinuities such as technological change. The survival of a population could be threatened by firms from other populations that move to capture segments of the market through the adoption of alternative technologies or aggressive marketing tactics. This sort of outcome has been seen in Tushman and Anderson's (1990) work on competency-destroying technological change. As the firms within a cognitive community develop overlapping competencies, they are less likely to be able to survive a competency-destroying technological change.

Proposition 2. The reduction in variation in structures, strategies, and beliefs within strategic groups over time can reduce long-term survival chances for the population.

Strength of Community Boundaries

The threat to the survival of populations described in the previous section is moderated by the permeability of the boundaries of strategic groups. Sources of variation may exist within existing strategic groups in the multiple overlapping professional communities that permeate the boundaries of firms in the group. These professional communities serve as reservoirs of cognitive and behavioral variety. One of the important implications of taking a situated learning perspective is the potential for recognizing variety in cognition, knowledge, and behavior persisting at deeper levels, even though observable behavior at the firm level may appear to be isomorphic with others in the community.

Brown & Duguid (1991, p. 53) suggested that organizations should be thought of as "communities of communities," meaning that numerous occupational and professional communities develop naturally within and across organizational boundaries. Organizations are collections of these communities. The legal or economic concept of the firm is but one way of drawing the boundary around organized activity and distributed knowledge. An organization can be conceived of as a larger community made up of smaller communities. Similarly, a strategic group can be thought of as a community consisting of smaller communities, and a population can be described as consisting of communities of strategic groups. In many cases, the communities that we think of as residing within the boundaries of an organization actually transcend a single organization, overlapping with other organizations and strategic groups.

Variability in beliefs and behavior may reside in the multiple occupational and professional communities that are represented by organizational members. The ongoing interactions of firm members with actors outside the "firm" from their occupational communities is a source of alternative identities, cognition, and behavior. These outsiders are a potential source of new ideas. Their relationships with insiders can be a conduit of external and innovative views into an organization (Brown & Duguid, 1991). The new media events that we highlighted earlier document the interaction of different communities during the evolution of a new, larger community. Participants in this emerging community are well aware of this: the advertising symbol of the 1998 Silicon Alley Conference was a Venn diagram representing the intersection of different communities, such as content, advertising, and commerce.

The outcome predicted in proposition 2 is more likely to occur when the flow of ideas among communities is hindered. The flow of ideas will be affected by the strength of the boundaries erected around a community. The stronger the boundaries, the less the community will permit legitimate peripheral participation by outsiders, who are a source of new ideas (Brown & Duguid, 1991; Lave & Wenger, 1991; Wenger, 1998). The mobility barriers erected around strategic groups to protect their competitive positions may have the unintended consequence of preventing the flow of new ideas into the community:

Proposition 3. The greater the mobility barriers erected around a strategic group, the fewer new practices will permeate its boundaries and the lower the variance in practices and beliefs within the group.

If variation in practice represents adaptive capability, then strategic groups characterized by variability in practices will have higher long-term survival chances than collectives with low variation in practices (Miner & Haunschild, 1995). Thus, in the long term, mobility barriers may actually create the very outcomes they are erected to prevent:

Proposition 4. Strategic groups with high mobility barriers will have lower long-term survival chances than strategic groups with low mobility barriers.

Communities within Communities

Populations are communities consisting of smaller communities—strategic groups. The configuration of these communities within the population, the identities that evolve within them, and the interactions among them will affect the behavior of firms in strategic groups and their long-term survival prospects.

Baum and Lant (1993) suggested that cognitive strategic groups may develop a tendency toward mutual forbearance, in which competitors exhibit less intense rivalry and establish stable, predictable patterns of behavior (Baum & Korn, 1996; Edwards, 1955; Karnani & Wernerfelt, 1985). Patterns of mutual forbearance have been observed in numerous industries, such as banking (Heggestad & Rhoades, 1978), airlines (Baum & Korn, 1996; Evans & Kessides, 1994), and telephone equipment (Barnett, 1993). These findings have been attributed to the rules of the game that evolve among competitors. Game theorists argue that firms recognize that their outcomes are interdependent and that they can often maximize their own outcomes through cooperation (Axelrod, 1984). From this perspective, mutual forbearance is based on the potential for future retaliation (Axelrod, 1984).

Members of cognitive strategic groups, by definition, anticipate future interactions, making them an important element in the forbearance process. Forbearance may be facilitated by the identity that evolves among members of a strategic group, because part of this behavior may be driven by the situated learning processes of *learning as belonging*, in addition to the individual assessments of member firms. Cognitive strategic groups that develop strong identities may be more likely to engage in cooperative behavior (Peteraf & Shanley, 1997). A sense of shared destiny may mitigate rivalry in many cases, especially in terms of actions that could undermine the shared goals of the group, such as maintaining a viable market, facilitating technological standards, or legitimating a new product market. For instance, in our observations of the emerging new media industry in New York City, we witnessed the pursuit of such shared goals, as evidenced in the following quote:

> ...there is a camaraderie amongst the interactive advertising community. It goes something like this: this will never be a viable industry unless we shift huge amounts of advertising dollars from TV, print and radio to interactive. Fighting over experimental advertising budgets is not going to rise the tide. In order for all the boats to rise the community needs to evangelize the potential of online advertising (Calacanis, 1997, p. 1).

There are many examples of competitive escalation that run counter to the notion of forbearance, such as airline fare wars and personal computer price and feature wars. From the perspective of situated learning, such competitive actions are most likely initiated by firms that do not share the identity of a strategic group, such as firms on the periphery of the group or those that belong to other communities within the population. For example, the greatest price competition in the airline industry tends to occur along routes served by small, low cost, regional carriers, such as Southwest Airlines. In the auto industry, aggressive competitive moves were instigated by Japanese competitors, not by the big three U.S. firms. These examples demonstrate that aggressive competition is more likely to occur between strategic groups, not within them:

Proposition 5. Members of cognitive strategic groups are less likely to instigate aggressive competitive moves that would adversely affect other members of their group than are firms outside of these groups.

At the level of the population, however, the existence of multiple strategic groups and peripheral, outsider firms may be key to the long-term survival of the population. New ideas can come from outsiders in the form of competitive actions. Those firms on the periphery of a strategic group will be less bound by a collective identity and socially constructed rules about competition. They will be less likely to engage in mutual forbearance. Since competitive threats provide equivocal experiences, often increasing uncertainty and decreasing the performance of member firms, member firms may experiment with new alternatives as a means of countering these threats. These experiments, although perhaps decreasing the chances that individual firms will survive, will increase the likelihood that the population as a whole will survive. A study of radio stations illustrates a similar pattern (Leblebici, Salancik, Copay, & King, 1991). Peripheral stations in the population innovated with new formats. The strategic group of firms consisting of the large, established networks started to fail and imitated the new practices of the peripheral stations. The large stations did not succeed in using these new practices, but by having used them, they legitimated the new practices, which were adopted by the whole population. It is also possible that new organizations may become members of existing communities, providing adaptive capability, new ideas, and different interpretations, without threatening the survival of the entire collective.

If incumbent firms can learn from new firms, then the population may be preserved, even as its membership and practices change.

Such a challenge is now facing the established recorded music industry, which is dominated by huge players such as Warner Music Group, MCA/Universal, Polygram, and Sony. A new Internet technology allows CD-quality music to be downloaded directly onto personal computers. This computer file format, called MP3 (Moving Picture Experts Group Audio Layer 3), allows users to e-mail audio tracks in file sizes from 3 to 5 megabytes. Some recording artists, such as The Beastie Boys and Billy Idol, have begun to release songs in MP3 format, bypassing the record labels. An item in the *Silicon Alley Reporter* described the problems this presents to the dominant firms:

> The major record labels have been fighting the MP3 format every step of the way. Afraid that rampant trading of MP3 files will circumnavigate their copyright-protection measures, the labels first hid their heads in the sand before slowly realizing they had to get involved with the technology that represents the future of their industry.... Couple the MP3 file format with the fact that recordable CD drives are dropping to the $200 price range, and you've got the makings of a major revolution. The corporate music companies, which have historically and almost universally dismissed the Internet, are now scrambling to figure out their value in a high-tech ecosystem where music is fast, free and hard, if not impossible, to control (Calacanis, 1999, p. 44).

As this example shows, competition can stimulate a strategic group to explore variations:

Proposition 6. Aggressive competitive actions from peripheral firms or between strategic groups, while lowering survival chances of individual firms, will increase long-term survival chances for the population due to increased variation in structures, strategies, and beliefs in the population.

DISCUSSION AND CONCLUSION

Adding the situated learning insights described above to the emerging sociocognitive perspective on strategic groups should enhance our understanding of population-level learning. In particular, understanding the dynamics of how strategic groups evolve and change over time contributes to our understanding of the distribution of practices in populations of organizations, in a number of ways.

First, by focusing on strategic groups as an important substructure within larger populations (e.g., industries), we gain insight into the relationships among learning at the organizational, strategic group, and population levels of analysis. For instance, we discover that the desirability of the outcomes associated with situated learning processes vary by level of analysis and over time. What is beneficial for firms in the short term may harm them in the long term. What is beneficial for the population may put individual firms at risk. Second, by following the assumptions of situated learning, we go beyond the individualist cognition and topographic view of organizational learning in the existing literature. We view strategic groups as learning communities, with actors from different firms interacting and collaborating as much as signaling and competing. Third, by focusing on self-organizing systems of activity, we are able to describe dynamics that transcend single levels of analysis. That is, organizations, strategic groups, and populations are locations in which actors, artifacts, practices, and interpretations flow, interact, converge, and diverge. Communities of actors that intersect with all three levels of analysis are the conduits through which interpretations and practices flow. These overlapping communities provide sources of variety and adaptive capability. Fourth, our view is dynamic, showing how the past influences the present and future. Fifth, by focusing on actors, artifacts, practices, and interpretations as key elements in a dynamic system, we can envision how stable patterns emerge as well as how novel recombinations of these elements lead to systemic change.

The novel insights that we gain from this perspective derive from three endogenous factors in these systems: the stage of development of a community, the strength of the boundaries around communities, and the distribution and actions of smaller communities within larger ones.

Populations go through stages of development. Early in the development of these communities there are numerous possible learning trajectories that they might create (Wenger, 1998). These self-designing systems are complex and unpredictable. The trajectory will be influenced by such factors as the strength of the boundaries that are created between communities within the population, the configuration of these communities, and their actions with respect to each other. By recognizing the probabilistic nature of the evolution of populations and by understanding some of the driving factors that influence their development, we can gain insights into the dynamics of population-level learning that have implications for both theorists and practitioners.

Most studies of population-level phenomena have been conducted by examining populations that have matured and looking back in time to find traces of their evolution (Baum, 1996). Although it is argued that these models represent dynamic systems (they use dynamic methods and trace event histories), they miss most of the real-time dynamics that characterize populations as they move through stages of development. We will only really understand the dynamics of population learning by studying the complex dynamics that characterize populations in early stages of development (Garud & Lant, 1998). As we know from studies of complex systems, these initial conditions can have a profound impact on the later characteristics of the system (Arthur, 1989; Stacey, 1996). At these early stages, strategic groups are just forming. As we saw in the Silicon Alley examples, approaches to doing business in this new community vary greatly across firms. Through interactive processes, strategic groups will emerge, structuration and identification will occur, and similarity among the members will increase. The reduction in variance occurs not only through the births and deaths of firms but also through changes in perspectives and strategic actions. This implies that managers can take an active role in creating and influencing the types of practices that are adopted by strategic group members. This perspective also implies that managers should be wary of the security they feel when they are a member of a strategic group with predictable characteristics and strategies. This lack of variance can be the source of their demise.

By considering the strength of community boundaries and the configuration and actions of communities in a population, we can uncover some ways in which strategic group formation is more or less likely to lead to ossification. The mutual forbearance exhibited by members of a strategic group benefits them in the short term, but strategic groups with strong boundaries make their members vulnerable to competitive actions by peripheral firms and other strategic groups. At the same time, however, the new strategies enacted by peripheral firms may provide the variation and adaptive capability that secures the survival of a population as a whole. As in our earlier example about the U.S. auto industry, the mix of firms and practices in the population may shift, but the population survives.

How might firms ensure that they are survivors of population shifts rather than casualties? Strategic groups that allow legitimate peripheral participation by maintaining relatively weak boundaries will allow the flow of different ideas into their community, thereby maintaining the raw material needed to adapt to population shifts. How do varying perspectives survive within strategic groups that evolve similar practices? We suggest that the mix of occupational and professional communities represented in the strategic group will influence the adaptive capacity of the group. These communities tend to maintain their own identities and perspectives and tend to flow across firm boundaries. In strategic groups dominated by a single occupational or professional community, the perspectives represented by firms will be isomorphic with those of the community. These groups will have little variation upon which to draw.

If our predictions are born out empirically, what would be the implications for managers, and how do these implications differ from those we would expect firm existing frameworks? First, our view would suggest that insurmountable mobility barriers are not as beneficial, in the long run, as would have been predicted by theories of economic strategic groups. The greater the mobility barriers, the less likely it is that variability will find its way into the strategic group. Second, the development of cognitive strategic groups does not always result in the myopia characterized by the Scottish knitwear makers. Within learning communities, there are mechanisms for maintaining variation—the interaction of multiple communities across firm boundaries. Given the tendencies for strategic groups to converge on limited sets of practices, the challenge for managers is to ensure that sufficient variation persists even while they capture the benefits of increased predictability. This tension between stability and change is a classic managerial challenge (Lant & Mezias, 1992), but it has not been considered a challenge for strategic groups as well as individual firms. As we hope that this chapter has demonstrated, however, because of the situated nature of learning, the tension between predictability and flexibility is an important factor in strategic groups and population level-learning and cannot be ignored.

ACKNOWLEDGMENTS

An earlier version of this paper was presented at the Academy of Management Meetings, Vancouver, BC, 1995. We would like to thank Phil Anderson, Raghu Garud, and the participants of the Organization Studies Group Seminar at the Sloan School of Management, MIT, for their helpful comments. We also thank Anne Miner and Thekla Rura-Polley for their constructive and helpful reviews of a previous version of this paper. This research was supported by a grant from the Tenneco Fund Program at the Stern School of Business, New York University.

NOTE

1. Arguably, this evidence encouraged Peteraf and Shanley (1997) to redefine the strategic group concept to stipulate that such groups only exist when they are acknowledged by industry participants and have meaning for member firms. Their definition is not tautological with respect to the evidence, however, because the definition was developed in response to the evidence.

REFERENCES

Abrahamson, E., & Fombrun, C. (1994). Macro-cultures: Determinants and consequences. *Academy of Management Review, 19,* 728-755.

Araujo, L. (1998). Knowing and learning as networking. *Management Learning, 29,* 317-336.

Argote, L., Beckman, S. L., & Epple, D. (1990). The persistence and transfer of learning in industrial settings. *Management Science, 36,* 140-154.

Arthur, W. B. (1989). The economy and complexity. In D. L. Stein (Ed.), *Lectures in the science of complexity* (pp. 713-740). Redwood City, CA: Addison-Wesley.

Axelrod, R. (1984). *The evolution of cooperation.* New York: Basic Books.

Bandura, A. (1986). *Social foundations of thought and action.* Englewood Cliffs, NJ: Prentice-Hall.

Bantel, K. A., & Jackson, S. E. (1989). Top management and innovations in banking: Does the composition of the top team make a difference? *Strategic Management Journal, 10,* 107-124.

Barnett, William P. (1993). Strategic deterrence among multipoint competitors. *Industrial and Corporate Change, 2,* 249-278.

Barney, J. B., & Hoskisson, R. E. (1990). Strategic groups: Untested assertions and research proposals. *Managerial and Decision Economics, 11,* 187-198.

Baum, J. A. C. (1996). Organizational ecology. In S. R. Clegg, C. Hardy, & W. R. Nord (Eds.), *Handbook of organization studies* (pp. 77-114). London: Sage.

Baum, J. A. C., & Korn, H. (1996). Multimarket contact and mutual forbearance in competitive interaction. *Academy of Management Journal, 39,* 255-291.

Baum, J. A. C., & Lant, T. K. (1993). *Cognitive categorization of competitor groups and perceptions of competitive intensity in the Manhattan hotel industry.* Working paper, Department of Management and OB, New York University.

Berger, P. L., & Luckmann, T., (1967). *The social construction of reality: A treatise in the sociology of knowledge*. New York: Bantam Doubleday Bell.

Bogner, W. C., & Thomas, H. (1993). The role of competitive groups in strategy formulation: A dynamic integration of two competing models. *Journal of Management Studies, 30*, 51-67.

Bogner, W. C., Mahoney, J. T., & Thomas, H. (1998). Paradigm shift: The parallel origin, evolution, and function of strategic group analysis with the resource-based theory of the firm. In J. A. C. Baum (Ed.), *Advances in strategic management* (Vol. 15, pp. 63-102). Greenwich, CT: JAI Press.

Brown, J. S., & Duguid, P. (1991). Organizational learning and communities of practice: Toward a unified view of working, learning, and innovation. *Organization Science, 2*, 40-57.

Calacanis, J. M. (1997, September). Editorial, *Silicon Alley Reporter*, p.1.

Calacanis, J. M. (1999). MP3. *Silicon Alley Reporter*, 3(1), p. 44.

Carley, K. (1992). Organizational learning and personnel turnover. *Organization Science, 3*, 20-46.

Caves, R. E., & Porter, M. E. (1977). From entry barriers to mobility barriers: Conjectural decisions and contrived deterrence to new competition. *Quarterly Journal of Economics, 91*, 241-261.

Caves, R. E., & Porter, M. E. (1978). Market structure, oligopoly and stability of market shares. *Journal of Industrial Economics, 26* (4), 289-313.

Clancy, W. J. (1993). Situated action: A neuropsychological interpretation response to Vera and Simon. *Cognitive Science, 17*, 87-116.

Cole, M., & Engestrom, Y. (1993). A cultural-historical approach to distributed cognition. In G. Solomon (Ed.), *Distributed cognitions: Psychological and educational considerations* (pp. 1-46). Cambridge: Cambridge University Press.

Cool, K., & Schendel, D. (1987). Strategic group formulation and performance: The case of the U.S. pharmaceutical industry, 1963-1982. *Management Science, 33*, 1102-1124.

Daniels, K., de Chernatoy, L., & Johnson, G. (1995). Validating a method for mapping managers' mental models of competitive industry structures. *Human Relations, 48*, 975-991.

Dess, G., & Davis, P. (1984). Porter's (1980) generic strategies as determinants of strategic group membership and organizational performance. *Academy of Management Journal, 27*, 467-488.

Dewey, J. (1938). *Experience and education*. New York: Mcmillan.

DiMaggio, P. (1991). Constructing an organizational field as a professional project: U.S. art museums, 1920-1940. In W. Powell and P. DiMaggio (Eds.), *The new institutionalism in organizational analysis* (pp. 267-292). Chicago: University of Chicago Press.

Dutton, J.E., & Dukerich, J.M. (1991). Keeping an eye on the mirror: Image and identity in organizational adaptation. *Academy of Management Journal, 34*, 517-554.

Edelman, G. (1987). *Neural Darwinism*. New York: Basic Books.

Edwards, C. D. (1955). Conglomerate bigness as a source of power. In *Business concentration and price policy* (pp. 331-59). National Bureau of Economic Research. Princeton, NJ: Princeton University Press.

Evans, W. N., & Kessides, I. N. (1994). Living by the "golden rule": Multimarket contact in the U.S. airline industry. *Quarterly Journal of Economics, 109*, 341-366.

Fiegenbaum, A., Hart, S., & Schendel, D. (1996). Strategic reference point theory. *Strategic Management Journal, 17*, 219-235.

Fombrun, C. J., & Zajac, E. (1987). Structural and perceptual influences on intraindustry stratification. *Academy of Management Journal, 30*, 33-50.

Garud, R., & Lant, T. K. (1998). *Navigating Silicon Alley: Kalaidescopic experiences*. Working paper, Department of Management and OB, New York University.

Glynn, M. A., Lant, T. K., & Milliken, F. J. (1994). Mapping learning processes in organizations: A multi-level framework linking learning and organizing. In C. Stubbart, J. Meindl,, & J. Porac (Eds.), *Advances in managerial cognition and organizational information processing* (pp. 43-83). Greenwich, CT: JAI Press.

Greeno, J. G., & Moore, J. L. (1993). Situativity and symbols: Response to Vera and Simon. *Cognitive Science, 17*, 49-60.

Hatten, K. J., & Hatten, M. L. (1987). Strategic groups, asymmetrical mobility barriers and contestability. *Strategic Management Journal, 8*, 329-342.

Heggestad, A., & Rhoades, S. A. (1978). Multi-market interdependence and local market competition in banking. *Review of Economics and Statistics, 60*, 523-532.

Hodgkinson, G. P. (1997). The cognitive analysis of competitive structures: A review and critique. *Human Relations, 50*, 625-654.

Hunt, M. S. (1972). *Competition in the major home appliance industry 1960-1970.* Unpublished doctoral dissertation, Harvard University.

Karnani, A., & Wernerfelt, B. (1985). Research note and communication: Multiple point competition. *Strategic Management Journal, 6*, 87-96.

Lant, T. K. (1999). A situated learning perspective on the emergence of knowledge and identity in cognitive communities. In R. Garud & J. Porac (Eds.), *Advances in management cognition and organizational information processing* (Vol. 6, pp. 171-194). Greenwich, CT: JAI Press.

Lant, T. K., & Baum, J. A. C. (1995). Cognitive sources of socially constructed competitive groups: Examples from the Manhattan hotel industry. In W. R. Scott & S. Christensen (Eds.), *Advances in the institutional analysis of organizations: International and longitudinal studies* (pp. 15-38). Sage.

Lant, T. K., & Mezias, S. J. (1992). An organizational learning model of convergence and reorientation. *Organization Science, 3*, 47-71.

Lave, J. (1988). *Cognition in practice.* Cambridge: Cambridge University Press.

Lave, J. (1993). Situated learning in communities of practice. In L. B. Resnick, J. M. Levine, & S. D. Teasley (Eds.), *Perspectives on socially shared cognition* (pp. 63-82). Washington, DC: American Psychological Association.

Lave, J., & Wenger, E. (1991). *Situated learning: Legitimate peripheral participation.* Cambridge: Cambridge University Press.

Leblebici, H., Salancik, G. R., Copay, A., & King, T. (1991). Institutional change and the transformation of interorganizational fields: An organizational history of the U.S. radio broadcasting industry. *Administrative Science Quarterly, 36*, 333-363.

Leont'ev, A. N. (1932). Studies in the cultural development of the child, 3: The development of voluntary attention in the child. *Journal of Genetic Psychology, 37*, 52-81.

Levinthal, D. A., & March, J. G. (1981). A model of adaptive organizational search. *Journal of Economic Behavior and Organization, 2*, 307-333.

Levitt, B., & March, J. G. (1988). Organizational learning. *Annual Review of Sociology, 14,* 319-340.

Luria, A. R. (1928). The problem of the cultural development of the child. *Journal of Genetic Psychology, 35*, 506.

Lyles, M. A., & Schwenk, C. R. (1992). Top management, strategy and organizational knowledge structures. *Journal of Management Studies, 29*, 155-174.

March, J. G. (1991). Exploration and exploitation in organizational learning. *Organizational Science, 2*, 71-87.

McGee, J., & Thomas, H., (1986). Strategic groups: Theory, research, and taxonomy. *Strategic Management Journal, 7*, 141-60.

Mezias, S. J., & Glynn, M. A. (1993). The three faces of corporate renewal: Institution, revolution, and evolution. *Strategic Management Journal, 14,* 77-101.

Milliken, F. J., & Lant, T. K. (1991). The effect of an organization's recent performance history on strategic persistence and change: The role of managerial interpretations. In P. Shrivastava, A. Huff, & J. Dutton (Eds.), *Advances in strategic management* (Vol. 7, pp. 129-156). Greenwich, CT: JAI Press.

Miner, A. S., & Haunschild, P. R. (1995). Population level learning. In B.Staw & L.Cummings (Eds.), *Research in organizational behavior* (Vol. 17, pp. 115-166). Greenwich, CT: JAI Press.

Nath, D., & Gruca, T. S. (1997). Convergence across alternative methods for forming strategic groups. *Strategic Management Journal, 18*, 745-760.

Palinscar, A. S. (1998). Social constructivist perspectives on teaching and learning. *Annual Review of Psychology, 49*, 345-375.

Pea, R. D. (1993). Practices of distributed intelligence and designs for education. In G. Salomon (Ed.), *Distributed cognitions: Psychological and educational considerations* (pp. 47-87). Cambridge: Cambridge University Press.

Peteraf, M., & Shanley, M. (1997). Getting to know you: A theory of strategic group identity. *Strategic Management Journal, 18* (Summer, Special Issue), 165-186.

Porac, J. F. (1994). On the concept of "organizational community." In J. A. C. Baum & J. V. Singh (Eds.), *Evolutionary dynamics of organizations* (pp. 451-456). New York: Oxford University Press.

Porac, J. F., & Thomas, H. (1990). Taxomic mental models in competitor definition. *Academy of Management Review, 15*, 224-240.

Porac, J. F., Thomas, H., & Baden-Fuller, C., (1989). Competitive groups as cognitive communities: The case of Scottish knitwear manufacturers. *Journal of Management Studies, 26*, 397-416.

Porac, J. F., Thomas, H., Wilson, F., Paton, D., & Kanfer, A., (1995). Rivalry and the industry model of Scottish knitwear producers. *Administrative Science Quarterly, 40*, 203-227.

Porter, M. E. (1979). The structure within industries and companies' performance. *Review of Economics and Statistics*, May, 214-27.

Porter, M. E. (1980). *Competitive strategy*. New York: Free Press.

Powell, W. W., & DiMaggio, P. J. (1991). *The new institutionalism in organizational analysis*. Chicago: University of Chicago Press.

Reger, R. K., & Huff, A. S. (1993). Strategic groups: A cognitive perspective. *Strategic Management Journal, 14*, 103-124.

Reger, R. K., & Palmer, T. B. (1996). Managerial categorization of competitors: Using old maps to navigate new environments. *Organization Science, 7*, 22-39.

Salomon, G. (1993). No distribution without individuals' cognition: A dynamic interactional view. In G. Solomon (Ed.), *Distributed cognitions: Psychological and educational considerations* (pp. 111-138). Cambridge: Cambridge University Press.

Stacey, R. (1996). *Complexity and creativity in organizations*. San Francisco: Berrett Koehler.

Stites, J. (1998, November 23). Building (and celebrating) a new-media community, *New York Times*, p. C-3.

Suchman, L. A. (1987). *Plans and situated actions: The problem of human-machine communication*. Cambridge: Cambridge University Press.

Thomas, H., & Carroll, C. (1994). Theoretical and empirical links between strategic groups, cognitive communities, and networks of interacting firms. In H. Daems & H. Thomas (Eds.), *Strategic groups, strategic moves and performance* (pp. 7-29). Oxford: Pergamon.

Tsoukas, H. (1992). Ways of seeing—Topographic and network representations in organization theory. *Organization Science, 8*, 71-83.

Tushman, M. L., & Anderson, P. (1990). Technological discontinuities and dominant designs: A cyclical model of technological change. *Administrative Science Quarterly, 35*, 604-633.

Vygotsky, L.S. (1929). The problem of cultural development of the child. *Journal of Genetic Psychology, 36*, 415-34.

Weick, K. E. (1979). *The Social Psychology of Organizing*. Reading, MA: Addison-Wesley.

Weick, K. E., & Roberts, K. H. (1994). Collective mind in organizations: Heedful interrelating on flight decks. *Administrative Science Quarterly, 38*, 357-381.

Wenger, E. (1998). *Communities of practice: Learning, meaning, and identity*. Cambridge: Cambridge University Press.

Wittgenstein, L. (1953). *Philosophical investigations*: Oxford: Blackwell.

CONSTRUCTING VARIATION:
INSIGHTS FROM AN EMERGING ORGANIZATIONAL FIELD

Thekla Rura-Polley

ABSTRACT

Using an evolutionary theory framework, this chapter explores population-level learning in Catholic children's institutions in Germany and the United States over a 75-year period. Through an analysis of variation in policy recommendations published in the major journals read by staff of such institutions between 1895 and 1970, the chapter shows that variation was not randomly distributed but was affected by the social, economic, and historic context in which the recommendations were published. The results suggest that variation is higher after periods of uniformity and monotony, during a general climate for change, and during or shortly after times of public debate of particular issues. This has important implications for population-level learning and strategic managers, as low variation among recommendations may increase the likelihood of implementation but lead to suboptimal performance in the long term. It also means that the content of what is being learned is not necessarily shaped at the selection and retention stage but by the variation that exists among a pool of options that are available to managers.

Advances in Strategic Management, Volume 16, pages 249-275.

ISBN: 0-7623-0500-2

INTRODUCTION

Evolutionary theories of organizational and industry change have a long tradition in the innovation and learning literatures, both at the organizational and the population level of analysis. Underlying these evolutionary theories is a repeated variation-selection-retention cycle. For example, at the organizational level, organizations may selectively retain idiosyncratic jobs (Miner, 1991, 1994) and thereby change their focus, goals, and structure over time. At the population level some organizational forms are more likely to survive—be selectively retained—than others, as population ecologists have shown in many industries (e.g., Barnett, 1990; Hannan & Freeman, 1989; Miner, Amburgey, & Stearns, 1990).

Much of the empirical research has focused on the selection and retention of organizational routines or organizational forms. Comparatively less empirical attention has been paid to the origins and antecedents of variation, particularly the social factors involved. Studies on technology innovation that have addressed the interaction between variation and cohesion, however, can inform such study of variation in populations of organizations. These include punctuated equilibrium theories (e.g., Tushman & Romanelli, 1985; Tushman & Rosenkopf, 1996) and technology cycle theories (Anderson & Tushman, 1990; Tushman & Anderson, 1986).

Social factors may affect not only the selective retention of routines and designs but the entire evolutionary cycle, including the variation stage. In the study reported here, I analyzed more than 2,200 strategic options published as policy recommendations for children's institutions in Germany and the United States over a 75-year period, some of which were later incorporated into organizations as routines, others not.

The study contributes to population-level learning research by showing that variation among policy recommendations is constructed within a social context and differs markedly over time. This constructed variation will have implications for the selective implementation of recommendations and, consequently, population-level learning. A brief historical overview of children's institutions in Germany and the United States provides the background for the study.

THE EMERGENCE OF THE FIELD OF CHILDREN'S INSTITUTIONS

Germany

Until the seventeenth century, orphaned and destitute children were not cared for in special children's institutions but in hospitals and poorhouses. Children were kept there until they were seven years old, when they were presumably old enough to provide for their own living by begging for alms. With the rise of mercantilism, children were kept longer and longer in such places, giving rise to special children's institutions in which children were used for weaving, spinning, and other production work. Children were expected to sustain, sometimes even make a profit for the institution through their work. Given the hard work, overcrowding of the facilities, bad sanitary conditions, poor ventilation, and rare breaks from work, diseases and the death rate among the children increased extraordinarily during that period (Kallert, 1964). Criticisms about children's institutions grew louder, and the subsequent "Waisenhausstreit," in which people argued about the best method of caring for orphaned children—institutions or foster care—led to the closing of most children's institutions in Germany. Toward the end of the nineteenth century, it became clear that foster care also had its share of problems, and the pendulum swung back toward institutional care, but with a difference: using trained staff and incorporating current childcare methods and pedagogy. This was the beginning of a new population of organizations emerging in co-evolution with and influenced by the rise of psychology, sociology, modern pedagogy, and modern medicine. Given the previously mixed experiences with institutional care, new forms, methods, and routines of childcare were called for.

United States of America

In the eighteenth and nineteenth centuries, poverty was widespread in the United States, mainly stemming from immigration and adjustments to the new society (O'Grady, 1931). Each immigration wave presented new problems. The early American development of Catholic charities was influenced heavily by immigrants from Germany and Ireland. While the immigrants themselves faced many social hardships and needed help, they also brought with them their knowledge and skills of doing charitable work, especially the nuns and monks. As Richan (1987, p. 149) noted, "the nuns simply continued practices that were well established in Europe." The earliest Catholic welfare institutions were orphanages, the first founded by Ursuline Sisters in New Orleans in 1727 (O'Grady, 1931). At that time, the number of Catholic orphans to be taken care of was relatively small. Catholic institutions often cared for only five orphans but offered educational facilities for another 100 children. With each immigration wave, the demands for Catholic charities increased, so that by the end of the nineteenth century more than 50 Catholic children's institutions existed in New York alone and another 30 in Illinois.

The institutions founded in the mid-eighteenth century were mainly concerned with the preservation of faith of the immigrants. American society was Protestant at heart, particularly when it came to public services and government. Moreover, Protestants actively proselytized to convert Catholics to their faith. In the 1850s and 1860s many Catholic orphans from New York and other East Coast cities were placed in the care of Protestants in the Midwest, via the so-called orphan trains (Youcha, 1995), partly because there were not enough Catholic adoptive or foster parents and partly because "the public" hoped to turn these children into good Protestants. Catholics became concerned about this practice and founded their own children's institutions. Raising these children in Catholic institutions and teaching them Catholic doctrine and values was seen as the best way to keep them within the Church. As Jacoby (1941, p. 8) described it, "Since Catholic charity is basically spiritual, it conceives of no greater service to the child than the preservation of his faith; this is the basic reason for the jealous insistence of the church upon its duty and right to take care of Catholic children."

Given that some of these institutions grew to taking care of more than 2,000 children at a time, conditions were obviously not always ideal for the children. As in Germany, the rise in medicine, pedagogy, psychology, social work, and related fields influenced and shaped the field of Catholic children's institutions in the twentieth century. There was the potential for population-level learning, which Miner and Haunschild (1995, p. 116) defined as "change in the nature and mix of routines enacted in a population of organizations, arising from shared experience."

The population-level learning perspective offers a coherent framework to analyze and interpret the changes in Catholic children's institutions. The rise of national umbrella organizations in Germany (Deutscher Caritasverband) and the United States (Catholic Charities) and the affiliated national publications offered an opportunity for the entire population of children's institutions to learn jointly from shared experiences as well as from one another rather than on a purely individual basis.

RESEARCHING VARIATION

Existing research in organization theory informs the study of variation in populations like the children's institutions. Campbell (1969, p. 73) suggested that socio-cultural evolution, which focuses on social processes that underlie social evolution, depend on three essentials: the occurrence of variation, consistent selection criteria, and "a mechanism for the preservation, duplication, or propagation of the positively selected variants." He claimed that "an evolution in the direction of better fit to the selective system becomes inevitable" under these conditions (p. 73). Variation seems to be the least problematic issue in Campbell's model, because "variation is continually taking place, so that this requirement is easily met" (p. 73). Variation may stem from differences between social groups or between individuals that lead to different executions of customs or actions. For evolution to occur it does not matter whether such variation is deliberate or unintentional, as long as it exists. The more numerous the variants and the greater the variation, the higher the likelihood for advantageous innovation. Factors that affect the number of variants and their heterogeneity include societies being at cultural crossroads or acting as melting pots, as well as cultural norms valuing change, progress, and innovation.

While in both biological and socio-cultural evolution, variation exists because of changes or differences in the environment, Weick (1979, p. 130) proposed that "ecological changes provide the enactable environment." For him, "enactment is to organizing as variation is to natural selection" (p. 130). Enactment involves people "creating the environments that impose on them" (p. 5). It is "action that produces the raw materials which can then be made sensible" (p. 133). Thus, variation does not necessarily describe the state of reality, but selection works on differently socially constructed enactments of an environment. These different enactments mainly work at the individual level, where individuals make sense of their perceived environment.

Many researchers distinguish between "blind" and intentional variation. Blind variation stems from organizations engaging in trial-and-error learning, incorrect or incomplete copying from others, mistakes, forgetfulness, and randomness (Aldrich, 1999). Intentional variation stems from institutionalized experimentation, direct and indirect incentives for individuals to produce variation, and tolerance for unfocused variation or pure playfulness (Miner, 1994). Other researchers think that variation occurs in waves. For example, Schumpeter (1934) spoke of creative destruction that triggers a new wave of economic evolution.

In punctuated equilibrium theory, variation is associated with periods of reorientation and turbulence. Proponents of punctuated equilibrium theory suggest that "organizations evolve through alternating periods of convergence and reorientation" (Tushman & Rosenkopf, 1996, p. 940). Instability and reorientation punctuate stable, convergent periods (Tushman & Romanelli, 1985). According to this theory, technological breakthroughs that emerge from environmental changes disrupt stable patterns of interaction and power relations (Tushman & Romanelli, 1985), leading to reorientation and divergence (Tushman & Rosenkopf, 1996). Empirical studies have shown that reorientation and turbulence may stem from technological or legislative crises, wartime jolts, or performance crises (Tushman & Rosenkopf, 1996; Meyer, Brooks, & Goes, 1990; Miner et al., 1990) and cannot be predicted. Thus, convergence periods can vary dramatically in length.

Management ideologies, which often grow out of policy recommendations, may also evolve in cyclical patterns of convergence and reorientation. Barley and Kunda (1992) found a dialectical relationship between rational and normative ideas on management in the United States. When the economy was expanding, rational theories surged, while normative theories were prevalent when the economy was contracting. Thus, they showed that macro-economic conditions affected the rational or normative content of management ideas.

In a similar vein, Abrahamson (1996) argued that management techniques follow a wave pattern that is normally associated with the fashion industry. In fact, he called "a relatively transitory collective belief, disseminated by management fashion setters, that a management technique leads rational management progress" a management fashion (p. 257). He argued that such management fashions cannot remain stable for too long or progress would not seem to occur. He proposed that socio-psychological as well as economic, political, and organizational forces shape the demand for management fashion and that management fashions would increase during periods of performance disappointment. One would expect that the content of the management fashion emerging from such disappointment would address the perceived performance problems. In his empirical test of the emergence of management fads, Abrahamson (1997) found support for linking performance disappointment, in terms of high voluntary turnover rates, to the number of human relations and personnel management articles published in the United States. Moreover, the welfare work rhetoric was also linked to voluntary turnover rates. Thus, the factors affecting the cyclical nature of management ideologies also affected the content of the ideology.

Technology cycle theories (e.g., Anderson & Tushman, 1990; Tushman & Anderson, 1986) similarly point to alternating periods of radical and incremental change, periods of increased discontinuities alternating with periods of increased fermentation. In contrast to punctuated equilibrium processes, the periods follow a more or less regular wave pattern. Eras of ferment, which are characterized by design competition and substitution, carry within them the seed for the eras of incremental change. These eras of incremental change follow the emergence of a dominant design and are characterized by elaboration of the dominant design.

The drivers of technological discontinuities are sometimes endogenous, sometimes exogenous to the industry (Fombrun, 1986). Tushman and Anderson (1986) used data from the minicomputer, cement, and airline industries to study technological innovation. When they differentiated between competence-enhancing and competence-destroying technologies, they noticed an interesting pattern. Apparently, competence-destroying technologies stemmed from new players, exogenous to the industry, while competence-enhancing technologies were developed by existing firms, that is, endogenous forces. They also found that competence-enhancing discontinuities were associated with decreased environmental turbulence. Competence-destroying innovations, in contrast, were associated with increased environmental turbulence. Even when a technology developed from endogenous forces, however, which technology emerged as the dominant design was affected by factors exogenous to the industry. As Anderson and Tushman (1990, p. 617) argued, "social or political processes adjudicate among multiple technological possibilities"; the dominant design "is an outcome of the social or political dynamics of compromise and accommodation between actors of unequal influence."

The question that arises from this research is, how do endogenous and exogenous forces affect variation within a population of organizations and what implications arise out of this for learning? In other words, to what extent can one detect systematic patterns in variation within a population of organizations that can be linked to the evolution of a population of organizations or to its social context? And subsequently, what might be the implications of systematic variation on population-level learning? This chapter explores these issues by systematically analyzing a wide range of policy recommendations. Thus, this chapter is consistent with earlier notions of the social construction of variation but moves the argument to a higher level of analysis, to consider two social contexts that may affect variation: the national context and the temporal context.

RESEARCHING POLICY RECOMMENDATIONS

In the organization theory literature, recommendations have been used to study the development and diffusion of innovations. As DiMaggio (1991) showed, a new form of art museum—the community art museum—emerged after a consultant recommended it to members of the Carnegie Foundation. Similarly, Rogers (1995) pointed to the importance of recommendations by both U.S. State Agricultural Extension Services and by consensus development conferences of the U.S. National Institutes of Health in the diffusion of agricultural innovations and health innovations respectively. Consensus development conferences are held to discuss a particular medical innovation using predetermined questions. At the end of the conference, a statement is prepared, to which attendees react. The final version is then published and disseminated within the medical community. Consensus panels may recommend for or against the use of a medical innovation, thereby fulfilling an important gatekeeping function for the diffusion of medical innovations (Rogers, 1995).

As the previous example showed, recommendations have generally been studied as an antecedent to implementation, rather than being an object of study themselves. Moreover, studies that have used them have often only focused on one recommendation or practice, tracing its implementation and diffusion (e.g., Tolbert & Zucker, 1983; Mezias, 1990; Davis, 1991; DiMaggio, 1991; Haunschild, 1993) rather than focusing on a set of recommendations. In other studies, recommendations have complemented analyses of population dynamics without being the focus of analysis (e.g., Baum & Ingram, 1998). In contrast to existing studies, recommendations themselves are the subject of this study. I examined all policy recommendations published over a 75-year period in the population of Catholic children's institutions, and compared recommendations from Germany and the United States to assess the variation embedded within a broadcast transmission process of learning. Broadcast transmission takes place when "a single source, such as an organization or governmental agency, is responsible for diffusing a new routine, practice or structure across a population of organizations" (Miner & Haunschild, 1995, p. 143). In this paper, the broadcasting agencies are the publishers or editors of relevant journals and the journals themselves.

I chose the particular setting because underlying similarities between the two countries with respect to the emergence of Catholic children's institutions allowed meaningful comparison of the two data sets. Catholic children's institutions in both countries were part of the worldwide Roman Catholic Church, so that the basic beliefs and doctrines were the same. Moreover, because the Catholic Church is hierarchical, textually prescribed, organizationally encoded, and authoritatively led, the majority of policy suggestions should be codified in writing. While the published policy recommendations are not an exhaustive pool of existing practices in the population, they represent legitimate strategic options in that they underwent an editorial review process and were available for experimentation in the field.

The study covers the period from 1895, when the first special journals for charity workers were founded, to 1970. I chose 1970 as the end point because in the 1960s the viability of children's institutions was contested for the last time in the recent history of children's institutions. They were considered to be too restrictive, artificial in their methods of raising children, and not family-like enough. In Germany some students "liberated" children from children's institutions and invited these children (often teenagers) to join students' communes in Frankfurt am Main and other cities.

The sources of the policy recommendations were the main Catholic charity journals for Germany (*Charitas*, *Jugendwohl*) and the United States (*St. Vincent de Paul Quarterly*, *Catholic Charities Review*). These journals started as quarterly or bi-monthly publications and later were issued monthly. I read every article, note, and editorial in these journals and extracted *all* policy recommendations addressed to Catholic children's institution staff. While other journals in the field of childcare in general existed, none was directed specifically at Catholic children's institutions, existed continuously for the entire time period, or published specific policy recommendations.

Although it is possible that other childcare journals may have influenced the policy recommendations published in the Catholic journals or staff may have used other publications as sources for recommendations, extensive reading of staff biographies and institutional reports indicated that the policy recommendations published in the Catholic journals captured the majority of recommendations in the field. The editors included summaries of formal and informal meetings of staff, printed recommendations given at meetings, and referenced recommendations published in other sources such as handbooks. Consequently, published policy recommendations largely represent the variation of strategic options available in the field.

There were amazingly few changes in editors over the years. In Germany, the first editor served from 1895 to 1912, the second from 1912 to 1919, the third from 1920 to 1931, the fourth from 1932 to 1957, and the fifth started his editorship in 1957. In the United States, there were also five editors over the 75 years. The first served from 1895 to 1916, the second from 1917 to 1931, the third from 1932 to 1961, the fourth from 1962 to 1965, and the fifth editor took over in 1966. Hence, there was consistency in editorial style over long periods of time.

For this study, I defined policy recommendations as statements suggesting how an organization's management might handle a particular organizational issue. An example drawn from the management of Catholic children's institutions reads like this:

> All institutions caring for or supporting more than 250 dependent children shall employ at least one visitor for every 500 children or major fraction of that number, whose duty it shall be to examine the ability of the parents or guardians of such children to support them in whole or in part at their own expense and to make report thereon at least once every six months to the Department of Public Charities and the Department of Finance (*St. Vincent de Paul Quarterly*, 1899).

I counted a statement as *one* policy recommendation when it dealt with handling *one* issue. In some cases, long (German) sentences actually contained more than one recommendation, in which case, I had to break the sentence apart into two or more recommendations. In other cases, a whole paragraph contained just one recommendation. The final population consisted of 2,261 policy recommendations.

Variables and Operationalization

Counting, categorizing, and rating the recommendations led to several measures of variation. Because there is no one widely accepted operationalization of variation, I operationalized it in several ways. The measures of variation included the number of recommendations published per page, the number of issues addressed within the recommendations per page, the diversity within issues, and the variation in economic, religious, and bureaucratic content ratings.

I counted the number of recommendations on an annual basis then divided that number by the number of text pages in the journals to create the variable, number of recommendations published per page. Immersing myself in the recommendations and using open coding schemes (Strauss & Corbin, 1990), I came up with 16 main issues addressed in the recommendations, e.g., nutrition, medical services, disciplinary practices, religious services, etc. A second rater and I then followed my classification rules to categorize all recommendations into these categories. Because these data were categorical, I assessed the reliability of the classification by Cohen's Kappa (Elder, Pavalko, & Clipp, 1993). After training sessions involving random samples of 50 policy recommendations and discussion of the classification, the interrater agreement was .84, which is high (Elder et al., 1993). Because of the expanding size of the journals in page numbers, I decided on the number of issues addressed in the recommendations by the number of text pages published in any given year to create the variable, number of issues addressed within the recommendations per page.

To take into account the variation within the categories, I assessed diversity within issues. Two trained, bilingual raters assessed how varied the recommendations within each issue were (interrater reliability $r = .87$) by reading all recommendations published in one year, sorted by issue. For each issue, they evaluated whether the recommendations within the category made essentially the same recommendation; addressed the same aspect of the category but differed slightly (e.g., within nutrition recommendations, to give children a half or a whole pint of milk daily); addressed different aspects of the category (e.g., recommendations to give milk daily and to feed children vegetables and fruit daily); or proposed contradictory actions (e.g., a recommendation to have the children drink a glass of wine with dinner versus another recommendation never to allow children to drink alcohol). The raters' responses were averaged, and the mean of the diversity ratings across the categories within a year became the variable diversity within issues.

I measured variation in the content of the recommendations from the ratings of two trained, bilingual raters (mean interrater reliability $r = .64$) who assessed the economic, religious, and bureaucratic content of each recommendation. *Economic content* was the extent to which a recommendation referred implicitly or explicitly to income, market, niche, differentiation, or competition. *Religious content* was the extent to which a recommendation referred implicitly or explicitly to divine order, Christian values, Church doctrine, liturgical life, or similar aspects of a Christian lifestyle. *Bureaucratic content* was the extent to which a recommendation referred implicitly or explicitly to bureaucratic and social stability, the state, or laws and requirements. For each year, I calculated the coefficient of variation and used it as a measure of the variation in content among recommendations, resulting in three measures, variation in economic content, variation in religious content, and variation in bureaucratic content.

VARIATION AMONG POLICY RECOMMENDATIONS

The overall research question that guided this research was how endogenous and exogenous forces affected the variation among recommendations for Catholic children's institutions. In other words, it asked to what extent one could detect systematic patterns in the variation of the recommendations and to what extent such patterns could be linked to the evolution of Catholic children's institutions or their social context? I will first describe some quantitative results and then report on some detailed qualitative insights.

The number of recommendations per page and the number of issues per page were highly correlated: .83 for Germany and .74 for the United States. In Germany, the number of recommendations published peaked between 1912 and 1925. Between 1900 and 1911 and between 1951 and 1963, very few recommendations were published. The years 1918, 1936, and 1969 were relatively high in their local context but may have been outliers rather than indicators of systematic trends. Similarly, the number of issues showed a clear peak between 1912 and

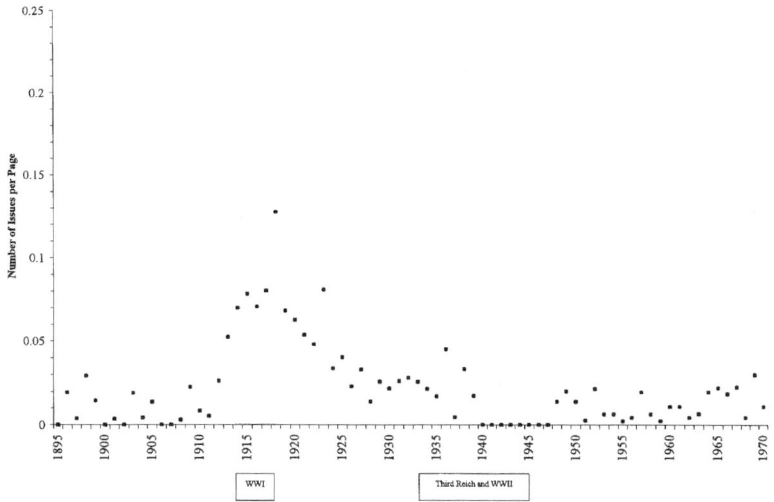

Figure 1. Number of Issues per Page in Germany

1925, as shown in Figure 1. There was a small rise and fall in the number of issues per page before the turn of the century, then a pronounced peak in 1917-18, which ended in a trough between 1939 and 1965 before another rise in the late 1960s. One might see a wave pattern in these data, going from zero recommendations and issues per page in 1895 to .008 recommendations and .03 issues per page in 1898, then decreasing until 1908, rising until 1913, and falling again until 1939. Between 1962 and the end of the study, there was another slight rise in the number of recommendations and issues.

The U.S. data do not show such clearly pronounced patterns, although they show a pattern of steady, small waves interspersed with two years of very high variation, 1939 and 1945. High peaks of these waves occurred in 1902, 1915, 1928, 1942, 1955, and 1968. The years 1927, 1939, 1945, 1955 and 1961 clearly stand out in the number of recommendations published. For the number of issues, graphed in Figure 2, the years 1939, 1945, and 1955 stand out. While one could interpret these years merely as outliers, they could also represent punctuations among seemingly stable small waves of recommendations and issues published.

The diversity ratings for Germany, in Figure 3, and the United States, in Figure 4, show a wave pattern in the German data but not in the U.S. data. In Germany, a trough in the early 1920s follows a peak between 1912 and 1917. A smaller peak in the early 1930s is followed by a trough between 1937 and 1959. An upswing in the early 1960s continues to the end of the study. While this last increase in variation seems quite small in terms of the numbers of recommendations and issues, the average diversity among those recommendations shows a substantial increase.

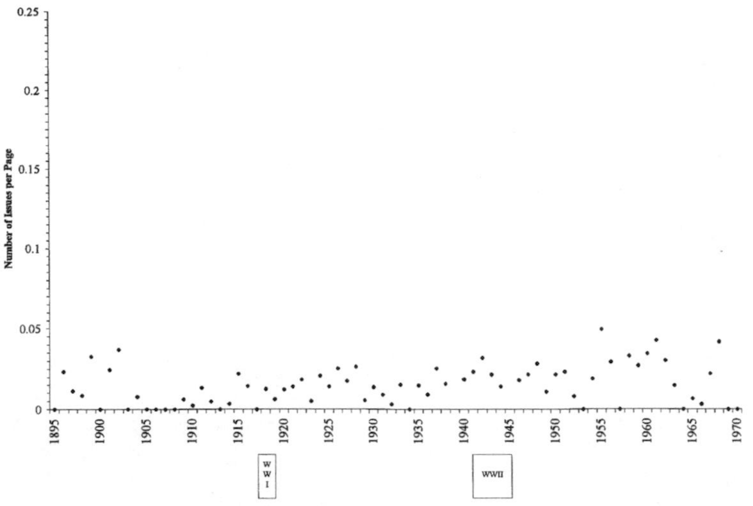

Figure 2. Number of Issues per Page in the United States

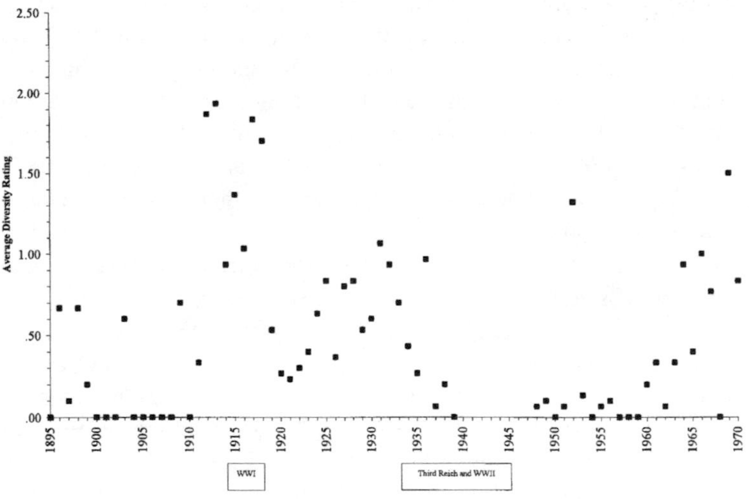

Figure 3. Average Diversity Rating for Germany

In the United States, in contrast, the diversity ratings seem to swing widely between very low and moderate diversity, with wider swings in the later periods of the study, but, no clear pattern can be detected.

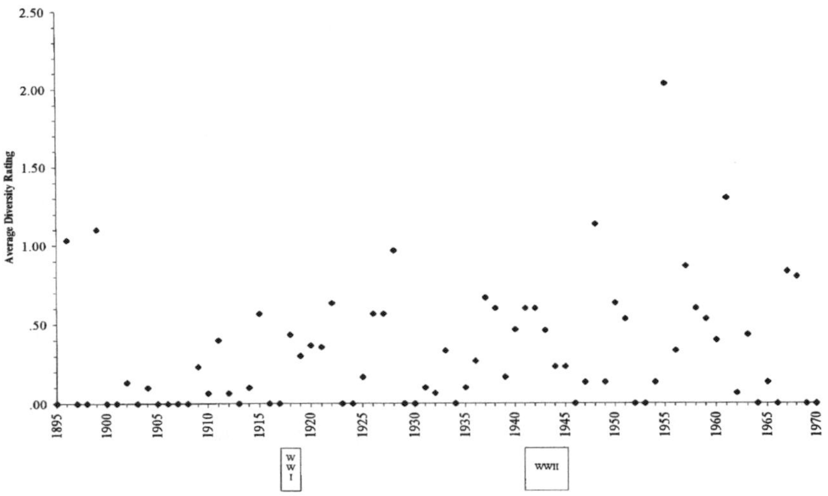

Figure 4. Average Diversity Rating for the United States

These quantitative results consistently suggest a wave pattern of one large or three smaller waves for Germany. For one large wave, the upswing would have started in 1911, peaked around 1918, and the downswing would have ended in 1939. Alternatively, as three small waves, the downswing of the first wave would have ended in the late 1920s, and a smaller second wave peaked in the middle of the 1930s, leading to a downswing until 1939. The upswing of a third wave might have started in the early 1960s but is difficult to verify because it runs into the end of the study period. Thus, one could conclude that a systematic cyclical pattern in variation existed in the German data. The question is whether these systematic patterns are linked to endogenous forces within the population of Catholic children's institutions or its social context. The U.S. data are not as unequivocal. While data on the number of recommendations and number of issues could be interpreted as showing small swings, in a small wave pattern, the average diversity ratings do not support such an interpretation. Hence, no clear conclusion about a systematic variation pattern can be drawn for the U.S. data.

Historical Events Associated with High Variation in Germany

In Germany, high peaks of variation occurred around 1898, between 1912 and 1919, in the middle of the 1930s and in the late 1960s. A quick review of history revealed a few events occurring around these times that could be associated with high variation. For instance, the late nineteenth century was characterized by change and reorientation, on the one hand, and by codification and coherence, on the other hand. The *Bürgerliches Gesetzbuch* (civil law code) came into effect on January 1, 1900. There were initiatives within the welfare sector to make it more coherent through national umbrella organizations; for instance, the *Charitasverband für das katholische Deutschland* was founded in 1897. At the same time, the first formal steps were taken toward professionalization through training courses and regular meetings of institutional leaders. A general change climate presents opportunities for experimentation and discussion of approaches, thereby indirectly encouraging different voices and variation. Thus, the general focus on change in Germany and in the welfare sector may account for the higher levels of variation before the turn of the century.

Starting in 1911 and up to World War I (1914-1918), the variation increased, peaked during the war and then declined. During that time Germany itself seemed to have become more unified. Chickering (1998), among others, talked about the "Spirit of 1914," which was seen as ushering in a new era in German history. According to him (p. 14), the period leading up to and the beginning of the war were associated with "a single great feeling of moral elevation, a soaring of religious sentiment, in short, the ascent of a whole people to the heights." Until then, the German Imperial state had consisted of 25 constituent states with fragmented institutions, as well as fragmented political and administrative structures. The Declaration of War stirred feelings of national unity, which were supported by new unitary national authority in political and administrative matters (Chickering, 1998).

The 1920s were characterized by renewal and rebuilding of social institutions, especially the mid-1920s, which were to some extent a golden era. The aftereffects of the lost war were ending. The Weimar Republic had not yet collapsed, hyperinflation was over, and life settled into a somewhat stable pattern. Energy that had been spent on individual survival could be directed toward the betterment of society. There was a strong push in the welfare sector to improve the system and the conditions of those in welfare institutions, influenced by the rise of sociology, psychology, pedagogy, and medicine in academia. While there was a change climate focussing on improvement, it was focused on incremental change, convergence, and stability, rather than on revolutionary change.

In contrast, Germany in the late 1920s and early 1930s experienced political instability, characterized by frequent elections and mobilization of fringe groups such as communists and Nazis. Unemployment was high, and traditional ways of living and sensemaking were no longer sufficient. For example, there were more than 2 million unemployed people in 1929. By December 1930, the number had increased to 4.4 million and by 1932 to more than 6 million. Unemployment could hit anyone, not just unskilled or lazy people. The rise of the Nazis, the dissolution of the Social Democratic Party, the burning of books in 1933, and the murder of political opponents by the Nazis in 1934 all show a state undergoing revolutionary change.

During World War II, *Charitas* and *Jugendwohl* were forced to cease publication, so it is impossible to know whether variation would have increased during the war years, as it did during World War I, remained stable, or decreased. Variation was quite low, however, between 1948 and the early 1960s. German society went through a rebuilding of the destroyed infrastructure as well as large migration movements at that time. The mid-1950s were the birth of the West-German *Wirtschaftswunder,* as well as West-German integration into Western political alliances such as NATO.

The late 1960s were a period of great change in the educational sector in Germany. It was the time of student revolts, university sit-ins, and the so-called liberation of children housed in institutions by students who invited them to join communes in Frankfurt and other big cities. Although the essence of housing children in institutions was questioned, it was also clear that not all children in need of care could be placed in foster families. Thus, there also was an impetus to make institutions more family-like, through group homes or living arrangements that resembled families. This climate of questioning and change may have contributed to the increasing variation in the 1960s. Overall, the historical events suggest that high variation in policy recommendations in Germany parallels periods characterized by revolutionary political change, such as preparations for wars, Nazism, or student revolts.

Historical Events Associated with High Variation in the United States

While no systematic pattern emerged in the U.S. data, the years 1939, 1945, and 1955 stand out as years of high variation in terms of the numbers of recommendations published and issues addressed, and later years were characterized by higher variation in the diversity ratings. These years corresponded to milestones in the development of social work in the United States. In 1939, it was agreed that two years of graduate studies and a Master's degree in social work were needed for recognition as a professional social worker. In 1945, the California Act for Certified Social Workers was passed that was very influential in the national development of social work. Finally, in 1955, the National Association of Social Workers was founded. It could be that increased numbers of recommendations and the issues addressed in them were influenced by the continuing professionalization of the social work field (Rura, 1995; Rura-Polley, 1996).

The links between high variation periods and historical events are, for obvious reasons, tentative and cannot support any claim for causal effects. If variation were socially constructed and affected by the social context in which it occurs, however, one would expect to find particular relationships between the content of historical events and variation in content. Thus, if a religious historical event were to have an effect, one would expect it to influence variation in the religious content of the recommendations. For example, a discussion about religious practice among a bishops' conference should affect the number and content of recommendations dealing with religion. To assess this link, I examined variation in the economic, religious, and bureaucratic content ratings.

Variation in the Content of Recommendations

Trends are evident in the coefficients of variation for economic, religious, and bureaucratic content in both countries. As shown in Figure 5, variation in economic content in Germany was moderately high at the beginning of the study but very low between 1901 and 1909—although this may be due to the low number of recommendations published during that time. Variation in economic content was highest in the second half of the 1920s and in the early 1950s. During World War I, variation in economic content was lower than before and directly after the war. Overall, the economic content was rather low in Germany (content-rating graphs available from the author), but whenever economic concerns featured highly in the recommendations, they seem to have been accompanied by public debate that was then reflected in variation in economic content. For instance, the years following the war evolved around economic problems and social upheaval. There were demands for reparations by France, a general strike, and hyperinflation, which may explain variation in economic content. Dealing with the economic reality was a core concern for the welfare sector. Hence, it is not surprising to find higher levels of economic content and variation in the recommendations. While some recommendations continued to be shaped by the underlying charitable philosophy and had low economic content, others honed in on the economic

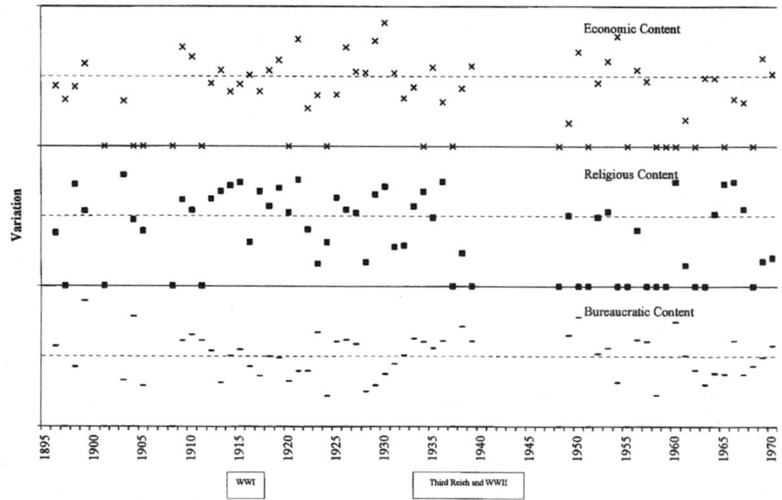

Figure 5. Content Coefficients of Variation for Germany

hardships, rationalization, and potential solutions. It seems that economic and social reality drove variation in economic content. A similar pattern occurred in the early 1930s and early 1950s, both periods of economic hardship in Germany.

Variation in religious content was generally higher between 1910 and 1935 than after World War II. Following World War II, years containing recommendations of no religious content were interspersed with years of moderate and high average religious content in Germany, but variation was generally low except for 1961 and 1964-1967. That is, the years immediately preceding and following Vatican II (1962-65) showed increasing religious content as well as variation (content-rating graphs available from the author).

No clear pattern of variation emerged in the bureaucratic content data. There was a general downward trend in the coefficients of variation between 1910 and 1923 and an upward trend between 1928 and 1939, interrupted by moderately high coefficients in 1925-1927. Before 1910 and after World War II, no trends are evident in the coefficients of variation, although the mean content ratings shed some light on the issue (content-rating graphs available from the author). In some years, there was a fairly high bureaucratic content in the recommendations, but also high variation, meaning that some recommendations were very bureaucratic and others were not at all (e.g., 1923, 1931, 1938, 1950, and 1960). While one might have expected that the bureaucratic content of recommendations would increase over time and then remain on a fairly high level in Germany, that was not the case.

Figure 6 shows that in the United States, variation in economic content seemed to have followed a downward trend over time. Economic concerns were barely addressed in the recommendations after 1938 (except for 1968), and variation in economic content was almost negligible during that time. The greatest variation in economic content occurred in the United States in 1913.

Variation in religious content in the United States was relatively high between 1896 and 1904 and between 1949 and 1963. During other periods, no clear pattern emerges. While the high variation pattern at the turn of the century is somewhat similar to Germany, in other periods it differs. When Germany experienced very low variation in religious content in the 1950s, the United States had high variation. When the United States had rather low variation between 1915 and 1933, Germany had comparatively high variation. Thus, it cannot have been a universal factor that accounts for the variation in religious content in both countries, even though doctrines, Church teachings, and the Vatican Council applied equally to both countries.

Variation in bureaucratic content seems to have decreased over time. For instance, in 1961, when 130 recommendations were published in the United States, variation in bureaucratic content was smaller than in 1909, when only four recommendations were published. With the rise of different organizational rhetorics and forms, bureaucracy and bureaucratic rationality seem to have lost favor among authors of policy recommendations.

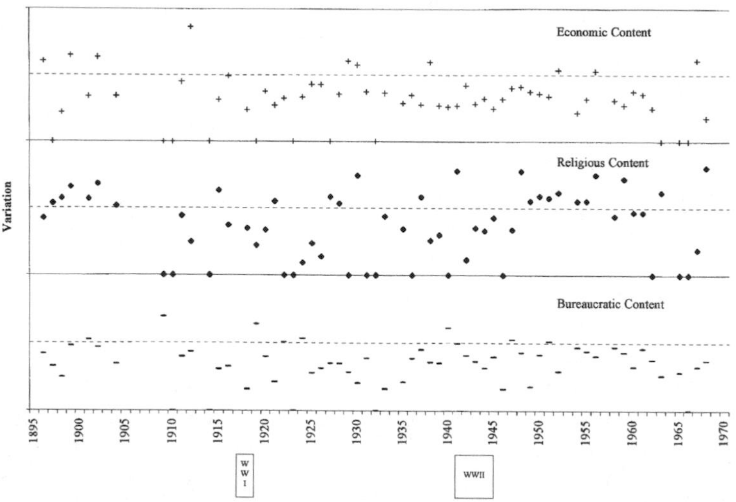

Figure 6. Content Coefficients of Variation for the United States

Another way to look at variation in content is to look at the text of the recommendations themselves, rather than at ratings of that content. Qualitative analysis of the recommendations led to different insights than the quantitative analyses.

CONTEXTUALIZING RECOMMENDATIONS, ISSUES AND THEMES

The policy recommendations themselves provide support for a cyclical pattern in Germany, as well as indicators of a cyclical pattern in the United States. In some years, recommendations specifically asked staff members to consider a variety of approaches, to consider the individual child, and to develop their own personal leadership and house styles. For example, in the years leading up to World War I, characterized by increased variation and the "Beginning of a New Era" in Germany, some authors argued for more variety in the vocational training for secondary students. One recommendation in Germany stated:

> So far, girls are given exemplary training in sewing, taking care of laundry, and ironing. The question arises, though, whether this monotony does justice to the demands of reality. It is unlikely that all students will remain in these vocations and find jobs within them. Thus, all who will have to find jobs outside this industry will not be suitably equipped for the daily struggles of life. Hence, it would be far better to ask girls either by choice or according to some predetermined schedule to engage in other occupations (*Jugendwohl*, 1912).

Other recommendations published during that time spoke strongly against uniforms and for individual clothing; a time where many young men actually took up uniforms to serve in the German army:

> The institution that raises school-age children must avoid making the external look uniform. This has to be taken into consideration when ordering fabric for clothing (*Jugendwohl*, 1915).

> Clothes have to be clean and neat. Uniforms are not recommended. It is best to buy leftover fabric from wholesalers; that is cheaper and provides variety (*Jugendwohl*, 1917).

Examples from the United States include flexibility in the daily schedule and attendance at daily church services:

> If the child were at home, he would rise at a given time, as a general rule, to either attend school or reach his job on time. Note this is the general rule, which admits of exceptions. Why could we not act likewise? (*Catholic Charities Review*, 1955).

> Another change over the years has concerned compulsory daily attendance at Mass. Where previously we had one fixed time for rising, we now have three, one for the Sisters, another for the high school students, and a third for the grade school students. Boys may attend Mass if they so request, and I like to think that such attendance means more to them because it is of their own choosing (*Catholic Charities Review*, 1955).

These illustrations show how flexibility and variation with respect to certain issues were highly valued at particular times. Thus, it seems that variation was not randomly distributed but followed certain patterns, for example representing counter points.

A look at particular issues and related variation in recommendations shows additional patterns. For example, in Germany variation about discipline occurred between 1911 and 1915 (in the years before and early in World War I) and then again in 1936 (in the period leading up to World War II). While uniform discipline is generally shegged during warm the recommendations emphasized variety. The following is a typical recommendation:

> We find it difficult to establish a disciplinary protocol for all Prussian children's institutions as planned by the royal government, because the educational material used in the individual institutions is too varied. The establishing of a disciplinary protocol sets back the fatherly-educational handling of each individual child. One would tend to fall back on the rulebook in the hand of the judge (*Charitas*, 1911).

Variation in recommendations about leisure activities was particularly evident between 1913 and 1918 (during World War I) and again in 1970:

> The first prerequisite is extensive choice in the environment—both instrumentally (toys...) and socially (several teachers to whom the child can relate closely)—in which the child can choose its activities and expect recognition and praise. Obviously, this activity is not entirely unconstrained, because it is limited by the supply. However, that is a sensible limitation as long as the teacher intends to keep the supply as broad as possible and allows the child truly free choice among the activities (*Jugendwohl*, 1970).

As mentioned earlier, variation in clothing occurred only between 1915 and 1918. Variation in recommendations about religion occurred only in 1966 and 1967, just after the close of Vatican II. At other times, these issues were not contested; the recommendations closely matched or complemented one another, with only slight variation.

> I recommend monthly confession. I generally use a comparison to explain this: If somebody is sick or likely to suffer repeatedly from sickness, it is good to see a physician on a regular basis (*Jugendwohl*, 1965).

> The same applies for participation at Holy Mass. We can offer those who refuse to participate the option to move to change into an inter-denominational institution (*Jugendwohl*, 1965).

> Mass on Sunday and a communal [school] Mass during the week should be offered and viewed as self-evident. If, however, a child truly does not want to attend Mass once in a while, no coercion should be used (*Jugendwohl*, 1966).

In the U.S. qualitative data, similarly fascinating patterns of high variation emerge among specific policy recommendations about a particular issue. For instance, vocational and educational training was a contested issue between 1955 and 1961. Institutions were called upon to provide flexible approaches, but it was hard to let go of the traditions. One contested issue was the schooling of the children, whether they should go to a school on the institution's premises or attend the local Catholic or public school:

> Delinquent girls are better off attending school in the institution for many reasons. Most of them have been placed in the institutions because of truancy from school and it is necessary for the staff to help give them a desire to attend school again. Most of their problems began in high school outside (*Catholic Charities Review*, 1955).

> Sisters—who hesitate to make a change from what has "always been," who are afraid to send children out to school for fear of upsetting what is now a smooth-running, well organized home of institution, have faith—take heart—read on a bit (*Catholic Charities Review*, 1957).

Accounting procedures were debated between 1960 and 1961. At issue was whether all institutions should follow a uniform system or design their own. Several recommendations called for variation, for example:

> Every system should be designed to serve each institution's particular need. Typical of the basic statistical records are books containing records of admission, discharges and deaths as well as days of care provided for residents (*Catholic Charities Review*, 1961).

Religious issues seem to have been debated in 1928 and then again between 1955 and 1957, as reflected in the earlier examples on flexibility about attending Mass. Variation in recommendations with respect to staff, job duties, and training occurred at a number of times, such as 1936, 1940, 1947, 1960, and 1962. There was a recurrent call for flexibility, especially in the later years of the study:

> A certain amount of regimentation is necessary for maintaining order. Routine, however, should not be emphasized at the expense of the child's individuality. The child is not made for the institution, but the institution for the child (*Catholic Charities Review*, 1940).

The issue of whether group homes were supposed to resemble family homes and should, therefore, be led by (married) houseparents or could be led by religious staff was hotly contested, as the following examples show:

> The cottage group is not supposed to approximate a family and therefore, adequate care and training can be given by Religious (*Catholic Charities Review*, 1947).

> In an institution conducted by brothers for boys, many of whom have been deprived of the usual mothering given children in normal homes, a mother-person would be conducive to more adequate treatment in individual cases (*Catholic Charities Review*, 1947).

These recommendations suggest that some social factors affected certain issues, but the aggregation of the data on an annual basis across all issues blurred such effects in the quantitative analyses. Overall, it seems that the content of the variation in Germany was shaped to some extent, by social factors, while no clear interpretation emerged in the United States. In Germany, three factors were associated with variation in the pool of options for managerial action. First, increased variation in the recommendations coincided with the end of a period of uniformity and monotony in the external environment of the children's institutions. During or shortly after periods of stressing uniformity in clothing, discipline, and education, recommendations called for increased variation in the approach to childcare. Second, variation increased during times characterized by climates favoring revolutionary change. This climate of change seemed to have opened windows of opportunity for experimentation, questioning, and searching for new approaches. This implies that windows of opportunity exist not only for managing selection and retention of routines but also for managing variation. Third, variation in content increased during or shortly after times when that particular content area was dominating public debate. In the United States, variation in the content of recommendations addressing particular issues seemed to have occurred during times of public debate and contest of those issues, which would have made them more salient. Neither war nor other social upheavals had broad overarching effects on the variation in policy recommendations in the United States.

The German findings, in particular are in line with findings by researchers of punctuated equilibrium and technology cycle theories (e.g., Anderson & Tushman, 1990; Tushman & Romanelli, 1985). Variation, measured by numbers of policy recommendations, numbers of issues addressed, and diversity ratings and evidenced in recommendations advising varied approaches to children and offering choice, suggests a systematic pattern in Germany but a less systematic pattern in the United States. These findings go beyond previous studies by showing that such patterns are not limited to the variation-selection interface, where the selection of a routine triggers a new wave of variation. Instead, variation itself already seems to follow a wave pattern. During some periods, variation is high, during other periods, variation is low, seemingly independent of the selection of particular routines.

Particularly in Germany, the cyclical patterns seem to have been affected by systematic environmental change, such as wars and social or political upheavals (Meyer et al., 1990; Miner et al., 1990). In contrast to Abrahamson's (1997) findings, the variation pattern did not seem to follow long-term economic waves, such as Kondratieff cycles, although empirical testing of macro-economic conditions and variation may reveal associations that this study, which mainly relied on descriptive data, did not reveal. The findings seem to support Abrahamson's suggestion that the content of management fads is affected by macro-economic and social conditions. Variation in economic, religious, and bureaucratic content showed some trends that could be associated with public debate and management fashion. For instance, variation in bureaucratic content declined in the United States, over time, showing some loss of interest in bureaucracy as a topic of management debate.

The question remains to what extent the variation followed a socially constructed reality or manifested objectively different best-practice childcare options. In many cases, the variation may have been socially constructed. In his study of American cement manufacturing Anderson (this volume) suggests that the joint social construction of interpretive structures shaped the industry and its routines. In the absence of scientifically justifiable best practices of childcare, the variation observed in the published policy recommendations may similarly have relied on a social construction process that subsequently shaped the field and its routines. The observation that particular themes dominated the debates at different times suggests that a large part of the variation was indeed socially constructed.

IMPLICATIONS

The results of this study show that thematic variation paralleled environmental conditions to a certain extent. Published policy recommendations may have been enactments of perceived environmental change or outcomes of collective debates. Periods of convergence and reorientation, of ferment and incremental change seem not only to characterize technical innovations and for-profit organizations but also social, administrative innovations in the non-profit sector. These results have interesting implications for population-level learning and strategic management. From an academic perspective, it seems that social constructionism extends not only to the selection and retention of phenomena but also to generation of the variation from which selection occurs. This would be consistent with Weick's (1979) social psychology of organizing and its attention to enactment. Such social construction may provide opportunities for experimentation, questioning, and searching for new approaches through the variations available. On one hand, shrewd managers may use their skills in managing resources, processes, and meaning to open up debates, as well as to create obligatory passage points for discourse within a population of organizations (Clegg, 1989). On the other hand, they may close down avenues for learning where they deem topics are no longer current or fashionable. This would imply that bids could be systematically mobilized (Schattschneider, 1960) at all stages in the learning process, not just in the selection and retention stages but also at the variation stage.

If variation is socially constructed or confined by social factors in ways that restrict both the amount and the content of variation, learning may be limited. As Campbell (1969, p. 73) wrote, "the more numerous and the greater the heterogeneity among variations, the richer the opportunities for an advantageous innovation." Small variation is likely to produce less innovative populations of organizations. Consequently, the long-term adaptability of the population of organizations may suffer.

Where variation is small, the choice between strategic options involves less complex search procedures. While small discriminations are easier to make in the shortterm, in the longterm they produce population inertia. Narrowly focusing on small variation may make managers lose the capacity to think about the big picture. Strategic foresight is likely to decline, and environmental jolts are likely to have greater impact without the availability of appropriate responses.

While low variation among recommendations increases the chances of selection for each variation, even such selection for trial may be a two-edged sword. On the positive side, if fewer choices are available, organizational members may come to a decision quickly about implementing a recommendation and may even reach consensus rather than mere compromise. On the negative side, selecting from a smaller pool of variation may lead to suboptimal performance over time. As Romanelli (1998) cautioned, populations may converge on satisfying rather than optimal routines. The possibilities of discovering potentially better routines will decline. Selection will occur from a limited set of strategic options; "there will no longer be grist for the selection mill" (Romanelli, 1998, p. 20).

FUTURE RESEARCH

Policy recommendations represent a pool of strategic options for managers in a population of organizations to choose from because they come from a broadcast transmission process of learning. They are suggested solutions to problems, suggested new ways of providing a service or creating a product, and so on. They are options rather than guidelines or requirements and, thus, offer more strategic options than existing routines or laws. To fully understand their impact on population-level learning, future research should look at the selective implementation and retention of recommendations. One question that arises out of this research is whether the implementation of a recommendation is more likely when variation is low and there are few recommendations to choose from. There may be low ambiguity about what path to follow and what recommendation to implement. Or is the rate of implementation higher during periods of high variation, which seem to occur during a general climate of change, or will there be more ambiguity about which recommendation to implement, decreasing the likelihood of choosing the recommendation most likely to lead to adaptation?

More broadly, a question arises about what factors drive the implementation of a recommendation. Is it supply driven or demand driven, that is, does a higher number of available strategic options make their implementation more likely, or do decision-makers evaluate each recommendation with respect to its content, its traits, as suggested by the diffusion of innovation literature? For example, recommendations perceived to offer high relative advantages may be more likely to be implemented (Rogers, 1995). In that case, a recommendation addressing the health of babies might be more likely to be implemented than some other recommendations.

An example of the early years of children's institutions helps to illustrate this point. Many institutions caring for orphaned infants hired wet nurses to nurse and take care of these babies, but there were many problems with these wet nurses because of their own poor economic living conditions. Thus, a recommendation was made that "besides receiving three meals, each wet nurse has a cup of chocolate at ten o'clock, tea at three, and a bowl of gruel at seven in the evening" (*St. Vincent de Paul Quarterly*, 1899). The motive, obviously, was to improve the health conditions of the babies, rather than the wet nurses per se, who were only the medium for improving the babies' health. The health of the babies was central to the core mission of children's institutions and, therefore, one might expect that this recommendation would very likely be implemented. In contrast, the following recommendation was less central to the organization's mission and, therefore, would be less likely implemented: "nurses and attendants should wear white gowns" (*Catholic Charities Review*, 1926).

Alternatively, recommendations that were compatible with existing routines, norms, and values could have had higher rates of implementation. As Rogers (1995) pointed out, innovations compatible with socio-cultural values and beliefs, existing routines, and needs are more likely to diffuse. Since the implementation of recommendations with high compatibility is less likely to face resistance by staff, creates less uncertainty for the organization, and reinforces current norms and values, compatible recommendations are more likely to be implemented. For example, in a Catholic children's institution, one would expect that a recommendation upholding the central values of the Catholic faith is more likely to be implemented than a recommendation contradicting the core values of the institution. Hence, the following recommendation might have a higher probability of implementation than some other recommendation: "religious instruction, therefore, is to be imparted daily, and at least monthly the children should receive the sacraments" (*St. Vincent de Paul Quarterly*, 1899).

Other traits identified in the diffusion of innovation literature concern the complexity of an innovation, its trialability, and observability (Rogers, 1995). Future research should examine whether certain traits affect the implementation of a recommendation. Alternatively, there may be other social or economic factors, such as the perceived legitimacy or the amount of slack resources available for experimenting with new routines, that might affect implementation.

CONCLUSION

This chapter explored the social construction of variation among policy recommendations published in two countries over a 75-year period. It showed that variation was not randomly distributed but seemed to have been affected by the social, economic, and historic context in which the recommendations were published. The results suggest that increases in variation sometimes coincide with the end of a period of uniformity and monotony, a general climate for change, and public debate of particular issues. Hitherto, the assumption has often been made that shaping and structuring of a strategic option occur during or after selection. These results show that shaping and structuring already occur at the variation stage. This has important implications for population-level learning. Low variation among recommendations may increase the likelihood of implementation but, at the same time, lead to suboptimal performance in the longterm. It also means that the content of what is being learned is not necessarily shaped at the selection and retention stage but by the variation that exists among a pool of options available to managers.

The broadcast transmission of policy recommendations studied here can affect population learning at several levels. In its variation, it can provide options for organizations to try different options and learn from their own experience, in a parallel organizational learning process. Organizations experimenting with variations in strategic options but confronting similar problems can then learn from other organizations, in a process of interorganizational learning. Finally, the population can experience and benefit from collective population-level learning at various times, strengthening common norms and practices that legitimate them as a population. This study of an emerging organizational field only begins to reveal the complexity of how these learning processes play out in children's organizations, but it points to directions for study in other populations of organizations.

ACKNOWLEDGMENTS

This research project received funding from the Internal Research Grant Scheme of the University of Western Sydney, Macarthur. Some of the data referred to in this paper were gathered for my dissertation, "Professionalization and Isomorphism in Organizational Fields: Catholic Children's Institutions in Germany and the U.S. from 1895 to 1970," which was funded by Cusanuswerk, Bischöfliche Studienstiftung, Bonn, Germany. I thank Joel Baum, Stewart Clegg, Pamela Haunschild, Anne Miner, and Berta Whitney as well as seminar participants at the University of Technology, Sydney and the Australian Graduate School of Management, Sydney for their valuable comments. Andreas Schwab provided tremendous help with the classification and rating of the recommendations.

REFERENCES

Abrahamson, E. (1991). Managerial fads and fashions: The diffusion and rejection of innovations. *Academy of Management Review, 16*, 586-612.

Abrahamson, E. (1996). Management fashion. *Academy of Management Review, 21*, 254-285.

Abrahamson, E. (1997). The emergence and prevalence of employee management rhetorics: The effects of long waves, labor unions, and turnover, 1875 to 1992. *Academy of Management Journal, 40*, 491-533.

Aldrich, H. (1999). *Organizations evolving.* London: Sage.

Anderson, P., & Tushman, M. L. (1990). Technological discontinuities and dominant design: A cyclical model of technological change. *Administrative Science Quarterly, 35*, 604-633.

Barley, S. R., & Kunda, G. (1992). Design and devotion: Surges of rational and normative ideologies of control in managerial discourse. *Administrative Science Quarterly, 37*, 363-399.

Barnett, W. P. (1990). The organizational ecology of a technological system. *Administrative Science Quarterly, 35,* 1-60.

Baum, J. A. C., & Ingram, P. (1998). Survival-enhancing learning in the Manhattan hotel industry. *Management Science, 44*, 996-1016.

Campbell, D. T. (1969). Variation and selective retention in socio-cultural evolution. *General Systems, 14,* 69-85.

Clegg, S. R. (1989). *Frameworks of power.* London: Sage.

Chickering, R. (1998). *Imperial Germany and the Great War, 1914-1918.* Cambridge: Cambridge University Press.

Davis, G. F. (1991). Agents without principle? The spread of the poison pill through the intercorporate network. *Administrative Science Quarterly, 36*, 583-613.

DiMaggio, P. J. (1991). Constructing an organizational field as a professional project: U.S. art museums, 1920-1940. In W. W. Powell & P. J. DiMaggio (Eds.), *The new institutionalism in organizational analysis* (pp. 267-292). Chicago, IL: University of Chicago Press.

Elder G. H., Pavalko, E. K., & Clipp, E. C. (1993). *Working with archival data.* Newbury Park: Sage.

Fombrun, C. J. (1986). Structural dynamics within and between organizations. *Administrative Science Quarterly, 31,* 403-421.

Hannan, M. T., & Freeman, J. H. (1989). *Organizational ecology.* Cambridge: Harvard University Press.

Haunschild, P. R. (1993). Interorganizational imitation: The impact of interlocks on corporate acquisition activity. *Administrative Science Quarterly, 38*, 564-592.

Jacoby, G. P. (1941). *Catholic child care in 19th century New York.* Washington, DC: Catholic University of America Press.

Kallert, H. (1964). *Waisenhaus und Arbeitserziehung im 17. und 18. Jahrhundert.* Dissertation, Johann Wolfgang Goethe-Universität, Frankfurt am Main.

Lant, T. K., & Mezias, S. J. (1992). An organizational learning model of convergence and reorientation. *Organization Science, 3*, 47-71.

Meyer, A., Brooks, G., & Goes, J. (1990). Environmental jolts and industry revolutions. *Strategic Management Journal, 11*, 93-110.

Mezias, S. J. (1990). An institutional model of organizational practice: Financial reporting at the Fortune 200. *Administrative Science Quarterly, 35*, 431-457.

Miner, A. S. (1991). Organizational evolution and the social ecology of jobs. *American Sociological Review, 56*, 772-785.

Miner, A. S. (1994). Seeking adaptive advantage: Evolutionary theory and managerial action. In J. A. C. Baum & J. V. Singh (Eds): *Evolutionary dynamics of organizations* (pp. 76-89). New York: Oxford University Press.

Miner, A. S., Amburgey, T. L., & Stearns, T. M. (1990). Interorganizational linkages and population dynamics: Buffering and transformational shields. *Administrative Science Quarterly, 35*, 689-713.

Miner, A. S., & Haunschild, P. R. (1995). Population-level learning. *Research in Organizational Behavior, 17*, 115-166.

O'Grady, J. (1931). *Catholic charities in the United States*. New York: Arno Press.

Richan, W. C. (1987). *Beyond altruism: Social welfare policy in American society*. New York: Haworth Press.

Rogers, E. M. (1995). *The diffusion of innovation* (4th ed.). New York: Free Press.

Romanelli, E. (1998). *Blind (but not unconditioned) variation: Problems of copying in socio-cultural evolution.* Paper presented at Variations in Organizational Science: A Conference in Honor of D. T. Campbell. Toronto, Canada, June.

Romanelli, E., & Tushman, M. L. (1994). Organizational transformation as punctuated equilibrium: An empirical test. *Academy of Management Journal, 37*, 1141-1166.

Rura, T. (1995). *Professionalization and isomorphism in organizational fields: Catholic children's institutions in Germany and the U.S. from 1895 to 1970.* Unpublished dissertation. University of Wisconsin-Madison.

Rura-Polley, T. (1996). *Professionalization: Isomorphism or heterogeneity? Evidence from Catholic children's institutions.* Paper presented at the Academy of Management Annual Meeting, Cincinnati, OH.

Schattschneider, E. E. (1960). *The semi-sovereign people: A realist's view of democracy in America.* New York: Holt, Rinehart & Winston.

Schumpeter, J. (1934). *The history of economic development.* Cambridge: Harvard University Press.

Strauss, A., & Corbin, J. (1990). *Basics of qualitative research.* Newbury Park: Sage.

Tolbert, P.S., & Zucker, L.G. (1983). Institutional sources of change in the formal structure of organizations: The diffusion of Civil Service Reform, 1880-1935. *Administrative Science Quarterly, 28*, 22-39.

Tushman, M. L., & Anderson, P. (1986). Technological discontinuities and organizational environments. *Administrative Science Quarterly, 31*, 439-465.

Tushman, M. L., & Romanelli, E. (1985). Organizational evolution: A metamorphosis model of convergence and reorientation. In L. L. Cummings & B. M. Staw (Eds.), *Research in Organizational Behavior* (vol. 7, pp. 171-222). Greenwich, CT: JAI Press.

Tushman, M. L., & Rosenkopf, L. (1996). Executive succession, strategic reorientation and performance growth: A longitudinal study in the U.S. cement industry. *Management Science, 42*, 939-953.

Weick, K. E. (1979). *The social psychology of organizing*. Reading, MA: Addison-Wesley.

Youcha, G. (1995). *Minding the children in America from colonial times to the present.* New York: Scribner.

COLLECTIVE INTERPRETATION AND COLLECTIVE ACTION IN POPULATION-LEVEL LEARNING:

TECHNOLOGY CHOICE IN THE AMERICAN CEMENT INDUSTRY

Philip Anderson

ABSTRACT

The most fundamental agenda for research on population-level learning is the systematic and deliberate examination of how levels and types of routines rise and fall in populations of organizations over time as a product of the interaction of experiences by individual organizations or the population as a whole (Miner & Haunschild, 1995, p. 155).

How does the nature and mix of routines in a population of organizations change as a result of experience? This is the central question of population-level learning (Miner & Haunschild, 1995). This paper responds to Miner and Haunschild's call for more detailed examinations of the rise and fall of levels and types of routines in a population via a detailed, quantitative study of technology choice in a population. It contrasts population-level learning explanations with other models of how

Advances in Strategic Management, Volume 16, pages 277-307.

ISBN: 0-7623-0500-2

routines shift over time, and extends population-level learning theory in three directions. First, I describe how "fitness," important in outcome-based learning, is collectively constructed. Second, I discuss the role of collective learning processes such as standard-setting and knowledge generation in changing the relative performance of rival technologies. Third, I examine how the collective construction of imitation neighborhoods influences allows uncommon routines to survive in local patches, that can nonetheless be invaded when multi-branch systems define differently what their local units will imitate. I report an empirical study of shifting industry adoption of two rival technologies: "wet" and "dry" cement manufacture. The rise to predominance and subsequent replacement of the wet process as the most common approach is explored.

INTRODUCTION: POPULATION-LEVEL LEARNING AND ITS RIVALS

How would we recognize population-level learning when studying changes over time in an empirical study of a set of organizations? What makes population-level learning a distinctive new area of inquiry? Miner and Haunschild (1995), suggest that the central question of population-level learning is: how does the nature and mix of routines in a population of organizations change as a result of experience? They add that an explanation of such a change should either invoke the outcome of learning interactions within a population, or should invoke collective routines.

Miner and Haunschild's emphasis on learning as a shift in the distribution of routines distinguishes this perspective from other definitions of learning in economics and organization studies (see Dodgson, 1993; Fiol & Lyles, 1985; Levitt & March, 1988, for reviews of the organizational learning literature). For example, studies of learning-by-doing (e.g. Arrow, 1962) conceive of learning as a reduction in costs over time, not as a shift in routines. For Argyris and Schön (1978), organizational learning occurs when individual actors detect mismatches between expected and observed outcomes, discover the sources of error, and invent new strategies to reduce the mismatch. This point of view underpins a large number of recent game-theoretic studies, which model learning as the reduction of error in understanding something about other players, such as their payoffs, strategies, or types. This work generally examines what can be seen as a special case of learning which is defined by its outcome: some form of performance improvement or variance reduction. Other scholars focus less on error reduction *per se* than on learning as the refinement of more accurate mental cause-effect models linking past and future actions (e.g. Duncan & Weiss, 1979; Fiol & Lyles, 1985). This work gernerally examines what can be seen as another special case of learning, in which the regularities that change over time are cognitive. In contrast, Weick (1991) explores a psychological tradition that casts learning as the production of different responses to the same stimuli.

If we accept a definition of learning as a shift in a collective property—the distribution of routines across individuals—then we still must distinguish population-level learning from three other streams of research that can explain learning, so defined. First, organizational ecology implicitly explains shifts in the distribution of characteristics (including routines) across members of a population as the outcome of differential selection. Distributions of characteristics shift when organizations with different bundles of attributes enter and/or exit a population at different rates.

Second, theories of the diffusion of innovation (see Rogers, 1996) account for shifts in the distribution of routines within a population over time. Various factors predict the likelihood that an individual firm will adopt a particular innovation, which can be thought of as a new routine or cluster of routines. At any given point in time, the prevalence of the new routine in a population reflects the past influence of these factors plus their influence in the present period.

Third, theories of social learning explain why the distribution of routines in a population change. Social learning occurs in any situation in which agents learn by observing the behavior of others (Gale, 1996). Individuals observe the actions and associated outcomes of other actors, and select behaviors that seem to be associated with superior performance on some dimension. [In the framework presented in Chapter 1 of this volume, social learning is interorganizational learning based principally on outcome imitation.] Selection may be direct or vicarious. Direct selection leads to behavioral learning, while vicarious selection produces inferential learning (Miner & Haunschild, 1995, p. 148). Social learning models frequently feature increasing returns to the adoption of a practice (frequency-based imitation), leading to herd behavior and adoption bandwagons (see Habermaier, 1989, for a review).

In all three of these cases, changes in the distribution of routines across members of a collective emerge from individual choices and outcomes. Individual firms enter or exit populations; individual firms adopt or do not adopt innovations; individual firms imitate or do not imitate successful others. Collective routines are not a feature of these perspectives, and interactions among agents influence outcomes only in very simple ways (e.g. population density may influence hazard rates, and imitation choices may be weighted by the present popularity of each alternative).

Can we construe the way actors interact with each other or act collectively in a stronger way, one that more clearly differentiates collective population-level learning processes from other ways of explaining shifts in the distribution of collective characteristics over time? This chapter describes and empirically illustrates three mechanisms that help distinguish this point of view from other perspectives that explain how the mix of routines in a population changes over time.

All three mechanisms draw upon a model of learning that locates a population of organizations on a rugged adaptive landscape (Levinthal, 1997). In this representation, individual organizations attempt to move "uphill" toward higher performance when the terrain around them is constantly shifting, because of the interaction between their own moves and those of others in the population. In order to adapt, they pay attention to and learn from the experience of some subset of the population they view as comparable.

The three mechanisms portrayed in this chapter are collective population-level learning processes. First, fitness itself—knowing what direction is "uphill"—is collectively defined. Second, the gradient of the fitness landscape can be altered by collective action aimed at removing bottlenecks that make one set of routines appear more attractive than another. Third, a collective definition of which organizations belong in each others' learning set shapes repeated interorganizational learning.

Three Mechanisms of Population-Level Learning

Collective Definition of Fitness

Daft and Huber's (1987) distinction between system-structural and interpretive perspectives on organizational learning provides an important key to understanding what is distinctive about the population-level learning framework. The former approach focuses on the way organizations acquire data, analyze it, then alter their behavior. The latter focuses on the ways in which organizations construct shared meanings from the equivocal data that environments present. In system-structural models, understanding leads to action; in interpretive models, action leads to understanding.

From an interpretive perspective, learning means creating choice sets, not just accumulating and analyzing information (Bianchi, 1992). Faced with a problem situation, firms, choose ways of defining the problem before they engage in error-reducing trials of prospective solutions. Organizations create the context to which they react (Weick, 1998), and attempt to influence the way other organizations interpret the context. Structuration is the production of interaction patterns and behavior from these intertwined influence attempts (Giddens, 1984). The meaning of environmental data emerges from interaction, not from summing up the interpretations of individual organizations (Weick & Westley, 1996). Sense-making is a collective enterprise, subject to social influence. Consequently, one way in which population-level learning may occur is through the interaction of firms competing and cooperating to control a population's collective definition of what the environment is saying.

Most outcome-based learning models (Haunschild & Miner, 1995) assume that individual learners hill-climb on a fitness landscape. Actions are associated with one or more performance outcomes, and subsequent actions reflect attempts to improve performance. But what is fitness? How does the learner decide which outcomes are more or less successful, on what dimensions?

The performance measures that learners use are subject to social influence, and the meaning of performance is socially constructed. For example, students of technological change broadly agree that competition among rival technologies is seldom settled on purely technical grounds (Bijker, Hughes & Pinch, 1987). Participants in a technology field socially construct a definition of the bottlenecks each technology must address (Hughes, 1983). One solution supplants others as the accepted, legitimated way to resolve these problems, and becomes a dominant design because of social factors, not objective technical superiority (Tushman & Rosenkopf, 1992).

To illustrate, consider Henderson and Clark's (1990) discussion of the semiconductor lithography industry. Seemingly small changes in the technology underlying the etching of circuits into semiconductors led to four changes in industry leadership within two decades, though the basic technological regime (x-ray lithography) remained unchanged. One reason why this happened is that dominant firms such as GCA and Perkin-Elmer believed that the key performance dimension for machines was throughput, the number of chips a machine could etch in an hour. Instead, as designers packed more and more transistors into a chip, feature size and yield became defined as the most salient dimensions of merit. Technologies that were inferior on the throughput dimension, such as scanning and stepping, succeeded because they could etch finer lines into chips with fewer errors.

Similarly, Christensen (1997) documents how leadership in computer disk drives shifted from one manufacturer to the next through a series of seemingly straightforward technological changes. Again, leaders were overturned when the accepted dimensions of merit underpinning their leadership were undermined. Customers told these leaders that they preferred the technology which could deliver the highest areal density (bits of information per inch of disk space) at the lowest cost. Therefore, they said they were not interested in drives that were smaller, but cost more per bit of information stored. Other manufacturers valued a different dimension of merit, however. 5.25 inch drives supplanted 8 inch drives, and 3.5 inch drives replaced 5.25 inch drives, because a new type of customer valued a different dimension of merit: smaller form factors.

If distributions in routines across a population change as a result of individual firms' efforts to climb a performance gradient, then population-level influences come into play when firms collectively define what performance is. Population-level learning of this sort can drive changes in the distribution of routines within a population when different routines appear to perform better on different dimensions of merit. A shift in the social definition of performance will result in a shift in the relative frequency of competing technological routines as a natural result of individual-level efforts to improve performance.

Collective Action to Alter Fitness Landscapes

Population-level learning can occur when firms undertake collective action to attack a particular technological bottleneck. If, as a result of collective action, a consensus emerges that the bottleneck has been removed (or at least appears to be less important), the population will shift away from routines whose value was predicated on the perception that they dealt more effectively with the bottleneck. Collective action can also be aimed at redressing the perceived shortcomings of a technological alternative, increasing its relative frequency within the population.

Such collective action frequently takes place within institutions such as trade associations or R&D consortia, such as the Microelectronics and Computer Technology Corporation (Gibson & Rogers, 1994) or SEMATECH (Corey, 1997). Such institutions are far more than meeting grounds where firms can pool resources to lower their joint costs of research (Sakakibara, 1997). They often help set an industry's agenda, both by advancing knowledge and by legitimating particular techniques. (Branstetter & Sakakibara, 1998). Initially, collective research institutions are often characterized by disorder and ambiguity, that is reduced when a set of norms and structures emerge that guide its progress (Browning, Beyer, & Shetler, 1995). The process by which the research agenda is set cannot be explained as a simple scaling-up of firm-level joint research agreements (Olk, 1998).

This process of creating a set of shared meanings is not driven by rational, technical criteria (Noble, 1984). Different interest groups inside a consortium contest the institution's agenda (Aldrich, 1998), employing influence tactics as part of a broader strategy of manipulation as a response to institutional pressures (Oliver, 1991). The outcome of this process affects the variation, selection, and retention of routines within the industry, creating population-level learning. New routines emerge through generative learning, the process of knowledge creation and discovery (see Fusfeld, 1986; Katz, 1986, for a thorough discussion). New routines compete with one another; typically, one emerges as a dominant design (Utterback & Anthony, 1975), a standard configuration of a product or service that is more widely adopted than all others combined (Tushman & Anderson, 1986). Because the dominant design is seldom if ever the routine with the highest technical performance (Anderson & Tushman, 1990), its selection is an institutional process (Tushman & Rosenkopf, 1992) that is influenced by managerial action (McGrath, MacMillan, & Tushman, 1982). Once a standard emerges, powerful forces tend to lock it into place (Katz & Shapiro, 1986) so that the distribution of technological routines becomes more homogeneous until another technological breakthrough occurs (Tushman & Anderson, 1986).

According to Miner and Anderson (this volume), a collective population-level learning process occurs when at least one learning step—such as knowledge discovery, retention or retrieval from memory—is collective. Both the knowledge-creation and standard-setting activities of industry-wide research groups exemplify this type of process.

Social Construction of Neighborhoods for Repeated Interorganizational Learning

Another way in which an interpretive perspective can help us distinguish population-level learning from other processes is through the social construction of interaction structures. Miner and Haunschild (1995) suggest that selective, imperfect copying of routines is one of the most important forces generating population-level learning. Selective copying is a two-stage process: organizations choose which set of peer firms to monitor, then select which routines to copy (e.g. those that are most prevalent within the comparison subpopulation, or those apparently associated with the subpopulation's most successful outcomes).

Many models suggest that imitative learning is localized (e.g. Ellison & Fudenberg, 1993). In such cases, firms only examine the actions and outcomes of actors they consider to be neighbors in some characteristic-space. In this volume, for instance, Ginsberg, Lomi, and Larsen allow the neighborhood within which organizations search for better performance to vary. Lant and Phelps' cognitively-defined strategic groups, Wade and Porac's core-periphery categories, and Greve's local-distal competitive regions, all described in this volume, are further examples of neighborhoods that influence repeated interoragnizational learning.

Environments make available many possible ways to interpret which firms are thought of as belonging to the same neighborhood. The definition of comparison sets is socially constructed in a collective way. Cognitive communities (Porac, Thomas & Baden-Fuller, 1989) emerge, whose members mutually observe each other. Shared meanings emerge that defining how a population is partitioned into blocs (Lant & Phelps, this volume).

Lomi and Larsen's simulation, reported in this volume, suggests that this partitioning has important consequences for the distribution of routines in a population. In their study, the proportion of cooperators and defectors, and the "patchiness" with which these two types are distributed, depends on how broadly each organization defines its neighborhood. Other things equal, the more a population is divided into small groups of firms who learn locally from one another's experience, the more heterogeneity in routines the population can support. First, it is easier for an uncommon routine to become predominant and persist in a small region than it is in a large one. Second there are more possible regions in which an unusual routine can gain a foothold. Third, it may be that a routine confers higher performance on the organization that executes it if it differentiates that organization from others. The more local learning regions a population contains, the more opportunities there are for an organization to prosper by adopting a routine that is unusual with respect to its neighborhood.

All three of the mechanisms I have described generate behavior that is difficult to explain by resorting to aggregated social learning (a form of repeated interorganizational learning) or traditional innovation diffusion. In general, innovation diffusion models lead to irreversible changes in the distribution of characteristics within a population. Innovation adoption usually follows the well-known logistic curve, suggesting that the cumulative percentage of adopters does not decrease from one period to another. Many social learning models that presume that the probability of adopting an alternative is a positive function of its popularity, also predict a steady increase in the relative frequency of the most popular routine. In contrast, changes in socially-defined adaptive landscapes, or in socially-defined imitative neighborhoods can cause a routine's relative frequency to wax or wane from one period to the next.

To summarize, the arguments presented here suggest that population-level learning can be generated by three mechanisms that are not discussed in Miner and Haunschild's seminal paper. In the rest of this chapter, I will present a concrete example of all three mechanisms in action, and discuss how they influence industry evolution in ways that social learning and organizational ecology explanations alone would not predict. The case studied here is particularly interesting because it shows how a particular technology started out more popular than its chief rival, fell out of favor for three decades, then through population-level processes became predominant once again.

An Illustrative Example: Cement Manufacture in the United States

Portland cement manufacture began in the United States in 1871, borrowing methods that had been developed in Europe over the previous 40 years (see Lesley, 1924; Anderson, 1988 for extensive histories of this industry). U.S. cement production began to grow rapidly in the 1890s, and the number of firms engaged in production rose from fewer than 20 in 1889 to in excess of 350 by 1930. Hundreds of organizations entered and exited the industry during that period (Anderson, 1988). Cement manufacture expanded from its original cradle, the Lehigh Valley of Pennsylvania, to every region of the country. The United States became the world's largest manufacturer of cement shortly after the turn of the century, and became a net exporter in this sector.

Portland cement (as opposed to cements that occur in nature) is an artificial stone made by mixing together in exact proportion a number of elements, principally limestone, clay, and gypsum. The limestone must first be crushed into a powder. Then, it is mixed thoroughly with the other elements. The mixture is then fed into a kiln, where slow heating causes the elements to begin to melt ("sinter") and combine into hard nodules called "clinker." Upon exiting the kiln, the clinker is cooled and ground into cement. See Peray, 1979, for a more thorough description of cement technology.

It is known today that the quality of the cement depends largely on the exact proportions of the ingredients, and on how thoroughly they are mixed before they are melted together. Historically, cement producers adopted one of two mutually-exclusive approaches to making high-quality cement. In *dry* production processes, the ingredients are mixed together in powdered form before being fed into the kiln. *Wet* methods combine the ingredients in a slurry, where they mix together intimately in suspension before being fed into the kiln.

U.S. Cement in the Nineteenth Century: Cost versus Quality

Demand for cement was fueled by the startling expansion and industrialization of the American economy that began after 1865. Cement flowed to the construction industry, and construction engineers were a cement maker's most important customers. The engineer in charge of building, say, a dam or a bridge, specified the project's requirement for cement, often by using particular brand names (Lesley, 1924).

Throughout the nineteenth century, the science of cementation was poorly understood (Meade, 1943). Different manufacturers used different proportions of clay, limestone, gypsum, and other raw materials, producing cements of widely different qualities. Cement testing was haphazard; different engineers employed widely varying specifications and methods of verifying that a given cement met their requirements. As the editor of *Rock Products*, the industry's leading trade journal described the situation in the industry's early years, "To enumerate the details of the hundreds of specifications issued by engineers and architects all over the country, all varying in their requirements for fineness, tensile strength, specific gravity, percentage of water, and every test to which a cement could possibly be subjected, or to relate the trials and tribulations of the cement manufacturer in his endeavor to produce a material to meet all the elements of these various specifications which differed daily in their component parts would take up many, many columns of this paper" (*Rock Products*, 1906).

In these days, cement making was an empirical art, not a science. As one pioneer described the state of knowledge in 1902:

> Scientists who tell you all about cement are ignorant, so to speak, though some of them would learn more if they did not think they knew so much already, but what I want to convince you about is the fact that cement behaves so queerly that it is impossible to lay down rules about it. I have taken samples of cement for testing, sending half of a given sample to one man for a test and the other half to another, and receive in return conflicting tests: so much so, in fact, that you would hardly believe that the tests were made on the same material. Wait, before you say that this may be explained on the ground that the men employed different methods, or something of the kind, for I am going to carry the subject further. I have taken two samples from the same bag of cement, one right after the other, and sent them to the same man to test, giving different names to the samples, and received the same conflicting tests that I did when I sent samples to two different men. I want to tell you again, however, that I am not seeking to cast reflections on the men who did the testing, for they were good, conscientious men, and the

> results came as they did from the fact that cement will not behave the same at all times—it defies hard and fast rules. That is why the more we study it the less we know about it (*Rock Products*, 1902).

Cement buyers in the industry's early decades were quite risk-averse. During the nineteenth century, a number of spectacular structural failures (e.g. bridge collapses) were traced to poor-quality cement, yet there was no widely-accepted theory explaining why some cements performed well for a year or two, then lost their integrity. Engineers paid attention to prices, because cement often constituted a significant fraction of a project's raw material costs, but they paid more attention to quality because the consequences of using bad cement were catastrophic (Lesley, 1924). Lacking the knowhow to certify quality by testing, they fell back on branding, reputation, and imitating the choices of respected peers.

During the American industry's first 40 years, manufacturers and customers jointly constructed an interpretive structure that defined quality as the most important dimension of merit (Lesley, 1924). Trade journals and other publications serving the industry were filled with articles that (a) debated the factors leading to high-quality cement; (b) widely reported structural failures, and trumpeted successes, naming by brand which cement had been used in important construction projects; and (c) set forth a variety of methods and rules-of-thumb for testing cement.

European firms had been making portland cement since the 1830s, and had an established track record of success. English and German brands were particularly well-known, and their makers were able to point to successful projects in Europe as evidence of their high quality. A number of famous American engineers flatly refused to use domestic cement, specifying particular foreign brands by name when drawing up their requirements (Lesley, 1924).

Before 1892, American portland cement typically was not competitive with cement imported from Europe in either cost or quality. Cement is a heavy product, and transportation costs are a significant fraction of the total value added. European cement competed successfully with American cement, particularly on the eastern coast, because it was used as ballast for ships. Even so, European manufacturers were able to charge a premium because quality was the central dimension of merit, and because branding and reputation were important signals of quality, absent objective, scientific methods of distinguishing good cement from bad. A self-reinforcing cycle ensued, because consumers often inferred that high prices signaled high quality—because American cement was cheap, they thought it probably was of dubious strength (Lesley, 1924).

Technological innovation and regulatory action combined in the 1890s to give U.S. manufacturers an edge in cost. In Europe, cement was made via a labor-intensive batch process. A small group of American cement-making pioneers pioneered the use of a continuous process that burned fuel lavishly, but was much less labor-intensive. Additionally, the McKinley Tariff Bill of 1890, which put a tax of 30.4 cents on each barrel of imported cement (Perazich, Woal & Schimmel, 1939). As a result, by 1896, American makers were able to meet or better the prices of their European rivals, but the fledgling industry still found it difficult to make headway against the European reputation for quality. Commented two engineers who were veterans of this era:

> Architects and engineers had tried the foreign product to their satisfaction and as we look back to 1896, when the prejudice was still strong against American portland, we cannot help but realize that the former were fully justified in their position on important work. In the year mentioned, the writers know that not a single brand was sound day in and out—the processes and methods of manufacture were such as to preclude uniformity; the raw material was coarsely ground, as well as the finished product, so that little dependence could be placed on American portland in the early years (Harrison & Schafer, 1919, p. 54).

Compounding this problem of technical credibility, between 1890 and 1905, dozens of fly-by-night operator promoters raised money to establish cement companies in the midwestern and southeastern United States, then went bankrupt or delivered a low-quality product. Related one expert:

> Michigan, apparently, was the first State in which the promoter found an opportunity to display his peculiar talents, and for a number of years, that State was dotted with prospective cement plants. Most of these flotations were capitalized excessively, owing to the fact that for the first time in the history of the industry, the stock was being sold to the public by promoters. Advertisements of stock for sale at 10 cents or $1 per share, with promises of 20 to 60 per cent dividends and with wonderful miscalculations as to operating costs, filled the papers of the Middle West during this period. After the Michigan boom had collapsed, leaving behind it a few good plants, a few poor ones, and a much larger number which had never come into existence other than in the prospectus, the promoter was for a few years scarcely seen or heard of. His reappearance took place when the Iola plant proved the profits in making cement in the natural-gas belt in Kansas, and for the last few years, there have been exaggerated statements of the profits awaiting the erection of cement plants in the States west of the Mississippi, notably in Kansas and Iowa (Eckel, 1907, p. 211).

Investors lost millions of dollars in these schemes, and it became difficult to borrow or raise capital to build a cement factory. As scandal after scandal was uncovered, the reputation of American cement producers suffered. As a result, the social consensus of the industry and its customers was reinforced: quality, as evidenced by reputation and branding, was the most important dimension of merit to consider when buying cement.

The American Triumph: Collective Action and Routinization

For important projects, customers typically favored German portland cement, "due to the more careful methods employed in German factories, which have resulted in a steady advance in quality, uniformity, and fineness of grinding"

(Newberry & Cummings, 1897, p. 38). Commented Robert Lesley, one of the pioneers of the American industry,

> When the cement industry was started in America and American cement and American mud were synonymous with many possible purchasers, the "Proceedings" of the Society of German Cement Manufacturers formed the Bible of the American manufacturer. After a long day in the works or with callous customers, it was necessary to put in a long evening with the hard German words of these reports, for in them alone could be found the information needed to establish the industry on this side of the Atlantic (*Rock Products*, 1904).

Why were the Germans the acknowledged quality leaders? The German Portland Cement Manufacturers Association was founded in January 1877, and established standard testing methods and quality specifications starting in 1878. This industry group took the lead in basic research and financed a Cement Technical Institute at the Technical School of Berlin (Platzmann, 1927).

Anxious to imitate the Germans, American manufacturers decided to imitate them, engaging in the collective learning process of copying a population-level routine from another population (*Rock Products*, 1906). In October 1902, the Association of American Portland Cement Manufacturers was formed, and at its inaugural annual meeting in December, 1902, one of the first committees appointed was that on Uniform Specifications. At its inception, the group, later renamed the Portland Cement Association (PCA), chose testing as its most important and heavily-funded activity, specifically the task of developing uniform, widely accepted testing procedures (Rock Products, 1904).

As early as 1885, the American Society of Civil Engineers had prescribed a tentative and very broad specification for testing cement, and in 1899 and 1901, the U.S. Navy and U.S. Army respectively put forth their own specifications. With the formation of the PCA, the manufacturers moved to create one universal standard for civilian and governmental use. The American Society for Testing Materials (ASTM) emerged as the consensus choice for a neutral, standard-setting body, and in late 1903, the ASTM appointed a committee to develop a unified testing specification for cement. The ASTM committee included all the members of the American Society of Civil Engineers committee on the subject, seven members of the Association of American Portland Cement Manufacturers, representatives from two leading cement testing laboratories, one representative of the American Railway Engineering and Maintenance of Way Association, four representatives of the leading railroads, one representative of the American Institute of Architects, and seven representatives of the ASTM (*Rock Products*, 1906). Its proposed standard was unanimously adopted by the ASTM in November, 1904, and was immediately accepted by the PCA.

The emergence of the standard knocked the chief support from under European manufacturers: given a legitimated test, customers no longer had to rely exclusively on reputation and branding as signals of cement quality. Furthermore, the PCA's stringent membership requirements provided assurance that any association member was a reputable businessman, not a fly-by-night promoter. Tests of American cement showed that many brands were technically the equal of their German rivals, and in the decade between 1903 and 1913, American portland cement virtually drove foreign cement out of the market (Lesley, 1924).

To summarize, a collective learning process—the establishment of an industry association and a coherent set of standards—led to population-level learning. The distribution of routines in American cement manufacture changed significantly, as extreme heterogeneity in cement composition and methods employed gave way to much more uniformity. The effect on industry structure, attractiveness, and evolution were dramatic. Dozens of independent firms serving new geographic markets were founded in the 1903-1913 period (Anderson, 1988), because ownership of an established brand was no longer a critical competitive advantage. This influx greatly changed the demographics of the industry and ensured that on a nationwide basis, it would remain fragmented instead of oligopolistic. The threat of foreign competition receded into the background, and the U.S. cement industry entered a period of unprecedented prosperity (Lesley, 1924).

From Dry to Wet Cement Manufacture

The traditional European batch process for cement-making used water to form raw cement material into bricks that were placed in a kiln to harden. The American continuous process developed in the 1890s dispensed with the need for water. Ground raw cement material was fed into the top end of a rotating metal cylinder (a "rotary kiln") that tipped downward, so that as the machine turned, its contents spiraled along the hot tube, fusing into clinker by the time it exited. The raw material could be fed to the kiln in powder form, dispensing with the brick-making step. Consequently, almost all American cement produced until 1905 was made by grinding clay and limestone together dry, mixing them during the grinding process, then feeding the powder directly into the kiln (Perazich, Woal, & Schimmel, 1939).

An alternative approach was forced on some manufacturers by exigency. In some locations, the raw materials were quarried from a wet source (e.g., the clay at the bottom of a lake bed) and entered the factory full of water. In such cases, the raw material naturally formed a slurry as it was ground up. As the particles of the raw mix were ground up finer and finer, they mixed thoroughly with one another, because they were suspended in water.

As cement chemistry began to be placed on a firmer scientific footing through the efforts of the Portland Cement Association, cement makers began to pay more attention to precision and control in the manufacturing process. Some manufacturers decided to add water when they ground and mixed *dry* raw materials together, so that they would blend together as thoroughly and intimately as possible. No scientific evidence demonstrated that the wet process produced better cement; the pioneers of this method adopted it because it made sense to them that mixing the raw materials together as closely as possible would yield a higher-quality product (Porter, 1925).

Wet cement manufacture had a built-in inefficiency: in the kiln, the water had to be evaporated before melting and clinker formation could occur. The production throughput of a slurry-fed kiln was inherently less than that of a kiln fed by materials that were already dry. Additionally, of course, the process required a new input: large quantities of water. Commented a German expert in 1911:

> The disadvantage of the thick slurry process is thus undoubtedly in the extra expenditure in fuel, and the increased cost of manufacture caused thereby. The thick slurry plant has some advantages which may be briefly stated as follows: (1) Smaller capital investment in the installation, (2) little dust, (3) the possibility of proper adjustment of the mixture without difficulty, (4) a simpler plant and fewer conveyors, (5) Saving of power in wet grinding....Gentlemen, I can only confirm this from the experience made by a company to which I formerly belonged and which altered one of its works to the thick slurry system. The factory in question works at much greater cost than the other factories with the dry process (*Rock Products*, 1911, p. 34).

Relatively unambiguously, the dry process was more efficient in operation than the wet. Whether the wet process produced higher quality was a subject of considerable contention, among both manufacturers and technical experts. As one engineer summarized the debate:

> Uniform chemical composition of the raw mix has been one of the most difficult problems to solve...After many years of experience with these [dry and wet] processes, there is a wide difference of opinion among cement-mill operators as to their relative merits. It is generally conceded that it is somewhat easier to obtain uniformity of mix with the wet process and there is some advantage in the cost of grinding the material wet. On the other hand, there is a decided economy of kiln fuel in the dry process and, in the writer's opinion, the full possibilities of obtaining uniform material through use of a series of mixing bins in the dry process are not generally appreciated or realized (Porter, 1925).

It was clear that every cement maker confronted a choice between two mutually-exclusive methods. A factory either employed a dry process or a wet process. It was uneconomical to install slurry-making capacity without using it full-time, and it would not make sense to advertise the superior quality of branded cement made sometimes via a wet process and sometimes via a dry one. The industry divided into wet and dry plants, the dry ones predominating (Perazich, Woal, & Schimmel, 1939).

Figure 1, drawing on data from annual issues of the *Directory of American Cement Manufacturers*, displays the relative proportion of American cement produced by each of these two methods. Wet cement manufacture is a complex cluster of routines that differ from the cluster of routines used in dry cement manufacture. A separate body of knowhow relevant to wet manufacture emerged, specifying best practices for feeding the raw materials into the mixing tank, agitating the materials, and ensuring that the materials were suspended together for

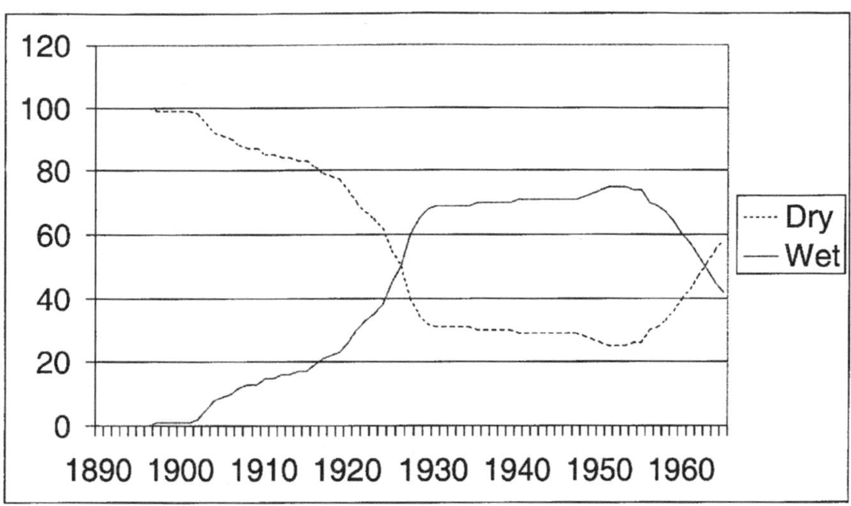

Figure 1. Relative Proportion of U.S. Cement Production Accounted for by Wet vs. Dry Methods

the proper amount of time (Peray, 1979). Dry-process manufacturers continued to construct their own body of knowhow, learning how to mix raw materials together more intimately to produce a more uniform product without suspending them in a liquid.

Figure 1 illustrates population-level learning, defined as a change in the nature and mix of routines in a population of organizations. Before 1904, virtually all U.S. cement manufacturers employed the cluster of routines associated with dry cement manufacture. In the 1920s, however, the wet cluster of routines became predominant and remained so until the 1960s, when the dry process once again prevailed. How did this shift in the distribution of routines occur? In an article written in the 1940s, the editor of the trade journal *Rock Products* explained:

> ...one aftermath of the 1914-1918 World War had been a poverty-stricken Europe, and manufacturers there were compelled to develop foreign markets. Foreign cement manufacturers entered the American market in appreciable volume not only with a cheaper but an early hardening product that came to be preferred by many engineers and architects. It was soon discovered that these imported cements owed part of their alleged virtues to fine grinding, and competition soon led to a race to make finer and finer ground American cements....American manufacturers, driven by domestic competition, as well as foreign, to finer grinding of cement, soon discovered that the secret of quick-hardening or high-early-strength involved a slightly higher lime content than the cements they had been making—more of the tri-calcium silicate in place of di-calcium silicate. It involved finer grinding and more complete blending of the raw materials, as well as much more accuracy in methods of proportioning and feeding. In fact,

> the introduction of high-early-strength cement manufacture in this country had done more than anything else to make the cement industry a scientific one and has given chemists a very important place on the plant staff—more important than some company executives are willing to concede. The introduction of the autoclave test about 1938 and the controversy over the effect of magnesia and the specifications a short time later for five types of cement, including for the first time chemical analyses, still further concentrated attention on the character and preparation of the raw mix; that is, on the chemistry of cement manufacture. At the start, these problems were more easily solved by the wet process than in the dry. Finer grinding and better blending were accomplished by introduction of hydraulic closed-circuit grinding methods, the use of large slurry thickeners, made necessary by much thinner slurries, and better devices for stirring or agitating the slurries up to the point where they are fed into the kiln (Rockwood, 1944, pp. 98, 106).

Had the wet process produced unambiguously superior cement, it might well have diffused more widely between 1905 and 1920. What produced a stampede in the industry toward a process whose merits had been debated for decades was a shift in the industry's collective definition of performance. The 1904 standards focused principally on the long-term strength of cement. More through the efforts of cement salesmen than customers (Rordam, 1930), attention was focused beginning in the early 1920s on how quickly a cement achieved high strength. High-early-strength cement seemed desirable to customers, other things equal, because the sooner that freshly poured concrete could bear a heavy load, the faster a construction project could proceed.

The industry's new, collective focus on high early strength meant that 49 of the 53 plants constructed during the period 1921-1935 employed the more expensive wet process, and many mills converted from dry to wet cement manufacture (Perazich, Woal, & Schimmel, 1939, p. 3). Wet materials could be ground in "closed circuit"—passed through mesh filters with up to 200 holes per square inch that returned coarser materials to the grinder—to a much higher degree of uniformity than dry ones could. Explained an expert:

> The first patent on a closed circuit grinding in a cement plant was issued May 23, 1916. The change to the wet process started when cement plant chemists recognized that while high-early-strength cement derived its desirable properties from its very finely divided state, further enhancement of its quick-setting properties could be obtained when the percentage of lime in the raw mixture was increased. Since a high percentage of lime could result in free lime in the cement and unsoundness, if the proper degree of combination was not affected during the burning process, the raw materials had to be ground uniformly and to well over 85 per cent minus 200-mesh and precise chemical control of the raw mixture had to be maintained. This was more readily accomplished by the wet process in which the raw ingredients are ground with water and later the slurry or pulp is blended to the proper chemical composition by intermixing slurry from two or more tanks equipped with agitators (Wolfe, 1947, p. 122).

No technological imperative generated the industry's shift in the mix of dry and wet manufacturing methods. High-early-strength cement was not necessarily better than standard portland cement. Commented the industry's leading trade journal in 1927:

> All the new plants that we are familiar with are able to make a 3-day cement—a cement that will give present 7-day strength requirements in 3 days. It is rumored throughout the industry that a new plant which cannot make a cement of early strength requirements had better not be built. As to what has brought about this marketing of early high strength cement at no greater price than the A.S.T.M. standard portland cement, there is some difference of opinion. It seems to us more a matter of voluntary competition on the part of manufacturers than any really widespread or insistent demand on the part of users. There is not, so far as we can determine, any proof that early high strength portland cements are of any greater ultimate value in construction than ordinary portland cement; and there is a possibility, although not a probability, that early high strengths are attained at the cost of ultimate strength and permanency in the resulting concrete....Finer grinding of the cement up to a certain point helps in making the cement quicker acting—at one new plant this was determined to be 88% through 200-mesh; beyond this point, the cement became too fine for the water to react on it readily; and for perhaps some other reason as well, there was no increase in the activity or resulting strength of the cement mortar from grinding beyond this fineness. To a certain extent then, early high strength in portland cement is an index of the care and thoroughness used in its manufacture. With it goes also the assurance of greater uniformity, because of more accurate chemical control (*Rock Products*, 1927c, p. 110).

In fact, later experience suggested that high-early-strength cement has significant drawbacks that were overlooked in the 1920s. Noted the leading trade journal, "There are certainly other qualities desirable in portland cement besides early hardening ability, especially in view of the facts, apparently well established, that the early strength cements do not have good keeping qualities, require more gypsum, make concrete more subject to shrinkage, and do not make so permanent a concrete when exposed to sea water, or perhaps any water" (*Rock Products,* 1931, p. 92). Added a leading technical expert, "It is well known that high lime cements, while yielding initially high strengths, tend to retrogress with time" (Blank, 1942). Another explained:

> Some of the quick-hardening cements may develop an initial strength which is two to three times higher than the corresponding strength of ordinary portland cement, but at later periods the difference is less pronounced. In some cases, an ordinary portland cement may show a higher strength at the 28-day period, although at the one and two day periods it had less than half the strength of the quick-hardening cement. It is by now pretty generally known amongst the makers and users of concrete that the strength of concrete is largely determined by the ratio between the water and the cement in the concrete mix. By controlling and regulating the water-cement ratio it is possible to make high-early-strength concrete with ordinary portland cement, and in a great number of cases calculations will show that the required early strength can be obtained cheaper by using ordinary portland cement (Rordam, 1930, pp. 45-46).

The industry's move toward the wet process and high-early-strength cement in the 1920s traded off perceived higher quality for losses in production efficiency. Noted a government study:

> While improvements in the quality of standard product and the development of special cements serve to enhance the effective construction capacity of a given volume of cement, they tend at

> the same time to restrict output and to increase labor requirements because of the additional processing which they require....In the making of standard portland cement, as estimated by one plant superintendent interviewed in the course of the NRP-NBER field survey, an additional output of 33 percent would be possible if cement were made according to 1920 standards of fineness instead of the more rigorous specifications of today. For another plant...the effective capacity of the kiln was decreased by approximately 20 percent when it was burning clinker for high-early-strength cement (Perazich, Woal, & Schimmel, 1939, p. 19).

But as the wet process gained momentum, its inherent inefficiencies were addressed, both by suppliers and by research supported by the Portland Cement Association. Two innovations appeared. The first was the use of filters, which took out 50-60% of the water from the slurry, reducing it to a moist cake as it passed from the grinding machinery into the kiln. The use of filters increased a kiln's capacity by 20-40%, reduced fuel consumption by 12-25%, and recycled the water strained out of the slurry (Coulson, 1926; Perazich, Woal, & Schimmel, 1939). Chain systems introduced about 1925 were another method of reducing the moisture content of slurry entering the kiln. They enlarge the heat-transfer area in the upper portion of the kiln, reducing the amount of fuel required.

As a result, for a time, the wet process became more fuel-efficient than the dry one. Noted a veteran executive:

> When the wet process was introduced during the years from 1917 to 1924, the fuel consumption in the wet process rotary kiln even increased from 100 to 150 pound per barrel and upwards. This increased fuel consumption was the greatest deterrent to the introduction of this process. Gradually the economy of the wet rotary kiln was improved, and from about 1925 new improvements in the kiln cut the fuel consumption in rapid strides, until the present day when it is possible to burn a wet mix in a modern rotary kiln with about 70 pounds of coal per barrel. Thus, in a wet process kiln, means were found to accomplish what the simpler dry process kiln had been waiting for more than 30 years....In the wet process rotary kiln, the heat transfer from the gases to the material is excellent while in the case of the dry burning rotary kiln, it is very poor (Lindhard, 1941, p. 50).

Social learning theory suggests that routines shift because actors imitate those with the best outcomes. In this case, however, the causality is reversed: the wet process became the most fuel-efficient because it was popular; it did not become more popular because it was the most fuel-efficient to begin with. Such a phenomenon, where an industry locks into an "inferior" technique because it is popular, may be the rule rather than the exception (Arthur, 1989).

In a similar way, population-level learning altered the productivity differential between wet and dry plants, arising from the slower wet-process throughput noted above. A government survey conducted in 1939 showed that during the period 1924-1935, wet-process plants underwent approximately one and one-half times as large a reduction in labor requirements as dry-process plants (Perazich, Woal, & Schimmel, 1939, p. 27). Adjusting for capacity utilization, in 1925, dry process plants built *before* 1915 required 7% less labor than wet process plants built prior to 1915. However, dry process plants built *after* 1915 required 27% more labor per barrel than wet process plants of the same vintage. The authors concluded, "The difference is probably due primarily to the fact that the wet-process plants included in the sample are of new construction, utilizing the latest technological improvements and are, therefore, more efficient than the older dry-process plants."

This story highlights the way that the three modes of population-level learning described by Haunschild and Miner (1995) intertwine. Once the definition of cement performance shifted in the 1920s from overall tensile strength and durability to high early strength, the wet process gained momentum. Firms employing frequency-based learning (which method is the most popular) or trait-based learning (what are the newest, most modern plants using) would have adopted it. Because it became widely adopted and a set of complementary innovations grew up around it, it eventually became the choice that outcome-based learning would select, if firms chose to imitate the most productive, fuel-efficient plants.

The Resurgence of Dry Cement Manufacture

Although almost all newly constructed cement plants through the 1950s employed the wet process and many cement factories switched from dry to wet grinding, the dry process continued to survive. Why wasn't it completely displaced?

The transportation cost of cement is high relative to its production cost. As a result, once quality standards took hold, the industry developed a structure of monopolistic competition in most regions (Loescher, 1959). The majority of cement plants dominated sales within a region, because their low transportation costs allowed them to undercut competitors. As a result, competition was localized; firms tended to pay attention to other firms within a radius of several hundred miles. As a result, patches of dry competitors survived in some regions, much like the patches generated in the simulation reported by Ginsberg, Lomi and Larsen in this volume. It was considered noteworthy, for example, when the first wet-process plant was constructed in the Lehigh Valley, the original cradle of the industry, in 1925 (*Rock Products*, 1925). Similarly, when the Colorado Portland Cement Company built a dry plant in 1927, it explained that water was scarce in Colorado, and cement of the highest quality had been made in the same locale for 25 years using the dry process (Van Zandt, 1928). U.S. cement manufacture became divided geographically into patches where an uncommon routine was able to survive because of distinctive local conditions and the geographic boundedness of competition.

The wet process typically invaded a formerly dry region when introduced by a diversified manufacturer who employed it in other regions. Non-local learning was propagated by branch systems, just as described by Greve's study of radio stations in this volume. The rise of the wet process coincided with a wave of mergers during the 1920s (Anderson, 1988). The International Cement Company exemplified the new, multi-branch firm. Founded in 1919 with two plants in Texas and three overseas, it had expanded to 11 mills in the United States by 1927. It annual report in 1927 proclaimed the virtue of leveraging technological knowhow across plants in different regions:

> Instead of being a local "branch" of a remote directing management, each International mill stands upon its own feet, and its operating heads are able to carefully attune its service to the needs of its territory. At the same time, the supporting strength of the International Cement Corp. makes available to each local subsidiary experienced commercial counsel, as well as technical and engineering skill which no one mill could of itself afford. The standards of quality set by the International Cement Corp. are steadfastly adhered to by each subsidiary. By means of the International wet-blending process, each mill is able to produce cement that not only exceeds standard specifications by a wide margin, but successfully maintains that quality day in and day out (*Rock Products*, 1927a, p. 83).

International's description of its wet-process technology clearly describes the ideology of scientific control and precision that underpinned this method of manufacture:

> This system (moving slurry from three large correcting basins, permitting complete chemical control) the manufacturer has termed the "International wet-blending process." The company is a thorough believer in the fact that the quality of cement is absolutely dependent upon uniformity of the slurry entering the kiln. The chemist must get the exact chemical proportions, and that he does is shown by the fact that the slurry never varies more than 1/10 to 2/10% on entering the kiln. This method of control of chemical content has enabled the company to manufacture a portland cement exceeding standard specifications by a considerable margin (*Rock Products*, 1926a, p. 49).

When International Cement took over a plant, it implemented its philosophy, regardless of local conditions. In a description of changes International made when it acquired a plant in Alabama, *Rock Products* noted, "The present dry-process plant of four 10x150 ft. kilns will be converted to wet-process, including lengthening the kilns. This is particularly significant as this plant, completed by the Phoenix Portland Cement Company in 1923, was the first dry-process plant built in this country in several years, and has been held up as a star exhibit of the survival of the dry process" (*Rock Products,* 1926b, p. 101).

How did patches of dry producers survive in the face of invasions from competitors such as International? Three significant collective learning processes allowed the dry routine to persist in the face of improvements in wet manufacture.

First, the dry manufacturers worked via the Portland Cement Association to adapt a technology that had been introduced into the industry in 1904. In the early days of the industry, once clinker was ground into powder, it was conveyed to storage tanks by conveyor belts that lost considerable amounts of the finished product. The Fuller Manufacturing Company introduced a pneumatic system that pumped the ground powder into storage using high air pressure, and the innovation diffused rapidly. Suspended in air, the powder as if it were a liquid.

Consequently, a few dry-process manufacturers pioneered the idea of mixing powdered raw materials in a turbulent air stream. In principle, it seemed to these manufacturers, particles finely suspended in air ought to mix with each other as well as particles finely suspended in water. Reported *Rock Products* in 1929:

> For nearly two years the Portland Cement Association has been conducting research work on closed-circuit grinding in collaboration with the United States Bureau of Mines at the Experiment Station at the University of Minnesota, and research work on particle size at the United States Bureau of Standards, Washington, DC. While the results of these researches have not been made public except to members of the Portland Cement Association, enough is known to predict they are almost revolutionary. While closed-circuit wet grinding had proved its efficiency and economy in metallurgy, and it only remained to convince portland cement manufacturers, the same was not true of closed-circuit dry grinding. The simultaneous development of both reopens anew the controversy of dry vs. wet process. The successful application of both, so far as the portland cement industry is concerned, hinged on the determination of the best particle size for the chemical reaction in a rotary kiln, and this appears to have been more or less definitely established, although it can vary a bit with the materials and conditions. During the last few years, with the increasing demand for quicker hardening cement and consequently the more careful proportioning of raw materials, the wet process with very long kilns and various devices for increasing heat efficiency, such as chains and slurry filters, has been by far the more popular of the two processes. In addition to more accurate preparation and easier control, the greater economy of wet grinding has sent the balance in favor of the wet process. Still greater economy in grinding, using a closed circuit with slurry thickeners, and in burning by use of slurry filters, or chains, have all the more increased the favor of the wet process....Now, it is reported, the use of air separators in closed circuit with dry raw mills and accurate control of the size of particle removal has almost revolutionized the relationship of the two processes. Some of the older dry mills, which seemed on the verge of becoming obsolete, have accomplished truly remarkable results in improved quality of product and in increased capacity of both grinding units and kilns. Of course, air separators, especially on the finish end, are by no means new to the cement industry, but the present type and adaptation of them are new. In the opinion of some of the most experienced cement manufacturers in the industry, this new closed-circuit dry grinding and use of particles of raw materials of the correct size for the product wanted, with up-to-date methods of dry blending, is going to be a life saver for many older dry mills (*Rock Products*, 1929, pp. 92-93).

The research conducted by the PCA allowed the dry-process manufacturers to imitate the scientific approach to mixing and control of raw materials that allowed wet plants to manufacture finely-ground high-early-strength cement or standard portland cement, according to demand. Noted *Rock Products*, "The Fuller Company has installed its Fuller-Kinyon dry blending system at eight cement mills. At one, the error of variation in the clinker was held within .5%, the tensile strength of the cement was increased 10%, and the actual kiln output was increased 10%" (*Rock Products*, 1928, p. 107). Dry plants were quickly retrofitted with new mixing systems. It was reported, "Pulverized, dry, cement raw materials of varying physical and chemical characteristics are being mixed and blended by means of the Fuller-Kinyon conveying system with very little additional equipment other than that normally required for conveying from finish mills to raw storage and from raw storage to kiln tanks...[placing] the entire system and its control under the direct supervision of the plant chemist" (*Rock Products*, 1927d, p. 162).

By the end of the 1920s, dry-cement manufacture was judged to have closed the gap in grinding fineness and mixture control that had initiated the shift toward wet grinding routines. Summarized one expert in a thorough comparison of the wet and dry processes, "We therefore find the industry at a state where construction costs of the two methods are about balanced. Operation costs of the dry mills are slightly lower, while the quality situation presents the spectacle of the wets a very few laps ahead of their dry brethren, who are speedily overtaking them" (Blaise, 1929).

Two more important collective-learning processes contributed to the survival of dry cement manufacture. First, the Portland Cement Association was persuaded to sponsor a strong line of research on dust control, which had surfaced as a major advantage of the wet manufacturing process when the wet technique began to predominate. Indeed, a number of firms had converted from dry to wet processes to hold down dust emissions near populated areas, not because they believed the wet process produced any better cement (*Rock Products,* 1927b). Local governments, observing the lower emissions associated with wet production, began insisting on cleaner mills with a vigor that had been unknown when the dry process predominated and the dust associated with it was taken for granted as the price of industrial progress.

Thanks in part to the PCA's research efforts, the gap was closed by the time the long hiatus in plant construction, occasioned by the depression of the 1930s ended. Commented the editor of *Rock Products* in 1939, "Progress in the elimination of dust from cement processing operations in the past few years has been so rapid that it is not unreasonable to believe that within a short time the industry from a practical standpoint will be comparatively free from this vexing problem" (Nordberg, 1939). Noted the journal's 1942 industry summary, "...it is generally admitted that so far as quality of product and control of manufacture are concerned, the modern dry process plant is in every way the equal of the wet process. Even the one-time potent argument of dust elimination in the wet process over the dry, has largely lost its weight in the newer installations equippd throughout with efficient dust collectors" (Rockwood, 1942, p. 63).

Second, the ASTM issued a new set of cement testing standards in 1939 that for the first time featured chemical analyses of a cement's structure. Whereas the 1904 standard applied uniformly to all Portland cement, the 1940 standard specified five different types of cement, each subjected to different tests (Loescher, 1959). The new ASTM standards legitimated the idea that high-early-strength cement was a separate type of cement, suitable for some applications and not others, instead of a superior form of cement for all purposes. They helped turn the tide against the notion that finer and finer grinding produced better and better cement, an important problem for dry-process manufacturers, because wet grinding produces finer particles than dry grinding does (Peray, 1979). Indeed, by 1946, 80% of cement manufacturers surveyed by *Rock Products* told the journal they thought the industry had gone too far in the direction of ever-finer grinding (*Rock Products*, 1946).

Although dry-process manufacture appeared to be technically competitive with wet-process manufacture, the postwar boom in kiln-building continued to favor the wet process. Noted *Rock Products* in 1952:

> A growing interest in long dry process kilns of high capacity... several conversions from wet process to dry operation have been made. Until these installations of long dry process kilns, the trend in recent years was almost entirely in the direction of continually longer wet process kilns. In either case the main objective was fuel economy, but the wet process was preferred because it has always been recognized that thin slurries could be blended to yield a much more uniform material for kiln feed. However, the perfection of special pneumatic and mechanical blending devices for raw materials, and, in some cases, the installation of blending tanks that consist of a large number of conventional individual units of modest size with flexible arrangements for handling and intermixing between has made it possible to approximate the holding point of some slurries...It may be anticipated that there will be more of the long dry process kilns installed in the future because they offer great potential savings in fuel, but the trend, according to numbers of actual installations, is still heavily in favor of wet process kilns.

The distribution of routines shifted back toward the dry process beginning in the late 1950s through the combination of innovation and a shift in the collectively enshrined dimensions of merit. It had been argued at least since 1928 that the throughput and fuel efficiency of a mill could be improved dramatically by pre-heating the raw materials in a turbulent stream of hot air before they entered the kiln (Blaise, 1928). Because the mix would enter the kiln quite hot and ready to fuse, kilns could be run at much higher speeds, and heat that would otherwise be wasted could be recycled for use in pre-heating. Preheaters was first installed in the Spokane Portland Cement Company in early 1930s (Perazich, Woal, & Schimmel, 1939), and the Coplay Cement Company had installed a preheater of its own design with great success at about the same time (Bell, 1957). However, because the wet process was so widespread, the idea lay fallow until a new type of air-suspension preheater, invented by a German firm, was installed by the Fuller Company (the American licensee of the invention) in the Evansville, Pennsylvania plant of Allentown Portland Cement Company in 1953. The throughput of the kiln was increased by 75%, while fuel consumption was cut by 60% (Nordberg, 1954).

In the late 1950s, full process automation was introduced into the cement industry (Anderson, 1988). This permitted a very rapid increase in the size and throughput of kilns, and as throughput became the dominant dimension of merit, suspension preheating diffused rapidly. By the mid-1960s, as Figure 1 shows, the dry process had once again become predominant.

Population-Level Learning Mechanisms at Work

To summarize, the formerly ubiquitous dry process of the nineteenth century gave way to the wet process during the first two decades of the 1920s. Eventually, however, the distribution of these two routines reversed, with the dry process again becoming the predominant choice. How can we explain this reversal?

Collective Definition of Fitness

Any technology can be evaluated on several different dimensions of merit. Gell-Mann (1994) points out that in general adaptive landscapes are not characterized by a single fitness dimension. Instead, performance is a composite construct, and there may well be tradeoffs between performance on one dimension and performance on other dimensions (Simon, 1996). Attention can be directed toward one at the expense of another, either via the functioning of a cognitive community (e.g., Porac, Thomas, & Baden-Fuller, 1989) or through repeated interorganizational learning (Henderson & Clark, 1990).

In its early days, American cement manufacture was more of an art than a science, and routines for both making and testing cement were quite heterogeneous. As a result, quality dominated price as the key dimension of merit. Reputation and branding were supremely important, and foreign cements commanded both high prices and a high market share. Through collective action, American manufacturers established a standard that was widely accepted as scientific, and permitted the evaluation of a company's product on technical grounds, not brand reputation alone. The result was the homogenization of routines in the industry.

The dry cement manufacturing process predominated until the 1920s, because it was demonstrably less expensive, and there was no evidence that the thorough mixing and fine grinding associated with the wet process produced any better cement. With quality more subject to objective assessment, production cost was the more easily observable performance dimension. The second wave of invasion by foreign cement makers in the 1920s altered the industry's definition of performance by stressing how much strength a cement displayed just a few days after being mixed into concrete. This shift in emphasis turned the spotlight on fine grinding and closely controlled mixing, which were viewed as the keys to making high-early-strength cement. Accordingly, the wet process gained momentum, which became locked-in even after most of the gap between the control and fineness attained via the two processes was closed. A shift in some performance characteristics was an antecedent, not a cause, of the trend toward wet-process production: for a time, wet production became more labor- and fuel-efficient than dry production, and dust control became much more salient.

In the end, a renewed emphasis on throughput combined with the innovations of suspension preheating and kiln automation led to a decline in installations that used the wet process. Innovation was only one contributor to this reversal of a decades-long trend, for the suspension preheater had been in existence for 25 years before it began to diffuse widely. It took a change in the industry's collective definition of performance for the lock-in of the wet process to be reversed.

Collective Action to Alter Fitness Landscapes

Collective action influenced the distribution of routines in cement manufacturing in two ways. First, the formation of an industry association and its cooperation with a multi-industry testing society led directly to the promulgation of widely-accepted standards. The 1904 ASTM standards eliminated the perceived quality advantage that foreign cement had enjoyed, and continued research by the Portland Cement Association over the years led American customers to accept that the U.S. industry was continually improving the quality of its cement in a rational, scientific manner. The revision of the industry's standards in 1939 had a less dramatic impact, but did put to rest the widely held belief of the 1920s that high-early-strength cement was superior to standard portland cements made with less finely-ground particles.

Second, the Portland Cement Association's knowledge discovery activities contributed materially to the survival of the dry process in the United States. Through cooperation with government bodies and suppliers to the industry, the PCA helped perfect and legitimize pneumatic blending techniques that gave dry manufacturers a close approximation to the fine control of raw materials so touted by advocates of the wet process. PCA-led research in dust control, which benefitted all manufacturers, was disproportionately useful to those employing the dry process. By eliminating most of the dust-emission differential between the two manufacturing methods, it helped arrest the tendency for existing dry mills to adopt the wet process, and paved the way for the eventual resurgence of dry production methods.

Social Construction of Neighborhoods for Repeated Interorganizational Learning

Had the wet process completely supplanted the dry process by 1940 or 1950, the advantages of suspension pre-heating might never have obtained in an American cement mill. The dry process never dipped below a 25% share of American production, because most cement manufacturers largely imitated nearby rivals; had each manufacturer engaged in frequency-based or outcome-based learning on a nationwide basis, the dry process might well have disappeared. On the other hand, the wet process was able to diffuse into new regions because more often than not, multi-branch systems adopted the wet process for all their new installations, instead of imitating local practice. As noted by several authors of chapters in this volume, population-level learning processes depend a great deal on the rules firms employ when deciding whose actions and outcomes to observe and imitate.

Rival Explanations

Innovation Diffusion and Social Learning

Many models from the innovation-diffusion and social-learning traditions have some difficulty explaining reversals of adoption bandwagons. In many of these models, the proportion of adopters in period t is one of the most important predictors of new adoptions in period $t+1$. The more popular an alternative becomes, the more pressure is exerted on non-adopters to conform to the prevailing practice.

Social learning models can in principle explain bandwagon reversals if their popularity-weighting terms are sufficiently small. In these models, firms not only imitate widespread practices (frequency-based imitation), they imitate practices that appear to be associated with success (outcome-based imitation; see Haunschild & Miner, 1995). Hence if underlying economic conditions change, it is possible that a routine that was formerly associated with success can give way to a routine that was formerly associated with lower performance. (Depending on the model, it is possible that organizations will become locked into inferior technologies anyway; see for instance Arthur, 1989.)

Social learning models may overlook the intertwining of frequency-based, trait-based, and outcome-based learning. It appears, for example, that in this case, firms rushed to produce high-early-strength cement through a classic bandwagon effect, characteristic of frequency-based imitation. Once the bandwagon gained momentum, the firms with the most attractive traits (e.g. highly visibile, modern plants) were high-early-strength producers. The popularity of the wet method led to dramatic performance improvements along the dimensions of merit (fuel efficiency and labor productivity based on throughput) upon which it had been inferior to the dry process. Outcomes appeared to follow adoption, not the other way around.

Many of the technological innovations described in this chapter existed for many years before they began to diffuse widely. An important challenge for social learning models is explaining such lengthy adoption lags. In this particular case, it would seem that collective processes outside the scope of standard social learning theory are critical to understanding why techniques that had been known about for years suddenly rose to prominence.

Organizational Ecology

An organizational ecology explanation of the reversal I observed would suggest that each process became predominant because new entrants employed it and because firms employing the "wrong" process had higher failure rates than firms employing the "right" one. There is a clear association between the survival of a routine and the survival of the firms who are that routine's carriers. Indeed, because there was a great deal of entry into and exit from the industry, especially in the 1900-1930 period, and a major factor explaining the rise of the wet process is that the overwhelming majority of new entrants employed it during the industry's boom years in the 1920s, when the number of cement makers expanded significantly.

However, in an analysis of plant-level survival rates reported elsewhere (Anderson, 1988), I show that the production routine employed had no effect on hazard rates, either as a main effect or interacting with the proportion of firms adopting that routine. There is no significant difference throughout the time period or in any particular era between wet-process and dry-process plants. It was the differential *growth* of wet cement plants, not their survival at the expense of dry plants, that altered the distribution of routines in the industry. This observation reinforces recent calls for a broader approach to organizational ecology than the study of entries and exits alone (e.g., Baum, 1996).

Summary and Conclusion

Miner and Haunschild have directed our focus toward learning interactions within a population and collective routines that lead to shifts in the distribution of routines within a population. In this case, I observed a shift in the predominance of two rival routines from one to the other and back again. Three important aspects of interaction and collection behavior help explain why this happened. All are rooted in the notion that learning is interpretive as well as systemic-structural.

First, a population reaches a social consensus on the key dimensions of merit that characterize and the key bottlenecks that confront its core technology. Collective routines may be mobilized toward addressing these perceived bottlenecks. Successful efforts to eliminate bottlenecks may contribute toward a shift in the socially-constructed view of what performance is, what the key dimensions of merit are. As a consequence, no routine dominates all others on all dimensions of merit, the distribution of routines in a population may change. What was formerly viewed as a lower-performing routine may be framed as higher-performing, given a new basis for evaluating tradeoffs. Furthermore, collective routines may contribute toward this change, as attention is given to solutions that seem more promising once the performance landscape is re-interpreted.

Second, populations can take collective action that alters the fitness landscape on which individual organizations learn and adapt. The two mechanisms highlighted here are standard-setting and generative learning, the creation of new knowledge by a collective organization. Neither process is purely technically rational; individual groups within collective associations vie to set the organization's agenda, and their relative success or failure in this struggle can determine the trajectory that performance improvement will follow. The actions discussed here are only a subset of a broader topic the actions of collective institutions not only influence fitness landscapes through their effect on technology, but also through their effect on regulations and taken-for-granted assumptions (Scott, 1995).

Third, collectively shared definitions define who learns from whom. Individual organizations make choices that are influenced by what they observe "relevant others" doing. The imitation set of relative others is socially constructed, and changes as firms enter and exit bounded regions of interest. (In this instance, those boundaries are spatial, but this need not always be the case.) Furthermore, some firms operate both inside and outside the region that defines a given organization's imitation set, and their distal operations can influence the lessons learned by firms that focus only on their local rivals.

The thrust of this argument is that collective population-level learning processes are important and distinctive, not that traditional social learning, organizational ecology, and innovation diffusion are irrelevant. Indeed, we argue in Chapter 1 (this volume) that repeated interorganizational learning—which would include both social learning and the imitative adoption of an innovation—represents an important source of change in the nature and mix of routines in a population, a claim explored by several chapters in this volume. As we refine theories about population-level learning, it behooves us to ask how it leads to unique insights that enhance our ability to understand and predict. Social learning and individual diffusion theories would not automatically draw attention to the collective processes illuminated by this study of the cement industry. Additionally, the overall population-level learning perspective directs research in novel directions by leading us to understand the distribution of characteristics in the population as more than the simple aggregation of individual choices and lessons learned.

REFERENCES

Aldrich, H. (1998). Information exchange and governance structures in U.S. and Japanese R&D consortia: Institutional and organizational influences. *IEEE Transactions on Engineering Management, 45,* 263-275.

Anderson, P. (1988). *On the nature of technological progress and industrial dynamics.* Unpublished doctoral dissertation, Columbia University.

Anderson, P., & Tushman, M. L. (1990). Technological discontinuities and dominant designs: A cyclical model of technological change. *Administrative Science Quarterly, 35,* 604-633.

Argyris, C., & Schön, D. A. (1978). *Organizational learning: A theory of action perspective.* Reading, MA: Addison-Wesley.

Arrow, K. (1962). The economic implications of learning by doing. *Review of Economic Studies, 29,* 155-173.

Arthur, B. W. (1989). Competing technologies, increasing returns and lock-in by historical events. *Economic Journal, 99,* 116-131.

Baum, J. (1996). Organizational ecology. In S. R. Clegg, C. Hardy, & W. R. Nord (Eds.), *Handbook of organization studies* (pp. 77-114). London: Sage

Bell, J. N. (1957). Radical preheater design proves practical. *Rock Products.* September, pp. 90-92.

Bianchi, M. (1992). Knowledge as expected surprise: A framework for introducing learning in economic choice. In W. J. Samuels & J. Biddle (Eds.), *Research in the history of economic thought and methodology* (vol. 10, pp. 43-58). Greenwich, CT: JAI Press.

Bijker, W. E., Hughes, T. P., & Pinch, T. J. (1987). *The social construction of technological systems: New directions in the sociology and history of technology*. Cambridge, MA: MIT Press.

Blaise, H. H. (1928). Practice vs. possibility in the cement manufacturing industry. *Rock Products*. February 18, pp. 61-64.

Blaise, H. H. (1929). The "Eighteenth Amendment" of the portland cement industry. *Rock Products*. May 25, pp. 57-60.

Blank, A. J. (1942). Evaluating high initial strength. *Rock Products*. August, pp. 70-71.

Branstetter, L., and Sakakibara, M. (1998). Japanese research consortia: A microeconometric analysis of industrial policy. *Journal of Industrial Economics, 46*, 207-233.

Browning, L. D., Beyer, J. M., & Shetler, J. C. (1995). Building cooperation in a competitive industry: SEMATECH and the semiconductor industry. *Academy of Management Journal, 38*, 113-151.

Christensen, C. (1997). *The innovator's dilemma*. Boston: Harvard Business School Press.

Corey, R. E. (1997). *Technology fountainheads*. Boston: Harvard Business School Press.

Coulson, D. C. (1926). Reducing the moisture content of portland cement slurry by filtration. *Rock Products*. December 25, pp. 166-169.

Daft, R. L., & Huber, G. P. (1987). How organizations learn: A communication framework. In *Research in the sociology of organizations* (Vol. 5, pp. 1-36). Greenwich, CT: JAI Press.

Dodgson, M. (1993). Organizational learning: A review of some literatures. *Organization Studies, 14*, 375-394.

Duncan, R., & Weiss, A. (1979). Organizational learning: implications for organizational design. In B. Staw & L. L. Cummings (Eds.), *Research in organizational behavior* (vol. 1, pp. 75-123). Greenwich, CT: JAI Press.

Eckel, E. (1907). Advances in cement technology, 1906. *Cement and Engineering News* (September), 206-211.

Edison Portland Cement Company. (1926). *The romance of cement*. Providence: Livermore and Knight.

Ellison G., & Fudenberg, D. (1993). Rules of thumb for social learning. *Journal of Political Economy, 101*, 612-642.

Fiol, C. M., & Lyles, M. (1985). Organizational learning. *Academy of Management Review, 10*, 803-813.

Fusfeld, H. I. (1986). *The technical enterprise: Present and future patterns*. Cambridge, MA: Ballinger.

Gale, D. (1996). What have we learned from social learning? *European Economic Review, 40*, 617-628.

Gell-Mann, M. (1994). *The quark and the jaguar: Adventures in the simple and the complex*. New York: W. H. Freeman.

Gibson D. V., & Rogers, E. M. (1994). *R & D collaboration on trial: The Microelectronics and Computer Technology Corporation*. Boston: Harvard Business School Press.

Giddens, A. (1984). *The constitution of society: Introduction to the theory of structuration*. Berkeley: University of California Press.

Habermeier. (1989). Competing technologies, the learning curve, and rational expectations. *European Economic Review, 33*, 1293-1311.

Hadley, E. J. (1945). *The magic powder: History of Universal-Atlas cement company and the cement industry*. New York: Wiley.

Haunschild, P. R., & Miner, A. S. (1995). Modes of imitation: The effects of outcome salience and uncertainty. *Administrative Science Quarterly, 42*, 472-500.

Henderson, R. M., & Clark, K. B. (1990). Architectural innovation: The reconfiguration of existing product technologies and the failure of established firms. *Administrative Science Quarterly, 35*, 9-30.

Hughes, T. P. (1983). *Networks of power: Electrification in western society, 1880-1930.* Baltimore: Johns Hopkins.

Katz, M. L. (1986). An analysis of cooperative research and development. *Rand Journal of Economics, 17*, 527-543.

Katz, M. L., & Shapiro, C. (1996). Technology adoption in the presence of network externalities. *Journal of Political Economy, 94*, 822-841.

Lesley, R. W. (1924). *History of the portland cement industry in the United States.* Chicago: International Trade Press.

Levitt, B., & March, J. G. (1988). Organizational learning. *Annual Review of Sociology, 14*, 319-340.

Lindhard, P. T. (1941). Reducing b.t.u loss in dry process kiln. *Rock Products.* April, pp. 50-52.

Loescher, S. M. (1959). *Imperfect collusion in the cement industry.* Cambridge, MA: Harvard University Press.

McGrath, R. G., MacMillan, I. C., & Tushman, M. L. (1992). The role of executive team actions in shaping dominant design: Towards the strategic shaping of technological progress. *Strategic Management Journal, 13,* 137-161.

Meade, R. (1943). *Portland cement: Its composition, raw materials, manufacture, testing, and analysis.* New York: Chemical Publishing.

Miner, A. S., & Haunschild, P. R. (1995). Population level learning. In *Research in organizational behavior* (vol. 17, pp. 115-166). Greenwich, CT: JAI Press.

Newberry, S. B., & Cummings, U. (1897). Production of cement in 1896. *Cement and Engineering News* (September), 37-38.

Noble, D. (1984). *Forces of production: A social history of industrial automation.* New York: Alfred A. Knopf

Nordberg, B. (1939). Making an industry dustless. *Rock Products.* August, pp. 29-31.

Nordberg, B. (1954). Cut fuel cost and increase output with suspension preheaters. *Rock Products.* October, pp. 68-72.

Oliver, C. (1991). Strategic responses to institutional processes. *Academy of Management Review, 16*, 145-179.

Olk, P. (1998). A knowledge-based perspective on the transformation of individual-level relationships into inter-organizational structures: The case of R&D consortia. *European Management Journal, 16*, 39-49.

Peray, K. (1979). *Cement manufacturer's handbook.* Chemical Publishing.

Perazich, G., Woal, S. T., & Schimmel, H. (1939). *Mechanization in the cement industry.* Works Projects Administration, National Research Project Report No. M-3, Philadelphia, Pennsylvania.

Platzmann, C. R. (1927). Development of the German cement industry. *Rock Products.* May 28, pp. 39-41.

Porac, J. F., Thomas, H., & Baden-Fuller, C. (1989). Competitive groups as cognitive communities: The case of Scottish knitwear manufacturers. *Journal of Management Studies, 26*, 397-416.

Porter, J. J. (1925). Manufacturing problems of the cement industry. *Rock Products.* February 21, pp. 46-48.

Rock Products. (1902). The colonel on cement testing. August, p. 8.

Rock Products. (1904).The Portland cement manufacturers association. April, p. 13.

Rock Products. (1906). Standard specifications. July, 33, p. 29.

Rock Products. (1911). Wet and dry processes. August 22, pp. 33-34.

Rock Products. (1925). A year of great development in production, financing and manufacturing processes. December 16, pp. 87-91.

Rock Products. (1926a). International cement company's new plant. April 17, pp. 49-63.

Rock Products. (1926b). A year of growth and technical developments. December 25, pp. 101-111.

Rock Products. (1927a). International cement annual report. April 16, pp. 81-83.

Rock Products. (1927b). San Antonio cement mill recently converted to the wet process. October 1, pp. 49-57.

Rock Products. (1927c). Fourteen new cement plants added to the fold in 1927. December 24, pp. 103-116.

Rock Products. (1927d). New development in mixing and blending dry raw materials for portland cement manufacture. December 24, pp. 162-168.

Rock Products. (1928). The Portland cement industry in 1928 and its outlook for 1929. December 2, pp. 105-209.

Rock Products. (1929). The Portland cement industry in 1929. January 4, pp. 84-93.

Rock Products. (1931). Cement industry has no new plants but gains 3,000,000 Bbl. capacity. January 3, pp. 90-97.

Rock Products. (1946). What cement executives are thinking. August, pp. 104-175.

Rock Products. (1952). Progress in cement. January, pp. 110-203.

Rockwood, N. C. (1942). Between wars. *Rock Products*. August, pp. 60-67.

Rockwood, N. C. (1944). Post-war cement industry. *Rock Products*. August, pp. 73-135.

Rogers, E. M. (1996). *Diffusion of innovations* (3rd ed.). New York: Free Press.

Rordam, S. (1930). High-early-strength concrete. *Rock Products*. August 30, pp. 45-46.

Sakakibara, M. (1997). Heterogeneity of firm capabilities and cooperative research and development: An empirical examination of motives. *Strategic Management Journal, 18*, 143-164.

Scott, W. R. (1995). *Institutions and organizations*. Thousand Oaks, CA: Sage.

Simon, H. A. (1996). *The sciences of the artificial* (3rd ed.). Cambridge, MA: MIT Press.

Tushman, M. L., & Anderson, P. (1986). Technological discontinuities and organizational environments. *Administrative Science Quarterly, 31*, 439-465.

Tushman, M. L., & Rosenkopf, L. (1992). Organizational determinants of technological change: Toward a sociology of technological evolution. In *Research in organizational behavior* (vol. 14, pp. 311-347). Greenwich, CT: JAI Press.

United States Federal Trade Commission. (1932). *Report of the Federal Trade Commission on price bases inquiry: The basing-point formula and cement prices*. Washington, DC: Government Printing Office.

United States Federal Trade Commission. (1933). *Cement industry*. Report in response to Senate Resolution no. 448.

Utterback, J. M., & Abernathy, W. J. (1975). A dynamic model of process and product innovation. *Omega, 3*, 639-656.

Van Zandt, P. C. (1928). Colorado portland cement company new dry process plant. *Rock Products*. June 23, pp. 42-59.

Weick, K. E. (1991). The nontraditional quality of organizational learning. *Organization Science, 2*, 116-123.

Weick, K. E. (1998). *The social psychology of organizing* (2nd ed.). Reading, MA: Addison-Wesley.

Weick, K. E., & Westley, F. (1996). Organizational learning: Affirming an oxymoron. In S. R. Clegg, C. Hardy, & W. R. Nord (Eds.), *Handbook of organization studies* (pp. 440-458). London: Sage.

Wolfe, J. M. (1947). What is in the future for grinding? *Rock Products*. January, pp. 119-151.